ORGANIZATIONAL PARTICIPATION

MYTH AND REALITY

FRANK HELLER, EUGEN PUSIĆ, GEORGE STRAUSS, and
BERNHARD WILPERT

OXFORD UNIVERSITY PRESS
1998

Oxford University Press, Great Clarendon Street, Oxford OX2 6DP
Oxford New York
Athens Auckland Bangkok Bogota Bombay Buenos Aires
Calcutta Cape Town Dar es Salaam Delhi Florence Hong Kong Istanbul
Karachi Kuala Lumpur Madras Madrid Melbourne Mexico City
Nairobi Paris Singapore Taipei Tokyo Toronto Warsaw
and associated companies in
Berlin Ibadan

Oxford is a registered trade mark of Oxford University Press

Published in the United States
by Oxford University Press Inc., New York

First published 1998

British Library Cataloguing in Publication Data
Data available

Library of Congress Cataloging-in-Publication Data
Organizational participation : myth and reality / Frank Heller . . . [et al.].
Includes bibliographical references (p.   ) and index.
1. Organizational behavior. 2. Organizational sociology.
3. Industrial relations. I. Heller, Frank A.
HD58.7.07378 1998 302.3'5—dc21 98–2531

ISBN 0–19–828851–4
ISBN 0–19–829378–X (Pbk.)

1 3 5 7 9 10 8 6 4 2

Typeset by Graphicraft Typesetters Ltd., Hong Kong
Printed in Great Britain
on acid-free paper by
Bookcraft (Bath) Ltd.,
Midsomer Norton, Somerset

ACKNOWLEDGEMENTS

The book was jointly planned and developed by the four authors who have professionally collaborated for many years. We made up the Editorial Board which produced three *International Yearbooks of Organizational Democracy* published by Wiley in 1983, 1984, and 1986, and three volumes of *International Handbooks of Participation in Organizations*, published by Oxford University Press in 1989, 1991, and 1993.

In producing this valedictory volume, we drew on the experience of these books of references as well as on our research. The work was divided in accordance with personal interests and availability and the authorship of chapters is indicated in the List of Contents. While each author retains responsibility for his own chapters, we planned the work together in four meetings in Europe, followed up with extensive discussions using all modern media including the Internet. We exchanged criticism and suggestions and introduced numerous changes and we have remained friends.

We are, of course, indebted to many colleagues not directly mentioned in the book. In particular we want to remember the important work of Rudi Supek in the analysis of participation and self-management.

Many funding bodies have contributed to the work with which the authors are associated: they are mentioned in the original publications. The Maison des Sciences de l'Homme in Paris hosted and supported all our meetings. We are indebted to Anne Theissen for her assistance in compiling and sorting out literature for Chapter 2 and to Hilary Walford, copy-editor for Oxford University Press, who drew our attention to a number of inconsistencies we had overlooked. The outstanding contribution of Pamela Hattingh is acknowledged separately.

We are grateful to Pamela Hattingh of the Tavistock Institute in London who, as Assistant to Dr Heller, was closely associated with the long gestation period for the present volume and its editorial and administrative arrangements as well as with the six international yearbooks and handbooks which preceded it.

CONTENTS

LIST OF TABLES

ABBREVIATIONS

BOAL	Basic Organization of Associated Labour
BSC	British Steel Corporation
BSE	bovine spongiform encephalopathy
CAPM	Computer-Aided Production and Management
CEO	Chief Executive Officer
CFTW	Cross Functional Team Working
CIM	Computer Integrated Manufacturing
DIO	Decisions in Organization
EBM	Employee Board Member
EC	European Community
EI	Employee Involvement
EIT	Earned Idle Time
EPC	Employee Participation Council
EPOC	Employee Direct Participation in Organizational Change
ESOP	Employee Stock Ownership Plan
EU	European Union
EWC	European Works Councils
FNV	Federatie Nederlandse Vakbeweging
GDR	German Democratic Republic
GM	General Motors
GNP	Gross National Product
HRM	Human Resources Management
IDE	Industrial Democracy in Europe
IPC	Influence Power Continuum
JIT	Just In Time
LOM	Ledning, Organisation och Medbestämmande (Leadership Organization, and co-Determination)
MOW	Meaning of Working
OLO	Open Learning Organization
OT	Organization Theory
PAR	Participatory Action Research
PDM	Participative Decision Making
QC	Quality Circle
QWL	Quality of Working Life
RPB	Representative Participative Body
SBA	Senter for Bedre Arbedsliv (Norwegian Work Life Centre)
SDWT	Self Directed Work Term
SI	Sound Incorporated

SMT	Self Managing Team
STSD	Socio-Technical System Design
TMC	Total Management Control
TQM	Total Quality Management
TUC	Trades Union Congress
WIDER	World Institute for Development of Economics Research
WSL	Whole System Learning

Introduction

The title of the book appropriately reflects the dilemma facing the authors, who have set out to describe and evaluate nearly half a century of research and experimentation with the democratization of organizational life. The reality of the experiments and the extensive support participation research and action have received in many parts of the world are undeniable. At the same time many questions remain unanswered and some are still ill-formulated. Protagonists and sceptics have found some common ground, but are still divided by ideology, political philosophy, and scientific orientation. Nowhere have the ideals of a fully participative organization been fulfilled, but then there is no agreement on what such an organization should do. Ideals easily transcend into Utopias. Leaderless and non-hierarchical organizations have been championed and may have worked in laboratory or small-group situations.

There must always be room for idealism and innovation; one recent movement merges participatory philosophy with action research[1] and is organized through local and world congresses that bring together scholar-activists to forge links between 'the academic and the popular, western and oriental and experiential' thinking (Cornell Participatory Action Research Network 1997).

The harsh reality of life in competitive organizations is different and has made participation into a hotly debated subject. Some proponents advocate it as a way of increasing productivity; others consider it to be desirable on a level with political democracy. There are several in-between positions, like the claim that participation increases job satisfaction or loyalty to the organization and consequently will have an indirect effect on efficiency. These various claims and others will be examined, but equal or even more importance can be attributed to the variety of perspectives and situations to which the term and its various derivatives have been applied. An extreme position is taken by economists, who use the term to describe the proportion of a given population who participate in—that is, take part in—work. Some behavioural social scientists, particularly in the USA, have tended to limit the term to group behaviour or leader-subordinate interaction—that is, sharing different degrees of influence between people. Others have started from the position that the phenomenon to be examined is power, and that its distribution in organizations includes various forms of decentralization, like delegation and subgroup autonomy, or semi-autonomous working groups.

The distribution of influence and power covers an enormous variety of behaviour. Minimally, it requires sharing information because, without information, no influence can be brought to bear. Even information-sharing can be from the top down, as advocated by the Industrial Society in the UK, or from the bottom up, as included in suggestion schemes, or as a two-way process sometimes called joint consultation.

Some of these processes are informal and voluntary, some are voluntary but highly structured, like the Kibbutz movement in Israel or various producer co-operative and joint-ownership schemes in most parts of the world. Then, particularly since the end of the Second World War and in Europe, there are legally prescribed methods of participation and power-sharing between different levels of employees and owners, with the German co-determination scheme as the best-known example. As we shall see in the next chapter, within this range a much greater variety of approaches to participation can take place, sometimes encapsulated within another schema, like Total Quality Management (TQM).

The words used to describe democratic organizational structures and behaviour have changed over the years and are espoused by different constituencies. Industrial democracy found favour in some Continental West European countries in the 1960s. Involvement was much in favour with some US and British organizations in the 1980s. Empowering has dominated much writing in the first half of the 1990s. Is it a case of 'old wine in new bottles' or does the changing terminology describe different practices?

We have chosen to stay with 'participation', the oldest and still most widely used term, although from time to time we will use other words, such as 'influence-sharing', to avoid repetition and boredom, or 'organizational democracy', to capture the flavour of certain European schemes. In the literature there are many definitions. We can live with several related approaches. One will be given towards the end of this introduction and others for more specific applications in other chapters, but even the mapping-sentence approach used in Chapter 2 is only a starting point for understanding a very complex and diverse phenomenon. There is no need to apologize for not offering a single definition to cover all the activities we will describe; the economist Joseph Schumpeter in his well-known *Capitalism, Socialism and Democracy* agonizes over seven pages in search of a definition for a political democracy, a concept which has received extensive attention since at least Aristotle.

There are four constituencies which operate in our field and use terms like participation: (1) organizational actors (employees at different levels sometimes roughly differentiated into managers, unions, and other employees); (2) researchers; (3) consultants; and, in some countries, (4) governments and political parties. Each of these groups has different interests and ideologies. In the case of political parties, the identification is not always clear-cut between the left and the right. In Britain, for instance, to some extent in the USA, as well as in Russia and several of its former satellites, the left wing had serious objections to industrial democracy, as it was then called. In West Germany in the early 1950s the only political grouping that opposed the new industrial democracy legislation on principle was the Communist Party. Among trade unions in Britain and the USA, particularly in the 1960s and 1970s, but to some extent still in the 1990s, employee participation was and is seen as a less acceptable alternative to collective bargaining (see Chapter 4).

Academic researchers tend to have humanistic values which sometimes make it difficult to remain neutral (Strauss 1963; Wagner and Gooding 1987*a*). Nevertheless, a considerable volume of research has taken a sceptical stance towards participation and has questioned its effectiveness (see Chapters 5 and 6). Consultants find neutrality and scepticism difficult to combine with their role as advisers, usually to management, who expect firm policy prescriptions. Consultants also tend to generalize from limited experience with small numbers of clients and methods which do not lend themselves to replication or independent assessment. Problems and failures are rarely reported by academics or consultants, and the latter's reports are usually available only to the client.

All these circumstances make it difficult to separate what happens from what some constituents think happens. Both advocacy and critique of participative practices are imbued with emotions, popular allegories, and metaphors. The Ancient Greeks drew a distinction between historians and mythographers. The former were thought to tell the truth about what really happened, while mythographers were thought to deal in fables, or at best improbable events, like Homer's stories and descriptions of the Trojan Wars. Then towards the end of the nineteenth century, when the amateur archaeologist Heinrich Schliemann excavated Troy, the improbable became probable. The Trojan Wars had taken place and some of Homer's myths were given credence (Warner 1983). Over time and with the accumulation of scientific evidence, the boundary between myth and reality changes or becomes blurred.

One can also speculate whether there is a connection between Romanticism in the arts and romantic notions in the social sciences. The term 'romanticism' derives from romance—that is, the telling of stories and myths. The artistic and philosophic movement under that name emphasized idealism, the use of metaphor as explanatory categories, and an opposition to rationalism and materialism (Cranston 1994).

It is possible to wonder whether the early German organizational democracy movement in the first decade of the twentieth century and its reincarnation into co-determination in the post-1950s also owes something to the spirit of Romanticism, idealism, and anti-materialism that characterized that movement and had repercussions in several other European countries. This would help to explain the different value positions which underpin the theory and practice of participation in Europe and the USA, as will emerge in later chapters.

In this book we set out to describe and evaluate the present landscape and reduce the gap between myth and reality wherever possible. We do not pretend that we have all the answers or that we have looked at every piece of writing. However, the authors have spent most of their working lives in and around the area of participation, and have read at least as much of the available evidence as most people. We have taken part in or been influenced by a number of research projects and in particular by two large scale cross-national studies—Industrial Democracy in Europe (IDE 1981*a*; 1981*b*) and Industrial Democracy in Europe Revisited (IDE 1993)—and by a follow-up longitudinal three-country Decisions in Organization research (DIO 1979). These studies will be described when we adduce evidence from them in later chapters.

The IDE research, and its replication ten years later, covered twelve European countries, 154 organizations, and 9,000 respondents; it was designed to assess the impact of external variables, principally national legislation, in support of organizational democracy with *de facto* representative and direct participation at all levels of organization. The extent of participation was then related to a variety of outcomes, such as satisfaction and organizational climate and the quality of management–employee relations as well as a variety of contextual and intervening variables.

The DIO study concentrated on seven organizations using participant observation, interviewing, and regular attendance at group meetings over four years combining quantative analysis with ethnographic data.

Since 1981 we have constituted the editorial board of a series of six yearbooks and handbooks on organizational democracy and participation covering 2,943 pages of material. The three yearbooks were published by Wiley; the three handbooks by Oxford University Press.[2]

These six edited books are a rich source of reference in our field and were for the most part divided into five sections: (1) Evaluation and Review of the Field, (2) Landmarks Revisited, (3) Recent Theoretical Developments, (4) Recent Research Findings, (5) Country Studies. The last book in this series contains Abstracts of all articles in the six volumes (Lafferty and Rosenstein 1993).

In this valedictory volume to the series we have decided that the time has come to write our own assessment of this field from a perspective which includes the point of view of the major disciplines that have contributed to it. After an overview chapter which gives the case for participation and defines, explains, and illustrates the various forms participation takes, Chapter 2 develops the view of psychology, Chapter 3 presents an approach from organization theory, and Chapter 4 takes industrial relations as a point of departure. Chapter 5 attempts to give a critical evaluation of available research evidence, Chapter 6 presents a rough assessment of the various factors which contribute to participation's success or failure, and the last chapter struggles, but we believe succeeds, in pulling together the main theoretical and practical outcomes that allow us to speculate about the future and in particular about which areas of this large domain are most likely to influence organizational life in the next decade. Inevitably there is some overlap and a limited amount of repetition. We think this is justifiable where the subject matter seems particularly important.

The four authors come from the USA, Germany, Croatia, and Britain. They have worked together for over two decades but have retained their individual ways of thinking and writing and little has been done to homogenize their stylistic approaches. While we have each taken major responsibility for assigned chapters, we have accepted suggestions from each other during successive revisions and allowed transfers of material between chapters to improve sequencing.

It should be made clear at the outset that at each stage of writing we had to make difficult choices about what to leave out. It is not only that the literature on participation itself is very large, as the six volumes we referred to earlier demonstrate, but that a substantial number of developments in organization theory and practice include participation as a central concept. An obvious, fairly recent example is TQM.

Going back to the 1950s and 1960s, there is the area of work design, starting perhaps with the Tavistock Institute's research into coal mining and leading to the seminal theory of socio-technology which has grown to require a 144-page bibliography of 2,685 entries (van Eijnatten 1993). From this work a broad multi-country movement developed under the name of the Quality of Working Life (QWL) in which work to redesign semi-autonomous working groups, multi-skilling, and participation played a central role. Team Working comes from the same stable, takes a variety of forms, and has its own bulging literature.

In addition to these major areas of development there are others which require participation in the pursuit of varying objectives—for instance, Self Learning Systems, Team Coaching, and Networking. De-layering is a fairly recent term used to describe eliminating one or more levels of an organization and is frequently a consequence of forming semi-autonomous work groups which, being self-regulating, do not usually require all the previous layers of supervision.

Finally, this is a field full of fads (Huczynski 1993; Watson 1994). A large number of new terms have sprung up which describe procedures that are similar or identical to one of those we have already mentioned: for instance, Self Managing Teams (SMTs); Cross Functional Team Working (CFTW); Self Directed Work Teams (SDWTs), or Cellular Working instead of Semi-Autonomous Teams; Whole System Learning (WSL) or Open Learning Organization (OLO) instead of Self Learning Systems; Cross Skilling instead of Multi-Skilling; High Involvement Management or Power Devolution instead of Participation or Influence Sharing; and so on.

By the time the reader has reached this stage of the book new acronyms and terms will have been developed as part of a competitive drive within *academe* or between consultants. In each case a moderate or small differentiation of practice or theory will be claimed for the new term. Genuinely new approaches may also surface. Recently there has been a backlash against the trend for social science to succumb to fashions. Hilmer and Donaldson (1996) argue that managers suffer from being led down ephemeral and false trails by the marketing of ready-made techniques which lead to 'instant coffee management'. Two consultants (Spitzer and Evans 1997) are equally sceptical of managers who believe that simple initiatives offer genuine answers to complex and idiosyncratic problems. Kieser (1997), in a hard-hitting but humourous critical assessment of current management fashions, compares modern managers to the seventeenth-century Austrian emperor who was one of many important political managers persuaded by Johann Joachim Becher to invest in a procedure which would create gold and 'yield at least 1 or even 2 per cent profit per week—which would thereby alone cover the cost of the investment' (p. 50).

We decided that we would not attempt to cope with a diversity of fashions and names. Instead, we believe that a review and assessment of the essential concept of participation, its management, and effectiveness would throw useful light on all the terms we have mentioned.

Each of the following chapters will indicate ways of conceptualizing our central term. In this Introduction it is sufficient to argue that participation describes how people interact with each other in an organizational context. More specifically, it encompasses a range of behaviour and choices rather than a standardized type of interaction between people. First of all, there must be access to information and to the process of decision-making; this can lead to involvement and consultation yielding various degrees of influence. Beyond this, participation can lead to agreement, consensus, or equality among people or groups, and, finally, there are degrees of self-determination and autonomy.

Conceptualizing participation as a range of influence over events or people from very little to a great deal explains why practices like multi-skilling fall within our area of interest. The more skills a person is able to use, the more varied the job becomes, and the more choices the employee has. This increases the influence he or she has over the nature of the task—for instance, in relation to priorities, timing and/or the use of tools. Similar considerations apply to the other terms.

Many accounts of our subject are written from a particular national perspective, from the point of view of a single academic discipline, or from a given value stance—for instance, rationality theory or postmodernism, which believes that all reality is subjective and best described in images and metaphors (Newton 1996). Many of these approaches have developed their own esoteric and stilted vocabulary which prevents dialogue between interest groups even when a participative activity called 'Democratic Dialogue' is put forward as a remedy for modern ills (Habermas 1990). We have attempted, but no doubt only partially succeeded, to minimize the problems derived from specialized communication channels.

Most adults spend about half their average day at work. It can be argued that the obligations we undertake and the rights we enjoy as employees are as important as those that apply to us as citizens, but the development of social policy has paid much more attention to the latter than the former. The subject matter of this book aims at redressing some aspects of this imbalance. Other imbalances can only be hinted at here. In many countries, citizens enjoy formal rights to information, to protection from arbitrary interference, to guarantees of defined human rights and the requirement of due process, to the untrammelled right of free speech without fear of punishment, and so on. The half of our waking day which classifies us as employees fails to incorporate some or many of these protections.[3]

While this book is about the myth as well as the reality of participation, we have already distanced ourselves from the original Greek contrast between *mythos* and *logos*, the latter implying a completely rational account of reality. We have shown that some of the original great Homeric stories have turned out to have some substance. More generally, modern social anthropology has argued that myths reflect important and enduring aspects of society and can provide a template for social action. The downside of mythologies, as Bronislaw Malinowsky has shown, is their endurance and unalterability implying strength as well as rigidity.

The concept of organizational participation is much younger than Homer's stories and the mythology is still evolving; can we hope to contribute to its shape?

NOTES

1. Action research derived from pioneering work by Kurt Lewin covers a variety of methodological approaches to applied social science. Usually the objective is to make sure that research evidence is used rather than simply published and filed (Clark 1976).
2. The three yearbooks are Crouch and Heller (1983), Wilpert and Sorge (1984), and Stern and McCarthy (1986); the three handbooks are Lammers and Széll (1989*b*), Russell and Rus (1991), and Lafferty and Rosenstein (1993).
3. An example of this is the case of 'whistle-blowers'. These are people who discover that their organization is doing something morally or legally wrong and are prepared to say so. They are frequently dismissed and thus deprived of their livelihood without due process or remedy. In the UK a registered charity was set up in 1993 to open a help line, give legal support, and achieve a change in the law.

1. An Overview

What do we mean by participation? What forms does it take? Why has it been subject to so much interest? This introductory chapter deals with these issues and raises some fundamental questions which will be explored in later chapters at greater length.

The Case(s) for Participation

Three broad arguments support participation: The first is *humanistic*—that is, that, by contributing to personal growth and job satisfaction, participation will enhance human dignity. The second argument, *power-sharing*, is that participation will redistribute social power, protect employees' interests, strengthen unions, and extend the benefits of political democracy to the workplace. The third is that participation will promote *organizational efficiency* (Dachler and Wilpert 1978).

Humanistic

Of the three arguments, the humanistic is most appealing to us. Described at greater length in Chapter 2, the argument is that participation helps satisfy employees' non-pecuniary needs including those for creativity, achievement, and social approval. It contributes to a sense of competence, self-work, and self-actualization. It makes use of the whole person. For employees, having a voice in how they do their work may be as important as how much they are paid for it. As it is sometimes put, 'A worker should not have to leave his or her head at the factory gate or office door.'

Indeed, it is argued, participation is a necessary antecedent to human psychological and social development. For example, experience in organizational participation may lead to greater participation in the community generally (Pateman 1970; Elden 1986). In any case, humanistic demands may become more insistent as employees become better educated and their basic needs for survival are better satisfied.

Power-Sharing

Advocates of this approach support participation for ideological and moral reasons, arguing that the traditional autocratic relationships are inherently unjust and inconsistent with the values of a democratic society (e.g. Vanek 1971 and Horvat 1983). Some do so on political grounds, others out of religious or moral conviction. (Indeed, Dachler and Wilpert (1978) distinguish between 'democratic' and 'power-equalization' theories.)

Although 'industrial democracy' or 'workers' control' has been a traditional goal of younger left-leaning people of almost every persuasion, they have differed as to how it could be achieved. Disillusioned by Soviet-style socialism, many younger radicals value the freedom of individual employees to direct their own work. By contrast, traditional communists rejected shop-level employees' control, as did many older socialists, most notably Sidney and Beatrice Webb (1920). Workers' control for these socialists meant public ownership and control of the economy on a fairly centralized basis. With employees' self-management, they feared, employees in each workplace might favour their own narrow interests rather than those of the working class as a whole.

Unionists today differ considerably in their attitudes towards participation. Some see it as a management tool, designed to capture employee loyalty and weaken union influence. Other unionists (and in other circumstances) view it chiefly as a means of curbing unilateral management power and of extending 'the frontiers of union control' to cover issues commonly subject to collective bargaining in unionized plants in English-speaking countries. (This issue gets more attention in Chapter 4.)

Power-sharing arguments were plentiful in the 1960–70s (in Britain, for example, in the Bullock (1977) report). According to some observers, workers involved in the wave of strikes which engulfed France and much of Europe in 1968 were protesting not just for higher wages, but also against bad working conditions and arbitrary management. They demanded 'a say in management, if not the introduction of some form of "workers' control"' (Pontusson 1992: 29; see also Crouch and Pizzorno 1978; Streeck 1995).

More recently, however, the discussion has focused on participation's organizational impacts (Lammers and Széll 1989*b*). Arguments have focused more on organizational efficiency than on workplace humanization or justice.[1] Why this shift towards more modest goals? First, experience with real participation in numerous contexts has demonstrated that, while participation has many advantages, it is unlikely to transform society or make the workplace into paradise. Secondly, the lengthy European economic recession has required greater attention to productivity than to social justice. And, finally and concomitantly, the political pendulum has swung generally to the right. Unions have lost power in most countries.

Organizational Efficiency

Explanations abound of the positive impacts of participation on organizational efficiency (e.g. Locke 1968; Lowin 1968; Miller and Monge 1986; Aoki 1990). Below we outline these arguments. (Note: whilst the discussion below focuses on employee participation, practically all the arguments apply to participation within management as well.)

1. Participation may result in better decisions. Employees often have information which senior management lacks. Further, participation permits different views to be aired and in this way the danger of groupthink is reduced.
2. People may be more likely to implement decisions they helped make themselves than decisions imposed on them from above. Not only do they know better what is expected of them, but helping make a decision commits them to it
3. Motivation is frequently enhanced, psychology has shown, by the setting of goals during the participative decision process (Locke 1968).
4. Participation may improve communications and cooperation; employees may coordinate each other, thus saving management time. Further, by disseminating the experience in employee problem-solving, participation may facilitate organizational learning. In so doing participation contributes to what Aoki (1990) calls dynamic (as opposed to static) efficiency.
5. Participative subordinates may supervise themselves, again making managers' and supervisors' lives easier.
6. Joint participation by employees and management to solve problems on a non-adversarial basis may improve employee–management relations generally.
7. On a personal level, employees may learn new skills through participation; leadership potential may be readily identified and developed.

In short, from an organizational point of view participation may change (*a*) how employees perceive their jobs, (*b*) how they do these jobs, and (*c*) how they and their unions relate to their employer.

Many of the foregoing arguments overlap. Participation provides what industrial-relations people call 'voice'. Voice is the key to influence-sharing. From a humanistic perspective, voice enhances personal dignity; from an organizational perspective, it reduces frustration, contributes to motivation and identification, and so lessens participants' need to demonstrate power through fighting management and restricting production. In so doing it may reduce turnover and absenteeism.

But note the tentative nature of the statements above. As we shall see in later chapters, these assumed advantages do not always translate into successful organizational practice. Indeed, for every advantage, participation has a disadvantage. Many of these disadvantages are substantial. More on this in Chapter 6.

Why has Participation Become so Popular?

While these arguments may be appealing, they do not completely explain why the concept of participation has become so popular in recent years. There are a numerous other explanations.

Technological Change

As we discuss at greater length in Chapter 3, recent technological and economic developments have considerably strengthened the organizational case for participation, especially in developed economies. As mass-production techniques have spread to low-wage countries, high-wage countries find it much harder to compete in the manufacture of standardized goods. Their comparative advantage rests increasingly on their capacity to adjust rapidly to technological and market changes and their ability to produce high-quality, high value-added, specialized, 'high-tech' products and services (Cressey 1991).

All this requires a flexible, better-trained, highly skilled workforce. These qualities are especially important in technologies where initiative is required and shirking difficult to detect. Under these circumstances there is an advantage in having employees who are willing and able (motivated and trained) to make decisions on their own. Further, teamwork and rapid communications are required. Thus participation may be the key to maintaining a competitive edge.

An example may illustrate this point. Women's clothing has been traditionally produced on a semi-mass-production basis. Dressmaking, for example, is divided into a series of steps, each performed by a different employee, with several days typically elapsing between steps and a resulting production cycle of a month or more. Because of the diversity of products, closer coordination is difficult. In the past this delay was not excessively costly because garments were normally ordered many months before they were to be sold.

But this system had two main disadvantages. First, despite the garment industry's relatively low wages, wages in developing countries are much lower; consequently much of the industry has moved overseas. Secondly, fashion (especially high fashion) is always a gamble. Designs which look hot to professional buyers in the spring may bomb in the fall. As a result a high proportion of each year's stock must be 'remaindered'—that is, sold at a substantial discount.

Several high-volume discount chains have revolted against the system. Through use of point-of-sale scanners, electronically connected to company headquarters, management can tell instantly its present stock of every model and size. Instead of carrying large inventories, management now operate a Just In Time (JIT) system: it orders goods as needed and insists on one-or-two week delivery (three days in the case of Wal-Mart). Meeting these short delivery deadlines has required an almost revolutionary change in the affected suppliers' manufacturing methods. Increasingly, production is assigned to 'modules' (teams) of multi-skilled employees who assign, schedule, and coordinate their own work, with full responsibility for meeting their customer-imposed deadlines. Each module makes an entire garment or a major part of one. Though moderately costly to install initially, modules have advantages in terms of labour costs, quality, and, of course, quick delivery (Berg *et al.* 1996; Dunlop and Weil 1996). We will have more to say about this case later.

Rapid technological change (plus increased competition) requires what Germans call 'flexibility' (Thelen 1991) and changes in what Americans call 'work rules' and the British call 'custom and practice'. Especially given the possibility of union and employee opposition, such changes were typically more easily accommodated when made participatively than when introduced autocratically.

Even where technology does not *require* participation, it may make it easier. For example, computers have made communications easier. It is no longer necessary for all messages to go through a hierarchy. E-mail, for instance, ignores status and departmental barriers. Anyone in the organization can instantly communicate with everyone else. And so, whether management likes it or not, e-mail makes it easier for employees to participate. Indeed if they are not allowed to use e-mail to participate in *making* decisions, they may use it to organize resistance to decisions made at higher levels. On the other hand, while e-mail, 'hot lines', and attitude surveys may provide management with essential information, they are poor substitutes for face-to-face participation. (We return to this issue in Chapter 7.)

Another factor contributing to the spread of participation is the growth of service work. By contrast with manufacturing, service employees' attitudes are an essential part of the 'product' they provide. A cheerful waiter or a concerned nurse provides a totally different product from one who is surly (Cobble 1994). To the extent that participation improves attitudes it also improves the quality of the service provided.

Further, new organizational forms, such as contingent employment, telecommuting, and networks (Miles and Snow 1986), all have some impact on both the desirability and feasibility of participation, though more study is needed. For more on this, see Chapters 6 and 7.

Overall Management Strategies

Growing international competition and financial adversity have led many companies to experiment with new forms of organization, including participation. Indeed, participation is a key ingredient in management strategies utilizing 'high-commitment' or 'high-involvement' policies (e.g. Lawler 1986). To use popular buzzwords, the purpose of these policies is to 'empower' employees and develop 'high-performance' or 'transformed' workplaces. Important elements in these policies include considerable individual autonomy, high investment in training, a multi-skilled workforce, job security, broad job descriptions, performance-based pay, and a heavy emphasis on organizational symbols and culture (Levine 1995). Indeed, as we argue later, there is considerable (but not conclusive) evidence that participation is less likely to be successful if it is not accompanied by such policies. High-involvement policies themselves are consistent with what Miles and Snow (1978; 1994) call a 'Prospector' strategy of continuously seeking new products and markets and what others call a 'high skill–high wage' strategy.

Concomitant with these developments at the workplace level has been the increasing popularity of managerial teams—for example, the cross-departmental team of designers, engineers, purchasing, manufacturing, and marketing experts which developed Chrysler's new Neon car. Through making it easier for individual departments to coordinate their own efforts, such teams reduce higher management's workload. Increasing participation within work groups is also consistent with growing collaboration between producers and suppliers in designing new products and ironing out quality problems. Many of these developments go under the heading of 'network organization' (Miles and Snow 1986; Marin and Mayntz 1991).

On the other hand, the 1990s have seen a considerable shift among companies worldwide from high-involvement policies to those of cost-cutting, 'downsizing', and 'restructuring'. These two sets of policies are incompatible, although management often seems unaware of this. Under these circumstance, participation is less appropriate and less likely to be adopted (but see Drago 1996, who argues that many companies introduce participation primarily to cut costs).

Fads

But participation is often a fad (Marchington *et al.* 1993). Indeed Ramsay (1983; 1990) argues that interest comes in cycles, with interest being greater when management's traditional rights are in question.[2] Various forms of participation are adopted because they are popular at the moment and are pushed by consultants and management publications. Bottom-up management, work humanization, and Quality of Working Life (QWL) programmes were all popular for a while and were then abandoned for new concepts which differed little from their predecessors except in name and buzz words used. Quality Circles (QCs), in their classical form, may now be on their way out (Applebaum and Batt 1994). Today the emphasis is on teams, Total Quality Management (TQM), and Employee Involvement (EI). Indeed, the term 'team' is often used for activities which ten years previously were called QCs (Work Practices Diffusion Team 1994).

Management's tendency to follow fads is a problem because in many cases it adopts participation programmes chiefly as a 'quick fix', a low-cost solution to problems of low productivity, poor quality, or whatever ails the organization—and does so without recognizing that these programmes require substantial changes in day-to-day behaviour, heavy investment in training, and often considerable reduction in managerial discretion. Management's failure to consider these facts helps explain why many participation programmes are short-lived and unsuccessful.

Managers are not the only ones to follow fads. There are similar fads among politicians, union leaders, and intellectuals. 'Autogestion' (self-management) was the French fad in the 1960s and 1970s. Meanwhile Charles de Gaulle espoused his own brand of 'participation', which featured a heavy emphasis on profit-sharing. In the USA during the same period there was considerable concern with 'Blue Collar Blues' and the Nixon Administration pushed heavily for QWL reforms.

Laws

The laws in many countries require various forms of participation (see discussion below). Indeed, laws and other legally binding rules provide a major explanation for differences in the extent of actual participation across countries (IDE 1981*b*; 1993). As we discuss later, recent European Union (EU) legislation may spread participation further.

In Practice: A Mixture of Reasons

In practice participation is adopted for a variety of different reasons, including many not discussed above. For example, according to Hartmann (1970; see also Thelen 1991), co-determination was reintroduced in Germany after the war because of the fortunate juxtaposition of numerous interests: the British occupying forces sought to curb industrialists' power, managers hoped participation would protect their plants from Allied dismantling, whereas Catholic liberals found it consistent with papal encyclicals. Though unions opposed the 1952 law establishing co-determination on a nation-wide basis, eventually they found the way to strengthen and dominate the process.

In Britain, in the mid-1970s the Labour Government offered unions 'industrial democracy', in part in return for acquiescence (through the social contract) in an incomes policy. Similarly, through much of Europe participation was viewed as a key element in 'corporatism'. And in the USA, participation is often a key part of a trade-off through which companies obtain union cooperation in reducing production costs in the face of serious competitive pressures. Non-union US firms often offer participation as a substitute for union representation. Many British firms have adopted similar strategies.

Various forms of participation, particularly worker ownership and self-management, have been proposed in an effort to spur development and foster a democratic society. This has been particularly the case in Eastern Europe (Kolarska 1984; Yanowitch 1991; Kostova 1993) and underdeveloped countries (McClintock *et al.* 1984; Putterman 1984).

Given the variety of reasons for which participation has been introduced, it is understandable that the parties have differing expectations as to how it should work and what it should accomplish. Nevertheless the reasons for which participation is introduced often have little to do with how it works in practice. Despite the original political and ideological reasons for fostering German participation, in actuality it has had a considerable effect on German economic success (see Chapter 6). By contrast many elaborate participation structures, introduced for the best reasons, have never taken off. Indeed the reasons for participation's initial introduction may have little to do with whether it is successful. Specific examples of this are provided in Chapters 5 and 6.

Defining Participation

Definitions of participation abound. Some authors insist that participation must be a group process, involving groups of employees and their boss; others stress delegation, the process by which the *individual* employee is given greater freedom to make decisions on his or her own. Some restrict the term 'participation' to formal institutions, such as works councils; other definitions embrace 'informal participation', the day-to-day relations between supervisors and subordinates in which subordinates are allowed substantial input into work decisions. Finally, there are those who stress participation as a *process* and those who are concerned with participation as a *result*.

For the moment we will define participation as a process which allows employees to exert some influence over their work and the conditions under which they work. Chapter 2 discusses definitional issues at greater length.

Varieties of Participation

Analytically forms of participation can be divided into three overlapping categories: requisite, informal, and formal (including both direct and representative participation). This book focuses on the formal and to a lesser extent informal approaches to participation.

Requisite Participation

This form of participation is required to get the job done. It is determined by the technology and organization of work. Athletic teams develop high levels of rapid coordination (participation), often doing so without verbal communications or advance planning. After all, things happen fast on a football field, too fast for a coach or captain to control events through endless explicit instructions.[3] Much of the same can be said about many work situations, regardless of whether the work is manual or intellectual. The more complex the work, the more important it is to have willing and committed employee participation.

As mentioned earlier, recent technological and economic changes have increased the extent of requisite participation. Traditional clothing manufacturing techniques required little participation (see above); management made the key work-flow decisions. The new module system made it mandatory that employees coordinate themselves. In some situations decisions have to be made so quickly and so much information needs to be processed that it is dangerous not to allow wide dissemination of decision-making power. For example, the safe operation of a 'high-reliability' system, such as a nuclear aircraft carrier, requires that substantial discretion be given all levels of personnel. Even the lowest ranking enlisted woman on a US Navy carrier is encouraged to halt a plane launch if she thinks safety is at risk (Roberts 1990).

Organizations may be designed either to require participation or to make participation unnecessary, regardless of the technical requirements of the decisions to be made. The traditional Tayloristic production system, with its close control over worker behaviour, was deliberately designed to make participation unnecessary and even impossible—or so some argue. Similarly, the design of computerized production systems in Britain kept control of the computer strictly in the hands of management and engineers; by contrast, German systems allowed blue-collar workers to do their own programming. In Britain computerization reduced workers' powers, in Germany it increased it (Sorge *et al.* 1983).

Between the extremes, in which participation is either essential or quite difficult, are situations in which the organizations have considerable choice as to forms of governance. For years the automobile line technology was viewed as making employee discretion impossible. Yet, as we shall see, high degrees of participation are possible even in this industry. Technology is not the only determining factor.

Informal Participation

Informal participation differs from its formal counterpart in that there are no explicit mechanisms involved. Likert (1961) describes the participative manager as one who listens to subordinates, encourages them to express themselves, grants wide discretion, is non-punitive in handling mistakes, and de-emphasizes status differences. The participative manager combines the functions of chair, team leader, and coach.[4]

Those studying informal participation approach it from two points of view. The first looks on participation as a *decision process* and is interested in how decisions are made. The second sees participation as a *resultant*, the extent to which subordinates are *in fact* able to *influence* decisions (or, more frequently, the extent to which they see themselves as influencing decisions). The latter is sometimes called *de facto* participation (IDE 1981*b*; 1993), while, to the extent that the decision process is mandated by law or union contract, it is called *de jure* participation (for further discussion, see Chapter 5).

In theory the extent of informal participation in a given situation can be located along three dimensions (Strauss 1977):

- whether decisions involve individual subordinates or groups of subordinates (this book is concerned primarily with group forms of participation);
- whether decisions are made formally by the boss, jointly, or by the subordinate(s);

Table 1.1. *Forms of decision process*

Decision made by	Decision involving	
	An individual	A group
Boss	Individual direction	Group direction
Jointly	Consultation	Joint discussion
Subordinates	Delegation	Group decision-making

Table 1.2. *Combining process and influence approaches*

Process	Subordinate influence	
	Low	High
Direction	Boss makes decision ignoring subordinate's preferences completely	Boss makes the kinds of decisions he thinks subordinates would want him to make—follows the polls
Consultation	Boss meets with subordinates, asks for agreement on a decision, but makes it clear by tone of view that he will accept no disagreement	Boss chairs the meeting but gives no indication of his preference
Delegation	Subordinate is formally free to make any decision he wants, but from prior experience he knows that he will be punished if he deviates from the boss's preferences	Subordinate is completely free to make decision on his own

- the extent of the subordinates' actual power or ability to influence these decisions.

The first two dimensions involve process. They can be combined in a matrix (see Table 1.1). The third dimension relates to influence. Both influence and process are critical and reinforce each other. Table 1.2 brings the two concepts together. Bosses who do not hold formal meetings with their subordinates may actually permit more influence than bosses who hold frequent meetings in which they mastermind subordinates until they eventually come up with the decision the boss wanted in the first place.

The distinction between formal and informal participation may be quite arbitrary.[5] A boss may meet her subordinates around a table to discuss work problems in pursuance of a written quality-circle plan; this is formal participation. Or the same individuals may gather informally to discuss the same problems around a water cooler; this is informal participation.

One of the advantages of formal participation is that it may encourage informal participation. Further, as we shall stress, formal participation is more likely to be successful if introduced in an atmosphere of informal participation. Unfortunately, as we discuss further in Chapter 5, managers often engage in 'manipulative' participation: they go through the motions of participation without allowing their subordinates any real influence (Heller 1971).

Formal Participation

Forms of formal participation can be classified under four headings or dimensions, as Table 1.3 illustrates. Under each heading forms of participation are ranged in a continuum, from weak employees' power to strong. The examples are designed to be merely illustrative. The German works council, for example, is not the only form of plant-level participation; many other examples could be cited—for example, Australian plant safety committees. Further, each individual form of participation fits somewhere on the four dimensions. For example, quality circles operate at the departmental level, they involve joint consultation, they deal with production methods, and they do not necessarily require employee ownership.

Organizational level. Perhaps the most important distinction here is between direct and representative (indirect) participation. Direct participation involves individual employees and includes such schemes as quality circles and work teams. Representative participation involves employee representatives, often selected by their union. Typically this form of participation is concerned with plant- or higher-level problems. Direct participation is more frequently initiated by management, while representative participation tends to be initiated by unions or is based on law.

Degree of control.[6] Consultation means that management listens to employees' suggestions and may even seek their ideas; nevertheless management retains the right to make the final decision. Joint decision-making requires consent from both sides. In theory, with self-management, employees give orders to management.

Laws in many European countries distinguish between three levels of influence: (1) information, (2) consultation, and (3) joint decision-making/negotiation (Gill and Krieger 1992)—or, as the Germans call it, co-determination.

A more elaborate and widely utilized approach to degree of control is represented by a measure called the Influence Power Continuum (IPC) (Heller 1971), a continuum with six points, ranging from 'no information' (in which the boss makes the decision without providing subordinates with detailed information about the decision made), through various degree of consultation, to joint decision-making, and, finally, subordinates making decisions on their own (for further

Table 1.3. *Major participation dimensions*

Dimensions	Illustrative examples
Organizational level	
Individual	Job enrichment
Small group	Autonomous work team
Department	Quality circle
Plant	German works council
Company	Worker directors
Degree of control	
Joint consultation	French works councils
Joint decision-making	Co-determination in the German iron and steel industry
Self-management	Yugoslavia (in the 1980s); producers' cooperatives; semi-autonomous work groups
Range of issues	
Wages	Collective bargaining in most countries
Personnel issues (e.g. redundancy and training)	Collective bargaining in the USA; works councils in Germany
Welfare benefits	French works council regarding medical service
Production methods	Quality circles, semi-autonomous work groups
Selecting managers	Yugoslav workers' councils
Major investment decisions	Supervisory board under German co-determination
Ownership	
No employee ownership	Typical company
Some employee ownership	Employee stock ownership plans
Complete employee ownership	Producers' cooperative

discussion, see Chapter 5). The IPC was perhaps the most significant measure used in the seminal IDE study.[7]

Range of issues. Participation may occur regarding a wide variety of issues. Table 1.3 lists only a few. IDE examined the decision-making processes regarding eighteen different issues, ranging from 'assignment of tasks to workers' to 'major capital investment'. These issues were aggregated into three basic categories according to 'time perspective'—short-term (e.g. working hours), medium-term (e.g. wage levels), and long-term (e.g. investment)—and again by subject matter, work/social conditions (e.g. personal equipment), personnel (e.g. dismissals), and economic (e.g. new products).

Table 1.4. *Two examples of extent of influence by task*

	Extent of influence 1	2	3	4	5	6
Work assignments			*		†	
Work layout				*	†	
Vacation scheduling				*		†
Redundancy	*		†			
Training	*			†		
Dividend policy	*					

* hypothetical average, formal UK joint consultative committee.
† hypothetical work team with broad discretion.

Notes: Extent of influence: 1. no or minimal information; 2. information; 3. opportunity to give advice; 4. advice taken into consideration; 5. joint decision-making; 6. complete control (autonomy or delegation). Note that the consultative committee has no influence over work layout or dividend policy, but it does have an opportunity to give advice over work assignments, redundancies, and training, and its advice is taken into account in scheduling vacations. The work team engages in joint decision-making regarding work assignments and layouts, but has no influence otherwise.

Participation regarding work assignments and production methods typically occurs at lower levels, while investment decisions are discussed higher up. In any case, the greater the range of issues discussed, the broader the participation. Table 1.4 illustrates the degree of influence which a hypothetical semi-autonomous work team and a hypothetical traditional British consultative committee might have with regards to six possible issues.

Chapter 3 distinguishes between participation regarding interest decisions and that regarding technical decisions. As the term implies, interest decisions relate primarily to participants' own, individual welfare—for example, wages, redundancy, training, and benefits—while technical decisions relate to organizational efficiency—for example, production methods. Meaningful participation in technical decisions is dependent on appropriate knowledge and information, more so than for participation in interest decisions.

Ownership. Ownership is sometimes called 'economic' or 'financial' participation. Employees may own all or part of a firm. Ownership can take various forms. Rather than highlighting legal ownership as such, Ben-Ner and Jones (1995) focus on what they call return rights which they contrast with control rights. Return rights relate to claims to income, such as profit-sharing and stock-ownership, while control rights refer to the degree-of-control dimension just discussed. Ben-Ner and Jones construct a two-dimensional matrix with control and return rights being the two dimensions.

As we shall see, employee-owned companies are often undemocratic, since employees have few control rights. Even return rights may be restricted. Often workers share profits, but may not sell shares until they leave the company. Or profits may be used for social amenities rather than paid to workers. To clarify these issues, Mygind (1992) distinguishes among three kinds of so-called 'democratic ownership'. In the first, decisions are made by employees themselves and they share the surplus (profits). The second differs from the first in that profits are shared collectively (devoted to social amenities), while the third is really government ownership in that decisions are made by democratically elected central authorities and the government takes the profits.

Decision-making stages. Heller, Drenth, Koopman, and Rus (1988) examine influence distribution at four decision-making stages: (1) initiation, (2) development, (3) finalization, and (4) implementation. Gill and Krieger (1992) have a somewhat similar scheme with three stages: planning, technology-selection, and implementation. Representative participation may be more common at the planning stage, whilst direct participation is more common during implementation.

Rather than consider each participative form in detail, this chapter deals with only three types of participation, direct participation, representative participation, and employee ownership. To save space, it will be concerned only with formal participation schemes and thus ignore informal boss–employee relations and also collective bargaining, even though the latter may be the most important form of all. (Chapter 4 discusses collective bargaining at length, whilst Chapters 3 and 5 deal with informal participation.)

Direct Participation

Direct-participation schemes, often called EI or QWL programmes ('work humanization' in Germany), represent an attempt to empower employees (Guest 1983). They constitute a reaction against Taylorism and the tendency to deskill employees. Their popularity derives also from their frequent association with Japanese management.

Among the most common forms of direct participation are *problem-solving groups* (such as quality circles) and *decision-making work teams*, also called semi-autonomous work groups (or, in some ex-communist countries, brigades). Decision-making teams can implement their decisions on their own, within specified limits, while problem-solving groups can only make recommendations to management.[8] TQM typically involves problem-solving groups. All are formalized means of taking advantages of employee ideas or what economists call their 'insider knowledge'. But they differ in the extent to which groups actually exert influence. (Other forms of participation, such as job enrichment, or of voice, such as suggestion systems, which provide autonomy for individuals, will not be discussed in this chapter, although they do provide important forms of participation.)

Problem-Solving Groups

Problem-solving groups (typically called QCs, but sometimes titled task forces, job-involvement programmes, labour-management production teams, or merely participation meetings) normally consist of small groups of employees from the same work area who meet together voluntarily on a regular basis.[9] Their chair may be their supervisor, a staff 'facilitator', or another employee. Frequently members of the group receive special training in such subjects as group dynamics and statistical analysis.

Despite their name, QCs typically deal with other subjects in addition to quality—for example, work flow, productivity, safety, and employees' welfare generally. Often such committees start with individual employees' gripes, move on to quality and working conditions, and later, as members gain confidence in working with each other and trust in management's receptivity to their suggestions, progress to questions relating to safety and eventually productivity.

Though the QC concept was originally developed in the USA (and has antecedents in the UK (Scott and Lynton 1952)), QCs were first widely adopted in Japan (Cole 1989). In recent years they have spread throughout the world. According to the limited figures available, QCs are more common in Japan than in the USA and much more common in both countries than they are in the UK (Marginson *et al.* 1988; Lincoln 1989; Millward *et al.* 1992; Geary 1994). Interestingly QCs are more prevalent in unionized plants in Britain than they are in non-union plants, while the evidence is less clear in the USA (Cooke 1988; Eaton and Voos 1992; Lawler *et al.* 1992; Osterman 1994*a*). According to both Australian and US surveys problem-solving groups were established at a rapid rate in these countries in the mid-1980s, though many have been abandoned since then (Marchington 1992*a*; Applebaum and Batt 1994; for German data, see Muller-Jentsch 1995: 126).

In some circumstances QC meetings may be little more than managerial pep talks, with little opportunity for employee input. When this happens, employees conclude that participation is a meaningless, 'Mickey Mouse' exercise. Sometimes, however, quality circles evolve into work teams or TQM (Stephen Hill 1991).

Among the advantages of problem-solving groups is the fact that they formalize the process of workplace innovation. Employees frequently think up ways of making their job more efficient, but they keep these to themselves or pass them on to close friends and hide them from management (Roethlisberger and Dickson 1939). Problem-solving teams encourage employees to reveal their innovations and make them 'public property'. Once formally approved, such innovations can be adopted by other employees department-wide and, if there are suitable communications links, disseminated throughout the organization. Thus they remain in the organization's memory. In this way problem-solving groups contribute to organizational learning (Adler and Cole 1993).

Total Quality Management

TQM goes beyond QCs in that it is typically an organization-wide effort involving teams of employees and managers (sometimes including even the Chief Executive Officer (CEO)). QCs, by contrast, solve problems in isolation. Further, TQM's overt, announced focus is on satisfying the needs of customers, both external and internal. TQM teams typically follow a set problem-solving procedure: starting with tracking the number and timing of problems (statistical process control), then analysing sources of error, generating a range of possible solutions, evaluating each alternative solution, picking one, implementing it, and finally checking whether the proposed solutions actually solved the problem. TQM is sometimes linked to ISO 9000, which requires that companies establish, maintain, and follow documented procedures for maintaining quality (although there is no requirement that these procedures be continually improved (Levine 1995)).[10]

To the extent that TQM facilitates communications of employee experiences in problem-solving it contributes to organizational learning. Further it makes quality management a normal method of operating. The functions of making recommendations and implementing them are linked together. Other forms of direct participation often bypass levels of management. By contrast, 'the extension of managerial participation under TQM is a significant gain for people, who like the employees they supervise, have a real interest in a more participative system of managing' (Stephen Hill 1991: 561). On the other hand, in practice TQM often permits little real participation (Tuckerman 1994). Delbridge, Turnbull and Wilkinson (1992) call TQM Total Management Control (TMC). TQM has been criticized as involving change from above.

Among the advantages of both QCs and TQM is the fact that they focus on a single generally accepted goal, quality. Employees and unions are rarely enthusiastic about productivity, since higher productivity may mean fewer jobs. Other goals, such as increased job satisfaction and motivation, are hard to measure—and may not be among top management's priorities. But no one objects to quality. Most employees prefer to do quality work, provided they are not too rushed to do this.

Decision-Making Teams

The concept of work teams developed out of research conducted by the Tavistock Institute in Britain on 'socio-technical systems' and later introduced extensively into Norwegian companies (Gustavsen 1983; Thorsrud 1984; West 1994). Work teams give employees fairly substantial discretion to organize their own work and operate without supervision.

The Tavistock's major research began with studies conducted in coal mines in the 1940s and 1950s (Trist and Bamforth 1951). At one time all the operations on the typical mine face were performed by small teams, each of which worked on a single shift. These teams had complete control of their work arrangements. There was no supervision; teams could pick their own members; and each employee was expected to acquire the complete range of skills required to do the entire job (such as drilling, handling explosives, and building elaborate supporting frameworks). Since group members were in close contact with one another, it was easy to devise solutions for problems as they arose. Each member felt responsible for the entire operation.

When a new technology was introduced, management tried to increase efficiency by working with much larger groups, each having specialized functions (thus seriously reducing skill diversity) and operating in the three-shift, 24-hour cycle. As a result of this division of labour, no single group felt responsible for the entire operation. As problems arose each shift developed the habit of shrugging them off and passing the buck to the next shift.

Trist and Bamforth discovered several mines which used the new technology but had not adopted the full mechanistic division of labour which prevailed elsewhere. Instead, they retained a degree of semi-autonomy and multi-skilling and this arrangement contributed to the concept of what was later called 'socio-technical systems'.

Teamwork proved to be highly efficient, at least in coal mining, and the socio-technical concept (though not the practice) spread rapidly, especially in Scandinavia. Its popularity was based on the belief that flexible, multi-skilled, decentralized, participative work designs are more productive than traditional, closely supervised, single-skill arrangements which allow little or no scope for employee initiative. From an employee's point of view there were two major apparent advantages of work teams: first, they were allowed to participate in shop-floor decisions, and, secondly, they were subject to much looser supervision.

Despite work teams' intellectual appeal, they have been adopted more slowly than QCs, in part because they require a substantial transfer of power from supervisors to the workforce.[11] For example, work teams have been given responsibility for safety, quality control, and holiday scheduling as well as for developing relations with suppliers, determining which operations are handled individually and which by the group as a whole, setting work pace, and repairing their own equipment (Gardell 1983; West 1994). In addition, they may select, evaluate, train, and sometimes discipline their own members. Often, too, individual workers are given the authority to 'pull the cord' which shuts down an entire production line. Such groups often meet every week or two (forty-seven minutes per week in the case of Saturn—see later). At times each group is given a room or alcove of its own where it can keep records, hold meetings, and perhaps display personal memorabilia.[12]

Sometimes work team members serve in roles normally reserved for staff personnel or supervisors: chairing the plant-safety committee, redesigning work equipment, or trouble-shooting customers' problems. The latter have more autonomy. Occasionally the job of supervisor is rotated among members of the group. At

Saturn-GM in the USA (discussed later) and Opel-GM in Germany team leaders are elected (Turner and Auer 1994). The introduction of team organization is often accompanied by the elimination of one management level and bestowing on the remaining first-line managers of new team-oriented titles such as 'coach' or 'consultant'.

Applebaum and Batt (1994) distinguish between three kinds of work teams with increasing degrees of autonomy: (1) supervised teams, (2) semi-autonomous work teams (a term quite common in Europe), and (3) autonomous work teams. In supervised teams the workers' role is primarily consultative and management still makes all critical decisions. Semi-autonomous teams report to 'team leaders' or 'coaches' but have broad autonomy. Truly autonomous teams, who receive virtually no direct supervision, are quite rare except in small producers' cooperatives or small organizations with members holding communitarian values (Rothschild-Whitt 1979). (The decentralized decisions in true autonomous work teams fit at the extreme point of the Influence Power Continuum (IPC) described above.) A major difference is between teams that meet with and those which meet without a supervisor present.

One of the most successful recent turnabouts in American industry occurred at NUMMI, the joint GM-Toyota venture located at GM's former drugs–absenteeism–poor-labour-relations-plagued Fremont, California, plant. Using almost the same technology and employees as the old plant, NUMMI productivity has roughly doubled[13] and it has the lowest absentee rate among US auto plants. Quality (as measured by number of defects) has also been excellent. Here 'work teams' are responsible for planning job rotation, balancing work assignments to equalize workloads, and engaging in 'kaizen' (continuous job improvement). Team leaders, who remain union members, are selected on the basis of recommendations of a joint union–management committee (Adler 1992).

At NUMMI the basic highly repetitive assembly technology, with its sixty-second job cycle, is retained.[14] Indeed the NUMMI form of production is an example of what Womack, Jones, and Roos (1990) call 'lean production' (see also Work Practices Diffusion Team 1994). Every operator's movements are carefully described and standardized. Through constant 'kaizen', workers engage in 'self-Taylorization', thus eliminating the few seconds of slack (or 'personal time') which might allow them to take a break or vary their work pace. A suggestion made by a work team, if accepted by management, is applied uniformly elsewhere. Thus the organization is a 'learning bureaucracy' (Adler 1992).

NUMMI-type participation has a major advantage: to the extent that workers participate in 'designing their own chains' they are more likely to accept the result as fair. On the other hand, job-redesign techniques capture the secret short cuts which employees could once use to make their lives easier (Adler and Cole 1993). Thus, as we discuss in Chapter 5, management can supervise them more easily.

In some Scandinavian experiments (e.g. in some Volvo shops) the technology itself has been changed: each individual employee performs a major portion of the total assembly process and the continuous assembly line has been eliminated.

With Scandinavian-style (socio-technical) groups substantial changes are required in technology, work flow, and work layout. The goal of the Scandinavian approach has been to adapt technology to the employees' needs, rather than to require employees to adapt to technology. Often employees are involved from the beginning in designing new work systems.

By contrast to the NUMMI approach, the Scandinavian approach to organization emphasizes work-team autonomy rather than team interdependence and coordination. Consequently substantial buffers (inventories) may be required between groups. Further, work teams may be too autonomous; they may fail to coordinate their efforts with other groups. Thus one team's innovations may not be passed on to the others, so inhibiting organizational learning. Adler and Cole (1993) suggest this may have happened at Udevalla. (For more extensive discussions of differences among various kinds of work teams, see Auer and Riegler 1990; Berggren 1991; Manz 1992; Applebaum and Batt 1994; Work Practices Diffusion Team 1994.)

For work teams to succeed, extensive cross-training is frequently required. At times, to reduce resistance to switching jobs, the number of job classifications has been greatly reduced, a process often called 'broad banding' or 'multi-skilling'. Thus, at NUMMI the eighty-five job classifications existing under previous GM management were cut to four. And, with 'pay for knowledge', compensation is based on the number of skills a employee has mastered and is willing to practise—rather than (as is traditional) the employee's primary job assignment.

As we discuss in Chapter 6, the introduction of work teams is often accompanied by the elimination of important management status symbols, such as separate parking lots and dining rooms.

Despite their current popularity, QCs and work teams often fail to live up to their promise. Management may give groups too little discretion. Multi-skilling may merely give management greater flexibility to move employees arbitrarily from one task to another. Thus 'multi-skilling' may mean only 'multi-tasking', in that a few new skills are learned but autonomy is not increased. Lengthening the job cycle does not necessarily mean more participation if employees have little discretion in determining the sequence and methods by which various portions of the cycle are done (Lawler 1986). Critics argue that, though nominally concerned with enlisting workers' ideas, EI plans serve chiefly to weaken work rules and gain employee acceptances for changes which may not be in their own interest (Chell 1983: 488). In short, they are instruments for potential employee self-exploitation or 'management by stress' (Parker 1985; Fucini and Fucini 1990).

Representative Participation

For a variety of reasons, direct participation may have only limited effectiveness unless combined with representative participation. Many important issues cannot be resolved at the workplace level: for example, more than one department may be involved, top management's approval may be needed to authorize change, or employees and supervisors may have differences which they cannot work out on their own. Further, innovations developed in one department need to be disseminated elsewhere. Finally, key issues, such as work-flow or employment conditions, have implications which extend well beyond any one particular department. In fact only relatively unimportant decisions are made at the workplace level. Really important decisions, relating, for example, to job security, are made higher up.

Arguably, since representative participation requires more careful deliberation, it improves the quality of decisions and gives them greater legitimacy (even though they may slow down the decision-making process). Further it may improve upwards and downwards communications. Two examples illustrate these advantages.

The US Scanlon Plan provides for 'production committees' (problem-solving groups equivalent to QCs) in each department (Schuster 1983). These make suggestions for productivity and quality improvement, many of which are beyond the foreman's power to approve. Rather than ignoring these, they are referred to a plant-wide 'steering committee', consisting of union representatives and top management leaders. This committee can authorize change. Thus direct and representative participation are neatly combined. (A second strength of the plan is its linkage with financial gain sharing, as discussed in Chapter 6.)

A large manufacturing company had two plants, one union and the other non-union. Both plants suffered from continuing complaints regarding the employee cafeteria. The non-union plant installed a cafeteria suggestion system and made continuous changes in its menu, all to no avail. The second delegated control of its cafeteria to a joint union–management committee. Complaints did not disappear, but greatly declined (and some of the pressure was shifted from the management to the union).

Some authorities (e.g. Likert 1961) have argued that supervisors can effectively represent employees' interests at higher levels and so there is no need for a separate representative body. In our view this is hardly enough. Supervisors have interests of their own and may be hostile to participation generally. Consequently employees need independent representation either through a union or through a 'representative body'.

Representative participation, in which committees of employees' representatives meet with management, take many forms. Participation may occur at the plant, divisional, or company levels; there may even be representation on the company board of directors. Participation may deal with narrow topics, such as safety, or broad ones, such as overall organizational investment policy. Employees may be merely able to make recommendations or they may have the right to block management action until agreement has been reached. Sometimes, as commonly in the case of university faculty senates, they may have limited power to make decisions on their own. Here we consider only three types of representative participation: consultative committees, works councils, and employee representation on boards of directors. (But let us stress again that in many countries formal and informal collective bargaining may be more prevalent and more effective forms of participation than any discussed below.)

Consultative Committees

Joint consultative committees (given a variety of names in practice) are perhaps the most common form of representative participation in English-speaking countries. These meet periodically with management for discussion, but have no power to make decisions. As of 1990, consultative committees existed in a majority of large UK establishments (and a quarter of all establishments).[15] Half these committees included union representatives yet slightly less than half met as frequently as monthly (Millward *et al.* 1992). Among the topics discussed most frequently at these meetings were production, pay, and employment. Consultative committees (Whitley Councils) also have a long history in the British public sector, though in recent years their role has diminished.

Similar committees exist in the USA. In Wisconsin (a typical state) 28 per cent of the unionized manufacturing firms had joint union–management committees which discussed general problems (other than collective-bargaining issues), while 43 per cent had committees to deal with *specialized* topics, such as safety (Voos 1987: 199; for comparable Canadian and Australian data, see Long 1989; Callus *et al.* 1991; Marchington 1992*b*).[16]

Committees vary considerably in their composition and function (Marchington 1994). As the Wisconsin data illustrate, there may be a single committee dealing with a variety of functions, or specialized committees, each dealing with a different function. Committees may function at the individual enterprise (plant) level, or, in the case of a multi-plant enterprise, at the firm level. Employee representatives may be selected by management, by the union (or unions), or (rarely) elected. Sometimes top-level managers and union officers participate in these committees and sometimes they do not. Committee may meet with various degrees of frequency.

US collective-bargaining contracts in the automotive industry have spawned a maze of consultative committees. Special plant committees have been charged with reviewing job design, new plant layout, changes in manufacturing equipment, and major new processes, all with the purpose of reducing stress and increasing efficiency. Plant-level committees permit exchange of information and the discussion of investment and other issues which might affect employment or employees' welfare generally. More on this 'jointness' process in Chapter 4.

Union–management joint consultative committees are common in Japan as well. In some companies these committees engage in traditional collective bargaining. In other companies the bargaining and consultative functions are kept separate. Quite often management shares confidential information with these committees, including details of major new investments and changes in policy.

Further, management normally revises its plans when faced with strong union objections (Morishima 1991).

Regardless of the country, consultative committees have had varying degrees of success. Employees' suggestions are too often ignored, and often the committees' scope is restricted to trivial matters of little importance to either side. In Britain they have sometimes been called 'tea-and-toilet' committees. Since committees lack the power to block management's actions, their influence may depend on management's faith and good will. According to a British study, 'the consultative machinery was of prime importance [only] where union organizations were weak and management was human-relations oriented' (Clarke *et al.* 1972: 80).

A common failure is that the parties fail to agree on the committees' mission and give low priority to committee activities. Management seeks to confine the discussion to safety, housekeeping, and similar problems, and occasionally production, whereas the employees want to deal with grievances and labour relations. Because neither side pays enough attention to the other, not much gets done. Downward communication is more common than upward communication and both are more common than joint decision-making (Marchington 1992*b*).

A four-year study of joint consultative procedures in two British companies looked at the relationship between formal structures, such as committees, and influence sharing between organizational levels (Heller *et al.* 1988). In spite of regular meetings between elected employees and senior management on a variety of topics, including incentive systems, new purchases, budget forecasting, safety, and the extension of a warehouse, employee influence over these decisions was very low. Management proposed the agenda, initiated discussions, proposed solutions, and in most cases, obtained agreement.

On the other hand, when management is truly interested in collaboration, such committees can be rather successful: they permit management to disseminate important information, they allow workers to voice grievances, they help solve production problems, and they may serve as a preliminary to collective bargaining (Marchington 1994).

Apart from 'trivia' most joint consultative committees seem to serve two functions. First, they facilitate upwards communications—chiefly expressions of discontent. And, secondly, they allow top management to pass on information, especially as to decisions that it has already made. Only rarely are these committees involved in decision-making itself, especially in the early stages of the decision-making process. Using Australian data, Marchington (1992*b*) suggests that there may be two kinds of committees. The first, primarily in small non-union or weak-union workplaces, is established by management, operates informally, meets frequently, and deals chiefly with performance and quality. The second type, established jointly by union and management, meets less frequently, operates more formally, and is concerned chiefly with working conditions (and, perhaps, what in the US context would be called grievances).

Other weaknesses of joint consultation are discussed in Chapters 4 and 5.

Works Councils

The main differences between works councils and consultative committees are that the former have generally more power and have jurisdiction over a broader range of issues; however, the differences among countries are great. This is especially true with regard to the topics with which works councils deal. In some countries their jurisdiction includes what might be called collective-bargaining issues, such as wages, hours, redundancy, work rules, and grievances; in other countries their functions are confined to less adversarial issues, such as safety.

Works councils are required by law in most Continental Western European countries for middle- and large-size companies. EU legislation mandates that by the end of the century firms with 1,000 or more employees and at least 150 employees in each of two or more EU countries must set up European Works Councils (EWCs) (or the equivalent), whose function will be consultation and information. Assisted by EU subsidies to defray the costs of negotiating sessions, the 'social partners' were given several years to agree upon 'the nature, composition, the function, mode of operation, procedures and financial resources' of an EWC. But if they fail to agree, 'subsidiary requirements' automatically come into force. These call for EWCs of between three and thirty members, with at least one member from each country in which the company operates (except the UK). The EWC must meet at least annually for exchange of information and consultation. Additionally, in 'exceptional circumstances'—such as 'reallocations, the closure of establishments . . . or collective redundancies', a special meeting must be called in which employee representatives must be consulted as to proposed measures. Consultation, however, as the directive makes clear, does not require agreement.

Only the UK was excluded from this requirement.[17] Over 1,100 firms employing some 15 million employees are expected to be covered. As of December 1995 voluntary agreements had been reached establishing works councils in roughly eighty EU firms. But as of that date there had been very little actual consultation (Rivest 1996; Schulten 1996). (See Chapter 7 for a discussion of EWCs' possible significance.)

Many councils owe their existence primarily to legal backing; rarely do they enjoy much more power than the law requires. Portuguese law, for instance, mandates that councils be kept informed of technological changes but not that they be consulted. Consequently Portuguese councils have little direct input into workplace governance but receive a great deal of information (Gill and Krieger 1992). German works councils, by contrast, have considerable power to block proposed management activities which lack their consent.

As discussed in Chapter 4, most councils are dominated by active unionists. Typically their members are elected (as is the case in Germany, Austria, France, Netherlands, and Toyota in the UK) with an electorate normally consisting of all employees but occasionally of union members only. Alternatively they may be appointed by the union (US) or even by management. Their terms of office may be set by law—for example, four years in Germany. Works-council elections are frequently hotly contested, especially where, as in France and Italy, there are rival unions.

In some cases management cannot move ahead without the council's approval. In Germany works councils have the right of co-determination with regard to a broad range of topics. Similarly larger Australian plants are required to have elected health and safety representatives who may 'in some circumstances unilaterally order the cessation of work' (Jamieson 1992: 165). Elsewhere works councils monitor compliance with governmental regulations relating to safety, health, and the like.

German works councils, along with employee representatives on company boards of directors (see below), have had a considerable impact. As Streeck (1984: 414, 416) puts it, 'Management under codetermination is essentially comanagement, especially but not exclusively in the manpower area. It is based on a close, symbiotic relationship between the personnel department and an increasingly 'managerial' works council . . . [which] not only shares in what used to be managerial prerogatives, but also accepts responsibility for the implementation and enforcement of decisions made under its participation'. Thus German works councils have made it considerably more difficult for management to lay off employees, thus forcing management to pay more attention to personnel planning, training, and internal mobility. In the former East Germany, 'In the fight for [plant] survival works councils collaborate closely with management in the introduction of innovation; in many cases the works council has pushed management (as opposed to the more usual vice versa) to invest in new methods and to remove or educate authoritarian-minded [supervisors] who stand in the way of modern, participative relations' (Turner, forthcoming: 24). Wever (1994) describes how works councils help increase productivity through (1) forcing management to articulate its reasons for decisions; (2) asking questions, pointing out problems which management has not considered; (3) making suggestions based on employees' experiences and suggesting alternatives to management's proposals, and (4) sometimes drawing on the experiences of works councils elsewhere.

The relationship between works councils and unions varies greatly among countries. Often there is considerable tension between them, as we discuss at greater length in Chapter 4.

A rather unusual form of representative participation is exemplified by GM's Saturn Division, which makes the Saturn car, once almost a cult fetish. Here a joint union–management committee formulated the division's strategy, determined its work organization, and designed its new plant. The division's stationery and the signs on its plant gate give equal status to the two co-sponsoring organizations. Major operational decisions are made jointly. First-level supervisors are elected. Higher levels of line management, up to Division Manager, are subject to co-management. For each managerial position there are two co-managers, one appointed by the union, the other by the company. Decisions are made jointly and they share the same large desk. When the company representative is on vacation, the union representative has full authority—and vice versa (Rubenstein 1993).

Representation on Company Boards

Most large companies in Austria, Germany, the Netherlands, and Norway are legally required to include employee or union representatives on their boards of directors (often called supervisory boards). Similarly there are union/employee directors in a small number of British (Chell 1983) and US firms (now including all major US steel companies), in the latter country often as a quid pro quo for union wage concessions, and also in some Australian publicly owned firms. In France a works-council representative is entitled to attend board meetings, but not to vote.

In the German steel and coal industries employees and management have equal membership (with a neutral selected to cast the tie-breaking votes). This has been required by law since 1951 and has worked well. In contrast an *ad hoc* arrangement gave labour and management equal representation on the British Post Office board in the late 1970s, but this experiment was halted by the Thatcher Government (Batstone *et al.* 1983; Taylor and Snell 1986). Before Yugoslavia broke down all Workers Council members (the equivalent of boards of directors) were elected. Elsewhere employee representatives are in the minority. Yet they have considerable influence in Germany, even with regard to major investment plans such as whether to invest overseas. In other places their influence has been less (Brannen 1983; Thorsrud 1984).

Employee members on company boards face numerous role conflicts. We discuss these in Chapter 4.

Employee Ownership

For some Marxists employee ownership of the means of production was the key to industrial democracy. Employee ownership has become increasingly common in non-communist industrialized countries, though this has not occurred as Marx had planned. As discussed below, in practice few companies are majority employee-owned and employee ownership is rarely associated with substantial (*de facto*) employee control.

In principle the most common forms of employee ownership in the Western world can be divided into three categories: (1) stock ownership, (2) employee 'rescues' or buyouts of financially troubled facilities that might otherwise be closed, and (3) producers' cooperatives established with the purpose of being democratic and highly participative. In practice these three forms overlap, differing mainly in the extent of employee ownership, the purposes for which it is established, and the extent of actual employee participation.

Stock Ownership

Employee Stock Ownership Plans (ESOPs)[18] have spread widely in both the UK and the USA. In 1990 such plans existed in almost a third of UK firms, although only 20 per cent of the employees in these firms actually acquired stock (Millward *et al.* 1992). As of 1994 about 11 million US employees worked in firms with ESOPs. Of these 1.5 million worked in firms in which employees owned a majority of the shares, with Avis (an auto rental firm)[19] and United Airlines being the best known. By contrast with the UK, most employees in US ESOP firms own at least some stock, but typically only a small amount. The vast majority of the firms listed on the Japanese stock exchange have ESOPs and 50 per cent of the employees participate in them (Jones and Kato 1993).

A major reason for stock ownership's spread has been the substantial tax subsidies provided in the UK and especially in the USA. But stock ownership plans have been established for other reasons as well: to motivate employees through giving them a sense of ownership and identification with their company; to inhibit takeovers by corporate raiders; and to permit the transfer of corporate control from one generation of top managers to another without requiring the sale of company shares to pay death duties. In the UK, stock-ownership plans and profit-sharing are offered more frequently by firms that espouse and practise consultation and participation (Poole 1988).

Ownership does not mean control, even where a majority of the stock is owned by employees (Russell 1989). Only in rare instances have individual employees or union representatives been placed on company boards of directors. Privatization plans in most ex-communist countries include provisions allowing (or encouraging) distribution of stock to employees. As of 1995 in many Russian plants the majority of the stock was technically owned by employees. Though few careful post-communist studies have been conducted of the impact of employees' ownership in Russia and Eastern Europe, evidence to date suggests that employees' ownership in practice has meant that the old top managers have retained control (Blasi 1994). Even where directors are formally elected by employee mass meetings, managers are able to manipulate the results.

Union attitudes toward employee stock ownership vary. European unions have traditionally opposed enterprise level schemes (Uvalic 1991). By contrast, in Sweden the labour movement proposed the Meidner Plan, which would eventually have transferred majority control of Swedish companies to their unions (but not to individual employees) (Ohman 1983). While leftist German unions at one time supported nationalization of the means of production in principle, they were suspicious of employee ownership of specific companies, being concerned that this might co-opt employees and also force them to take undesirable risks (Gurdon 1985). Although US unions originally opposed employee ownership, recently they have begun to demand payments in stock as a condition for granting wage concessions to financially troubled firms. 'If you can't give us money,' unions seem to be saying, 'give us stock'. United Airlines employees won majority ownership of their firm, for example, in exchange for substantial wage concessions.

Though the impact of stock ownership has been extensively studied in the USA, the findings are somewhat mixed, particularly as to whether stock ownership *alone* affects profitability, productivity, or union–management relations (Winther 1995).[20] There is evidence that it increases commitment among employee owners, but only mixed findings as to satisfaction and motivation (for an extensive review of studies of the impacts of worker ownership worldwide, see Uvalic 1991 and Kruse and Blasi 1995; see also Conte and Svejnar 1990). On the other hand, there is stronger evidence that stock ownership, *when—but only when—combined with participation*, does increase productivity. Put another way, stock ownership and participation tend to reinforce each other (US General Accounting Office 1987; Hanford and Grasso 1991; Jones and Pliskin 1991; Poole and Jenkins 1993). An EU-sponsored study concluded 'both econometric and more informal studies suggest that the combination of financial with decisional participation can have significant beneficial effects' (Uvalic 1991: 189).

Plant rescues. 'Plant-rescue' buyouts have occurred in the UK, USA, France, Canada, Sweden, and the Netherlands when employees (and managers) have taken over facilities that might otherwise have been closed, either because they were financially troubled or because they no longer fitted their parent companies' strategy (Paton 1991). The most famous British buyouts—at Scottish Daily News, Meriden Motorcycle, and Kirkby Manufacturing—were organized in the mid-1970s, and all were failures. More recently, in the UK, the National Freight Corporation was sold to its employees as part of the Conservative Government's drive for privatization. As of 1997, it has been very successful.

Typically buyouts are financed by a combination of employee-equity contributions, bank loans, government loans and grants, and wage cuts. Changes in ownership, however, rarely mean that employees take control, even though individual employees are occasionally elected to boards of directors. In fact, 'buyout' arrangements are often put together so hastily that little thought is given to how the firms are to be run. Employees' prime motivation is to save (not change) their jobs and radical new ideas might scare off financial support.

Buyouts often appear successful at first: profits improve, productivity climbs, and apparently hopeless plants are restored to seeming prosperity. At least three factors seem to be at work: (1) wages and manpower have been cut, thus increasing profits, (2) the newly purchased plants are freed from the requirement to contribute towards corporate overhead, and finally (3), once the often formidable barriers to employees' ownership have been overcome, employees feel a sense of triumph; in turn this leads to an immediate burst of enthusiastic cooperation as the parties enjoy the hope that, by pulling together, their previously threatened jobs can actually be saved.

Often, after a year or so of employee ownership, disillusionment sets in. Employees move 'from euphoria to alienation' (Whyte *et al.* 1983). Once fear of job loss subsides, employee ownership, by itself, seems to have little impact on either productivity or satisfaction. For the average employee, the job and the boss are unchanged. As one observer put it, 'People are happy their jobs were saved and the company is doing well . . . On the other hand, insiders say, many employees do have a vague if unarticulated demand for greater involvement in participation—and they feel frustrated that they've been denied it' (Zwerdling 1979: 78). In several prominent cases frustrated expectations contributed to a dramatic increase in labour–management and internal union conflict (Hammer and Stern 1986). To avoid this problem, unions in many recent US buyouts have insisted that, in exchange for wage concessions, employees' rights of control be formally guaranteed and that high levels of participation be introduced.

A high percentage of buyouts involve technologically backward plants in troubled industries plagued by overcapacity. These firms are economically too weak to be saved. Others needed new capital to survive. At least three once totally employee-owned steel companies in the USA (Republic Engineered, Weirton, and Oregon Steel) have been forced to sell part of their stock to provide funds for necessary investments (*Employee Ownership Report*, May 1995). On the other hand, some of the more successful employee-buyouts were sold back into private ownership, with the employee-owners garnering the profits. Thus, some lessons have been learnt from earlier mistakes.

A perhaps unique US phenomenon has been union efforts to displace unfriendly managements either by taking over the company through a leveraged buyout (as at United Airlines) or throwing its support (and votes as a stockholder) to one of several contenders in a fight for management control (as at TWA). Today United Airlines are majority employee owned.

Producers' Cooperatives

Producers' cooperatives (often called 'labour-managed firms') are employee owned and in most cases have been designed from the beginning to allow high degrees of employee participation. There have been producer cooperatives in the UK and USA since the early 1800s and today they are found through most of the world, including in underdeveloped and communist countries.

The Israeli kibbutz, in which members live as well as work communally, may be the logical extension of this kind of organization (see Chapter 5), but small employee-owned and democratically controlled firms are common in many parts of Europe. An estimated 500,000 people are employed by producer cooperatives in Western Europe, especially in France and Italy (Signorelli 1986; Estrin *et al.* 1987). Professional partnerships in law, accounting, and medicine constitute another form of producers' cooperative (Russell 1991; Tolbert and Stern 1991).

Perhaps the best-known producer cooperative is Mondragon, located in the Basque section of Spain (Whyte and Whyte 1992). With 27,000 employee-owners and £1.3 billion in annual sales, Mondragon is a federation of linked organizations, including manufacturing companies, a large savings bank (which generates money to invest in the manufacturing firms and also provides new firms with technical assistance), and technical schools. The governing boards of all the manufacturing firms are elected by their member owners.

Yugoslav workers enjoyed 'social ownership' and 'worker self-management' until that country's break-up. Though subject to indirect control by the state through the banking system, elected Workers' Councils had the right to hire and fire management and to make major decisions. Yugoslav workers' self-management has now largely disappeared; however, its experience provides some important lessons, as we discuss in Chapter 5 (Horvat 1983; Rus 1984).

Counterculture producers' cooperatives have been formed for a variety of reasons. Often calling themselves 'collectives', they 'represent one of the enduring legacies of the anti-authoritarian movements of the 1960's' (Rothschild and Whitt 1986: 7; see also Ehrenreich 1983; Rothschild-Whitt 1983; Jackall 1984). They have been formed by people wanting to escape bureaucratic hierarchies, formalization, and labour specialization. Their members typically subscribe to a philosophical belief in a collectivist society. These firms are concentrated in fields that require low capitalization. Many are craft shops, non-conventional schools, medical clinics, food stores, legal collectives, or alternative newspapers.

In their purest form, producer cooperatives meet the following conditions: (*a*) *all* employees are owners, (*b*) *only* employees are owners, and (*c*) every employee-owner has an equal say in making major decisions. In practice these principles are often relaxed. Employees exert relatively little influence, for example, in two of the better-known British employee-owned firms, John Lewis and Scott Bader. Further, many so-called producer cooperatives hire non-members, at least for temporary jobs.

Proponents of producer cooperatives cite many potential advantages of this kind of organization, including increased productivity, satisfaction, and commitment. On the other hand, a substantial literature predicts that, even when successful at first, cooperatives will degenerate over time. Potential problems include: owner-members lack needed managerial skills; they are unwilling to make hard decisions, to take orders, or to discipline their colleagues; and factionalism develops. Further, from the employee-owners' viewpoint, this may be a bad investment: if the firm fails, they loses both their investment and their jobs.

There are predictions of financial problems as well. Pessimists argue that the initial members will bring in too little capital. If firms are forced to raise capital from their own members, they may be starved for investment. But borrowing from outside sources will be difficult because cooperatives are so unconventional. Potential lenders fear that owners will pay themselves high wages rather than investing for the future. Consequently, because of inadequate capital cooperatives will 'self-strangulate' (Jones 1980).

Further, if the firm is successful, present owners may hesitate to share their good fortune with newcomers. Instead, as the firm expands, new employees are denied ownership rights, the original owners become bosses, and so the organization loses its unique characteristics as a cooperative (Grunberg 1991). Even if this does not happen, as members approach retirement age they may be unable to find replacements able to buy out their investment. Instead they may sell out to a capitalist organization—or simply shut down. In short, theory suggests that cooperatives will be short-lived (e.g. Ben-Ner 1984; Russell 1985).

Fortunately these problems may be exaggerated (for reviews of cooperative success generally, see Cornforth 1989*a*; Abell 1983; Bonin *et al.* 1993; van Waarden 1986; Estrin and Jones 1992; Kruse and Blasi 1995). Evidence as to whether worker-owners overpay themselves is mixed. On balance they seem to prefer employment stability to higher earnings (Bonin *et al.* 1993; Craig and Pencavel 1992).

Increasing evidence suggests that cooperatives can survive as long as do conventional small firms, if not longer (Ben-Ner 1984; 1988*a*). After all the mortality of small firms generally is high. At first cooperatives are as productive as their capitalist counterparts, and some times more so, especially 'in firms with the most co-operative features' (Jones 1984: 52); unfortunately, this advantage may decline over time (Estrin *et al.* 1987). Cooperatives may survive best in certain niches—for example, in craft (e.g. construction) and professional work which requires little capital. In any case, they are a viable form of organization. And some, such as Mondragon, have been very successful.

Conclusion

There is growing interest in participation as a principle, though the principle is applied differently in various countries. In the post-war period and the 1970s European unions pushed for representative participation, especially co-determination and work councils. Their objective was to increase union power. More recently management has promoted direct participation. Today there is a growing constituency for shop-level QWL-type participation. Better-educated employees want more variety and discretion in their work, and management is increasingly convinced that participation pays off in terms of a more committed and responsible workforce and greater flexibility in deploying manpower. Participation may be most needed when creativity, innovation, and commitment are at a premium.

Formal structures of representative participation are in place in much of Continental Europe. They serve as the locus for plant- and firm-level bargaining in these countries, much as stewards and bargaining structures serve in English-speaking countries. Though producers' cooperatives exist in many countries, as yet they play only minor roles.

All these issues will be discussed at greater length in the chapters to come. As mentioned earlier, participation provides benefits for both the individual and the organization. In Chapter 2 we approach participation from an individual, psychological point of view. In Chapter 3 our perspective is organizational. Chapter 4 is more specialized: here we examine how participation impacts on industrial relations. Chapter 5 deals with the 'dark side' of participation—it summarizes the problems which participation faces—whilst Chapter 6 describes the conditions necessary for participation to be successful. Our final chapter is more personal. Here we shed our attempted objectivity and list the lessons we think we have learned from a quarter century's research.

NOTES

1. The 1995 report of the US Commission on the Future of Worker–Management Relations (the Dunlop Committee) presents a strong case for direct participation, but justifies it in terms of economics rather than psychology or morality.
2. In the USA, on the other hand, representative participation schemes have been more common when unions are weak, especially in the 1920s (Jacoby 1983).
3. Even so the coach will encourage team participation and minimize go-it-alone behaviour.
4. A closely related line of research concentrates on job characteristics such as variety, task identity, autonomy, and feedback, leading to semi-autonomous types of job design (Hackman and Oldman 1980).
5. 'Formal participation', as the term is employed here, is the equivalent of 'prescribed participation' and 'participative structure' as these terms were used by IDE. According to IDE (1993: 4), participative structure refers to 'the formal, written-down framework of participation in organizations. It may be based on national laws, bargaining contracts, or managerial policies.'
6. In some classifications what we call 'degree of control' is called depth, while 'range of issues' is breadth.
7. The IDE (1981*b*; 1993) group made use of three measures of what is here called 'control': (1) 'intensity of proscribed participation', also called participative structure; (2) 'involvement'; and (3) the Influence Power Continuum. The first is viewed as a measure of *de jure* participation while the last two are measures of *de facto* participation.
8. A distinction is sometimes made between 'on-the-line' groups, in which members work together, and those which are 'off the line', with members continuing to work separately (Applebaum and Batt 1994; Work Practices Diffusion Team 1994). Levine and Tyson (1990) distinguish between 'consultative' and 'substantive' participation. Regalia (1996) uses the terms 'consultative' and 'delegative' participation.
9. For analytic purposes a distinction can be drawn between the 'problem-solving groups' discussed here, which deal primarily with workplace or departmental issues and often consist of volunteers—and *representative* 'consultative committees' (to be described later) which deal with firm or enterprise-level issues and whose members are typically elected by employees or appointed by their unions. In practice these two forms of participation may overlap.
10. ISO 9000 series of quality standards have been proposed by the International Standards Organization and have been widely adopted by countries in the EU.
11. According to the MIT Motor Vehicle Project, based on a worldwide sample, the percentage of auto assembly workers in work teams increased from 16 in 1989 to 46 in 1993–4 (Pil and MacDuffie 1996).

12. Russian 'brigades' were touted during the late Soviet period as being the equivalent of self-managing teams. There is considerable debate, however, as to how many were given real freedom to manage themselves (Van Atta 1989).
13. Under the prior management it required 48.5 hours to assemble a vehicle. After two years NUMMI averaged 19.6 hours (Krafcik 1989).
14. Under the old GM management employees worked an average of 33–43 seconds out of a sixty-second job cycle. Under NUMMI the average is closer to fifty-seven seconds (Adler *et al.* 1995).
15. The incidence of joint consultative committees in the UK declined from 1984 to 1990, primarily due to a decline in the proportion of large unionized firms, in which such committees are most common. During the same period consultative committees became more numerous in Australia (Marchington 1992*b*).
16. Representative committees may be less common in US non-unionized firms, in part because their existence is legally questionable if they deal with terms and conditions of employment.
17. In spite of the Conservative Administration's opposition, several large UK companies decided to introduce works councils because they believed they would be to the advantage of both sides.
18. Stock ownership should not be confused with profit-sharing, although the two forms of benefit are granted for much the same reasons and have somewhat similar impacts. Some authors view profit-sharing as a form of participation. Our definition excludes this.
19. Avis was bought out by another firm, with employees receiving an average of $30,000 each for their shares.
20. In Japan, 'on average, the net effect of introducing an ESOP is to increase productivity by almost 7%' (Jones and Kato 1993: 331). No evidence is given as to the independent impact of participation.

2. A View from Psychology

This chapter approaches participation from a psychological perspective. A full-fledged review of the voluminous psychological literature on the subject seems to be impossible. In fact, already by the mid-1970s reviewers began to lament the abundance of the available literature, which 'is so enormous that to achieve a complete "review" is virtually impossible' (Locke and Schweiger 1979). Rather, this chapter uses the discipline to raise some questions which have not been discussed sufficiently.

The chapter intends to introduce some conceptual clarifications, to identify some of the main themes, findings, theoretical, and methodological developments, and to address important lacunae in the ongoing psychological discourse on participation.

But psychology, organizational psychology in particular, is only a starting point. Participation is a complex problem with many different parties taking an ideological, political, scientific, or practical interest in it. The analysis of its very complexity requires a liberal interpretation of what is traditionally viewed as psychology. Our treatment will be somewhat 'macroscopic': besides the individual aspects of participation, we will discuss a variety of social and environmental issues normally considered within the bailiwick of sociology, anthropology, and political science. This approach is a deliberate choice based on Lewinian action theoretical positions, which affirm that any behaviour, hence also participation, can be understood only as a function of the total situation—that is, all factors must be considered which are relevant for an action.

More than fifteen years have passed since we attempted a similar systematic reflection of the theme of organizational participation (Dachler and Wilpert 1978). Since then, the world of work in industrialized countries has undergone a variety of important changes which provide new demands, constraints, and opportunities for participation. Further, theorizing about and practical experience with participation in organizations have advanced. Hence, the renewed effort. It follows the following five steps: 1. conceptual issues; 2. prerequisites of participation; 3. forms of participation; 4. consequences of participation; 5. summary.

Conceptual Issues

There are at least two major issues here: one concerns what may, in philosophical terms, be called the 'finality'—that is, the ultimate goals[1] or purpose of participation in its instrumental function; the second is the problem of defining participation.

The Finality of Participation

The previous chapter defined participation rather simply, as 'a process which allows employees some influence over their work and the conditions under which they work'. Here we adopt a more complex definition which allows us to focus on participation's ends or goals. But before proposing this definition, let us examine several approaches to participation which we feel are inadequate.

The question here relates to how different forms of participation should be evaluated. Vroom and Jago (1988: 2) do so exclusively 'in terms of their contribution to the goal of effective performance, not as ends in themselves'. Thus, they reject the view that participation may be valuable in itself, that it may represent a moral imperative irrespective of practical consequences. (In addition, they acknowledge a possible third position that is linked to a leader's authentic self-realization: autocratic persons should act autocratically, but participative persons participatively.)

Locke and Schweiger (1979) take a similar position in their review essay on Participative Decision Making (PDM). They severely criticize a so-called moralistic, ideological, and mainly European orientation which favours participation as an end in itself. The authors go on to contrast this ideology-ridden perspective with a purportedly ideology-free 'basis on which to advocate participation' (p. 273)—namely, its role in contributing to organizational efficiency. A related position is taken in reference to work satisfaction: 'From the point of view of an organization, employee satisfaction must be considered a means to an end (e.g. a necessary condition for long-term profitability), not an end in itself' (p. 328). We will, at this point, contain the temptation to discuss their supposedly ideology-free position.

The authors just mentioned accept an instrumental role of participation (efficiency, satisfaction as a condition of long-range profitability, leader authenticity) and juxtapose this instrumental conception with a presumed, mainly European 'value-in-itself' position which would imply participation to be a terminal value in itself. We agree that it makes little sense to postulate that participation is an end in itself, because organizational participation can be conceptualized only as goal-directed behaviour. It follows that it is not a terminal value in itself. But again: *cui bono* = what ends does participation serve? While the above-mentioned authors locate the rationale for participation exclusively in organizational goal contexts or the superior's self-realization, we argue that participation serves a much more fundamental anthropological individual and social function. This is what we mean by finality of participation. Thus, it cannot simply be justified in terms of organizational goals or leaders' interests alone.

The wider context in which participation has to be seen can be illustrated by a useful distinction adopted by Lammers and Széll (1989*a*). Placing the notion of participation into the context of democratic theory, they distinguish between functional and structural democratization. Rather than focusing on a given level of democratic behaviour, they address the direction into which the given system is moving. Structural democratization denotes for them a zero-sum game in which a gain of power of one group necessarily leads to a loss of the other actor; thus a process of power equalization can take place. Structural democratization, therefore, redresses an imbalance of power distribution among organizational actors. Functional democratization, on the other hand, refers to a non-zero-sum game in which power can expand or contract. An increase of lower level power will in all likelihood lead to an increase of organizational efficiency and/or effectiveness with the overall power of the system being expanded.

Towards a Definition of Participation

Participation has been defined in a great variety of ways. Depending on a given author's preoccupation, definitions stress the purpose of participation, its scope (the topics included in participation), or behaviours included or excluded (see Table 1.3 for the range of approaches). Misunderstandings may arise then as a consequence of authors claiming that their respective definition represents the ultimate truth and forgetting that 'definitions are conventions which are related to a limited reference point in time and are linked to interests' (Mambrey 1985: 37).

Locke and Schweiger (1979) use participation and PDM as synonyms and accept the Oxford 1961 definition: a sharing with others, by which they mean the sharing of decision-making, specifically 'joint decision-making' by groups of subordinates or among superiors and subordinates. This explicitly excludes delegation, which other authors would painstakingly include (Heller 1971; IDE 1981*a*; Cotton *et al.* 1988). Besides, this definition does not include the type of finality of participation which we consider as being crucial.

Therefore, we suggest the following definition of participation in the form of a mapping sentence (see also Wilpert 1994):

> Participation is the totality of forms, i.e. direct (personal) or indirect (through representatives or institutions) and of intensities, i.e. ranging from minimal to comprehensive, by which individuals, groups, collectives secure their interests or contribute to the choice process through self-determined choices among possible actions during the decision process.

This definition underscores that participation is more than simply a content-free method of reaching decisions (Locke and Schweiger 1979: 275).

- It explicates the finality of participation in terms of securing interests through choice among possible options for policy or action.
- It always implies goal orientations in the actions of individuals and of collectives.
- It covers direct-personal as well as indirect-representative securing of interests.
- It recognizes differential effectiveness in securing one's interests—i.e. in some situations goals may be achieved more through participation than in others.

For example, since some participatory apparatuses (joint committees, etc.) have only limited power, they are less likely to achieve their goals.

The definition links participatory processes and activities to the interests of persons or collectives of persons affected. It also covers the whole gamut of participation forms from informal consensual decision-making between boss and subordinate to adversary, conflictual decision-making in formal collective bargaining. In other words: not so much the process of decision-making but the relative influence of interested parties on decision outcomes comes into focus.

Prerequisites of Participation

The term 'prerequisite' may have two alternative meanings. It may refer to the basic requirements for participation to occur at all, or it may relate to the conditions (contingencies) associated with participation to be successful. Depending on the issue at stake we use both meanings. Further, in the following we distinguish between individual and social prerequisites.

Individual Prerequisites

Motivational bases. Ernest Becker (1968; 1971), in directly referring to Dewey's normative behaviourism, postulates that participation is a fundamental requirement of any individual and social growth. On philosophic–anthropological grounds he argues that learning and 'organismic growth' depend on interaction with the person's life space ('action domains'). An individual's well-being and his or her endowment—i.e. the expansion of his or her action potential (which he denotes as 'funding')—is dependent on influencing those action domains.

Lafferty (1975; 1979) has elaborated Becker's approach into a social psychological theory of 'normative symbolic interaction':

> Participation is a basic well-being. It is basic because not to participate in the decisions which affect my funding possibilities is to give up that which is most essential to expand my control over object-action-symbol possibilities. To not participate in decisions which symbolically control the emotional value (status, legality, worth, etc.) of my action world is quite simply to choose a lesser degree of humanism (actually a form of organismic sickness) for both myself and my community. (Lafferty 1979: 10)

Similarly G. W. Allport (1945), in fervently advocating the growth of a democratic society underlines the extraordinary significance of participation:

> . . . people have to be active in order to learn . . . to build voluntary control . . . *unless (a person) is in some areas ego-engaged and participant, his life is crippled and his existence a blemish on democracy . . . unless we try deliberately and persistently to affect our destinies at certain points . . . we are not democratic personalities, we have not balance as wholeness, and society undergoes proportionate stultification.* (p. 127; emphasis in original)

Allport differentiates simple activity from personal participation. The latter implies ego-involvement, which is propelled by the individual's striving for social prestige, self-respect, and autonomy. Because such ego-involvement tends to spill over to other personal life spheres, participation becomes a necessary precondition for individual self-realization and for development of society at large.

Some may agree with Locke and Schweiger (1979) in classifying these approaches as 'representing the essence of tribalism and the Dark Ages' (p. 328). However, such classification may run into difficulties when we consider the position taken by White (1959) in his much underrated paper reanalysing motivation theories up to that date. In discussing Freud and Hull and their followers, among others, he points out that concepts such as drive and instinct fall short of explaining exploratory behaviour, playful object manipulation, and mastery of the environment. Instead he concludes that a more encompassing explanatory principle is called for—a general need for *competent person–environment interaction*, in which 'competent' means effective control of the environment. This need he considers as a universally valid motive to produce effects in one's environment and to master it, at least segments of it. One's own ability to influence and control one's environment ('making things happen') produces 'affectance' or, more generally, 'competence motivation' (Wilpert 1991*b*: 156).

Bandura's (1977) concept of self-efficacy seems to be related to White's notion of affectance. However, it differs from it in so far as it denotes a cognitive more than a motivational aspect in terms of 'a judgement of one's capability to accomplish a certain level of performance' (Bandura 1986: 391).

White's theory of affectance provided the basis for the psychological theory of self-determination (Deci 1975; 1981; Deci and Ryan 1985). Competent environment mastery here is a critical condition of intrinsic motivation. A person's opportunity to choose self-determinedly among actions to affect his or her environment is central to the theory of self-determination—that is, persons must feel themselves to be the origin of causal effects upon surroundings ('locus of causality', as Heider (1958), and De Charms (1968), put it). This is somewhat different from Rotter's concept of 'locus of control', which refers to the person's experience of an event being contingent upon one's own behaviour. 'Locus of causality' refers to the source from which an action is initiated and controlled. In this sense, the concept is related to action-control theoretical notions (Oesterreich 1981), which were based on the writings of Rubinstein (1977) and Leontiev (1977).

Deci and collaborators have demonstrated the validity of their theories through research in a large variety of settings. In a similar vein, Erez (1993) has discussed the socio-dynamic (commitment), motivational (sharing in goal-setting and individual efficacy), and cognitive (information-sharing) concomitants of participation.

In short, the universal need for competence motivation is the central psychological theoretical point of reference for participation. We may consider it as a fundamental anthropological, i.e. universally valid, motivational disposition to carry out self-determined (self-chosen) and competent (effective) actions in one's environment. In saying this we answer also the *cui bono* question: participation is not an end in itself. Participation responds to the basic human need to interact effectively with one's environment. It facilitates learning and competence endowment, individual growth, and development (Wilpert 1989). It is not an end in itself. But to see its instrumentality solely in terms of superficial notions of organizational efficiency or employee satisfaction would be a great mistake.

The motivational theories mentioned so far might be characterized as process theories since they focus on dynamic aspects and largely neglect content. To put it differently: process theories explain the *general processes* which induce people to participate, but they say little about why people participate in a *specific situation* or *organization*. A new and still-to-be-developed theoretical approach may offer a key to this crucial question: a theory of psychological appropriation of the workplace (Wilpert 1991). The approach goes back to the theory of self by William James (1890), who argues that material and immaterial property objects are essential for the development of the individual self. Sustained utilization and interaction with such objects lead to their integration into the self by virtue of the 'law of mental association by contiguity'. Social valuation further supports this process. Furby (1978) has shown in empirical studies that control over the use of an object is the most important characteristic of property sentiments, irrespective of legal title. Assuming now that employees feel control over their organization, it follows that they will develop property sentiments towards their organization. This, in turn, may express itself in various forms: commitment, involvement, participation, or responsibility.

Participatory competence. We hope to have established that the need for competence, in the sense of effectively interacting with one's environment, is the central psychodynamic driving force for participation (a foundation). However, it must not be overlooked that competence is also both a requirement for and a consequence of effective participation. We are dealing here with individual skills for participation.

A contingency hypothesis would claim that the extent of an actor's participation will depend on the extent to which his or her participatory skills can be mobilized. For Locke and Schweiger (1979) this skill is reflected in the knowledge available to solve a given problem. This knowledge competence might be called the job-related 'functional' competence—that is, the technical skills and knowledge base required to solve workplace problems adequately.

However, technical know-how alone may generally be a necessary, but insufficient, condition for effective participation (IDE 1981*a*: 174). Fricke (1975) stresses this point by demonstrating that 'extra-functional, innovatory' skills are required in participation in order to respond competently to the 'dualism in work settings which consists of work process demands [*Sacherfordernisse*] and of interest demands [*Interessenlagen*]' (Fürstenberg 1984). Fricke (1975) categorizes these qualifications as social or 'micro-political' skills. They represent individual resources for goal-oriented action and facilitate the articulation of needs, the effective negotiation and implementation of one's interests. With Lammers (1989) we might speak of skills in the plural rather than in the singular. And it follows that it should be an adequate 'skill match' (Heller 1991) between participatory demands and respective personnel qualifications.

In a research effort involving dyads of close to 1,600 top-level managers in eight countries we studied the contingencies for informal, direct participation among boss and subordinate. Our findings show clearly the complex, multifaceted nature of participatory skills and their significant impact on participation (Heller and Wilpert 1981). The Decisions in Organization (DIO) study (Heller *et al.* 1987) of matching organization samples from three countries similarly demonstrated the close positive relationship between skills and participation.

But are we not now in a cul de sac: how can we claim, on the one hand, that participation is a major individual prerequisite for learning and competence development and, on the other hand, that participation is contingent upon requisite competence and skills? A classical chicken or egg problem, indeed. We shall come back to this problem later.

Uncertainty and conflict tolerance. Our conceptualization of participation as a realignment of decision outcomes with the interests of parties involved implies uncertainties for all parties simply due to the fact that interests hitherto latent receive a chance of being articulated. Such articulation, in turn, increases the chance of bringing latent conflicts out into the open. In other words, participation leads to ever-increasing demands to cope with uncertainties and the potential of manifest conflict. An important further individual prerequisite of participation is therefore the readiness and ability of organization members to engage in potentially conflictual situations, which often lead to greater uncertainty until they are resolved.

Participation is more likely to be successful if employees, their representatives, and management all trust each other. Trust contributes to a sense of certainty. From this perspective participation is akin to the prisoner's dilemma. For participation to be successful, workers and managers have to trust each other. But trust–trust relationships are volatile; either party can defect at any point in time, and participation will suffer.

Little research seems to have dealt with these aspects which affect, of course, motivation to participate. The IDE (1981*a*) project found that higher levels of participation were positively related to the frequencies of disagreement. This is counter-evidence to the hope that participation would reduce conflict (Coch and French 1948). This raises the issue as to whether conflicts are perceived as being functional or dysfunctional for the conduct of organizational tasks. Some managers will say that conflicts are sand in the smooth functioning of organizations, hence, counter-productive, and to be avoided. Others take the position that they facilitate innovation and consensus. Thus, Nightingale (1982) showed that, compared to non-participative organizations, participative ones are more likely to use 'problem-solving' as a conflict-resolution technique rather then 'forcing' or 'ignoring'. (For similar findings see Hoffman *et al.* 1962.)

Social Prerequisites

Organizational structures. The size of organizations as an important influence or moderator of various organizational characteristics has long been identified (Blau and Schoenherr 1971). What about its impact on the level of influence and participation? The IDE (1981*a*) study, still the largest and most comprehensive international comparative research on participation, reports contrary evidence for participation: size does not significantly predict the level and influence of participation. Neither does vertical differentiation (numbers of hierarchical levels) have any measurable predictive power. In contrast, horizontal differentiation, as measured in terms of functional differentiation, and formalization show a positive relation to participation. The latter finding may be counter-intuitive because formalization is often considered as an indicator of bureaucratization and thus to be an impediment to participation. But a different view has also been expressed: formalization provides also protection from managerial whims and arbitrariness by giving employees clear-cut responsibilities (Crozier 1963; Gustavsen 1973).

One of the few psychological theories which relates hierarchical organizational structures directly to participation has been developed by Mulder (1977). His is a theory of power, defined as the ability to determine others' behaviour. The experience of power is pleasurable and goes hand in hand with the experienced closeness of persons in one hierarchical level to the next higher one. In order to expand this hedonistic experience people try to reduce their power distance to the next higher hierarchical level and to increase their power distance *vis-à-vis* their next lower hierarchical level. Power, in Mulder's power-distance-reduction theory, is an addictive drug. The more you have, the more you want. On first sight, Mulder's approach may strike one as too simplistic, but on re-examination and confronted with everyday experience the hypotheses derived from his theory gain considerable credibility.

Technology. According to the IDE (1981*a*) study, technology as such had no significant impact on participatory intensity, except for automation, which was positively related to the influence of representative bodies.

The dramatic diffusion of new information technologies in all sectors of industry seems to herald a new era of the role of participation in work settings. Kern and Schumann (1984), two industrial German sociologists, went back to the same companies they had studied some ten years earlier. By contrast to their original study, a new trend in management seemed to have emerged which they labelled 'new production concepts'. We seem to be witnessing here an ironic twist of history. While the introduction of new technologies was originally meant to increase managerial control over the production process and to minimize the role of employees, technological advances today involve greater capital intensity. Consequently, machines have become more vulnerable and competent maintenance is required. Combined together, these factors increased the importance of the human component of socio-technical systems. Given the highly developed technological work environment, the human component appears to provide the only remaining reservoir for further economic rationalization and improved competitiveness. 'New production concepts' then mean managerial strategies which give more responsibility, more autonomy, more influence to employees (see also Piore and Sabel 1984). What is important here is to see that technology *per se* does not impact deterministically on participation (IDE 1981*a*; 1993). What counts is the managerial strategy, the social use made of technology.

However, the introduction of new technologies which have impacts on the whole work organization such as the switch from mechanical printing to computer-assisted photoprinting or the introduction of robotics presents a variety of problems and challenges for participation on at least four levels (Koubek 1985):

1. *National and international level.* The new technology is often strongly influenced by national and international R&D programmes of state governments, intergovernmental bodies, or multinational corporations. A case in point are telecommunication technologies in Europe. Relevant decisions regarding basic research and development policies are far removed from the influence of individual employees or their representatives on the company level. The only possible way to influence national and international laws, rules, regulations, and standards seems to be through high-level representatives of unions and employer associations. However, in some international corporations we find international representative bodies such as international corporate work councils which may some day exert some influence (see Chapter 4).

2. *Strategic corporate planning level.* The high capital intensity of some production technologies requires long-range corporate planning horizons which, in turn, imply high degrees of uncertainties regarding the outcomes of implementing new technologies. These uncertainties are shared by management and employee representative bodies because neither knows for certain what, at the end of the day, the ultimate utility of such long-range technological decision will be for the company. Open communication and efficient dialogue structures among the parties involved seem to be required here in order to guarantee that decisions are continuously readjusted to emerging conditions.

3. *Level of detailed project planning.* This is the domain of representative bodies on the company and establishment level. Time and again studies show, however, that employee representatives often lack the requisite technical competence to get effectively involved (Wilpert and Rayley 1983; see also Chapter 4). The training of representatives in requisite technical and social skills as well as the development of a joint learning climate among management and representatives seem to be critical conditions for participation (see Chapter 6).

4. *Level of implementation and use.* This is the place where the knowledge and experience of middle management and of operators themselves seem to

present the best opportunities for effective direct involvement. After all, it is in the implementation and routine utilization phases of introducing new technologies that the experience and tacit skills of the employees at the immediate man-machine interface must by necessity be employed if the new system is to be used optimally.

The four levels are intertwined with different phases of the introductory process (planning, selection, implementation, evaluation) which offer different opportunities for participation of affected parties (see Chapter 1). This has clearly been shown in various studies, such as DIO (1988) and those by the European Foundation for the Improvement of Working and Living Conditions in Dublin, which use IDE measures (Fröhlich and Krieger 1990; Cressey 1991). In general it can be said that the advent of new information technologies and their introduction in workplaces offers new opportunities also for participation.

Participative structure. Participative structures have been defined as 'the totality of all formal (i.e. written down) operative rules and regulations that prescribe a certain involvement of various groups in intra-organizational decision making' (IDE 1976: 181). The definition covers all formal rules, including managerial regulations pertaining to participation, not just legal norms. Those rules may provide for certain bodies (e.g. work councils) to function as institutional settings for such involvement.

Whether formal rules and structures are necessary or superfluous elements of participation has been contentious among theoreticians as well as practitioners. For example, some Anglo-American writers fear the limiting consequences of rules and regulations and, therefore, favour 'voluntarism' also in the adoption of participatory practices. So, according to Locke and Schweiger (1979: 267) 'most Americans still favor freedom, at least to some extent'. This is not the place to go into the complexities of legal theory, which discusses rules as independent causes of intended change, rules as a consequence of social change, or rules as a result of interactions between both (Nagel 1970). Generally we may say, however, that the Continental European tradition favours rule-making and statutorily intends to facilitate employee participation as a matter of right as opposed to a result of 'voluntary' managerial generosity.

King and van de Vall (1978) studied in systematic measuring fashion rules and regulations (participative structures) in an international comparative research. However, they remained on the level of comparing legal structures without scrutinizing their behavioural consequences. Hence, the authors were unable to answer the question: what do we know about the consequences of participative structures, irrespective of their formal bases, whether they be laws, collective agreements, or managerially proclaimed formal regulations? The IDE (1981*a*, *b*) study appears to be the only research which has systematically studied this relationship by measuring *de jure* participation structures and their impact upon *de facto* participation behaviour. The intensity of prescribed participation proved to be the strongest predictor of *de facto* participation in the first round of the twelve-country study. The replication of that research 'ten years later' in the very same establishments which participated in the original research aimed to test the robustness of the first findings. Although additional mediating factors entered the model, participative structures proved again to be among the best predictors of *de facto* participation (IDE 1993). The findings thus indicate that participation is to a significant extent a result of socio-political will.

Another IDE finding further corroborates this thesis: 'employee mobilization' as measured by union density and the percentage of employees with experience in a representative role (e.g. works-council membership) had a significant positive relation with *de facto* participation. Apart from underlining the importance of the readiness of employees to articulate their interests, this result also supports what has been said above about participatory competence which can be assumed to grow with participatory activity.

Mulder's theory referred to above is a theory of individual power-distance reduction in hierarchical—that is organization structure—contexts. It helps to understand why individuals participate in organizational settings. However, what is missing is a theory which goes beyond individual motivation and behaviour in organizational contexts and covers collective and representative interest articulation and participation in work organizations.

Another topic which deserves further theorizing and empirical research relates to the psychological dynamics of property and ownership titles. In as much as ' "property" denotes a bundle of rights, ownership, and also the objects of these rights' (Eugen Pusić 1991: 137), property titles may be viewed as making it easier for title holders to participate in decision processes and to influence their outcomes. This participation then is derived from the formal or informal rules, regulations, and rights associated with these titles. Thus, these rules fall into the category of participative structures discussed here. From a psychological perspective the questions that call for further scrutiny are posed by the still poorly understood triadic interaction between legal property titles, psychological ownership, and their behavioural implications (Wilpert 1991). As was pointed out in Chapter 1, stock ownership, for instance, may not necessarily imply psychological ownership and therefore may not lead to effective participation.

Organizational processes, organizational culture. Lowin's early review (1968) of PDM research takes subordinates and managers to be equally crucial actors. Given this, he speculates extensively about the potential influence of organizationally shared participation attitudes and ideologies on PDM. His summary of findings, however, remains equivocal concerning his criteria which refer almost exclusively to PDM effectiveness. So he concludes: 'It is abundantly clear that any simplistic PDM hypothesis is too gross to be proven or disproven' (p. 99).

How actors in the participation game perceive themselves is an important moderator of participation effectiveness. Bothe (1987) investigated the effectiveness of German works councils in representing their clients' interests. In distinguishing three modal-type councils in terms of how they perceived their relationship to management she found that 'conflict-oriented' councils provided consistently more effective interest representation than did those which were either 'passive-appeasement oriented' or 'management oriented'.

So far we have discussed values and attitudes, organizational structures, and technology as intra-organizational prerequisites of participation. Espoused attitudes and values in and of themselves do not guarantee their enactment. And structures or technology, although setting certain framing conditions for behaviour, do not necessarily determine specific desired outcomes such as a certain level of participation. We should also consider the behavioural processes within the organization, especially the organization's 'folkways', its custom and practice, the manner in which things are accomplished, the procedures, communication flows, and quality of social interaction among organization members—in short, the ensemble of organizational features which is sometimes considered its organizational culture.

To illustrate the role of behavioural processes, let us look at how managerial strategy influences participation in the context of introducing new information technologies in work organizations. At least three basic strategic models of technology change can be distinguished: the life-cycle model, the replacement model, and the evolutionary model (Mambrey 1985). The three differ considerably in the opportunities they provide for participation.

The *life-cycle model* is oriented towards the life phases of a technical system. These can ideally be divided into system development phases (conception, systems analysis, design, specification, construction, test, and implementation) and systems operational phases (systems acceptance, operations, maintenance, adjustments), and finally a systems decay or death. This is a highly logical and sequential conception of the introductory process leading to a rather static end result which is difficult to modify. If participation is meant to have any impact at all, it must come in at the development phases which demand considerable technical know-how and hard-to-achieve judgements about the system's consequences.

The *replacement model* is more flexible. Rather than planning a system comprehensively and completely, it focuses on modular planning of individual systems components. It is relatively easy to replace small subsystems or systems components by improved modules if the need arises to adjust the system. Participation under the premisses of this model is a continuous process which allows employees to articulate their needs and to bring in their competence in each stage of incremental improvement.

The *evolutionary model* is characterized by the assumption that systems ought to be developed incrementally rather than all at once. It uses rapid prototyping of individual modules early on in the systems planning. Such modules can easily be tested and corrected on the basis of experience; hence, prototypes display a high degree of reversibility and ideally the end result benefits from the feedback loops of an organizational learning system which profits from the competence gained by the users. Thus, the evolutionary model goes furthest in offering opportunities to participative inputs.

Apart from managerial behaviour which is exemplified by these different modes of introducing new technologies, particular attention should be paid to *custom and practice*, which is quite important in facilitating or impeding participation. Custom and practice are indeed the folkways of organizational behaviour which, although never formalized, have a normative influence and an impelling normative appeal. The *ringi* system of decision-making in Japanese companies which enables employees at various hierarchical levels to participate in shaping the ultimate decision outcome may be taken as an example (Misumi 1984). The area of custom and practice, that grey zone between structure and factual rules, seems to be quite under-researched, in spite of its significance for participation.

However, as pointed out before, managerial practice alone will not do the trick of guaranteeing participation. As Lammers (1989: 351) emphasizes:

> the general organizational regime which is a function not only of the 'style of governance of dominant élites' in organization, but also of the 'style of organizational effort arising from the norms and tactics of rank-and-file groups' . . . is in all likelihood significant for the viability of most forms of organizational democracy and of efforts to increase the level of competence of those involved in it.

Lammers includes here participative leadership style, cooperative norms, and social interaction style of all organizational constituents as significant contingency factors for the quality of participation. Thus, he comes close to describing the essential features of organizational culture. In short, participation is more likely to thrive when the organizational culture is favourable.

Organizational environment. We usually conceptualize organizations as living open systems. A necessary conjecture from systems thinking is that internal organizational processes, such as participation, will be influenced by environmental factors. While it is easy to formulate the conjecture on a theoretical level, it is difficult to prove the point empirically, because organization–environment interaction requires a demonstration of effects across various systems levels (Wilpert 1992). The difficulty consists in systematically measuring environmental characteristics and relating them to organization and individual level variables such as participation. Our managerial behaviour study (Heller and Wilpert 1981) showed the positive relation of perceived environmental turbulance to participation. In the IDE replication research (IDE 1993) we found that perceived tight labour markets, presumably creating uncertain employment condition for employees but higher levels of certainty for management, were negatively related to participation. Given that perceptions may err, it is, however, a question whether a specific perception of an organizational environment is an aspect of the external environment or an intra-organizational perceptual characteristic ('percept–percept studies' (Wagner and Gooding 1987*b*)).

Taking more objective measures of environment we find further evidence which supports the hypothesis that uncertainty is conducive to participation. Managers in foreign-based multinational companies in Germany (presumably experiencing high environmental uncertainty) are more participative than their colleagues in German multinationals (medium environmental uncertainty). And German managers in purely German-owned companies (low environmental uncertainty) are the least participative ones (Wilpert 1977). However, as Lincoln, Kerbo, and Wittenhagen (1995) show in their study of German and Japanese firms, local decisions may be reached more participatively, while strategic decisions of conglomerates may be made more centrally at headquarters. Further, sometimes foreign management may be unable to use efficiently available institutions of participation such as works councils.

These findings raise a more general point which is related to the growing internationalization of enterprises. A multinational company entering a new country with an affiliate will be confronted with new structural and legal bases for the enforcement of participation. New rules and regulations apply for the conduct of participation, new patterns of custom and practice are in operation. Will host or guest traditions survive? The IDE finding that participative structures (mostly externally induced rules and regulations for participation) are highly predictive of participation appears to be another example of a successful demonstration of environmental factors impacting upon intra-organizational behaviour (cross-level effects). It would be important to study how multinational companies adjust to and cope with such participatory structures in comparison to strictly national companies.

However, it seems plausible that whether given rules and regulations for participation are enforced depends on the perceived costs incurred to a party to enforce these rules. If, for instance, national law stipulates that management must pay the legal costs of a representative body trying to enforce a participation rule, representatives will be more likely to take management to a labour court.

But what about changes in political climate or *Zeitgeist*, reflected, for instance, in changes of governments? What about changing societal value patterns —for example, the emergence of a 'new breed' (Yankelovich 1979) of workers with different work values, including expectations and aspirations regarding the quality of their workplaces (MOW 1987)? No doubt, changing value preferences in the population influence the degree of participation, especially since these value changes seem to be linked to an overall growing level of formal education in industrialized countries with its ensuing rise in the level of aspirations.

Furthermore, even stable societal value patterns may provide favourable or unfavourable conditions for organizational participation. Thus it seems to be more than just a very plausible hypothesis that in egalitarian cultures the implementation of participative practices in organizations will be more likely than in more hierarchical traditions (Strauss 1982; Putterman 1984).

A dramatic instance of environmental impacts upon participation is given by the Yugoslav system of self-management. Some twenty-five years ago, in Dubrovnik in 1972, many of us gathered at the first international sociological conference on participation and self-management and studied with eagerness the problems and advances of this giant national experiment. Now we can only study historically the internal Yugoslav and international environmental factors which for a limited period of some fifteen years or so made the system of self-management fairly succesful but eventually eroded its promising beginnings and subsequent achievements (Rojek and Wilson 1987; see also Chapter 5 of this volume).

Another perspective is employed in research studies which try to identify the link between changing societal conditions and predominant theses and methodological approaches to participation research such as the interesting study by Wagner and Gooding (1987*a*). There it was shown that dominant societal issues at a given point in time seemed to have influenced the conduct of research on participation in terms of the type of questions pursued. Their results suggest, for instance, that between 1976 and 1985 general societal conservatism in the USA made researchers favour studies of observable, material outcomes of participation rather than resulting individual satisfaction.

Forms of Participation

Chapter 1 described various forms of participation: formal/representative, informal/direct, and participation as (co-)ownership. In this chapter we have adopted a definition of participation which stresses the behavioural aspects of securing one's interest. It is therefore worth nothing that informal/direct participation is also called personal participation, and formal/representative participation is often called indirect participation. We will, therefore, use these alternative terms and deal with the following important differences of form: direct/personal versus indirect/representative participation (Lammers 1967; Cotton *et al.* 1988). Ownership can, as pointed out above, be considered as a possible social prerequisite of participation in the sense that the legal ownership title may serve as a facilitating factor by setting ground rules of control.

Direct Participation

Participative Management. The literature on participative management and PDM is vast and illustrates it to be the favourite informal form of participation from an Anglo-American perspective with all its presumed advantages, limits, and barriers (Lowin 1968; Locke and Schweiger 1979; Cotton *et al.* 1988). The readiness of management to offer participatory opportunities to subordinates will undoubtedly remain a crucial condition for the survival of all participation processes, no matter whether this managerial readiness is a consequence of personality characteristics, belief in the instrumental use of participation, enforcement of respective rules and regulations, or humanitarian philosophy.

Quality Circles. Heller (1991) pointed out that the concept of quality control through circles of operators originated in British experiments in the late 1940s. Why a hiatus of several decades prohibited the wide use of this social technology in Western countries is in itself a question worth of study. However, today the new wave of utilizing employee competence and commitment through orthodox Quality Circles (QCs) *à la japonaise* or a variety of local adaptations, often complemented by Total Quality Management (TQM), seems still on the rise in many industrialized countries. Although QCs are implemented on the basis of entrepreneurial initiatives, as opposed to the legally stipulated French or Dutch work groups, the actual content of their deliberations and their objective function are quite similar. An important distinguishing element may be the voluntary involvement of QC members—the main (and perhaps most significant) difference being the presumed voluntary nature of QC participation. In Japan the involvement is often expected and therefore virtually compulsory. An autonomous choice of employees to become a QC member may very well prove to be of critical difference, since it may, according to our theoretical reflections above, imply an increased affectance motivation. Systematic comparisons of these different forms of participative groups are still missing, although some observations give first hints to their differential consequences (Moire 1987).

(Semi-)autonomous work groups. The introduction of (semi-)autonomous work groups is usually attributed to be a consequence of socio-technical systems thinking. However, during the early 1920s Lang and Hellpach (1922) experimented with 'group production', which in many ways must be considered a genuine forerunner of the experiments later developed and propagated worldwide by members of the Tavistock group after the Second World War (Wilpert 1990*b*). All requisite characteristics of autonomous work groups were already present seventy years ago:

> (1) employees with functionally interrelated tasks who collectively are responsible for end products; (2) individuals who have a variety of skills so they may undertake all or a large proportion of group's tasks; and (3) feedback and evaluation in terms of the performance of whole groups. (Wall *et al.* 1986)

This again is not the place to speculate why these early beginnings of autonomous group thinking were interrupted and more traditional Tayloristic work structures prevailed for several decades. What is important to note here is that autonomous work groups present one of the most advanced forms of self-determined choice for employees to organize their work according to their needs and interests. Many benefits have been claimed from autonomous work groups: increased satisfaction, motivation, performance, and organizational commitment as well as lower turnover and better mental health. How many of these benefits can be achieved has not been demonstrated by research (see Chapter 6). Nevertheless numerous companies are adopting the principles of autonomous-work-group design, doing so under the guise of various concepts such as 'lean production', 'tightly coupled work groups', or 'new production methods' (see Chapter 1). We have referred to the possible explanations why this is so above:

we seem to enter a new stage in thinking and implementing participation whether we use the term or not.

Legally stipulated direct work-group participation. Direct worker participation under the auspices of the 'laws Auroux' in France and the programme of *werkoverleg* in the Netherlands (Drenth and Koopman 1984) may be cited as examples of the introduction of work-group participation through laws. The laws Auroux (of 1982 and 1986) aim to facilitate the direct expression of worker interests on the basis of 'frame agreements'. These agreements are negotiated by management and unions and, thus, constitute collective-bargaining agreements. Such agreements stipulate the modalities (e.g. participants, frequency of meetings) and topics to be treated by work-unit groups to be established in all companies with more than 200 employees (optional for smaller ones). Management was obliged to respond to the proposals developed by work groups.

Goetschy (1991) reviews the main studies evaluating the impact of the laws Auroux. She concludes that the intricate mechanisms of implementing the legal stipulations through first representative negotiations and then a semi-autonomous operation of the work groups resulted in a tripartite power play which was bound to affect the outcomes of the work groups: 'While the purported aim of the plant-level negotiations was to empower workers, both unions and management were anxious also to preserve their own respective powers' (p. 241). Management was unwilling to introduce major organizational changes, unions were wary of weakening their traditional bargaining bodies. Rank-and-file employees in turn, who were not included in the original negotiations of the frame agreements, were reluctant to enter as a third party in the new structures. Lukewarm managerial responses to work-group demands then contributed to considerable employee apathy. Nevertheless, participatory learning and improved communication among employees took place and may be the most tangible result of the laws Auroux so far: 'through formulating requests, ranking them, and writing them in minutes, participative groups learned how individual claims can (and cannot) be made collective' (p. 243).

Indirect/Representative Participation

Specific psychological aspects. Authors, mainly of the so-called revisionist democratic-theory persuasion (Dachler and Wilpert 1978), see indirect/representative participation as the royal road in the pursuit of collective interests. In fact, virtually all European countries have legislated and implemented some kind of such collective, representative form of participation. Therefore it is rather surprising that no social psychological theory of indirect/representational participation has been developed which would correspond to the psychological theories of individual participation discussed above. Such a theory would conceptualize indirect/representational participation and explain the conditions for its success and failure, its functions and dysfunctions.

Nevertheless, the practical implications and problems of indirect participation have been long known. In the late 1950s Fürstenberg (1958) explained some of the problems of German works councils as stemming from their boundary positions, wedged in between management, employee, and unions. The IDE (1981*a*) study demonstrated the trends of employee representatives to develop into a quasi-professional élite apparently clinging to their roles, thus keeping their clienteles in a dependency relationship. Others have contemplated the endemic fate of all organizations (including representative bodies) eventually to show signs of oligarchization and estrangements of representatives from their mandators (Lammers 1993).

Kirsch, Scholl, and Paul (1984) were among the first to develop theoretical underpinnings of indirect participation. Theirs is a marketing approach to interest representation. They conceive of marketing as a form of taking account of presumed (consumer) interests where decisions, although made without those affected by the decisions, are taken in view of their presumed needs. Indirect/representative participation encompasses both decision-making by intermediaries and reaching these decisions without prior consultation with those represented. However, similar to marketing decisions, these decisions aim at satisfying presumed needs of those for whom the decisions are made. The next election of representatives then gives an opportunity to correct possibly incorrect assumptions of representatives about the needs of employees. The requisite empathy of representatives for the needs of their clientele may be analysed with theoretical concepts of symbolic interactionism, of social perception and the psychology of communication, thus expanding this approach into a veritable theoretical framework. Here is also the point where it becomes evident that the phenomenon of participation, like other forms of organizational behaviour, cannot be understood as objectively true and valid, but rather as socially constructed and negotiated reality.

Structural aspects. Emergent oligarchization of representative functionaries has for long been perceived as a danger for the true interest representation of clienteles. The danger seems intrinsic to any representative role. Measures such as term limits, reduced tenure, and systematic rotation of representatives may be considered as mitigating this danger. On the other hand, Edelstein and Warner (1975) have shown in union studies that electoral procedures may also foster the very dysfunctions described.

Inter-organizational aspects. Inter-organizational cooperation seems to be growing in a variety of fields: for example, in unions and employer federations, intergovernmental organizations, industrial consortia, national or international professional or scientific associations. Network members may have different sizes: small unions join a federation with large powerful ones, multinational giants cooperate with a specialized firms. Hence, the constituents of such federative structures seldom have equal weight when it comes to policy-making and the implementation of decisions. Thus it may happen that parts of the network may become partially or totally disenfranchised from participating in the steering of the cooperative network. Inter-organizational connectedness often implies reduction of autonomy and of influence for the smaller, weaker members. This is the context from which the notion of 'inter-organizational democracy' originates. Participation of a network's subsystem is usually guaranteed by some form of indirect/representative participation of individual members in boundary spanning roles: 'representative intermediaries' (Lammers 1993). This situation raises a variety of practical problems. How to cope with member dissimilarities in kind, size, and weight in such networks? How to organize appropriate decision-making mechanisms (one organization, one vote?)? How to deal with oligarchic tendencies? How to set up rules of interaction? (See also Chapter 1.)

In discussing the 'network form of organization' emerging in industry, Miles and Snow (1986) deal with the same basic problem. Although they do not raise explicitly the issue of inter-organizational democracy, they direct attention to an important dynamic consequence of organizational interconnectedness: worldwide competitive pressures seem to propel the development of networks of cooperating firms. Such inter-organizational networks push member firms to increase the rate of boundary-spanning positions in order to raise their 'connectability'. This happens through switching from top-down control to wider internal self-direction of employees, thus establishing appropriate fits between internal and external structures and processes. The net results are greater autonomy and latitude to rank-and-file members who increasingly function as 'representatives' of their companies (Snow and Miles 1994). Little is known about the requisite competences of employees in these emerging roles.

The psychological conditions and consequences of indirect/representative participation are poorly understood and in need of deeper theoretical penetration and empirical scrutiny.

Consequences of Participation

Turning to consequences of participation we shall try to deal with some of the main current themes in a multi-level perspective.

Individual Level

Satisfaction. Individual satisfaction or morale as co-variates or consequences of participation have been favourite topics of scientific investigation as well as dominant assumptions among managers. The equivocal empirical findings of the gigantic literature regarding this alleged relationship has stimulated many attempts to model and conceptualize the nature of the relationship between participation and satisfaction (Miles 1965; Heller 1971; Locke and Schweiger 1979). Considering, first, direct/personal participation, the empirical evidence is that sometimes there exists a moderate positive relationship popularly assumed to run from participation/PDM to satisfaction, sometimes it does not exist, and sometimes it is negative (Locke and Schweiger 1979). The relationship seems to be moderated by a host of variables such as employee needs for independence, leader characteristics, nature of task and skill match, and skill utilization (Srivastva *et al.* 1975; Strauss 1992). The IDE (1981*a*) study found correlations between personal involvement in decision-making and satisfaction in the fairly low range from 0.10 to 0.23, which may be considered as representative for many studies showing a positive relationship (see Chapter 6).

Turning now to indirect/representative participation, we have to note that only a few studies investigated satisfaction of employees with the given indirect/representative participation system. The IDE study (1981*a*: 260–5) assumed that *de facto* participation of representatives would be positively evaluated by employees. However, this was true only for Yugoslav workers. But the evaluation of the participation system in the different countries correlated positively with the given prescribed rules and regulations—in other words, the extent of legally available possibilities to participate and not the *de facto* participation of representatives. Deci's theory of self-determination, which stresses the importance of self-determined choice among options, might be used to explain this initially surprising finding. In countries with far-reaching prescriptions for participation (e.g. Germany) employees evaluate the possibilities for self-determined action of their representatives positively, more so than the actual level of *de facto* representative participation.

Rising aspirations versus demotivation. The average level of formal education of the population in industrialized countries is rising. One of the consequences of this epochal trend is a general change of expectations regarding the nature of one's work which are directed towards increased autonomy and self-realization potential (MOW 1987). Apart from this general societal trend it is, however, participation experience itself which tends to shift the level of expectations. According to Mulder's theory, power experience is a drug (Mulder 1977) which motivates people to repeat that experience at ever new and higher levels. The correlations between actually experienced and desired participation range from $r = 0.40$ to 0.74 (IDE 1981*a*), which suggests that participation experience constitutes a self-reinforcing dynamic of spiralling aspirations, a reciprocal relationship of 'double interact' to participate ever more intensively. Similar observations have been made by various other authors (Drago and Wooden 1991; Carrie *et al.* 1992).

It cannot be excluded, however, that social desirability plays some role here as well as in the sense that in our society people are expected to say they want more participation, regardless of whether in practice they really take advantage of available participation opportunities. Note, however, that this relationship between actual and desired participation, which increases with higher levels of formal education, refers exclusively to direct participation. Furthermore, the difference between actual and desired participation generally turns out to be small or medium in size

(Wall and Lischeron 1977; IDE 1981*a*), a phenomenon which ought to comfort unrealistically frightened managers worried about a wholesale loss of their prerogatives. Regarding the relationship between experienced direct participation, on the one hand, and desire for representative participation, on the other, the little available evidence is contradictory (Gardell 1977; Koopman-Iwema 1977; IDE 1981*a*).

Another problem of considerable importance relates to the individual and organizational psychological conditions and consequences of frustrated participatory aspirations. We may draw on Brehm's (1966) theory of reactance to formulate some hypotheses about the nature and direction of presumable response patterns. In line with White and Deci, Brehm postulates that people are motivated to experience themselves as directors of their own behaviour. If circumstances threaten this experience by limiting a person's choice options or forcing a person to act in undesired fashion, reactance develops—that is, the person tries to recapture or defend the threatened freedom of choice. We may assume that many industrial conflicts arise as a consequence of reactance to unilateral restrictive measures of management.

However, often it is apathy instead of conflictual reaction which develops as a consequence of frustrated aspirations. To help explain such a course of events we may resort to Wortmann and Brehm (1975), who have related the concept of reactance to the theory of learned helplessness which postulates that a sustained exposure to stress and a lack of control leads to resignation and inactivity (Seligman 1977). The parameters of their model are control expectancies, on the one hand, and the extent of helplessness learning, on the other. Thus, they are able to describe reactance as well as the demotivated state regarding participation as a consequence of learned helplessness. If participation fails in one situation, people seem to become 'immunized' against trying again (Miles 1974). Empirical verification of these theoretically derived propositions is urgently needed. Also unstudied are the conditions under which large mismatches of participatory motivation and corresponding participatory opportunities lead to apathy or burn-out. A related process in terms of stagnating motivation to participate has been discussed under the notion of 'plateauing' (Miles and Rosenberg 1982)—when easy problems have been solved through active participation and some participatory learning has taken place, but the pay-off from further increased participation is then perceived to decline, frustration and resignation result.

Personal development and competence acquisition. How participatory experiences influence the development of an individual's personality has been the subject of extensive speculations. Ulich (1978) assumes that participation will impact positively on self-regulatory, cognitive, and social competences, because participation means goal-directed interaction in the work organization, goal-setting, and interest articulation. Thus, both functional job-related and extra-functional competences may be enhanced. First research evidence seems to confirm these hypotheses (Baitsch and Frei 1980; Baitsch 1985; Széll *et al.* 1989).

But back to our chicken-and-egg problem: what comes first—participatory competence or the experience with participation? We suggest that we confront here again the dynamics of 'double interact'. Learning through participation may be conceived of as a circular process (Mulder 1977): the pleasurable power experience motivates people to reduce further their distance to the next higher hierarchical level. This, in turn, increases the pleasurable power experience, further raising aspirations. Kißler (1980) sees this process intimately linked to the acquisition of functional skills (demanded by the particular features of the work tasks) as well as extra-functional ones (competences developed through working, but of broader relevance also in other life spheres such as social skills), ultimately leading to professional autonomy. Gardell (1983) provides first evidence for the validity of these assumptions. We deal with this issue also in Chapter 5.

Career implications for representatives. So far, we have mainly addressed consequences of direct personal participation. As discussed earlier, the attitudes of employee representatives with regard to the given system of indirect participation differ strikingly from attitudes of their clienteles (IDE 1981*a*). The readiness of representatives to run for representative offices and their interest in participation is drastically more developed among representatives than among rank-and-file employees. At least three different explanations may be offered:

- representatives know better from their personal experience that they can affect decisions in the interest of their constituents;
- owing to their participatory involvements representatives reduce possible cognitive dissonances of their own accomplishments and given aspirations and, hence, develop a positive attitude towards their function;
- power is addictive and the competence acquisition as a consequence of participatory involvement leads to a professionalization of the representative role (Hartmann 1979), which increases chances for re-election. Besides, management might offer additional benefits to representatives in the hope of increasing their cooperativeness.

The overall consequence may therefore be that representatives experience their role as a parallel career pattern alongside the ordinary career within their organization. (For further discussion of this aspect, see chapter 4.)

Learning transfer to other life domains. Whether 'spillover effects' from participatory learning in work settings to other spheres of a person's private life (family, leisure, religious community, voluntary groups, children's schools, etc.) can be observed is a totally under-researched field. One reason may be that theoretical conceptualizations of the interaction dynamics of different life spheres are poorly developed. Bamberg (1986) has demonstrated this lacuna for the relationship between leisure and work. However, some authors have begun to demonstrate transfer effects from work life to other life roles (Kohn and Schooler 1983).

Organizational Level

Organizational climate, culture, identity, and image. The collective social representations of how members perceive and evaluate their organization and how these perceptions impact upon participation have been neglected. This is probably due to theoretical conceptualizations of the relevant terms still being rather fuzzy (Wilpert 1995). This relates to concepts such as commitment, climate, culture, and organizational identity. The terms refer to holistic features of the general intra-organizational regime. They encompass as important elements also the general participatory milieu, the folkways, and the organization's specific custom and practice of dealing with interests of different constituent groups of the organization. Such holistic features may be considered from both perspectives, as prerequisites and as consequences of participation, although we probably face here again that dynamic circular relationship which we have encountered before. Since member commitment, member identification with organizational goals, and collective evaluations of an organization are usually considered to be part of such molar concepts, we can expect them to be closely related to the practice of participation as well.

The participatory image of an organization, in contrast to the just-mentioned concepts, relates to how a particular organization is perceived by its relevant environment. It is again a theme which has hardly been looked at in any systematic fashion, although it may very well influence the ability of an organization to attract goodwill, manpower, and material resources from the environment as long as societal value preferences favour participation. Furthermore, it seems that management is often quite sensitive to the danger that internal conflicts with work councils might become widely known and thus damage a company's reputation (Teulings 1989*a*). On the other hand, the widespread publicity given to Volvo–Saab in the 1970s ('Volvo—Made by Happy Workers') and to Saturn and NUMMI in the USA undoubtedly helped and helps sell cars and recruit motivated workers.

Productivity, and quality of product and of decisions. When we asked managers why they would use participatory decision styles with their subordinates, their answer was invariably 'to improve the technical quality of decisions' (Heller and Wilpert 1981). Participation, in this rationale, serves as an instrument to improve company operations. Findings that participation indeed improves the quality and efficiency of the use of company facilities seem to be accumulated in connection with studies on participation in the introduction of new information technologies. They demonstrate that participation improves the acceptance of the new devices and leads to better use of them (Jansen *et al.* 1989).

More specifically, the business economist's perspective of the participation–productivity relationship has been the object of various meta-analytical investigations of studies based mainly on materials from the USA (Locke *et al.* 1980; Guzzo *et al.* 1985; Miller and Monge 1986; Wagner and Gooding 1987*a*, *b*; Macy *et al.* 1993; Levine and Tyson 1990. See also Chapter 5). In this type of research the kind of the methodology that was employed seems to be of particular importance in determining findings: percept–percept studies (studies using questionnaires asking the same respondents about perceived participation as well as about perceived outcomes) generally yield higher correlations than multi-source studies (e.g. studies using questionnaires for the measurement of participation and independent economic outcome measures). This suggests that a great deal of the variance explained by percept–percept studies may be a methodological artefact. However, it is important to note that at least modest positive relationships between participation and productivity measures are found in most studies irrespective of their methodological approach. Using meta-analytical results, we may, therefore, safely say that participation is at worst a neutral, often a positive factor in relation to productivity. Such a cautious statement may not be sufficient to argue that participation may also be considered as a social technology to increase productivity. But it is sufficient to weaken the a priori negative attitudes towards it. Besides, studies in other countries also tend to show positive relationships between participation and productivity (Cable and FitzRoy 1980; Rosenberg and Rosenstein 1980) and a recent US-governmental commission on the future of management–labour relations claims that employee participation is a significant contributing factor to productivity and viability in the USA (Dunlop 1994).

Societal Level

Social theorizing and social-scientific reflections suggest (Pateman 1970) that participation in one life sphere will 'spill over' to others and, thus, contribute eventually to democratizating society. This will mainly depend on the extant degree of learning transfer from work organizational participatory experience to political life roles of individuals and a possibly ensuing fostering of public democratic climates. We have little empirical evidence for these conjectures so far. Societal outcomes again remain a vast open field to be studied.

From an organization theoretical perspective, however, an open socio-technical systems approach would make this almost inevitable. This is simply because intra-organizational participation is always bound by and impacting on the surrounding industrial relations system—that is, the institutional environment. An example may illustrate the intimate connection between the organizational and societal levels and some of the analytic dilemmas these create. Collective bargaining has become decentralized through much of the developed world in recent years, typically from industry-level to company-level negotiations (Teulings 1989*a*; Trinczek 1989). Is this shift towards greater democracy or less? As we discuss in Chapter 6, arguments can be made both ways.

The issue of inter-organizational democracy discussed above is already a clearer case in point, because high levels of participation in inter-organizational networks are most likely to influence factors which will co-determine the overall democratic climate in a country and between countries. This again remains a wide open field to be investigated.

Summary

At the root of any participation lies the general dispositional need of people to interact effectively with their environment. The concept of participation lies in the intersect of individual development, organizational viability, technological and social development. Thus it highlights and offers substantial promise to bring into focus many different problems and to integrate various subdisciplines in psychology and other social sciences.

There are significant differences in theorizing and methodological approaches between Anglo-American and European Continental writers, the former stressing the instrumental role of participation for social and economic efficiency, the latter emphasizing the significance of participation as a fundamental anthropological role essential for personal development.

The most promising and urgent future research topics in the area of participation are following on from a psychological perspective:

- individual and social consequences of participation, such as competence acquisition or learning transfers from a work organizational experience of participation to other life domains;
- new historical challenges, such as new technologies and participation;
- new methodological approaches to the study of participation, such as the analysis of cross-level effects and longitudinal studies;
- the development of a theory of indirect/representative participation which complements the fairly well-understood psychological bases of personal/direct participation.

Participation as an issue for theory, research, and practice is alive and demands continued and even increased scientific attention because of technological, educational, and societal value changes which should revitalize an important topic on the social agenda precociously predicted by many to be dead.

NOTE

1. The use of the term 'finality' as referring to ultimate goals may be strange to some readers. However, the term is related to an important 1970s debate among European social scientists as to the role of science in society.

3. Organization Theory and Participation

In a sense, participation is the essence of organization in both its empowering and its limiting aspects. Participation implies a field of self-determined choices, but among possible actions (cf. Wilpert, Chapter 2, this volume). And what is possible is predetermined by, among other criteria, the participants' commitment to collective activity—just as organization itself is the enhancement of individual effort through the differentiated and integrated work of many and at the same time the constraint of coordinated cooperation imposed upon individual will and representation.

Organization theory is the study of this relationship—a study meandering in its lifetime from the pole of enhancement to that of constraint and back again before breaking through to the insight of their dialectical link. Adam Smith (1937: 3) tends to become lyrical about the empowering advantages of the division of labour: 'The greatest improvement in the productive powers of labour and the greater part of the skill, dexterity, and judgment with which it is anywhere directed, or applied, seem to have been the effects of the division of labour.' Karl Marx prefers to harp on about its constraining aspects. By the division of labour the workers are impoverished in their 'individual labor force' and 'brought face to face with the intellectual potencies of the material process of production, as the property of another, and as a ruling power' (Marx 1889: 335). Max Weber (1968: 973), again, reverts to Smith's optimism, as it were on a higher technical level:

> The decisive reason for the advance of bureaucratic organization has always been its purely technical superiority over any other form of organization. The fully developed bureaucratic apparatus compares with other organizations exactly as does the machine with non-mechanical modes of production. Precision, speed, unambiguity, knowledge of the files, continuity, discretion, unity strict subordination, reduction of friction and of material and personal costs—these are raised to the optimum point in the strictly bureaucratic administration, and especially in its monocratic form.

While Georges Friedmann (1961: 120) arrives at what amounts to a final negative judgement about the whole process of division of labour in the age of the machine: 'The subdivision of jobs, constantly on the increase during the development of the machine age from the end of the eighteenth century onward, will in future appear, not as a one-way process of unlimited duration, but as a transitory form of labor, and often a pathological one, if we consider it in relation to some of our deeper human needs.'

Organization Theory (OT) took time to get hold of both aspects of the organizational phenomenon, its instrumental, goal-directed, rational, Weberian aspect of people pursuing their interests in cooperation, and its reverse side of power-seeking, domination, frustration, alienation, its Marxian and Freudian aspect of people pursuing their interests in conflict with each other. The links between the two aspects are people and the perennial ambiguity of their relations between cooperation and conflict, dependence and independence. This is why people in organizations and in contact with organizations are the necessary focus of OT. And this is also why the problem of participation is inextricably linked with the whole development of OT: 'one can think of participation as a central concept of organizing' (Dachler and Wilpert 1978: 1). The double-faced nature of organization as cooperation and as conflict parallels the opposition between the empowering and the constraining effects of organizational participation—and leads also to the changing emphasis in the study of participation on participation-as-working-together and participation-as-sharing in the results. Who are the people that participate in organizations? In what kind of decisions do they participate? How do they participate, what is their weight in shaping the outcome of decision processes? What are their chances of satisfying their interests in the organization or in relation to it, particularly if these interests conflict with those of other participants?

We will start with *conceptual* clarifications, then sketch those aspects of *social change* we consider decisive for the emergence of the contemporary problem of participation in organizations, in order to turn, first, to *interaction* producing the characteristic tension in organizations between techniques and interests, structure and action, internal and external sources of change, and then to the *specific implications* of this tension for participation in cooperation and conflict, for producing dependence, and for encouraging independence in organizations, leading to the *conclusions*.

Concepts

Organization

Organizations are groups of people pursuing some of their interests by being formally committed to a common purpose, to a type of mutual relations at work, and to given methods of work. Organizations function in a physical world and need resources in the appropriate form of matter energy—human physical and intellectual energy, non-human sources of energy, financial resources, etc. They also function in an informational world of conscious actors and need information in the appropriate form—knowledge, tools and instruments, data, etc. Finally, they function in a social world of interests, values, and rules, of individual and collective actors. And they interact in their functioning with all these aspects—physical, informational, social—of their environment. By their formal commitment to an organization people are committed to cooperation. In the reality of their mutual relations cooperation is linked to the possibility and actuality of disagreement or outright conflict. People in organizations become dependent, symmetrically and asymmetrically, and tend to assert and reassert their independence.

Definitions of organization are getting more complex, more inclusive, and more dynamic. 'We propose that organizational analysis has been evolving toward more complex, paradoxical, and even contradictory modes of understanding' (Jelinek *et al.* 1983: 331). But people are a constant element in all of them. Fayol (1949, first edition, 1916) understood organization as 'the double structure, material and human, of an undertaking' (pp. 5–6). The authors of classical administrative science in the USA saw organizations as 'the arrangement of personnel for facilitating the accomplishment of some agreed purpose through the allocation of functions and responsibilities' (Gaus *et al.* 1947), and in the UK as socio-technical systems—i.e. 'a combination of technology (task requirement, physical layout of the plant, work flow, available machinery) and a social system (a system of relationships between those who must perform the job)' (Kassem 1976: 8). Newer models are more intricate, such as Fombrun's (1986), where organization is seen as a three-layered system of infrastructure (technology), socio-structure (relations among people at work), and superstructure (norms, values, beliefs) 'converging', i.e. stabilizing and 'diverging' in interest conflicts among participants, in the midst of a population of similar organizations, in a community of complementary organizations, within the wider environment of a society (pp. 403–21). But, though people are essential in all the definitions, in the beginning they are treated as a resource ('human structure', 'personnel'), to evolve later into a more independent 'social system', in order to become 'participants' with legitimate interests.

Participation

Participation, according to Wilpert (Chapter 2, this volume), is 'the totality of forms and of intensities . . . by which individuals, groups, collectives secure their interests through self-determined choices among possible actions' in the context of organized interaction; or, 'a process in which influence on decision making is shared between hierarchical superiors and their subordinates . . .' (Wagner and Gooding 1987*a*: 241). What does it mean to participate? Practically, it means to influence decisions made in the organization, on whatever level and on whatever subject. The decisions being influenced belong to one of two broadly defined groups: *technical decisions*, related directly to the work in the organization and only indirectly to the interests of the participants—from the typing of a letter to an overall production plan—and *interest decisions*, related directly to the interests of the participants and only through these interests to the functioning of the organization—from an individual pay rise to an overall holiday plan. The key question about participation is the equality or inequality among participants in their ability to influence decisions, both technical and interest decisions, made in organizations.

Technical decisions are related to the work performed in the organization. The work of the organization, however, though in principle common to all participants, is not of one kind. People participate as sources of energy doing manual work, or they participate as sources of information performing intellectual work. Actually, almost all manual work requires some knowledge, some informational competence, and the question, therefore, is of more or less informational elements present in all work, than of people doing exclusively one or the other. Intellectual work, as well as the intellectual element in manual work, can be distinguished according to the generality and the complexity of the information involved. Information is more general when it is relevant for a larger area of the organization's activity. It is more complex when it includes more diverse elements, and their understanding and utilization have more diverse prerequisites. A possible gradient of inequality among participants in an organization results from the way information is distributed among the members along the two dimensions of generality and complexity. The more skewed the distribution, the fewer people control a larger part of the general and complex information needed in the organization's functioning, and the greater the technical inequality among participants and, consequently, the inequality of their chances to influence decisions. From the purely technical point of view, the optimal distribution of information in an organization along the dimensions of generality and complexity varies with the size and the overall complexity of organizations. In small and simple organizations the more equal distribution of the necessary information among participants tends to be preferable because it increases the possibility of individual contribution, thereby improving the overall effect. With increasing size and complexity the concentration of complex information within the organization tends to become more profitable because it reduces the needed number of expensive participants qualified to contribute and to use complex information. The same goes for the concentration of general information because of its coordinating and integrating effect when concentrated. Beyond a certain higher level of size and complexity of the organization, however, the transfer of complex as well as of general information to organizational subunits and to individuals becomes unavoidable because total concentration of complex and general information in large and very complex organizations tends to paralyse their functioning.

To influence interest decisions in an organization means also to share in whatever the organization produces or has to offer as means of interest satisfaction: products, profits, salaries and wages, security, solidarity, companionship, recognition, experience, growth. But these decisions, as well, include an element, larger or smaller, of information. And in order to take part, usefully from the point of view of the overall effect for the organization, the participants have to acquire relevant information and be competent to use it. The two meanings of participation—participation as taking part and participation as sharing in the results, influencing technical decisions and influencing interest decisions—are not strictly separable; they shade over into each other and depend on each other.

The distinction between participation as influencing technical decisions and participation as influencing interest decisions about sharing in the results of the organizations' functioning brings up the question, who is to be considered a participant? The two circles are not necessarily congruent: some share in the results who do not contribute to the work, even if we count the contribution of resources as tantamount to work. As well as the other way round, some take part in the work—e.g. by regulating it—without sharing in its results. Also, there are those who are not members of an organization but are so vitally affected by its activities—e.g. as users of a service—or do so vitally affect the organization—e.g. as providers of essential inputs—that the normative order is inclined to treat them, in some respects, as participants and give them some influence upon the organization's decisions.

Organization as interaction. Organizations are forms of interaction and thus subject to the tensions that interaction normally produces. Interaction may take the form of cooperation, working together to achieve a common purpose, or the form of conflict, working against each other in order to achieve alternative purposes. The term 'conflict' is used here generically, in order to stress its dialectical relation with cooperation; it includes all shades of conscious differences that arise among people in protracted contact with each other. Organizations, though conceived as cooperative systems, provide a stage for on-going interaction and are therefore the scene of both cooperation and conflict. Conflicts can arise about cognitive disagreements on technical questions, as well as from confrontations on questions of interest. They can also originate in a difference of ideas without immediate relevance to either technical or interest questions, or in a discrepancy in evaluating a situation and its implications for interests. Most conflicts have a mobilizing effect and can in this way be a source of cognitive and normative innovation. Most conflicts also generate emotions and it is the possible escalation of emotions by mutual induction that makes conflict potentially explosive and destructive. Cooperation in organizations itself is the source of conflict on both dimensions of participation: conflict on how to cooperate, how to function, how to take part in the organization's activities; and conflict about how to share what the organization has to offer. Both the aims of cooperation and the likely sources of conflict are influenced by the organization's structure. The actors in both cooperation and conflict are the participants; both cooperation and conflict are ways to participate consciously in the life of the organization.

Beside the opposition between cooperation and conflict, there is also the tension between the autonomy of the participants to pursue both cooperation and conflict as dictated by their interests and the limits imposed on this freedom of movement by the organization's structure—its purposes, relations, and methods of work. Relatively enduring structures create dependence of some participants on others or mutual interdependence. Dependence, however, gives rise to strivings for independence, in so far as it reduces the chances of interest satisfaction for those who are dependent. Independence, however, can only be asserted within the limits imposed by the organization's structure. Again, the life of the organization is lived and participation is experienced as tension between the necessities of dependence and the promises of independence for its participants.

Organization and entropy. That organizations are structures means that they are areas of non-random events. Thus they are subject to the universal influence of the Second Law of Thermodynamics in the sense that all non-random arrangements tend towards ultimate dissolution into randomness, and therefore need, in order to maintain their structure, constant inputs of energy to achieve *negentropy*, to sustain their non-randomness, or to increase it through *morphopoiesis*, the creation of form. Energy, however, is scarce in principle, for the same entropic reason just mentioned. All organizations function under the limitation of scarcity and the same limit applies to participation. Participation, on the one hand, consumes energy—the time and attention of people—but, on the other, it also mobilizes energy by motivating people to additional inputs that would otherwise remain unutilized for organizational purposes. Organizations 'import' energy, i.e. negative entropy, by co-opting people as agents doing physical–intellectual work and as highly complex physical–mental structures themselves. The main source of energy for doing the organization's work as well as for integrating its differentiating elements are its participants. Also, the main source of friction born of dependence, the main origin of conflict within the organization, are again its participants. In relation to people, scarcity is specific. First, organizations do not need just any kind of people, but people with given types of training and particular combinations of experience, people that may be scarce even in the presence of high unemployment. Secondly, participants can share only in what is available. If their interests are concentrated on a particular scarce resource—for example, money in a poor environment—conflicts about this resource will tend to dominate the scene of interaction in the organization. These conflicts will channel participation into antagonistic forms—for example, workers versus owners, trade unions versus management, blue collar versus white collar, production versus sales, etc. Some of the more frequent conflicts 'inherent in organized activities' develop 'among sales, engineering staffs and between staff specialists who design comprehensive management systems and the managers who often oppose their implementation' (Aram 1984: 473). It is likely that concentration of interests on material rewards will be proportional to general scarcity and will slacken with increasing general affluence (Maslow 1968). A consequence is also the effort of management to influence participants towards reorienting their interests away from material and in the direction of non-material benefits—for example, companionship and a sense of belonging in the human-relations movement—or the proliferation of honorific roles—for example, in self-management practice in former Yugoslavia—ahead of the material conditions for a change in interest orientation. On the other hand, material rewards can become so deeply rooted in the value system of a society that they come to stand as a symbol of success as such and become resistant against reorientation even after reasonable material needs have been met.

Organization and information. Organizations are information-using and information-processing systems. They depend on information in all of their activities. Technical knowledge is the basis of their productive—in the widest sense—enterprise; it is relevant for their integration as well as for managing their relations with the environment. The initial and boundary conditions of the productive process are defined as information in the form of data. For participation, the availability of necessary information and the competence to use it are fundamental preconditions.

There is, for organizations, the risk of both dearth and over-abundance of information. The knowledge necessary for operations may simply not be there, so that the main productive activity of the organization cannot proceed at all or not at the required and expected level of quality. It is not that just information is a scarce resource. Information may be, theoretically, available, but, given the maximum possible span of attention, it cannot be absorbed and used.

> The centrality of attention allocation to decision making in social institutions is a standard feature of behavioral theories of collective choice . . . What happens depends on which rule is evoked, which action is initiated, which value is considered, which competitors are mobilized, which opportunities are seen, which problems and solutions are connected, or which world-view is considered. Consequently, a major means of intentional control over institutions is the management of attention. (March and Olsen 1989: 61)

More often, however, the lack of information will manifest itself at the level of the organization's relations with its environment. Not to know what is happening in the organization or how the relevant environment is likely to react produces uncertainty in the organization's members.

Uncertainty has a wide range of influence upon behaviour, from stimulating initiative and inventiveness to paralysing all activity. How it will affect conduct depends on the pertinent combination of personal and situational characteristics in and for each individual. It can be seen as a welcome openness of the situation, as chance and opportunity, but also experienced as absence of essential orientation and as unreliability of the environment, inhibiting action.

Participation in the sense of increasing responsibility for and influence upon decision-making in the organization can reduce uncertainty as well as increase it. Reduce it because participation provides greater personal control over uncertainty: one is able and expected to contribute to decisions about what are, for the participant, major sources of uncertainty: his or her personal status in the organization, the job, higher wages or salaries, the chances of the organization to continue to exist and to function. But participation can also increase uncertainty if the participants feel that more is expected of them than they are able to contribute, that their time budget is overtaxed, that participation is formal, and that it does not really change the relations of power in the organization. And here as well, uncertainty is ambivalent in its influence upon behaviour. People may lose interest in participation, reduce their input into decision-making, turn to other methods to further their interests. Or they may try to use the institutions of participation for what they are worth, seeing in them a chance to further their own personal interests even if not in accord with the initial intentions and the logic of the institution.

Organization and environment. Organizations exist and function within societies. They are themselves systems of meanings, rules, values, cognition, stabilized in a process of habitualization, and dependent on their social milieu in two directions. First, people as members of an organization bring into it their mental make-up, the specific semantic, normative, and cognitive structures that serve as filters for all inputs from the world as well as from their organic infrastructure, structures derived from and built into the process of socialization and internalization of the corresponding elements in society at large. The behaviour of people as members of organizations, and thus also their participation in decision-making, does not only depend on the rules regulating their organizational roles. In an important part it is predetermined by the mental structures that members carry with them into the organization, 'by some underlying structure of meaning that persists over time, constraining people's perception, interpretation, and behavior' (Jelinek *et al.* 1983: 337). And, secondly, the most significant part of the environment of an organization is the other organizations and institutions that may be classified into categories that are symbolic, regulative, productive, complementary to the semantic, normative, and cognitive filters present in the mental make-up of each individual. These institutions produce and reinforce the meanings, rules, values, and cognition that channel and practically limit what people on the average will see, think, feel, and do inside the organization as well as outside it.

Besides providing the framework for participation by the organization's members, the correspondence of the mental and the institutional components of the social environment suggests the idea of the 'external' participant. Customers, clients, users, etc. do not only depend upon the organization and its activities; in the aggregate they are also in a position to influence it. So are the regular suppliers, the inspectors and other agents of public regulatory and supervisory agencies, as well as people active in an organization fulfilling a complementary function (e.g. producing components of the organization's product). As the network of interdependence and interrelationships is becoming more dense in the course of increasing overall social density, the role of the external participant is becoming more pertinent to the organization's concerns. An indication of this concern is the theoretical developments towards seeing organization as a combination of problems, solutions, decision-makers, and choice opportunities, converging and diverging, meeting and separating, without clear distinction of 'inside' and 'outside' (Cohen, March, and Olsen 1972).

Social Change

At the centre of our attention here are those processes that alter the ways in which people are working together pursuing purposes, having stabilized a given type of relation among themselves, and applying given methods. In other words, we are interested to find out how social change influences the participation of people in organizations. This intention determines both the time span and the priorities among the dimensions of change. The time span is that of the dominance of urban industrial societies from the second half of the nineteenth to the last decade of the twentieth century. The widespread discussion today about post-industrial or postmodern society, about post-structural relations and post-materialistic values, about risk society or emerging global society is a sign that consciousness of fundamental social change and the accelerating rate of change is becoming more general and more intensive. Not only the past but also the present is already history.[1]

Under the general label of social change, the most important dimensions in transforming the organized interaction of people are those of *technology*—that is, the transformation of tools and methods of work, as well as of the modalities of the division of work—and *legitimacy*—that is, the widening circle of individual and group interests that are accepted to be articulated and pursued in a social context. There follow the dimensions of *productivity*—the measure of affluence in society—and *density*, including demographic (people/territory), ecological (degree of urbanization), communicational (networks of transportation and communication), and organizational density (the part of human work that is performed cooperatively). Organizational density is an aspect of the division of labour in society that leads directly to the specific phenomena of organizational change and, consequently, change in the position and the radius of action of the individual participant.

Technology

Technological change shall mean, in the present context, such change in the 'tools, devices, and knowledge that mediate between inputs and outputs (process technology) and/or create new products or services (product technology)' (Tushman and Anderson 1986: 440). We assume that this change modifies the position of the organization's members in taking part in the work and/or in their chances to share in its results.

The source of technological change is, generally, the advance in experience and understanding. During the last 200 years or so this has meant, essentially, the advance of science, a cumulative and gradually accelerating process. Within this time span technological change replaced human and animal physical strength as a source of energy with other sources, it amplified human physical capabilities with the use of machines, and it began to amplify human intellectual capabilities with the use of information processing systems. 'Since the first industrial revolution, social scientists have called attention to the central role played by technological change . . . in shaping the evolution of organizations and in affecting the relations among individuals, groups, and the organizations within which they work' (Tushman and Nelson 1990: 1).

The influence of these changes upon the position of individual participants in their work roles as well as in their interest roles was considerable—and ambiguous. Freeing people from the burden of being a source of physical energy and amplifying their physical and intellectual capabilities strengthened the position of the individual in organizations. At the same time, however, the machine unfolded a new dimension of the division of labour. Traditionally, the division of labour meant the partitioning of a field of activity and interest into more narrow areas where more concentrated effort made it possible to penetrate deeper into reality or to deal with it more efficiently. In the age of the machine the division of labour had shifted from the field of activity to the individual work process. The work process was divided and subdivided, broken down, some say crumbled (Friedmann 1956), to the level of single physical movements repeated endlessly on the production line. This meant that the traditional craftsmen were, as industrial workers, deprived of their skill: their skill was made pointless, they were 'de-skilled', their 'competence was destroyed' (Barley 1990) in the mechanized factory. In consequence, the necessary overall information relevant to the work process had to be concentrated at the top of a technologically underpinned hierarchical pyramid, the work process started to be divided down to the practically information-less repeated motions on the bottom of the pyramid, in order to be reintegrated towards the final product by this very hierarchy. With relevant information concentrated at the top, hierarchy became the most economical way to communicate in organizations, besides being the most natural way to dominate them.

The invention of information-processing systems meant, in the beginning, a reinforcement of the concentrating effect of mechanization, as computers expanded the reach of central control. It is only in the further course of its development that electronic data-processing began to manifest a different potential. The emergence of automation and robotization meant that work that could be broken down into simple single motions could also be transferred to computerized machine systems where the whole work process could be completed practically without human intervention. What could be crumbled could also be automated. The accent in the division of labour is shifting back from work process to field of interest where the partitioning and narrowing could serve to deepen knowledge in each of the subfields.

In this perspective human work in organizations would be needed only for those processes that, for any reason, could not be broken down into elementary operations. Their elements might be too complexly interwoven, the process as a whole might depend on indivisible blocks of information, or on the emotional–moral engagement of the individual worker (e.g. in nursing or in social work). This would lead to organizations with, on the average, more highly skilled and highly educated participants than today. Therefore, not only would their taking part in the organization's work be more meaningful; their bargaining position would also be stronger and, as a consequence, their chances of interest satisfaction, of sharing in the results of the work, better. Also the development of information-processing includes telematics—that is, more differentiated and more efficient ways to communicate at a distance—and the implied perspective that the separation between living space and working place, dominant since the first Industrial Revolution, would be reversed; the spatial concentration of the work of an organization would no longer be necessary.

However, we are not there yet, and, thinking of the many other variables on which the reality of human relations in organizations depends, including the potential of technology for reintroducing close and detailed control, we might never be. Technology by itself cannot change what people might do to each other. It is simply that technological developments in the last decades have opened the *possibility* for fuller and more meaningful participation of people in organizations.

Legitimacy

Political developments in the last 200 years, when considered in the long run and discounting the many relapses, can be reduced to the common denominator of a progressively widening circle of interests that are considered legitimate—that is, whose public articulation and open pursuance is socially accepted. It began in the democratic reforms and revolutions of basic human rights to life and liberty, in the political interests of people who had become citizens from being merely subjects, and in protection against the arbitrary exercise of political power. It continued with the legitimacy of economic and social interests in the reforms leading to the Welfare State and in the social-democratic and socialist reforms and revolutions. These movements included a particular emphasis on the position of workers in industrial and other organizations, the workers' movement. Industrial workers also began individually to develop a special psychological link to their workplace, a feeling that this place, in a sense, belonged to them, a sort of 'psychological appropriation of the work place by the worker' (Wilpert 1991). First people as citizens and then people as producers became social roles seen as fundamental to a legitimate social order. The process continues with the recognition of ecological interests, of the rights and interests of minorities, with anti-discrimination movements and claims to social justice in an increasing number of areas.

Again, the bestowing of legitimacy to a class of interests does not by itself guarantee that these interests are going to be satisfied. It is certainly true that the twentieth century saw the most blatant disregard of some of the most elementary human interests and rights on historical record.

In addition to technological development and the expanding legitimacy of interests, there is a growth of productivity and of social density, partly caused by technical and social innovation, and partly complementary to them.

Productivity

Technological advance and changes in the division of labour have led directly to a gradual increase in the productivity of human work measured by the relation of value of product to the time spent in its production (the record is less clear when the measure is value of product to quantity of raw materials used or to energy spent). This means a greater possibility of affluence at higher levels of development and with less pressure of scarcity. In organizations, greater general affluence increases the possible share of each participant and in this way the chance for rank-and-file participants to satisfy their material interests by sharing to a greater extent in the results of the organizations' work.

However, not only does the realization of these possibilities depend on the outcome of numerous interest conflicts in the world, in every society, and in each individual organization. The tendency towards increasing productivity itself is slowing down worldwide during the last decades of the twentieth century and its possible ultimate limits are implied in a number of factors discussed under the theme of 'limits to growth' (Meadows *et al.* 1972).

Density

The improvements in the conditions of life through increasing affluence are leading to more people surviving and thus to increasing social density in its general demographic dimension as well as to greater ecological, communicational, transportational, and organizational density. More of the work done in a given society is performed in some form of cooperation with other people, even if better communicational technology should make it unnecessary to place all of them in spatial propinquity. Whatever the risks and the drawbacks of increasing social density, growing organizational density means that more and more people will find themselves interdependent with others with whom they cooperate and disagree as the case may be in an organizational setting. Also greater density makes possible the shift from direct to indirect methods of control, meaning less emphasis on control through hierarchy in organizations.

The various dimensions of social change are interconnected. They influence and stimulate each other. All point to the increased importance of people in organizations, to the strengthening position of the individual participant, and in this way to a greater possibility for members of organizations to participate—that is, to share more fully in what the organization has to offer. On the other hand, it is a world where increasing density gives more opportunity for conflict, in organizations no less than in other forms of human interaction—conflict with its stimulating effect but also with its load of the unexpected, the uncertain, the destructive. The growth of knowledge and of technological capacity can be used for destructive just as well as for constructive ends. More extensive and more encompassing systems in all fields of human activity are increasingly vulnerable to specific types of ecological accidents (nuclear, oil, chemical) and catastrophic destabilization (e.g. Eastern Europe). Already visible and potentially possible limits to the capacity of our planet to accommodate us and the fallout of our activities (population explosion, pollution, etc.) foreshadow the progressive rise of uncertainty in the future. They create today a high-risk environment for many organizations. The realization of these possibilities, positive as well as negative, depends on all contingencies besetting human relations generally. It is also interdependent with the concrete alternatives in structuring organizations and in their functioning, to which we now turn.

Interaction and Participation

Organizations are forms of intentionally continuous human interaction. As such they are subject to the tensions characteristic of interaction between the opposites of cooperation and conflict, dependence and independence, owing to the 'fact that an organization is simultaneously a system of competition and a system of cooperation' (Morgan 1986: 195).

Participation in organizations, therefore, means to influence decisions, both technical and interest decisions, that are a part of cooperation as well as those related to conflict, decisions that create or express dependence and decisions meant to assert independence, decisions that are in response to environmental pressures to change and those that reflect internally generated change processes. These fundamental oppositions produce the main ambiguities of both organization and participation. Participation is constrained by the character of organizations as instruments for achieving cooperatively stated purposes. It is also determined by organizations being groups of people in conflict pursuing their interests to whom stated purposes are at best a résumé and at worst a pretext—techniques versus interest. Participation is constrained by the structure of organizations—that is, restrictions on human behaviour that is made dependent upon rules, habits, situations. It is also oriented towards action guided by motives and in principle opposed to any restrictions—structure versus action. Organizations are changing; change is the result of both internal processes and external causes to which organizations react. Participation can be both cause and consequence of changes in organizations internally as well as externally generated—internal versus external sources of change.

Techniques versus Interests

Organizations do not just happen. They are an act of human consciousness, created to achieve some human purpose, no matter whether it is the purpose declared in the charter or other formal foundation document. This basic fact of organizational life makes organization an instrument, a means towards an end, whatever else it is or will be from any other point of view. Does this mean that people who are members of the organization, who work for the organization, who are the organization, are also instruments? That they depend on the organization and on those having power in it, that they are one of the resources, along with money or technology, to be used in the achievement of the organization's purposes? Or can organizations function also when people in them have achieved the status of independent participants?

Organizations are groups of people—people working in the organization, leading it, investing money in it, controlling it, or also and increasingly people buying from the organization, consuming its products, utilizing its activities, using its services, supplying it regularly with whatever it needs, people inspecting it, or people depending on it, for whatever reason, in a more than transitory manner. People have interests, defined broadly as any relatively stable motive; or, more elaborately, as 'a complex set of predispositions embracing goals, values, desires, expectations, and other orientations and inclinations that lead a person to act in one direction rather than another' (Morgan 1986: 149). These interests they have brought into the organization when joining in any capacity, or have developed them in the organization or in relation to the organization, no matter whether these new interests originate in the association or flow from other sources. Their behaviour in the organization or in relation to the organization is motivated by their interests. This basic fact of human association describes organizations as interest groups or interest arenas, whatever else they may be at the same time. People cooperate in order to satisfy interests but they also compete and conflict about the distribution of scarce means by which interests can be satisfied. The result may be an organization where some people's interests permanently dominate over the interests of others, or an organization where the interest conflict is institutionalized and as such has become part of the normal functioning of the organization, or an organization based from the outset on a compromise among the interests of all members.

The classics of OT—Taylor, Fayol, Gulick—though committed to an exclusively instrumental view of organizations, are not unaware of interests. They simply assume that pursuing the formal goal of the organization is normally in the interest of all participants: owners, shareholders, managers, workers. Frederick Taylor, formerly lathe-operator and engineer completely familiar with the practice in the factory, had developed in his *Principles of Scientific Management* (first published in 1911) the model of an efficient factory-organization, directed primarily against the 'negligent', i.e. undependable worker, wanting to discipline him as necessary. All shortcomings of the organization of work in his time Taylor explained by the excessive autonomy of the worker. He criticized that the worker has 'nearly complete responsibility for the execution of the work, generally as well as in relation to details, and in many cases also responsibility for his tools, and that the workers because of their professional experience and their knowledge appear as "the true masters of the factory", even if they have no power to dispose of the manufactured products' (Glaser 1988: 106–7). The criticism of this position—for example, by the human-relations school—does not deny the instrumental character of the organization nor the view of workers as a resource of the organization rather than its members. It only approaches in a different way the problem of how to control the workers, and how to motivate them.

Whether people in organizations will tend to be treated as a resource, as a cost, or will be given recognition as participants may depend on the overall economic level as well as on the ups and downs of the economic cycle. Stewart Clegg (1981: 554) refers to the 'long waves' in the rise and decline of the rate of profit, the acceleration and deceleration of accumulation. It is plausible to expect people to be treated as a resource when they are more expendable, more easily replaceable from a larger reserve of unemployed labour.

> The organization is seen not as an incentive distributing device, abstracted from the relationship of its members, but as a marketplace in which incentives are exchanged . . . if the power of organizational members is seen as an expression of their ability to contribute incentives to other members, then the relative power possessed by the individuals in any particular relationship would seem to rest on their replaceability and dispensability. (Georgiou 1973: 306–7)

It is also a function of the social use of technology. Technology that corresponds to the 'crumbling' of work into elementary operations almost without any information content will condemn the base of the organizational pyramid to function simply as resource. This, however, is not necessarily a permanent condition. General social organization, the prevailing values of a strongly stratified society, whatever its criteria of stratification—aristocracy, plutocracy, meritocracy—will tend to create a corresponding attitude in individual organizations. 'Political domination in the workplace is one reflection of the larger dynamics of capitalism. Events seemingly far removed from the workplace itself impose important constraints on workplace relations. In this light the worker–management struggle in organizations is to be seen, simply, as a microcosm of the wider arena of class society' (Astley and Van de Ven 1983: 265). On the other hand, increasing recognition of the value of the individual human being will tend to give legitimacy to the demand of each member in the organization to be recognized as participant. The respect for persons 'is entailed in the proposition that individual human beings are ends in themselves not merely resources or means to organizational well-being' (Keeley 1984: 11). The circle of legitimate interests in the organization is becoming wider. There is also more awareness of the variety of interests present in the organization and around it. There are interests common to all participants in an organization: 'It is nevertheless assumed that participants share interest in aggregate organizational consequences which constitute very general means to everyone's particular ends . . . It is a widely accepted belief that harm minimization (in some sense) should take precedence over other organizational concerns' (Keeley 1984: 14, 20). The prevailing position, however, is to ask about the distribution of interests within an organization: 'The point is that goal-based measures of effectiveness, whether single or multiple, are rather insensitive to the distribution of outcomes, whereas organizational participants usually care a great deal about how outcomes are distributed' (Keeley 1984: 3). Probably the most important difference is between *transactional* interests, of members who take part in the work of the organization more or less exclusively for the sake of the immediate benefits, primarily material, the organization has to offer, and *organizational* interests, of those who have, in a measure, identified with the organization and linked their whole working life and hope of success to the organization and their career in it. Most decisions have, in fact, both technical and interest aspects.

Structure versus Action

The dilemma between structural and 'interactionist' perspectives—'the "structural" perspective specifying abstract dimensions and contextual constraints, and the "interactionist" perspective of symbolic mediation and negotiated processes' (Ranson *et al.* 1980: 1), appears in OT as the opposition between deterministic views of organizations as preordained by the logic of structure and voluntaristic views of organizations as depending on the will and the conscious activity of participants direct or indirect. Both classical OT and its criticism are essentially deterministic. Alternative views, derived from sociological action theory, tend more towards indeterministic models of organizations as institutionalized arenas for the action of their members as participants. Action in organizations is related either to the organization's goal or to the maintenance of the organization. In both varieties, however, it is structured or constrained action. The structuring becomes first evident in the concept of organizational role. 'The basic components of structure are roles. These predefine the set of behavioral expectations, duties, and responsibilities associated with a given position' (Astley and Van de Ven 1983: 248). Roles are, in fact, rules, stabilized expectations of behaviour within the organization as well as in relation to it—that is, constraints on behaviour and thus structure. There is the inherent opposition between the 'potential inherent in human agency and the constraining influence of organizational structure' (Reed 1988: 42).

The structure of the organization limits the extent to which interests of participants can be accepted as legitimate. And thus structure limits participation, in the sense of freedom of participants to pursue their interests. On the other hand, structures that are, in a sense, residues of participative action, such as formal work councils, can and do facilitate participation. Experience, though, here again documents the limitations of normatively prescribed structures of participation. The attempt to base organizations exclusively on self-managing interest groups is likely to reduce the efficiency of such organizations below the economically tolerable limit. The main reason for this is the 'logic of collective action' (Olson 1971) inducing participants to limit their contribution to results from which they cannot be excluded or, alternatively, inducing them to use to the limit and beyond it all possibilities to satisfy their interests, under the assumption that if they do not the respective resource will not be economized but will be simply used by others.

Internal versus External Change

Organizations, in a sense, are structures under tension. These tensions lead to change. In their 'Central Perspectives and Debates in Organization Theory' Astley and Van de Ven (1983) see all main currents of contemporary OT, agreeing that organizations change and disagreeing on how they change (p. 247). Change as a mode of existence, was obvious to the classics as well as to the moderns.[2] On the other hand, OT, particularly in its beginnings, pays special attention to how organizations achieve even the relative stability they have. Fayol (1949: 133) sees organizations as creations of the natural order. Systems theory operates with the concept of homeostasis, stay-the-sameness, and even defines organizations as entities that are relatively stable in a changing environment. 'Organizations are entities maintaining themselves in a complex and changing environment by stabilizing the difference between its interior and the external world' (Luhmann 1984: 143). At present, change in organizations over time is a recognized fact. 'The life process of organizations is an exchange relationship with its environment over time. Hence, only by systematically integrating the time dimension in our thinking and researching will we have a chance to make sense of the dynamically changing organization–environment relations' (Wilpert 1990*a*: 22). The question is not whether organizations change but how and why they change. Change is seen, on the one hand, as the product of differentiating organizational structure or of a change in its internal integrating framework, and, on the other, as caused by forces in the environment (for example, natural-selection theories). Changes called 'internal', though, depend as well, in most instances, on an external cause, the increasing complexity of the organization's relevant environment. The evident complementarity between internal and external causes of change is significant for the role of participation. The interests of participants in all positions, internal as well as external, are one of the media through which the various causes, internal or external, affect behaviour that leads to change. A relatively greater emphasis on internally caused processes of change will assign a greater weight to the interests of internal participants, members of the organization in any capacity. Seeing change as primarily caused by external factors leads to paying more attention to external participants—suppliers, customers, consumers, users, etc.—and to their evolving interests.

Organizations as instruments for achieving a purpose are necessarily confronted with the question 'whose purpose', while organizations as interest groups imply the question 'whose interests have what chance of getting satisfaction'. The focus on organizational change brings also to our attention the role that conflict, as well as the tendency towards independence both within the organization and in its environment, plays in changing organizations and their position in the world.

In the short run there is an alternation between less and more emphasis on people in OT since the time when Taylor's and Fayol's views were criticized by the human-relations school. The overall result, however, here as well, is that organizations are recognized as groups of people. This is indeed a prerequisite of these people's status as participants.

But this in no way predetermines the mode in which people participate and will interact in organizations. Their interaction as before will take the form of cooperation and will lead to conflict, it will result in some people becoming dependent on others and it will stimulate strivings for independence, however small or large the circle of those who are in a position to influence decisions taken in organizations.

Participation—Specific Implications

Participating in organizations, people act. Their action is motivated by their interests. Interests are relatively stable motives, and thus introduce a first constraint into the otherwise unlimited variability of human action. Then, action in a social context is interaction—that is, action additionally constrained by the expected response of others. Interaction in organizations is cooperation with the simultaneous chance of conflict. Cooperation constrains behaviour down to practical previsibility, but the dialectic of cooperation and conflict is the source of irreducible uncertainty in organizations.

The implications of this dialectic for participation will be considered in the light of the opposites characteristic of organization: participation both in technical and in interest decisions in organizations is made dependent on *changing structure* and strives towards independence in *changing action*, in the *changing* setting of a relevant *environment*.

Changing Organizational Structure and Participation

By organizational structure we understand the three dimensions of purpose, relation, and method ordered and stabilized in a given pattern. Within the framework of their environment, changing along the three parallel dimensions and differentiating on several levels, individual organizations change their structure under the impulse of both external and internal factors. The process of change in organizations appears as differentiation and integration. Hierarchy, applied almost universally since the first Industrial Revolution to integrate organizations, has two sides, two functions. It is, on the one hand, a type of arrangement for communicating inside the organization, for coordinating. In organizations where the quantity of knowledge and information necessary for functioning is limited, so that it can be concentrated in one place, the most economical way to communicate is through that place. 'Organizations, like cultures, have been considered communication phenomena, that is, entities developed and maintained only through continuous communication activity among its participants' (Schall 1983: 560).

On the other hand, the method of dividing work by splitting the work process introduces a systematic difference among the organization's members as to their ability to see the whole organization and, therefore, to participate in decisions concerning the whole organization. This ability decreases as we descend the hierarchical scale. The bottom of the pyramid—representing the majority of the organization's members—is pushed into the position of a resource to the organization and all their interests conflicting with or simply irrelevant to their instrumental role have to be controlled or neutralized lest they interfere. All organizations are confronted with 'problems of organizational members holding divergent goals, some of which conform to the organization's and some of which conflict. In short, organizational members do not always work toward organizational goals, know how to complete tasks, or work cooperatively with others. In order to ensure that employees work toward objectives, organizations institute control mechanisms in particular combinations and patterns' (Peterson 1984: 574). The top of the hierarchy is not only the coordinating centre in the communication net of the organization. It is also invested with formal authority to control and check all extraneous interests and influences, keeping the rank and file to their restricted roles.

In the course of the process of differentiation, both functions of hierarchy are becoming problematical. Knowledge and information necessary for functioning are growing and have to be spread among many positions, and cannot any longer be usefully concentrated in one place. The optimal span of control is shrinking with the increasing level of expertise of the positions to be coordinated. Hierarchies are becoming taller, with reduced spans of control, and are no longer above discussion as the best method of coordination. To coordinate through hierarchies is more and more time-consuming and produces resistance in the professionals so coordinated. Also automation, computerization, etc. make it, in principle, possible to transfer routine work to machines and in this way to remove the bottom of the hierarchical pyramid.

So the argument that hierarchy is the most economical way to communicate in organizations is becoming less and less valid. Meanwhile each specialist is a centre of information and the most economical way to communicate among them is an arrangement permitting direct contact of each with each. The position of the professional-specialists in organizations is becoming stronger, and their claim to participate in decision-making more convincing. At the same time, with widening circles of legitimate interests in the organization, it is becoming both less necessary and less possible to neutralize the interests of organization members that, to management, appear irrelevant to the organization's purpose.

Generally, relations cease to be the fulcrum of integration in organizations as the accent moves to the dimension of methods. Therefore, relations have more degrees of freedom to vary. The requirement of direct communication among specialists will tend to favour the form of *teams*—groups of specialists linked by the complementarity of their expertise in relation to a defined task. Thus, 'task forces, project teams, and quality circles become more prevalent in the corporate world . . .' (Gladstein 1984: 499). 'These experts are housed in specialized units for administrative and housekeeping purposes, but are deployed in temporary teams to work on their project; the structure thus takes the form of a matrix' (Mintzberg and McHugh 1985: 192). The many concrete forms that team-like arrangements take have the common characteristic that superordination and subordination in them are less emphasized and mutual equality is more so. Leadership is present, but it is not based on formal authority: 'The dilemma of leadership in managing adhocracy lies in trying to exercise influence without being able to rely on formal controls' (Mintzberg and McHugh 1985: 192).

To differentiate and be integrated on the dimension of method means that organizations will differentiate by acquiring information, knowledge, and data, in forms that can be integrated into a framework defined by the problems they are confronted with and by the capacity of the organization's members to utilize information. This is going to be a framework, in a sense, more tolerant than that of hierarchical relations, excluding less of the personality of organization members, but also more demanding as to their informational capacity.[3] Information processing machinery makes relevant information accessible to more people given that capacity.

The expectations regarding the consequences of automation and computerization, however, are not uniformly optimistic. Some experiences point to the phenomenon of polarization of the workforce, with a highly trained 'upper class' planning and guiding the work process and the 'pariahs' feeding raw data into the machines. André Gorz (1986: 77) calls the expectation that automation should reaffirm the professional status of the skilled worker 'dangerous nonsense'. This would require professional personnel with long and extensive training and education. This would mean the distribution of a shrinking total quantity of work among fewer people, a 'workers' élite' and would only strengthen the dual stratification of society (Glaser 1988: 108–9).

The new forms of integration are still in their beginnings. In the light of existing examples, there are the different forms of *lex artis*, the rules of professional performance in all fields. How highly trained specialists in research institutes, or the faculty of a university, or the medical staff of a hospital are going about their work depends more on their education and experience as professionals than on anybody's command. The technological hardware employed by an organization, as condensed information, orients and programs its activities. More adaptable computer programs of work processes integrate the activity of people who participate in the processes in any capacity.

There are still important differences in the informational content of various jobs in the organization, from simple to highly complex, and, consequently, in the ability of their incumbents to participate significantly in decisions presupposing complex knowledge with a larger number of possible repercussions.

However, the relative number of professional–specialist jobs in organizations is increasing, because of the necessary decentralization of knowledge and information throughout the organization as well as because of the transfer of information-poor routine work from people to machines. When this relative number reaches some sort of 'tipping point', the whole atmosphere in the organization is likely to change, along with the structural regime. It is becoming legitimate for professionals in the organization to participate in technical decisions on the ground of their expertise, but then also to participate in decisions concerning their personal interests: 'managing professionals is not too different from managing non-professionals except for professionals' emphases on academic credentials and participation in decision making' (Guy 1985, in Haddock 1987: 299). But these decisions do not, in principle, presuppose expert knowledge in the first place. Everybody is qualified to judge what is in their interest, and also to assume the responsibility for deciding what the organization should be expected to do about it. It is likely that the participation of the relatively numerous professionals will, sooner or later, also induce the participation of the rank-and-file at least in those decisions that directly concern their interests. The ambiguity of the decision-making situation in organizations pointed out by a number of authors (following upon Cohen, March, and Olsen 1972) is the consequence of the legitimacy of personal interests of the majority of an organization's members (the examples are mainly from universities and similar institutions, where highly trained professionals are in the majority). Where there is no longer hierarchy to 'control'—that is, to exclude interests that to management appear as irrelevant—the many interests that enter, overtly or covertly, into the decision processes produce, especially when compared with the classical 'controlled' organization, the impression of ambiguity. Participation, in order to become effective, has no longer to depend on particular participative institutions; it is becoming 'systemic' (cf. Teune and Mlinar 1978).

The crucial point here is that in the most important decisions in organizations—for example, decisions about major investments or about the introduction of new technology—the technical and the interest dimensions are inseparably linked. Participation in these decisions presupposes technical competence but it presupposes at the same time legitimacy of interests. This legitimacy depends, not on formal criteria, such as membership of the organization, but on who is contributing the resources that are at risk in such decisions. So the quality of participant in these critical decisions will depend on the overall organization of the economic system—that is, on who controls the funds out of which major risky decisions are financed.

In the longer run the process of change in organizations by differentiating and integrating structures is at the same time the process by which the initial and boundary conditions of organizational participation are changing characteristically and dramatically. The depersonalization of organizations and the consequent deformation of participation had two main sources: the peculiar form of dividing labour by splitting the work process, and the appropriation of automatic ascendancy in organizations by those who controlled the assets. The resulting impersonal purpose, defined in the charter, impersonal relations among jobs, not people, and impersonal methods prescribed by blueprints and imposed by hardware were not conducive to organizational participation. Participation can be motivated only by personal interest and consists in personal engagement. What is happening in organizations today is a return, at least partially, to a personal description of method, relation, and purpose. Methods depend on the personal knowledge and skill of specialists, relations are increasingly relations among persons associated in teams, crews, circles, and even the goals of organizations are given reality by the informational potential of its educated members and are not simply imposed by the design of the machinery against their will and judgement. Personal interest and personal judgement can again motivate participation in influencing decisions and in claiming a share in the outcome of the work. This tendency may well be the deeper current of development beyond the ups and downs of economic and political cycles.

Changing Organizational Action and Participation

Participating in organizations, people organize in order to act. Their action stabilizes, congeals in a sense, into structure in order to facilitate action, to carry action, to make it less problematical by answering certain questions about the course of action in advance, resolving priorities, establishing patterns of communication, adjudicating claims to resources, allocating responsibilities, prescribing procedures. Structure is useful only in so far as it does this and so long as it does it. When it does not, it has to be changed by action, action that must first overcome the inertia, the resistance of former repeated action coagulated into the independently existing structure. One of the fundamental questions of participation is, precisely, how far can the action of participating be transformed into structure, into fixed institutional forms, into institutional participation (in the sense of Teune and Mlinar 1978; cf. also Heller *et al.* 1988 on status power) without losing its essence, the spontaneous motivation by felt interests of the participating individuals?

Action in organizations is interaction. Therefore, it carries into organizations the specific dynamics of interaction, the ambiguity of cooperation and conflict, the potential for creating dependence among people and in this way stimulating their striving for independence. Action not only transcends structure at every point in time of the organization's duration; potentially at least it contradicts structure.[4] The dialectic of action and structure crystallizes around the three salient points of purpose, relation, and method that are the determinants of structure and also, in a mirror image, the anchoring points of action in organizations. First, organizational purpose, defining structurally what the organization is supposed to do, coincides with or deviates from interests, what people in organizations are motivated to do. Secondly, organizational relations establishing the formal pattern of links among organizational positions, allocating power to a given position, in part channel but to an extent also inhibit the network of actual communication, of ongoing cooperation and conflict among organizational members. Thirdly, organizational methods sometimes prescribe how people should act pursuing organizational goals, but not always. Members will be confronted with necessity in their choice of methods, or they will be free to choose how to proceed according to their own lights. This situation will be seen as serving the interests of the actors or as thwarting them, and will be treated accordingly.

Purposes and interests. On the action dimension, participation is motivated by human interest and constrained by organizational purpose.

The reasons why people join an organization are not necessarily the same reasons as those that keep them from quitting. Why people work well has almost nothing to do with why they joined and why they stay, and is seldom identical with the causes of their feeling well or otherwise in their organization. Motives that guide the action of individuals are multiple and are changing. Organizational participation is genuine only if people feel that by participating they can influence what is happening and thereby further their actual felt interests. The form that participation is taking depends, therefore, on the degree of dispersion of interests, on the width of the circle of legitimate interests, and on the competence of participating members to understand the decision situation.

While the interests of participating members are concentrated on material rewards, their motivation to participate will tend to remain restricted to that issue. With increasing dispersion of interests, if and when this occurs for certain categories of members, their motivation to participate is likely to broaden. Motives evolve with increasing security, from seeing the organization exclusively as a source of material rewards, through valuing, in addition, the chance to satisfy needs of belonging, of companionship, of recognition, and of social status, towards experiencing the organization as an opportunity to pursue optimally one's quest for excellence in professional work and in human relations alike.

While all interests of members outside those specified by the work contract are considered non-legitimate, their participation will tend to take the form of conflictual action, the organization being experienced as an antagonist, not as a partnership. With the progressive widening of the circle of legitimate interests more and more interests are accepted to be articulated and aggregated within the organization—participation might become multiple and the chances of the organization being perceived by members as a partnership, a 'we'-association, is likely to increase.

While members, on account both of their role in the work process and of their general educational development have not the capacity to understand complex issues of organizational decisions, their motivation to participate in these decisions will remain low. If participation at this low level of competence is introduced and institutionalized by general law, it is likely to remain formal only or to be redirected at secondary purposes and interests not relevant for the decisions in which people formally participate, as was amply demonstrated by the experience of self-management in former Yugoslavia. With growing competence, their motivation for participation is likely to become more compelling (cf. IDE 1993).

All these conditions—dispersion of interests, legitimacy of interests, competence—tend to develop in directions favourable to strengthening the motive of organizational members to participate. The effects of the information revolution, as well as the shift from primary and secondary production to higher sectors of economic activity, are changing the proportion of professionals to non-professionals in organizations in favour of the first category. Professionals as a group are likely to have a more dispersed palette of interests and greater competence to understand and to influence complex issues. Widening circles of legitimate interests in society generally are a discernible tendency for the last two or three hundred years and it is natural to expect that this tendency will reflect also on the legitimacy of interests of organizational members.

Whatever the motives to participate, the actual possibility to do so and to influence effectively organizational decisions in the sense of one's interests are constrained, in principle, by the purposes of organizational action. But here as well a process of change is at work. Organizations produce an output, sometimes predicated upon a fairly stable technology, and this output is their purpose. But in organizations of any complexity the output differentiates into a lengthening list of different products, services, and effects, opening thereby the possibility of conflict about priorities, importance, and perspectives on further differentiation. Organizations have to go on existing in order to produce; to ensure their continuing existence can be understood as their purpose. But the conditions of their existence are multiple, and here again the question is what comes first, what is essential, what should command attention. The existence of the organization can become a focus only after the conflict of views about what it is that this existence depends on is settled one way or another—and it rarely is. Organizations have outlays, the cost of existence as well as the cost of functioning, and they have to secure intakes to cover the outlays. A positive balance of intakes over outlays in most cases is a condition *sine qua non* of organizational viability, and thus can be enthroned as purpose. But this is too general to be helpful. It excludes too little, covering the whole gamut of organizations from the maximally successful to the barely surviving, from forced labour camps to academies of equals. Purposes, whatever they are, differentiate also on a vertical dimension into subpurposes, instrumental and intermediate goals, and operational tasks down to elementary operations and change at all these levels, independently, to an extent, of each other.

The differentiation of organizational purposes produces, on one side, more favourable conditions for participation. More purposes in the organization offer simply more opportunity for participation. In fact, 'organizational' interests often coincide with subpurposes of the organization as the members identify not with the organization but with one of its subunits that are the base for group formation in organizations. In this way a large part of ongoing conflicts in organizations is triggered not by its members' original interest but by interests induced through their organizational position (Friedkin and Simpson 1985: 377, 392). The multiplicity of purposes makes it increasingly important to create a 'we'-feeling among the membership in order to integrate the organization as a human association. On the other side, however, differentiation of purposes will tend to make the decision situation more complex and, thus, demand higher competence of the participating members. Finally, organizational purposes, however multiple, will continue to face members as a limit of the possibility to satisfy their individual interests. The tension between organizational purposes and individual interests will continue to exist and to influence the atmosphere in organizations, but also in a sense to make it more bracing, to provide the necessary *tonus* and resilience in action.

Participation in the organization's decision-making depends on one's security, on the reduction of one's one-sided dependence on the centres of power in organizations. The possibility of participating can itself become a motive for members of the organization, a source of satisfaction, a reason to identify and feel responsible for what is going on. It can also be a source of disagreement (IDE 1981*a*; Heller *et al.* 1988).

Power and participation. From the original, aboriginal, meaning of superior strength, understood as the potential to harm another, power in organizations was from the outset a more balanced concept, the administration of both rewards and punishment. The origin of power in organizations was identified in the peculiar type of organizational division of labour. As a complex objective was broken down into progressively simpler tasks down to elementary operations, positions at each level of this gradual, from the top down, simplification process remained as steps for a simultaneous process of stepwise integration of action, from the bottom up. Each of these positions was formally invested with the necessary power to integrate—that is, to coordinate and to control all positions on the scale resulting from the further subdivision of the work assignment that it itself represented. This logical link of organizational positions to that higher position of whose jurisdiction they were, in a way, parts was called functional dependence. The term is well chosen, because it points to the first important limitation of power in organizations: power does create dependence, but in organizations power was allocated only in so far as it was required by function, within the limits of the task as specified at each level of the hierarchy, as necessary for the integration of the organization in its functioning.[5] However limited to the facilitating of function, organizational power is still power and does create dependence of some people on other people.[6]

The next step towards changing the character of power in organizations, functional as it may be, is when the dependence is no longer directly on people, superiors on the hierarchical scale, but on one or the other objective factor of the situation in the organization or in its environment. 'Building on the dependency framework (Emerson 1962), the strategic contingency and resource dependency frameworks (Hickson *et al.* 1971; Salancik and Pfeffer 1977) posit that power (the inversion of dependence) derives from control of relevant resources' (Brass 1984: 519–20).

After that came the definition of power, not as one-sided ascendancy but as a relation, where the power of *A* over *B* is more or less balanced by the power of *B* over *A*. In this sense there is talk of the bargaining power of interest coalitions in the organization (Cyert and March 1963), of shifting power centres in teams (Marshak 1955), of the limited power to influence outcomes in one's favour in games (Von Neumann and Morgenstern 1949), and in conflicts generally (Shapley and Shubik 1954; Black 1958; Kaplan 1960; Attali 1972), of the constraints of acceptability, credibility, and scarcity of power (Cotta 1976: 186). In a postmodernist context of the Japanese firm, as understood by Stewart Clegg (1990), power within the organization is supplemented by 'spiritual training' together with 'empowerment on the shop floor', 'suggestion schemes', 'management rotation', tenure for workers (pp. 191–3). And power around the organization by a 'relatively stable capital market' and by public policy (pp. 194–5). Maffesoli (1988: 49) distinguishes *pouvoir*—power in the sense of external imposition upon others—and *puissance*—power as internal potential of an individual or a social group. He sees postmodernity as a shift of emphasis from the first to the second.

How many subordinates could a superior exercise his or her functional power over? From the beginning the answer was: it depends. The span of control was wider when the positions to be controlled performed routine tasks and it became narrower with the growing complexity of the work controlled. The other factor was the intensity of supervision expected. The less the organization could rely on the initiative of its members, the more intensive supervision had to be. On both accounts the necessary information had to be concentrated at the top of the hierarchical pyramid. Only then could the division of labour by splitting the work process be pushed to the extremes of the assembly line, where the bottom operations were almost completely emptied of informational content and at the same time closely controlled by the assembly line. Gradually, as the sum total of information necessary to the organization's functioning grew, it could no longer be concentrated at the top. Spread throughout the organization among its expert, specialist, professional positions, knowledge could not remain the reason for power in its hierarchical one-dimensionality, though it continued to be the source of power: expert power, decision-making power, competitive power, the power conferred by the control of information (Pusić 1974). The information revolution of the 1960s made it then, in principle, possible to transfer all tasks that could be simplified by splitting the work process into routine operations from human labour to machines that were able to perform routine tasks with greater speed, precision, and economy. The reflection of this development in OT can be seen in the reaffirmation of the human personality in the work role, in the more egalitarian distribution of control in the organization in the various forms of participation.

The other change in relation to power in organizations is the wider circle of legitimacy of interests of the organization's members. The classical work contract was based on the assumption that it represented the sale of the worker's workforce for the price of the agreed wage or salary. No other interest of the worker entered, normally, into the work contract, and could, therefore, not be legitimately pursued by the worker during working time. The evolution of labour law traces the changes of this initial understanding towards a widening circle of legitimate workers' interests leading ultimately to various forms of participation in decision-making, profit-sharing, co-responsibility, and co-ownership encountered in present-day organizations.

For some observers the question is not whether power is any longer instrumentally necessary in organizations, but when and under what conditions the powerful will be ready or could be forced to abandon their dominant positions. The power distance among people in organizations is, in this view, always a matter of contention and struggle (cf. Mulder 1974). Mulder's closer look at power in organizations led him to distinguish formal, sanction, expert, and referent power, and to the conclusion that, if the first two variants were becoming less important, the second two have lost none of their effectiveness, even after the introduction of formal participation. If power in organizations, however, is increasingly based on the control of information and that form of control is increasingly decentralized, the readiness of the hierarchical power-holders to abandon the gratification of their position does not depend only on their will but more and more also on their possibility to maintain this position in the face of the new patterns of information control.

From the classical Weberian concept of power (*Macht*) as the 'chance to impose one's will also against opposition' (Weber 1921: 28) the meaning of power is evolving towards concepts of authority, responsibility, facility, and influence. In these meanings it is no longer the negation of participation but rather the condition for it. Participating members share in these forms of a power that is, actually, an aspect of their competence. Utilizing this competence, organizations are likely to reduce the extent of under-utilization of skills that was identified as a major source of diseconomies in organizations (Heller 1991: 267–81).

Necessity and choice in organizational methods. Organizational methods are methods of action in organizations. They become structure in so far as they are stabilized, thus becoming necessary and removed from the choice of the actors. Stabilization of method is achieved by norm (enforceable rule), by prescription (non-enforceable rule of technical correctness), by hardware (e.g. assembly lines), or by control of information (e.g. data banks), or any combination among them. Methods, however, are also the main avenue to organizational innovation, and, in order to keep this avenue open, the choice of the actors must be kept as a possibility.

For participation, the meaning of the opposition between necessity and choice is ambiguous on several levels. The information revolution and its technical consequences—automation, robotization, and computerization—are moving basic technological choices to an ever higher strategic level. These choices are necessarily risky and depend, therefore, increasingly on those who bear the risk in a direct financial sense, leaving less room for the participation of the rank and file. But, once introduced, they reduce uncertainty in the organization's operations and, thus, the need for hierarchical supervision, so that non-hierarchical, participatory forms of cooperation in organizations are likely to spread. On the level of programming operations, the new technology introduces choices that did not exist before, permitting the diversification of production that formerly was running in large series. In this way the organization can take into account wishes of individual customers, transforming them into a sort of external participants. The firm Benetton in Italy is more 'an organized network of market relations' than an organization with a clear identity. It consists of a centre with a data bank and very developed information technology, about 200 small enterprises linked to the centre by contract, and about 2,500 independently managed and financed shops. This network produces clothing in large quantities but according to individual orders, with a minimal inventory, and the ability to fill each order within ten days (cf. Stewart Clegg 1990: 120–5).

On the other hand, the growing capacity of the hardware involved produces by itself pressures towards concentration and centralization. There are several reasons for this:

1. Removing ever larger parts of routine work from the action of people to the functioning of machines increases the average level of demands upon the capacities of people.

> Each minute while production stands still, possibly because the controller of the system has not discovered and corrected a mistake in time, costs the entrepreneurs a lot of money. A select part of the industrial labor force is confronted with new demands that transcend specialties. Self-reliant thinking, a sense of responsibility, concentration, flexibility, the capacity for quick decisions in emergencies. There is demand for a new type of employee, with significantly greater self-reliance. It is impossible to install the most modern technology, but leave hierarchical relations as they were, i.e. based on command and obedience. (Glaser 1988: 108)

Even if we assume that the median of capacities will climb—industrialization in its successive technological steps was able to educate its labour force—it is likely that the group of those only marginally employable will expand. The number of jobs in automated and robotized factories as such will decrease and those that remain will not be within the capacities of a large part of the workforce. The crucial technical decisions might be even more beyond the grasp of the average organization member than they are today and thus restrict the potential of participation.

2. The destructive side effects of work on the assembly line or in bureaucratic routinized organizations might be repeated on a higher level in automated systems. People get used to adapt to the system, to accept the preconditions on which the system functions, and, without being tied to any routine in their actual individual work, abandon their overall choices to the necessities of the system.

3. With increasing stakes in large concentrated systems, the divergent interests motivating the participants will push up the costs of participation. Though the more valuable technological infrastructure with fewer and more informed workers is likely to strengthen the bargaining power of each individual,[7] other factors, such as spatial deconcentration, might reduce it. It is to be expected that management will go on attempting to control all interests of participants that might put into jeopardy the technical rationality of the complex large system.

Changing Organizations in Changing Environments

The trends of change in the world and in the environment of organizations have transformed some of the basic conditions of participation.

That markets decide the fate of organizations was clear ever since there were organizations that produce for markets and markets that functioned as independent regulatory devices. It was clear as well that markets are institutionalized forms of conflict. But OT was slow to build this fact into its theoretical edifice. In more recent theorizing some went to the extreme of asserting the absolute primacy of the forces of the market, and thus of the conflict perspective, over the organization's own policies and decisions, and its endeavours at collaboration (population ecology theory: Hannan and Freeman 1977; Aldrich 1979).

The concept of contingency in OT was born of dissatisfaction with the assertions and authoritative recommendations of classical OT about how organizations should be organized. These pronouncements were of very limited practical usefulness. The concept of contingency attempts to explain why—because 'it is possible to understand the differences in the internal states and processes of organizations on the basis of differences in their external environments' (Lawrence and Lorsch 1967, in Pugh 1984: 104).

Contingency was taken one step further by Niklas Luhmann (1976), who links the concept to its roots in theology as the negation of both necessity and impossibility. Contingency is 'everything that is also possible in other ways' (p. 97). The novelty of Luhmann's idea is in his assumption that the two contingencies linked together limit each other's free variability and in this way achieve something which is not necessity, but greater probabilistic previsibility, theoretically 'a more complex pattern that admits the discontinuity between system and environment and interprets it as both an increase in and a self-restriction of other possibilities' (pp. 98–9).

Systems theory applied to organizations provides a more general explanation than contingency theory of the dynamic relations between organizations and their environments. Organizations as homeostatic open systems are threatened by the potentially destabilizing influences of their environment. In order to neutralize these threats organizations have to develop ways of reacting to them. These ways have to be no less diversified than are the sources of possible destabilization. This relationship, formally defined by W. R. Ashby (1963) and named the 'law of requisite variety', has far-reaching implications.

Looking at the environment from the point of view of organizations, environment is no longer a single concept. It differentiates in concentric circles, where the individual organization is the centre. The widest circle includes ecological (climate, soil, subsoil, etc.), biological (distinctive biological and psychological traits of human populations), demographic (density, population increase, morbidity, etc.), and cultural (technology, artefacts, ideas, values, science, etc.) elements, in part affected and structured by the above trends. The next narrower circle is the institutional repertory of society, the symbolic (language, art, etc.), regulative (government, law, education, etc.), productive (goods and services), and associational (societies, clubs, political parties) institutions, affected by the general trends of social change as the case may be, but also subject to human planning and action to a greater degree than the wider circle of the 'natural' environment. The narrowest circle is the task environment—J. D. Thompson classifies external participants as belonging to the task environment of the organization (Keeley 1980: 351)—as we approach its 'life space' (Lewin 1950).

The gradual 'integration' of organizations with their task environment has two important consequences for participation. First, with more of their interests becoming legitimate in the organization, the members are reasserted as whole persons. There is less reason to separate their organizational role from the rest of their personality and to classify the first as 'organization' and the second as 'environment'. When people participate, they can think and act only as whole persons, not as incumbents of roles, because participation is in principle unstructured and presupposes that all interests of the participant will be relevant for participation. Therefore the trend towards accepting members as persons is a first prerequisite for participation. This trend is strengthened by reopening the moral problems inherent in organizational relations, advocating the 'responsible' and the 'just' enterprise. The social responsibility of industry cannot be asserted 'while . . . its workforce (is) excluded from membership of the company' (Goyder 1987: 94–5). Secondly, the task environment of the organization includes people, members of other organizations, public agencies, user groups, the public generally, and there is no reason why they should not be counted as participants, treated as such and given the opportunity to influence decision-making in the organization whenever their interests are involved. On the other hand, it is plausible to expect that the increase of uncertainty stemming from conflicts around the organization will influence unfavourably the chances of participation, both its acceptability to management and the capacity of the rank and file to participate meaningfully.[8]

Conclusion

Processes of change within organizations, changes of structure, point in the same direction. Organizations are seen as changing through a dialectical process of differentiation and periodic change of their integrating framework, where all dimensions of organizational structure and action—purpose, relations, and methods—are in turn emphasized. As the accent moves from relations to methods, differentiation no longer means an increase in the number and variety of positions in organizations, but the growth of quantity and complexity of information, a characteristic of the dimension of methods. The exclusive accent on hierarchical relations as a means of coordination and control is replaced by a wider range of patterns where teams and team networks play an increasingly important role. From a view of organizations as dominated by the interests of the owners, theory is moving towards the model of organizations as coalitions among various interests where the interest of the owners/managers is only one component. With efforts towards the reduction of power distance in organizations, power is not disappearing but appearing in new forms. Instead of a one-sided technological determinism, views of mutual influences among technological infrastructure, organizational structure, and the superstructure of norms and values in organizations are prevailing. Notions of environments in which organizations exist and operate are becoming more complex and organizations are seen not only as competing but also as cooperating with each other. These changes are, under normal conditions in the foreseeable future, irreversible. And they increase possibilities of participation in a way that is independent of convictions or ideologies, of contingencies of the economic cycle or the political arena.

OT also sees the other side, that especially the institutionally more developed forms of participation are vulnerable to crises from any source. Participation remains a problem; it is not *per se* a solution for organizational problems. OT, on its applied side, will have to find answers for a number of practical questions arising from the conflict between the mainly centrifugal tendencies of participation and the essentially centripetal requirements of organizational integration.

Participation, that did start as a moral idea, a democratic, socialistic, human growth ideal (Dachler and Wilpert 1978: 3), is becoming a matter of more people in the organization and around it having access to information that gives them the possibility to influence decisions, and of more interests in the organization and around it that are accepted as legitimate. What will actually prevail in organizations, however, will depend, as before, on the ongoing process of interaction with its dialectic of cooperation and conflict, dependence and independence. That gives room, as before, to moral commitment, to ideals of a more humane world. As all ideals, they demand permanent striving that cannot be replaced once and for all by any structural, institutional solution, including institutions of participation.

NOTES

1. There is wide divergence, though, about the content and precise character of the changes considered. As, for instance, between Stewart Clegg (1990: 178–207), for whom post-

modernity in organizations brings diffusion of goals, democracy in relations, the market as regulatory device instead of specialization of function, bureaucratic relations, and hierarchical control (p. 203) as exemplified in contemporary Japanese organizations, and Baudrillard (1990), who writes about postmodernity as a source of 'total confusion' (p. 18), the 'disappearance of the proletariat' along with 'the political [*le politique*]' generally (p. 19), of a 'radical agnosticism' in aesthetics (p. 30), the 'destructuration of value' (p. 41), and the emergence of a 'transeconomy of speculation' (p. 79).

2. Max Weber, writing about the bureaucratic form of organization, wrote of *Bürokratisierung* (bureaucratization) as a process, a historical process parallel to the process of 'rationalization', the prevailing of rational approaches to the affairs of society. 'Bureaucratic structure is everywhere a late product of development. Its emergence and growth had . . . everywhere a 'revolutionary' effect in that particular sense in which the advance of *rationalism* usually affects all areas' (1921: 677–8; emphasis in original).
3. Stewart Clegg (1990: 180–1) maintains that organizations he calls postmodern dedifferentiate, reversing the trend towards differentiation considered characteristic for organizations since Weber. It seems probable that the examples he gives—job enrichment, job enlargement, multi-skilling, emphasis on the team—are the consequence of the shift from relations to methods as the main dimension of differentiation-integration. Organizations now differentiate by acquiring and using new information in their data banks, their specialists, or otherwise and are integrated by using the information in their decision-making. Relations are now free to vary as they are less and less the crucial supporting beam of the construction that they used to be. Information-processing machinery makes relevant information accessible to people to an extent independently of their initial specialist training and skill.
4. In Luhmann's view (1964: 269) organized systems not only adjust to contradictions; they actually need them in order to be able to exist in an uncertain environment.
5. It was F. W. Taylor (1967; first edition, 1911), a man not under suspicion for being committed to organizational democracy, who came up with the curious idea of decomposing the hierarchical pyramid into a system of eight functional foremen for each worker on the line, simply by following the notion of the functional character of organizational power to its logical conclusion.
6. Dependence is sometimes understood as the obverse of uncertainty, as does Crozier (1963); or 'occupants of certain positions in the organization's workflow will encounter more uncertainty than those in other positions and thereby will have more opportunity to cope with uncertainty and thus establish a base of power' (Brass 1984: 523).
7. Large firms unconsciously provide workers with resources that allow the latter to achieve their goals of improving wages and more favorable working conditions . . . The fact that they are extremely capital intensive makes companies dependent on skilled labor to operate and maintain their equipment and thereby strengthens the bargaining position of the employees' (Finlay 1987: 50).
8. But what is plausible is not always true: 'we expected to find a reversal since the late 1970s of the process of de-concentration that originated in the 1960s. However . . . we encountered hardly any evidence of an overall tendency towards the breaking down of the democratizing process in Western work organization. On the contrary, several authors observe that some forms of participation or co-determination have spread further or gained in strength' (Lammers and Széll 1989*a*: 315).

4. Collective Bargaining, Unions, and Participation

Collective bargaining and representative participation can be viewed as alternative forms of employee representation. This chapter is concerned with the relationship between the two. Though our primary focus is on tensions between unions and Representative Participative Bodies (RPBs), such as works councils, we will consider two other issues, the attitudes of unions towards participation, and the extent to which either collective bargaining or participation adequately represents employees' interests.

In view of the great variety of industrial-relations arrangements throughout the world, this chapter makes no pretence at being comprehensive. (It ignores, for example, developments in Asia, Latin America, and Eastern Europe.) Instead it places considerable (but far from exclusive) emphasis on Germany and the USA, both because there has been more relevant research done in these countries and because (as we shall see later) they may represent opposite ends of a continuum.[1] This necessarily limited and unrepresentative coverage has a particular purpose—namely, to concentrate on certain chosen issues which allow us to prepare the ground for the final chapter, where we will draw policy conclusions that, hopefully, will have application to large parts of the industrialized world.

Given the chapter's length the reader may like a road map. Here is our itinerary.

1. Assuming collective bargaining can be viewed as a form of participation, how effective is it in practice? Our first section discusses various problems which make collective bargaining less effective as a form of participation, though later we suggest that many of these same limitations apply to other forms of participation. For example, both union officers and works-council members may communicate poorly with their constituents.

2. What are the main differences between collective bargaining and representative participation, viewing them as separate systems? We discuss these first in general terms and then illustrate these differences through comparing two quite different systems of workplace employee representation, workplace collective bargaining in the USA and works councils in Germany.

3. In practice, in most industrialized countries, participation has developed as a supplement to collective bargaining. Despite major differences in overall industrial-relations systems, unions in most countries were ambivalent about participation at first and only gradually cast aside their initial suspicions. The debate over participation has given rise to considerable intra- and inter-union political skirmishing.

4. For a variety of reasons, as this next section discusses, participation is more likely to be successful if it has union support.

5. The remainder of this chapter is concerned with RPBs. We begin by discussing their institutional framework and functions. As we point out, these vary greatly among countries.

6. RPBs serve many of the same functions as unions, yet in most cases exist separately. Indeed, along with management, they may be looked upon as separate power centres. This section, our longest, examines the sometimes competing, sometimes cooperative relations between RPBs and four other power centres. These are national unions, local unions (branches), direct participation institutions (such as quality circles (QCs) and work teams), and rank-and-file employees.

7. Our last major section deals with another form of representative participation: employee representation on company boards of directors. Employee board members are subject to most of the problems faced by employee representatives generally plus some others unique to their position.

8. Our conclusion deals with several issues, especially the extent to which either unions or RPBs effectively represent members' interests.

Collective Bargaining Viewed as a Form of Participation

Given our initial description of participation, in Chapter 1, as 'a process which allows employees to exert some influence over their work', collective bargaining qualifies as a form of participation in the wider sense of the term—at least it is so formally. But for it to be so effectively requires that two conditions be met. First, the union which is the employee's representative in collective bargaining must be participative itself, and, secondly, the collective-bargaining process must in fact 'exert some influence'.

Participation in Unions

Here we argue that, if collective bargaining is to be effective in influencing management, then the union should be participative itself—that is, it should be democratic.[2]

Not everyone agrees with our position. The opposing view is that the 'end of trade union activity is to protect and improve the general living standards of its members and not to provide workers with an exercise in self-government' (Allen 1954: 15). The union's chief contribution to the larger democracy—it is argued—is as a counterfoil to management, not through internal self-government. For some, democracy means factionalism, and factionalism may divide or paralyse the union.

As with organizational participation generally, we can distinguish between two forms of union democracy, direct and representative. Both forms have advantages. First, direct democracy (see below) has many of the advantages of direct participation discussed in Chapters 1 and 2. Secondly, representative democracy permits ineffective leaders to be replaced through the election process, thus making leadership more responsive to members' needs. Thirdly, through facilitating debate, democracy increases the likelihood that officers are aware of their members' interests and priorities. And, finally, democracy helps develop leaders.

Direct Democracy

Opportunities for direct democracy in unions are fairly limited, and rarely do more than a few members take advantage of them. Among the available forms of direct democracy are the following.

Meeting attendance. Many union branches (called locals in the USA) hold regular membership meetings, often monthly, which all members can attend. Though in some unions in English-speaking countries such meetings provide the main avenue for direct participation, in many European countries branch unions are non-existent or weak. Even where branch meetings occur, union structure may deprive them of any meaningful function. Employees in a given British or Australian plant, for example, may belong to half a dozen different unions, each representing a different set of occupations. Members of each union have the right to attend the meetings of their own branch, but, since branches may encompass all the members of that union in a large geographical area regardless of employer, those who attend may have few common interests, especially regarding shop-floor questions. Under these circumstances attendance is minimal (Ben Roberts 1956; Davis 1987).

The situation is only slightly different where unions are organized on an industrial basis, with all the employees of a given employer belonging to the same union and where there is a separate branch meeting for each large or medium-sized workplace. Even here attendance is usually low, and for a variety of reasons: the meeting may be held at inconvenient times and places; more time may be spent on union organizational minutia and political factionalism than on workplace issues; and the officers may discourage individual participation. In any case, members may find better uses of their times—for instance, being with their family, watching TV, or engaging in sports. Despite this sorry picture, attendance may be high when important matters are being considered—for example, contract negotiations.

In Australia and the UK meetings are sometimes held at lunchtime, or immediately after work, and even during working hours (at times stopping production in violation of a union's peace obligation). This may be an effective form of participation.

Balloting. Depending on the union, members may vote for union officers, decide whether to go on strike, ratify a contract, or accept a proposed change in the union constitution. Voting is a meaningful form of participation only when members have real choice. Experience indicates that, when voting takes place at convenient locations, say at the workplace, participation rates may run to 60 per cent or higher.

Filing grievances. In many countries members can protest management's actions through filing grievances with their union steward or works councillor. Such grievances may allege that management has violated its labour contract or the law of the land, or merely acted unfairly. This is a highly personal form of participation.

Industrial action. Strikes, showdowns, working-to-rule, and even sabotage are potent means of exerting influence. Sometimes these forms of participation are formally called or orchestrated by the union, and on other occasions their purpose may be to embarrass union leadership. Strike rates vary greatly among countries. In Austria and Sweden strikes are rare; in Italy and Canada rates are relatively high. But as unions have become generally weaker since the mid-1980s strike rates have declined in most countries.

Informal communications. Informal channels of union participation are widely used. For example, rather than attend a union meeting to express their opinions, members may make their wishes known privately to officers on the job.

A considerable literature discusses the determinants of direct union participation (Gallagher and Strauss 1991). Unfortunately most studies have been confined to English-speaking countries (exceptions: van de Vall 1970; Klandermans 1986). Typical of the questions seemingly relating to participation rates are the following. Are meetings held in convenient places? Do those who are eligible to attend have occupational interests in common? How homogeneous and cohesive is the membership? How likely is individual participation to make a difference in the final result? Do members feel safe to participate without fear of discrimination?

Extent of participation varies greatly, from highly militant unions, where members engage in frequent industrial action, to situations where members' sole opportunities to participate are to pay their dues and re-elect their officers. By and large participation in most unions is confined to a relatively few members who view their union as a hobby or a cause. For this hard core of activists union participation provides an often rich sense of creativity as well as an opportunity to socialize. This hard core is critical, because it serves as a communications channel between the top leadership and the rank-and-file members. (Similarly, as we discuss in Chapter 6, only a minority of employees take part in other forms of direct participation, such as QCs.)

Representative Democracy

Since union members typically spend little of their time participating personally, most participation occurs through representatives, the union's elected and appointed officers who actually engage in bargaining. So the critical question becomes: how effective is representative participation in ensuring that union leaders actually represent their members' wishes?

Although many (possibly most) union leaders try to listen pretty closely to their members and so respond to their desires, communications are difficult in a large union and there is a strong tendency toward oligarchy. As Michels (1958: 401) put it (though referring to political parties), 'Everywhere the power of elected leaders over the elected masses is almost unlimited. The oligarchical structure . . . suffocates the basic democratic principle.' Once leaders become established in their positions, they adopt different life styles and values and may lose contact with their members. Indeed research suggests that union leaders frequently misjudge their members' bargaining priorities (Strauss and Warner 1977) and often convince themselves that they know better what the members should want than do the members themselves.[3] In any case, they put the institutional needs of the union above the individual needs of its members.

Potential opposition is the best antidote to oligarchy. If leaders cease being responsive to the members, the members should be able to replace them—and to do so relatively easily. Often this is not the case. Of course most unions are technically democratic, in the sense that their constitutions provide for regular elections. Further, there are laws in many countries which guarantee these rights. But opposition in large unions is difficult. Typically the leadership controls the channels of internal communications, such as the union newspaper; it is has a monopoly of information; and it has ways of rewarding supporters and punishing opponents. On top of this, many union leaders work full time for the union, which means that they can campaign for re-election while on the job, though their opponents often can do so only after work. Thus in a large union it may be fruitless for a single member or small group of members to oppose an entrenched leadership on their own.

Effective opposition is most likely to develop when there are *centres of countervailing power* which have sources of support independent of the incumbent leadership. Typically these centres take the form of organized factions or parties or they are arranged around full-time officers who are elected independently of the top leadership and often from a different constituency (Edelstein and Warner 1975). For instance, a regional vice-president might run against a president.

The hard core of branch-level volunteer union activists may play a key role in preserving national-level democracy. Volunteers are not subject to the same pressures as paid union staff, and so the existence of a strong hard core of volunteers generally increases union responsiveness. Both opposition and incumbent national leaders campaign to enlist their support.

All of these factors make it easier for incumbent officers to be defeated. In most countries, however, officer turnover is, in fact, rather low. Paradoxically this may be a testimony either to members' satisfaction with their current leadership or to the strength of oligarchical forces—usually a bit of both. Nevertheless, fear of election defeat is not the only means of facilitating representative responsiveness. The typical union has a variety of legislative and consultative bodies, such as conventions and executive boards. Whether these contribute to overall responsiveness depends on their own influence and the extent to which they, themselves, are responsive to membership preferences.

In closing this section, let us stress that most of the factors that limit the extent of member influence and participation in unions also operate to limit participation in works councils and the like.

Limitations on Collective Bargaining as a Form of Participation

Though the union itself may be participative, this does not mean that collective bargaining constitutes an effective means of influencing the larger organization whose employees the union represents. There are at least three reasons why: (1) the union may be too weak to represent its members adequately, (2) it may focus its limited strength on objectives other than employees' 'work and the conditions under which they do their work' (for example, national politics), and finally (3) the collective-bargaining process, as practised, may not constitute an effective form of representation.

Union strength. Numerous factors contribute to union strength—for example, the size of its membership and treasury; the percentage of the relevant product and labour markets it represents; the state of the economy generally and of the industry or employer specifically; the union's cohesion, loyalty and commitment of its members; and the legal arrangement under which it operates.

Union focus. The traditional focus of many left-wing Continental European unions was on politics—that is, to mobilize the working class to change the power structure of society. For these unions politics came first and workplace issues were of secondary importance. Indeed some argued that concern with the minutiae of workplace issues would distract employees from larger, more important objectives.

More conservative Continental unions were concerned chiefly with industry-wide bargaining. Their objective was (and still largely is) to establish a 'level playing field' and a 'common rule' which treats all employees and all employers alike. They sought to equalize wages so that companies would be prevented from competing with each other on the basis of labour costs. Thus they traditionally avoided negotiations with individual companies.

Neglect of company-level and work-level issues was the result in part of deliberate union policy and in part of other matters receiving higher priority. On top of this, employers in many countries (for example, France and the Netherlands) fought hard to 'keep the union out of the shop'. As a consequence, by the 1960s there was a clear 'representation gap' in much of Europe, with unions exerting more influence nationally and industry-wide than they did at company, plant, or workplace levels. Today, in much of Europe this gap is filled by works councils.

By contrast, in the USA and UK, despite considerable difference in labour-relations procedures, unions in both countries have been relatively effective at the local level (at least until recently). Unionized plants in both countries have a strong steward structure, and formal (in the USA) and informal (in the UK) workplace bargaining is common. For this reason, among others, works councils never took hold in these countries in the way they did in Continental Europe.

But there is another 'representation gap' which is worldwide. Even at the shop level in the UK and USA, the focus is on economic issues, such as job security, rather than psychological issues, such as satisfaction with accomplishment. It is partly because of a deficit in this area that forms of direct participation, such as work teams, have become so popular.

The bargaining process. A final problem: Arguably collective bargaining is not an efficient way of resolving problems and therefore not an effective form of participation.

Scholars distinguish between two aspects of bargaining, 'distributive' and 'integrative' (Walton and McKersie 1965). Distributive bargaining assumes an adversarial relationship—that is, that the parties have opposing interests and will not voluntarily accede to the other's preferences. Thus there is a 'zero-sum' or 'win–lose' relationship in which one party can gain only at the cost of the other. Consequently each party exaggerates it own demands as well as its willingness to fight rather than make concessions. Bargaining power (the ability to inflict pain on the other) becomes more important than rational argument. Information which may lead to solutions beneficial to both sides is often withheld, on the assumption that the other side will use it for a bargaining advantage. Discussion often concentrates on who is right or wrong, rather than how to resolve common problems. At times the differences become personal and parties attack each other. They distrust not only the other side's arguments but also its good faith.

Thus among the disadvantages of distributive bargaining are that it inhibits free communications, exaggerates differences, and institutionalizes conflict. It focuses on areas of difference, making it harder to discover productive solutions and areas of agreement. In economists' terms, it often fails to maximize 'joint welfare'.

Integrative ('win–win' or 'mutual-gains') bargaining is the conceptual opposite of distributive bargaining (Fisher and Ury 1981). It assumes the possibility of 'variable-sum gains'—that is, if the parties search with an open mind, they will find solutions to their problems from which both parties gain. The hope is to make bargaining less adversarial and to develop more harmonious relations. Parties who engage in integrative bargaining seek to understand the other side's needs, focus on underlying problems ('interests') rather than demands ('positions'), evaluate a range of alternative solutions rather than advocating a single one, and above all concentrate on developing solutions ('yesable propositions') rather than meeting both parties' needs simultaneously.

Experience suggests that parties who utilize integrative techniques are better able to negotiate contracts amicably and without resort to industrial action (Walton, Cutcher-Gershenfeld, and McKersie 1994). But doing this is not easy. Past history and suspicions are often too strong to overcome. Further, integrative bargaining will not automatically leave both sides better off. It works better with problems for which there are solutions from which both parties in fact can gain—for example, holiday schedules or arranging a new production method. It works poorly with regards to problems for which no such solutions are available—for example, whether there should be a wage increase. Thus integrative bargaining does not eliminate the need for distributive bargaining. Through facilitating value-creating trade-offs, integrative bargaining may increase the size of the pie to be distributed. But once pie size is maximized, the distributive question of how to divide it remains. In practice most bargaining is 'mixed motive', a combination of both forms.

Complicating matters further is the fact that 'inter-party bargaining' takes place in a context of 'intra-party bargaining'. There are numerous interest groups within both management and union. On the union side, for example, older employees may want better superannuation plans, while the top priority for younger ones may be an immediate pay increase. Similarly, within management the finance department may be interested chiefly in keeping costs low, while the manufacturing may be more concerned with easing work-rule restrictions. Until these internal differences are ironed out, agreement between the two main sides may be difficult. In short, adversarial bargaining may be an imperfect form of representation or influence. (Note that there are similar problems with other forms of participation. Works councils must obtain some sort of consensus before they negotiate with management.)

With this in mind let us briefly contrast collective bargaining and representative participation.

Contrasting Collective Bargaining and Representative Participation

Distinguishing between collective bargaining and participation is not easy, even if they are accepted as separate phenomena. It is largely a matter of perspective or degree. We see at least three differences: (1) in the extent to which the parties' interests converge or diverge; (2) in the means adopted for problem-solving, and (3) in the topics with which the process deals. In practice there is a good deal of overlap.

Similarities or Differences of Interest

Collective bargaining is based on the *pluralist* assumption that, though there are basic differences between employees and management, the parties accept common values, and are prepared to resolve their differences in a relatively peaceful fashion. The parties fight, but the struggle is restrained by well-understood and accepted rules. Each side accepts the other's right to exist; neither seeks to destroy the other. Nevertheless the relationship is adversarial. The union's job is to counterbalance management's power.

Collective bargaining is thus inconsistent with the *unitary* assumption that the interests of labour and management are one and the same, with apparent differences being caused by misunderstanding and 'poor human relations'. It is also inconsistent with the radical assumption that the differences between the parties are irreconcilable. (Not all bargainers accept pluralist values, of course. In France and Italy, during the immediate post-war period, bargaining was often viewed as merely an extension of the class struggle, while in pre-*perestroika* socialist countries the logic of labour agreements made sense only in terms of the unitary model.)

By contrast with bargaining, the assumptions underlying participation are far from clear—and vary, depending on the form of participation involved. In most cases they are unitary: participants are expected to accept common organizational goals. The German Works Constitution Act, for example, requires works councils 'to work together in trustful cooperation in the interests of the employees and the firm'. However, the goal of some advocates of participation is to restrict management, as in the pluralist model, while in the immediate post-war period there were radical advocates of 'industrial democracy' as a means of wresting control from management. In practice, therefore, participation schemes vary considerably in their position along the cooperative–adversarial continuum.

Another difference may be only symbolic. Unionism and collective bargaining have been associated with commitment to class (class solidarity) in most countries (not in the USA); in contrast, participation may signify commitment to one's employing organization.

Means of Problem-Solving

In principle, participation is integrative and bargaining distributive. But this is over-simple. For example, the technically participative relationship between works councils and managements in many German companies includes much bargaining; certainly it is often adversarial. On the other hand, quite ingenious integrative solutions are often developed in a formal bargaining context. Thus, in practice, both participation and bargaining involve 'mixed motives'. As a means of workplace problem-solving, what has been called 'union–management cooperation' or 'mutual gains bargaining' closely resembles the smooth working of the works-council system.

Levinson (1996: 133) reports that Swedish codetermination is moving towards 'integrated participation' in which unions are involved 'during the early days of change, when new ideas and concepts [are] still crystalizing'. He contrasts this with 'separated participation' in which the union's main function is to react to management's proposals. As described, however, integrated participation in Sweden seems much like union–management cooperation in the USA.

Although bargaining typically involves attempts at persuasion, the force that leads the parties to agreement is not so much logic as 'clout', the ability of each side to harm the other economically through industrial action or otherwise. By contrast, there is an implicit expectation in most participative schemes that agreements will be reached amicably, through rational discussion, and without coercion. In other words, the parties have interests in common and will work together for the common good.

Topics

At least in theory, collective bargaining should cover topics regarding which one side can gain only at the expense of the other (zero-sum gain), while participation is best suited for issues regarding which solutions can be found from which both parties gain (variable-sum gain). Wages presumably are best suited for bargaining, while holiday or vacation scheduling and quality improvement are presumably more appropriate for participation. In practice, however, collective bargaining in Continental Europe deals with major issues, such as wages, regarding which uniform standards can be set which affect large numbers of employees and firms, while participation is concerned with workplace issues, such as staffing ratios. In Anglo-Saxon countries, both types of issues are handled by collective bargaining.

In principle, participation should be concerned with strategic long-term problems, while collective bargaining deals more with short-term, tactical issues. In typical practice, both forms of employee representation devote most of their efforts to the short run.

To conclude, the distinctions between collective bargaining and participation can be considerably exaggerated. Each involves both adversary (distributive) and cooperative (integrative) elements. Much bargaining takes place within the various bodies (works councils, etc.) established by participatory schemes. It is entirely possible to have close cooperation without establishing two distinct systems, one for adversarial relations and the other for cooperative ones.

Germany versus the USA

Though in practice the processes of collective bargaining and representative participation may overlap, there are some important differences in formal structure and assumptions. To illustrate we compare the industrial-relations systems in Germany and the USA, emphasizing the main avenues of employee voice available in these two countries (for a more extensive comparison, see Summers 1987). We take these two countries as examples because their industrial-relations institutions are highly developed and may represent the extremes of a continuum:

heavy reliance on works councils in Germany and a limited role for their counterparts in the USA.

For explanatory purposes, too, we focus on unionized multi-plant firms in manufacturing. These firms may be broadly representative of industrial relations in Germany and illustrative of the (now small) unionized sector in the USA.

Unionized employees, in both countries, are represented by national unions which negotiate the basic collective-bargaining agreement. They do so with regional employers' associations in Germany and, typically (not always), with company management in the USA. The main (and important) difference is that German contracts deal primarily with overall wages, total hours of work, and benefits, while US contracts cover a much broader range of topics. Among these are vacations, pay for specific jobs, promotional and lay-off sequences ('seniority'), safety, and overtime. Including appendices, US contracts may run for hundreds of pages. In both countries, if an agreement is not reached, the union may strike and the employers may lock out their employees. But, as long as the contract is in effect, both are subject to a 'peace obligation' (called a 'no-strike clause' in the USA). The typical German agreement lasts for one year; in the USA it is three.

Enterprise-level structures. There are union and participative structures at the plant level of both countries. But in the USA the union structure is of primary importance and the participative one is secondary. The reverse is true in Germany.

At the plant level US blue-collar unionized employees are represented by strong local unions with an elaborate framework of elected officers, stewards, chief stewards, bargaining committees, and monthly membership meetings. Stewards are especially important. Elected by the members in a ratio of one for every 30 to 300 members (depending on the contract), they represent the first step in the grievance procedure (discussed below).

In Germany, the main functions of the US local union are performed by works councils. However, the correspondence between the two bodies is far from perfect and they operate in different ways. The US local union is merely one part of the overall union organization: its powers and procedures are typically set by the national union's constitution. Though the typical Germany works council is dominated by its union, it is legally independent; its powers are derived from the law, which applies to all companies, regardless of whether they are unionized.

In addition to work councils, there are union stewards in many German plants and sometimes a stewards' assembly (*Vertrauensmanner*), but their role is largely confined to mobilizing support for union positions. Recent years in the USA have also seen the growth of a network of joint union–management consultative committees, but they are distinctly subservient to the union officers. Their influence is far less than that of German works councils.

All non-managerial employees (union members or not) are eligible to vote in German works-council elections, while only union members can vote for US union officers. Further, white-collar employees in US manufacturing are rarely unionized and supervisors (a much broader category than German managers (*Leitende Angestellte*)) have no representation rights at all. This means that US representation is confined largely to blue-collar employees.

Nevertheless, German works councillors and key US local union officers enjoy somewhat similar privileges. Often they are excused from their normal duties so that they can serve as full-time employee representatives; the company assigns them offices of their own; they have telephones and even secretaries and technical experts to give advice. Beyond this they can call on the national union for counsel.

The powers of German works councils and US local unions are somewhat (but only somewhat) similar. US local unions negotiate plant supplementary agreements covering local issues such as parking, training, work rules (for example, the assignment of work to different occupations), and even the operation of the plant restaurant. These plant agreements often require the national union's approval.

Works councils negotiate (co-determine) many of the same issues plus numerous others which are covered by national agreements in the USA but left to local determination in Germany. Negotiations over the circumstances in which overtime can be worked, for example, are conducted at the works-council level. There are other topics over which works councils have the right to 'consultation'. Additionally, unions in both countries have the right to certain forms of company information, but the German right is far, far more extensive. Works councils are also charged with enforcing national laws, such as safety regulations. If works councils and management are unable to agree regarding matters subject to co-determination, the matter may be referred to the labour court.

Some key differences. Despite some elements in common, there are some important differences between the two systems. In the USA a sharp distinction is made between negotiations over what should be in a new contract after an old contract has expired (called negotiations over 'interests') and questions regarding how an existing contract is to be interpreted and administered (called disputes over 'rights').[4]

Once a contract is ratified, the US union's function changes considerably. Its job now is to enforce and administer the contract primarily through a fairly legalistic 'grievance procedure'. Employees who feel their rights are being violated may file a grievance which specifies the sections of the contract which are alleged to be violated. If the steward is unable to resolve the grievance with the first-level supervisor, it may be submitted to the 'second step', typically a chief steward and a second-level supervisor. If this is unsuccessful, it can be referred to a third step, and so on. If settlement is reached at none of these steps, all specified in the contract, the dispute goes to an impartial arbitrator, whose decision is final and binding, but must be based on the contract.

True, the US process is not entirely legalistic. No long-term contract can anticipate every possible future development. Thus rather than specify exactly what must be done in every conceivable situation, some contract clauses are little more than guidelines. Applying these guidelines provides considerable opportunity for bargaining. On balance, however, workplace rules are applied on a somewhat more legalistic fashion in the USA than they are in Germany.

Contrasting approaches to redundancy. The issue of redundancy may illustrate this point (we follow Summers 1987). In the USA a clear distinction is made between lay-offs and discharges. Lay-offs are presumably temporary; employees retain their seniority rights of recall if work becomes available. Discharge is for cause; it is permanent. The distinction is less clear in Germany.

With regard to lay-offs, the typical US contract gives management an almost unrestricted right to reduce the number of employees owing to lack of work. However, who is laid off is determined strictly by seniority. How seniority is measured is set by the contract—it may be by time in job, department, or company. But, once seniority is determined—a mechanical process—neither company nor union has much discretion. Indeed, a union which fails to uphold a member's seniority rights is subject to suit for damages on the grounds that it has violated its 'duty of fair representation'.

The situation in Germany is very different. The company must negotiate with its works council on a case-by-case basis *whether* there will be a lay-off. Usually the council will insist in a 'social contract' providing for redundancy pay and sometimes retraining.[5] As to *who* will be laid off, German law requires

> consideration should be given to several factors—seniority, age, skill, family responsibilities, and ability to find other work. Although works councils can negotiate guidelines giving each of these factors defined weights so that the results can be objective and predictable, few works councils do so . . . The door is thereby opened wide to arbitrary judgement, favouritism, and discrimination. The works council may, on the other hand, abdicate its function. Unwilling to make choices between employees, the works council may simply accept the choices made by the employer. (Summers 1987: 348–9)

In discharge cases in the USA the burden is on management to prove 'cause' or 'just cause'. 'Although such vague terms might seem to give the union a wide range of discretion' (Summers 1987: 349), in practice, rather than make an independent judgement, the union acts chiefly as a defence attorney. Except in obviously hopeless cases or where an agreement can be reached on a lesser penalty, unions normally take discharge cases to arbitration. Not to do so might again subject them to civil suit.

Again the German approach is different. Works councils can object to (but not prevent) dismissals. But in practice they do so only about 10 per cent of the time (Summers 1987: 349). Regardless of the works council's position, the employee may appeal to the labour court (the German equivalent of US arbitration).

To close, German works councils and US local unions perform much the same functions but there are some important differences in emphasis.

1. Particularly in theory and somewhat in practice local and national unions are more closely integrated in the USA than are national unions and works councils in Germany (more on this later).
2. In terms of contract administration, the German system is more flexible. The US system emphasizes substantive rights, embodied in written agreements; the German system emphasizes procedural rights (Cutcher-Gershenfeld and Verma 1994). As the German manager of a US subsidiary of a German company put it, 'The US system is predictable, even though it is rigid. In the end the German system may give management more freedom, but it's very time consuming.'
3. There is considerable bargaining in both systems. Much of it is highly distributive and adversarial, especially regarding wages. But there is also a good deal of what US scholars call 'union–management cooperation', integrative problem-solving which seeks mutual gains.

Nevertheless there is a major, if only symbolic difference between the systems. By law, works councils are obliged to cooperate with management in 'a spirit of mutual trust' for 'the good of the employees and the establishment'. In theory, then, the German approach is expected to be integrative. In practice, most observers agree that, although German works councils have broader authority than US unions, by and large (not always) they are more likely to exercise it with the interests of the overall organization in mind.

US unions, following the pluralist model, have traditionally viewed themselves chiefly as employees' advocates and their function has been to press hard to maximize their members' individual (at times short-run) benefits.[6] Nevertheless recent economic pressures have convinced many US unions that their employer's survival is their concern and numerous innovative participative schemes (such as at NUMMI) have been adopted with union support. However, old adversarial inclinations die hard.

In practice, therefore, the two systems have tended to converge. But they start from different historic positions and values—and this is significant. One important difference may be linguistic. The German terms *arbeitnehmer* and *arbeitegeber* suggest functional rather than power differentials. In English 'owner' versus 'employee' or 'manager' versus 'worker' convey more confrontational meanings.

We end this section with a disclaimer. There are many styles of collective bargaining. The US style is only one. The traditional British industry-wide contracts and the traditional Australian awards were far less detailed than the typical US contract. In both Australia and the UK much is left either to management discretion or to informal local-level bargaining (depending on the union's local-level strength). Germany, Sweden, the USA, and Australia all have unified union movements. Competing unions in France, Spain, and Italy all add to complexity not found elsewhere.

The previous section compared collective bargaining and participation as separate systems. We now examine the relationship between the two in practice, beginning with union attitudes towards participation.

Union Attitudes towards Participation

Though industrial-relations practices differ among countries, one can discern something of a pattern regarding works councils, especially in Continental Europe (Streeck 1995). Councils with primarily consultative powers were established immediately after the war, as unions and managements united to restore their war-torn industries. Except in Germany and partly in the Netherlands, these bodies atrophied, with unions afraid they would develop into rival power centres and management unwilling to cede them power. But the late 1960s wave of semi-spontaneous strikes and the growing need for technological flexibility in an increasingly competitive economy gradually led both parties to become more tolerant of workplace participation. New laws in most countries gave councils greater powers. Often the political–intellectual arm of the labour movement began to support participation before its union branch. Then, as unions learned to live with and later dominate these councils, their attitudes changed towards first acceptance and later enthusiastic support.

Here we examine both the nature of these changes and the reasons for them. First we discuss attitudes towards participation generally and then at those relating to direct participation. In each section, we look first at the experiences of a few individual countries and then generalize from them.

Germany. Established initially as part of Bismarck's programme of paternalistic social welfare, works councils have existed in Germany for over a century. Unions opposed them at first, with August Babel, a leading socialist, calling them a 'mere fig leaf for capitalism' (Muller-Jentsch 1995: 53). The councils were re-established in different form by law after the first World War, in part to pre-empt the then spreading soviet-style revolutionary workers councils. When demonstrators marched to the Reichstag to protest against the new Act, they were met by machine-gun fire, with forty-two being killed.

Unions in Germany generally opposed the 1952 Works Constitution Act, with the national union federation calling its passage a 'black day in the development of democracy' (Muller-Jentsch 1995: 54). The majority feared that the new law would weaken their position at the workplace level and establish works councils as rival power centres. They objected also that the new law gave councils in most industries less power than those given in the recently passed law for the iron-and-steel industry. Other objections were that unions were placed in a minority position on supervisory boards (board of directors) and that the lines between union and councils were drawn too sharply. Not till a Social Democratic regime amended the Act in 1972 to give councils more power and unions captured the vast majority of works council seats did their suspicions moderate (Thelen 1991: 17).

Sweden. During the post-war period, in accordance with the famous Swedish model, Swedish unions were concerned chiefly with raising and equalizing wages and providing a full-employment economy with substantial social benefits. In return, the unions were prepared to let managements run their companies as they wished (Turner and Auer 1994). The union influence was felt at the national level and labour relations were highly centralized. On the other hand, local unions (clubs) were relatively active, compared, for example, with Germany.

Early proposals to establish effective works councils met with union scepticism. As in Germany, it was feared that they would compete with unions and threaten union solidarity. In the 1970s increasing rank-and-file dissatisfaction with workplace conditions and wildcat strikes highlighted the deleterious effects of excessive centralization. Alarmed, unions moved to fill the workplace representation gap and in 1976 they won a Co-Determination Act; however, no provision was made for separate works councils. Instead, the co-determining power was vested in the local union and various joint union–management committees. In fact, 'Swedish trade unions have always been sceptical of council arrangements' (Brulin 1995: 189). Instead, there is co-determination through collective bargaining, with the union as the only channel of representation.

Norway. Historically, Norwegian unions appear to have been less interested in economic democracy than their Scandinavian cousins, one reason being the greater role of the state in their society. It was the Labour Party and not the unions which made the initial proposal for union representation on company boards of directors. The union reaction was 'scepticism' and fear that board representation might threaten the principle of centralized bargaining. Moreover, unions feared that the issue might threaten their consensual relationship with management. Eventually a system of co-determination was established, including union representation on company boards and works councils with only consultative powers (Dolvik and Stokland 1992).

Netherlands. After the Second World War the three rival national unions were unable to agree on a position regarding workplace representation. Meanwhile, works councils were established by paternalistic employers. As these councils became more active, unions began to fear that they would 'become the springboard for company- rather than union-based forms of solidarity' (Visser 1995: 101). To establish an independent form of workplace representation, the socialist union (Federative Nederlandse Vakbeweging (FNV)) began organizing plant union committees. Once these failed to take hold, the FNV changed its tack: it began working through the councils, which have now gained considerable strength.

United Kingdom. Support for participation in the UK has been stronger among left-wing intellectuals than practising unionists. The Labour Government in 1975 established the Bullock Commission, which recommended that union members be added to company boards of directors. Meeting strong management opposition and a divided union reaction, the recommendations were shelved. The idea remained dormant during the Thatcher administration; however, prior to the 1997 election Labour announced plans to revive the plan in some form once it returned to power. The main union contribution to the discussion was to insist that there be 'single channel representation'—that is that the union (or unions) be the sole employee voice in any participative body. Illustrating UK union attitudes in 1982 the Transport and General Workers' Union opposed the employee buyout of the National Freight Corporation (Pendleton *et al.* 1995).

USA. The situation here is somewhat different. Employee Participation Councils (EPCs) (often called 'company unions') were established by many companies in the 1920s and early 1930s. Superficially these functioned much as works councils, though their powers were limited largely to making suggestions. Their purpose in many cases was to keep 'real' independent unions out. Then in 1935 the National Labor Relations Act banned all company-dominated representation plans.

Participation Councils became controversial again in the 1980s and 1990s. Hoping to establish some sort of participation short of unionism, numerous non-union companies began to seek means of circumventing the law. Meanwhile, because unions had become generally so weak, a number of generally pro-union scholars began to argue that elected EPCs should be made permissive or even mandatory (e.g. Weiler 1990; Gould 1993; Kochan 1994). Basically their argument was that some sort of participation was better than none. The issue split the union leadership. Some viewed works councils as a step towards real unionism. A majority saw this proposal as a 'Trojan horse' policy playing into management's hands. In 1995 the national Dunlop Committee, appointed to consider changes in the nation's labour laws, recommended that participatory mechanisms be permitted, but only under limited conditions (Commission on the Future of Worker Management Relations 1995). In 1996 the Republican Congress sought to resolve the issue by lifting all restrictions on participation plans, management controlled or not, but President Clinton vetoed their proposed act. Meanwhile, as discussed in Chapter 1, a variety of participative forms—both direct and representative—were established in unionized companies. Indeed, by contrast with much of Europe, direct participation was introduced in the USA before its representative counterpart.

Why Suspicion?

Why should unions in so many countries be so suspicious of participatory schemes?

In the first place, there is the (often justified) fear that management will use participation as a means of establishing rival power centres and so weaken unions and take away functions which are properly theirs. There is the further concern that participation might divide employees into pro- and anti-union camps and draw employees away from the union (Eaton and Voos 1992).

Secondly, participation plans have been installed in some unionized companies, without consultation with the union or with the union given little voice in their operation. Understandably, under these circumstances they meet with resistance.

Finally, the traditional union role has been adversarial. Shifting is not easy. Most forms of participation involve some sort of accommodation with management and some acceptance of common objectives. Union leaders are often divided and uncertain as to how desirable such cooperation might be. In this regard there are considerable differences in union perspective among countries.[7] Until recently, most US and British unions opposed participation, believing that collective bargaining might serve them better, especially since they already enjoyed well-established systems of shop-floor labour relations. Representative participation was also seen as creating impermissible conflicts of interest (as will be discussed below). Unionists feared that participation would subject them to changes of having 'sold out' to management.

On the other hand, some unionists view participation as a means of protecting employees' interests, making jobs more desirable, democratizing the workplace, and extending union power (the 'frontier of union control'). This has become the dominant view in many countries. Even in the USA the United Steel Workers used up scarce bargaining power to win a priority demand, representation on company boards of directors; the union argued that it needed the information and ability to influence policy that board membership would presumably provide. (The contract also guaranteed union access to a wide range of company plans and financial information which hitherto had been kept secret.)

Unions in most countries view representative participation more favourably when overall union–management relations are good and unions feel strong and secure (Marchington 1994; the USA may be an exception (Jacoby 1983)). Indeed, participation rarely takes root when overall relations are hostile, as was traditionally the case in France.

Despite initial opposition, today unions in most industrialized countries endorse representative participation, with Canada being a major exception. Nevertheless, in doing this unions are more interested in protecting job security and fair treatment than in influencing production methods.

Direct Participation

As with attitudes toward works councils, union attitudes towards direct participation vary from country to country. By contrast with representative participation, support for direct participation came first from management. But unions have gradually changed their position. Today, for example, after original hostility most European unions are beginning to accept work teams (Mueller and Purcell 1992). Support for workplace restructuring has entered union rhetoric. In most countries, however, this is a low-priority demand, below higher wages, for example, job security, or expanded union-controlled representative participation.

Germany. That was certainly the history in Germany. Though IG Metall initially opposed experimentation with QCs (Thelen 1991: 198), Muller-Jentsch (1995: 126) reports that the main source of opposition today is from middle management rather than works councils or unions.

German unions joined in a 'coalition for industrial modernization' designed to rationalize production as early as 1955. But they did so reluctantly and only in return for steadily increased wages and benefits. Union interest in what was called 'Groupwork' started with the wildcat strikes of 1969–73, which were in part directed against Taylorism, especially by younger employees. The Social Democratic Party developed a 'humanization of work' programme in 1970s. In 1973 one Metal Workers contract prohibited work cycles shorter than ninety seconds. In a step toward job enrichment, IG Metall agreed to merge fifty-four previously separate trades into ten. It also developed a twelve-point set of objectives (*Eckpunkte*), including longer cycle times, QCs, technology redesign to permit group work, paid group meetings of at least one hour a week, making participation voluntary, and supervision of the entire process by joint union–management committees (Turner 1991).

The big union push for humanization lasted till the 1980s. Then management, facing the recession, called for work reorganization, not to humanize work but to increase production. This gave unions the chance to trade off increased productivity against improved working conditions, doing so through individual works councils rather than uniform national contracts (Thelen 1991). As a consequence there is much variation from one workplace to another (Bunmdesmann-Jansen and Frerichs 1996).

Today many works councils take a proactive role in advocating decentralization of decision-making and introduction of self-directed work teams and other new forms of work organization (Turner and Auer 1994: 47–8; Wever 1994; Muller-Jentsch 1995). Works councils 'figure prominently in the unions' current strategy of going beyond securing compensation for workers adversely affected by new technology to actively influencing the organization of production itself . . . The union sees work organization as central to the defence of workers' skills and incomes' (Thelen 1991: 181) and as a first step towards 'co-determination at the workplace'.

Sweden. The famed early Swedish experiments with direct participation and job redesign were largely initiated by management. Swedish unions were originally suspicious of work teams and other forms of employee involvement. Then, once they won co-determination rights, they became less fearful that participatively introduced workplace changes would leads to speed-ups (Thelen 1991: 205; Applebaum and Batt 1994; Turner and Auer 1994). In any case, as long as there was full employment, they were relatively unconcerned that improved efficiencies might lead to job loss. On the ideological level, unions have given direct participation their full support.

By 1971 Swedish union clubs (locals) were energetically pushing to extend teamwork and other forms of direct participation (Berggren 1991: 107). They are often highly involved in the design of new workplace arrangements, more so than in Germany (Turner and Auer 1994). On the other hand, based on several studies, Kjellberg (1992: 130) concludes that, of the four stages of the change process (initiation, development, formal approval, and implementation), the union is active chiefly at the approval stage, leaving initiation largely to management. As Turner and Auer (1994: 54) put it, although 'the drive toward new work organization has been for the most part management led . . . the union in recent years has moved towards its own proactive stance on group work, and has tipped the balance within management towards more autonomous, "human centred" forms of organization'.

Norway. Norway has a reputation of encouraging direct participation. The 'Cooperation Project' of the 1950s and 1960s was co-sponsored by the main union and employer federations as well as the state. Based on the Tavistock Institute's socio-technical approach (Emery 1959), the project's goal was to reduce employee alienation through use of autonomous work groups. Nevertheless, according to Dolvik and Stokland (1992: 154) this 'emphasis on workplace-oriented industrial democracy met with union scepticism; from the end of the 1960s it was clear that the union's main strategy for industrial democracy was through the extension of collective bargaining and legislation . . . The effects of the project . . . seem to have been limited . . . partly because it was initiation from "above" without sufficient motivation at the workplace.' In short, Emery and Thorsrud's 'model of successful demonstrations did not work well in Norway' (Qvale 1989: 99). (More on the Norwegian experience in Chapter 5.)

The principle of direct participation has received strong support from both unions and the Labour Government (Brundtland 1989). Nevertheless 'new forms of work organization . . . have largely resulted from management initiative' (Dolvik and Stokland 1992: 162). Unions seem to have adopted a generally supportive but reactive role. Kalleberg (1993) ascribes this limited success to lack of 'know-how' (or, as we call it, 'competence'—see Chapter 5).

Explaining these attitudes

Why the union's somewhat ambivalent feeling regarding direct participation in so many countries? Apart from the reasons for union uncertainties as to participation generally—suspicion of management's objectives, concern that employees might be co-opted, and reluctance to blur the union's adversarial role—there are three other reasons why many unions have been slow to embrace the practice of direct participation.

Historically, the thrust of collective bargaining in many countries (but especially in the USA) has been to rigidify and codify personnel practices. In the typical unionized plant, decisions as to the allocation of work among employees are made on the basis of collectively-bargained seniority and job-demarcation rules. These rules determine job assignments, promotions, lay-offs, and even vacation schedules (the senior employees get first choice). Many employees believe strongly that these rules give them quasi-property rights in their jobs, rights they are willing to fight hard to preserve.

Broad banding (discussed in Chapter 1) requires combining some jobs and blurring the boundaries between others. Decision-making work teams tend to erase the sharp line between employees and managers, a distinction which unions have long sought to maintain. New career patterns disturb established promotional ladders. Job rotation goes against union traditions emphasizing seniority. In plants with the most advanced of the new forms of participation, decisions as to the allocation of work and even pay and discipline are made by the work teams on a flexible *ad hoc* basis. In short, by contrast with collective bargaining, which leads to what the Webbs called the 'common rule', the whole participation movement promotes experimentation and diversity. Further, if employees make personnel decisions by themselves and if first-line supervisors are elected, how is the union to handle grievances filed by disgruntled employees? We have more to say about this later on. (This is a serious problem at GM's Saturn division, as we discuss below).

Job demarcation is an important issue in many countries. It is difficult to combine jobs or to set up work teams where employees belong to different craft unions, as in the UK, or to blur the lines between white-collar and blue-collar employees, where, as in Sweden, the two kinds of employees belong to different unions (Brulin 1995). Many German employees have gone through a lengthy craft apprenticeship. Having earned their position in this way, each craft fears that sharing its work with those trained under a different apprenticeship scheme would downgrade their skill. Similarly Spanish unions have opposed measures to increase occupational or geographical mobility (Escobar 1995).

A second problem is related to the first. The new forms of work organization tend to decentralize decision-making. Decisions previously made by management, perhaps in conjunction with union officers, are now made by ordinary employees. Problems are resolved at lower levels, leaving both union leaders and management with less to do.[8] No wonder union leaders are suspicious as to what's happening at the workplace levels. 'Are they selling out the contract? Are our members giving up rights we fought to obtain?'

Finally, much participation today involves what was once known as 'productivity bargaining'. In the face of growing competition (especially foreign competition), management seeks greater flexibility in how it uses its employees. Its main purpose is not so much happier, better-satisfied employees, but employees who work more efficiently. Some of management's proposals, particularly broad banding and the establishment of work teams, are arguably in the interest of both employees and management. On the other hand, many unionists see this as a speed-up ('work intensification' in Germany): each employee takes on more responsibilities, more work, and for the same pay. Workplace reform was hindered in

Australia by employee fears that this would threaten their overtime (Rimmer 1992). And other 'reforms' are chiefly in management's interest, at least in the short run; in the long run, however, if they save jobs, they may be in employees' interests as well.

Under these circumstances, neither the union nor the works council is likely to make concessions unless they get some consideration in return. The nature of this consideration varies, depending on the circumstances. Often it consists of greater union (or works council) input into management decision-making. If the company is profitable, the consideration may include higher wages; if the company's economic position is marginal, the consideration may be a stronger guarantee of job security; and if the company is in truly bad shape, then the consideration may be a greater chance to survive.

In much of the world, this bargaining involves more than a simple quid pro quo. Unions (and works councils) in many countries are making active contributions to the restructuring of production. 'Productivity coalitions' have developed in many places. These are 'collaborative joint approaches to change and flexibility in the interests of corporate competitiveness and hence of the permanent work force . . . [At times] unions have accepted management's objectives in exchange for influence over their achievement' (Ferner and Hyman 1992: pp. xx, xxvi). This is occurring not just in Europe but to some extent in Australia and the USA. But productivity coalitions require the adoption of an overall co-operative, integrative relationship—and above all, trust—between the parties. When this relationship is not achieved, the productivity coalition is in trouble (for further discussion see Chapter 6).

In many countries participation has been introduced in the context of concession bargaining. Participation has been sold to union members as a means of saving jobs. Thus member attitudes towards participation are coloured by their attitudes towards concession bargaining specifically and more generally to the question of how militant the union should be in its dealings with management. Internal union debate as to the desirability of these concessions has been intense and the controversy has affected attitudes towards participation (see discussion below). Under these circumstances the success of workplace participation depends heavily on the quality of overall union–management relations.

Nevertheless, unions have become increasingly receptive to various forms of direct participation. Their position regarding worktime flexibility is illustrative. In the face of rapidly changing technology, many managements have sought greater freedom in setting work schedules. Most unions' reaction at first was to oppose this, or to offer to accept it only in exchange for some concession—for example, higher penalty rate for non-standard hours. More recently their position has begun to change, especially in Sweden and Germany. Rather than opposing flexibility, they are demanding flexitime as a right, with the hours to be determined by employees' convenience, rather than management's (Terry 1994).

Our next section deals with the political controversies that participation has helped to generate.

Participation and Internal Union Politics

The related issues of participation and militancy have lead to political conflict and election battles (1) within unions, (2) between unions, where, as in France, there are competing unions, and (3) in works-council elections.

Union attitudes toward cooperation with management in the USA are spread along a continuum, with the two extremes labelled the 'militant' and the 'co-operativist' (Katz 1986; Gershenfeld 1987).[9] These differences and uncertainties carry over to attitudes towards participation. Noting that participative programmes have been introduced into some militantly anti-union companies, many unionists view these as chiefly union-busting techniques (Parker 1985). They see participation schemes as forms of manipulation and 'speed-ups in disguise' and as attempts to 'co-opt' employees into management's fold. 'Cooperativists', by contrast, view the militant position as almost suicidal. They see cooperation as helping business to survive and thus saving jobs. They argue that shop-floor participation may yield valuable non-economic benefits. However, by contrast with some European counterparts, few US unionists have developed an ideological interest in industrial democracy. Indeed, attitudes are determined less by ideology than by economic circumstances. As a union adviser put it, US participation 'isn't a social revolution; it's a deal' (Koenig 1984) and is supported chiefly by unions whose members' jobs are most severely threatened (Cappelli 1985).

Together, participation and concession bargaining have become issues in numerous US union elections, with some officers being defeated because they were viewed as being co-opted by management. Indeed, in unionized workplaces with participative schemes, it is almost a rule that opposition factions in contested elections will charge the 'ins' with 'being in bed with the boss'. In the Auto Workers 'New Directions', an opposition group, practically an opposition political party, has been formed largely around the question of concessions and participation. NUMMI members voted their pro-participation shop chairman out of office. The victor was prepared to continue the present work arrangements but promised to be more militant in protecting the interests of individual members. The NUMMI situation is not unique. Indeed, a high percentage of the local union officials most closely involved in the best-known examples of US employee participation have suffered strong electoral opposition and even defeat (for election fights at Saturn, see Shaiken 1995).

By contrast, opposition to social partnership in Germany is quite mild, but it exists and was stronger in the 1960s and 1970s. At that time

> there were strands of union opposition with militant [stewards] as their backbone. Especially in IG Metall and IG Chemie . . . rank-and-file activists organized unofficial strikes, opposed established works councils, and became the representatives of discontented groups . . . But the rivalry ended with a victory [for the Councils. Nevertheless] in several cases, oppositional trade unionists have scored spectacular successes. (Muller-Jentsch 1995: 64; see also Jacobi *et al.* 1992: 244)

Opposition groups won a notable victory at Opel-Russelsheim in 1975; as of 1990 this upstart group was itself being opposed as being too conservative (Thelen 1991: 141).

Much of the recent German opposition has come from two sources: first, active union stewards, especially in the automobile industry 'where the more politicized nature of plant policies . . . is reflected in (and reinforced by) more active and vocal shop steward committees' (Thelen 1991: 141); and, secondly, from non-union and occasionally foreign employees (Jacobi *et al.* 1992: 244). In any case, compared to the USA, participation appears less frequently as an issue in German union politics.

There is somewhat the same situation in the Netherlands, where in the 1970s radical unionists talked of replacing works councils with union-shop committees (Visser 1992: 175). The Italian scene has been marred by on-and-off hostility between national unions and 'autonomous' workplace councils (Regalia 1995). Historically, French and Italian radicals have viewed RPBs as bureaucratic and distant from members. They seemingly have preferred 'spontaneous' shop-floor action to either RPBs or national unions. More recently, disputes have occurred at Fiat between non-communist unions who support participation and the communist CGIL, which prefers traditional adversarial relationships ('never sign anything') (Meardi 1996: 279).

The situation is less chaotic in Austria, where works-council elections (which include non-member employees) are tests of the strength of as many as seven union factions and the results are used as the basis of allocating seats in higher-level union bodies (Traxler 1992: 281). And in countries with divided union movements (France, Spain, Belgium, and Italy) there is sharp competition between unions for works-council representation. Eaton (1994) reports that direct participation is less likely to survive in US plants where there is more than one union (see also Gill and Krieger 1992).

Are Unions Necessary for Participation to Succeed?

Although we know a good deal about the impact of unions on productivity (e.g. Freeman and Medoff 1984), there has been little research on the impacts of unions plus participation, as opposed to that of unions alone. Hypothetically, union support should be critical to participation's 'success', regardless of whether success is measured in terms of improved working conditions, increased productivity, or just programme survival. The limited empirical (mostly US) evidence generally supports this view (for a review, see Eaton and Voos 1994). For example, unionized firms are more likely to *introduce* various forms of direct and representative participation (Eaton and Voos 1992: 185). QCs and similar programmes are more likely to *survive* in unionized firms (Drago 1988), in part because they are more likely to be associated with representative participation (Cutcher-Gershenfeld *et al.* 1991: 8)). Forms of representative participation, such as works councils and safety committees, are more likely to be *successful* if backed by a strong union (Kelley and Harrison 1992). Participative schemes are more likely to *impact* productivity favourably if the firms introducing them are unionized and if the union gives these plans its support (Kelley and Harrison 1992; Eaton and Voos 1994 contra Fitzroy and Kraft 1987). Summarizing the US data, Eaton and Voos (1994: 99) conclude that participation programmes 'should have a larger positive impact in the union than the non-union sector only when the union is involved in program administration, something that is far from universal'.

Joint consultative committees are twice as common in unionized than in non-union UK firms (Streeck 1995: 661). Basing their opinions on observations and interviews, Visser (1995: 204) and Turner (1991) both agree that union support is critical for RPB success in Netherlands and Germany. Finally, according to IDE (1993: 98–9), 'the degree of employee mobilization, measured in terms of workers' membership in trade unions and representative bodies at the plant . . . was found to be positively related to the influence of both workers and their representatives at the plant'.

Why should this be? (For lengthier discussions, see Eaton and Voos 1992; Cooke 1994.) In the first place, unions increase employee job security; consequently employees are less likely to fear that increased productivity caused by participation will cost them their jobs. Indeed unions often stress that the issue of job security must be addressed before becoming involved in participation programmes.

Beyond this, unionized workers have greater freedom to be outspoken. As we discuss later (Chapter 6), participation is often resisted by first-line supervisors and middle management, who fear that employee suggestions will expose their mistakes and generally threaten their authority, status, and even jobs. In a non-union situation, such supervisory opposition may stifle participation; however, unions can protect critics from management reprisals.

Obviously any participation programme is in trouble if the union actively opposes it. But even by being passive, the union threatens the programme's success. In workplaces where the union is weak or non-existent, management may impose participation programmes without consulting the employees who are supposed to do the participating. But if employees feel forced, for example, to enter work teams involuntarily, they may sabotage them. By contrast, unions provide employees with a voice in designing and implementing these programmes. Further, union approval increases the chance that changes will be viewed as fair and legitimate. At NUMMI, for example, 'union voice channels have added equity, credibility, and legitimacy—and thus commitment and effectiveness to the production system [participative] channel' (Adler *et al.* 1995: 10). US experience is that it is hard to develop effective representative participation without strong shop-floor union organization. A union needs to be strong enough so that it does not seem to be co-opted by management (Streeck 1995: 605).

In Europe 'the local union acts as an integrator of the specific bodies for participation, the employees in general, and the external environment. Thus, the bodies created are more efficient in democratizing if there are unions present' (IDE 1981*b*: 330). Beyond this, experience in union activities may increase members' competence and effectiveness as RPB members.

With a union it is participation among equals. 'Only with a union—with workplace level groups supplemented by plant or firm level institutions of collective bargaining—do we get real productivity bargaining' (Eaton and Voos 1992: 212). Since the presence of a strong union makes it possible for employees to say 'No' to participation, it also makes their 'Yes' more meaningful. For management, union agreement makes employee behaviour more predictable. Non-union firms, by contrast, lack mechanisms to bring differences out in the open and to negotiate the compromises necessary to win employee acceptance.

Moreover, for employees to accept and implement new ideas they must feel that they will gain from them. A union can negotiate how to share the benefits of increased cooperation. A non-union firm will be sorely tempted to expropriate these for its own purposes. As we discuss later (Chapter 6), there is considerable evidence that participation is generally more effective when associated with complementary human-resources practices such as training. Without union pressure, the company might ignore these complementary practices. With a union employees are less likely to feel taken advantage of.

An example may illustrate how unions may facilitate the participative process. Repetitive strain injuries are common in automobile assembly plants with lean production systems. This was the case at both NUMMI and Isuzu in the USA. At NUMMI union pressures (reinforced by government inspectors whom the union had invited in) forced management to give the matter high priority; thus the problem is less likely to reoccur. Here the union contributed to organizational learning (Adler *et al.* 1995). At non-union Isuzu, little was done, thus contributing to employee disillusionment with an ostensibly participative teamwork system (Graham 1995).

Both unions and RPBs can protect employees so that change occurs less rapidly and less painfully than it would otherwise. But RPBs and unions cooperating can do this better than can RPBs alone.

No participation programme is perfect. Glitches often occur. In resolving problems, a union can bring perspectives which management lacks. Union staff can sometimes provide expertise which is not available locally. Unions, for instance, can force management to take RPB suggestions seriously. Union weakness may go far to explain why, despite their fairly substantial legal power, French RPBs generally have so little influence.[10]

Experience suggests that lack of union support for participation may divide workers into two camps, one which engages in participative activity and the other which supports the union (Verma and McKersie 1987; Cutcher-Gershenfeld *et al.* 1991: 7). Beyond this, participation's success depends to a considerable extent on a united union and good (not necessarily excellent) labour–management relations (Eaton 1994).

A final point: one of IDE's major findings was that 'Participative Structure' or '*de jure* participation' (rules, chiefly laws, requiring participation) was an important determinant of 'Power Distribution' (*de facto* participation). Here we argue that union support is another critical factor. We hypothesize further that, with both union and legal support, representative participation is more likely to be 'successful' than with just one alone. With neither, representative participation has little chance.

Representative Participative Bodies

In Chapter 1 we listed three forms of representative participation, consultative committees, works councils, and employee or union representation on company boards of directors. Since the boundary between consultative committees and works councils is somewhat fuzzy (with the main difference being extent of power), the two will be discussed together, often using the generic term Representative Participative Bodies (RPBs) to cover both. A separate section deals with board representation.

Institutional Framework

RPBs may be established by law (as in much of Europe), by union contract, or unilaterally by management. Laws may have various degrees of detail. The rights of French enterprise councils, for example, are less precisely defined than those of German works councils. Sweden's legislation merely provided a framework; the parties themselves had to bargain out the details. In 1991 the Australian Industrial Relations Commission required that parties seeking a wage increase should satisfy the Commission that they had established a 'consultative relationship'.

Law and practice often provide that there be more than one representative body. RPBs in most countries spawn subcommittees. In large German firms there are separate plant and company works councils, each with subsidiary finance and training committees. French law provides for four independent, often competing representative bodies: *Enterprise Committees* receive information, are occasionally consulted, and manage funds provided by the firm for employees' social and cultural activities; *Personnel Delegates* can present grievances, but have no right to make formal agreements; *Union Delegates* are appointed by their unions and can bargain with management (if management is willing); and *Health and Safety Committees* (Tchobanian 1995: 244) monitor workplace conditions. As we have seen, US auto union contracts mandate a multitude of committees at both plant and company levels. In general RPBs are larger and the entire framework more elaborate in large companies.

As mentioned earlier, RPB members frequently enjoy substantial prerogatives. Typically they are protected against dismissal. Often RPBs can hire their own professionals and staff. The average total cost of RPBs to employers, including lost time, meeting facilities, and RPB staff, has been estimated at 2 per cent of the payroll in the Netherlands (Visser 1995: 110) and at DM 440 per employee per year in Germany (Muller-Jentsch 1995: 65). Ford in the USA spends $60 million annually on 'jointness' activities. General Motors (GM) estimates the cost as 1 per cent of the payroll.

Most European RPBs consist of employees only, but in some instances (e.g. Norway and typically in the USA) they are joint bodies, consisting of both employee and management representatives. Separate meetings may help ensure that employee representatives are truly independent (however, little stops employee members of joint councils from holding pre-meeting caucuses). In the early post-war period RPBs in the Netherlands met jointly with management, with management often setting the agenda and chairing the meeting. A 1979 law separated Dutch RPBs from management and increased their independence (Visser 1995: 93).

RPB Functions, Formal and Informal

Chapter 1 suggested a typology according to which forms of participation might be classified by organizational *level*, range of *issues*, and degree of *control*. Below we deal quickly with RPB powers in terms of this typology.

Levels. The primary impact of RPBs is at the firm and plant level, though RPBs often monitor workplace (direct) participation.

Issues. The issues RPBs handle differ greatly among situations, depending heavily on their legal rights and the union's political power (Thelen 1991). When RPBs are weak, many subjects are viewed by either unions or management to be too important to be subject to the participative process and so are *formally* reserved either to management's sole discretion or to collective bargaining. Thus the effective influence of weak RPBs may be confined to 'tea and toilet' issues such as safety, training, and workplace amenities. In practice, on the other hand, RPBs may exert considerable influence over issues formally outside their jurisdiction. German and Dutch RPBs, for example, exert considerable authority over matters, such as overtime or redundancies, which in the USA are subject to collective bargaining. More generally, as we discuss below, sharp lines between topics subject and not subject to RPBs' jurisdiction are hard to maintain.

Especially with regards to their formal rights, RPBs have greater power with regards to what IDE (1993) calls 'short-term' decisions, such as task assignments or working conditions, than over 'long-term' decisions, such as investments or new products. In many countries RPBs' most significant activity in recent years has been to engage in productivity bargaining (see, for instance, Muller-Jentsch 1995: 67). Indeed, a major RPB function has been to permit modification of work practices on a fairly continual basis and in manner which provides reasonable protection for present employee rights.

Aside from the issues just mentioned, RPBs in some countries (e.g. Germany and Spain) have the right to monitor management's conformity to government regulations. In some cases, as in France, they may also administer welfare and retirement funds, cafeterias, and medical services.

Degree of control. Even RPBs which are otherwise weak have the right to be *informed* about significant company developments. As a broad generalization, employee representatives receive considerably more information today than they did formerly. In the USA, for example, as a result of 'jointness' (union–management cooperation) agreements, union committees in many steel and auto plants now receive regular reports on production plans, financial results, and proposed technological changes.

Beyond this, RPBs generally have the right to be *consulted.* Though many managers treat consultation seriously, this process can easily be perfunctory. At times, consultation consists of little more than downward communication (Marchington 1992*b*), although even this may be useful for union representatives desirous of learning management's plans. Legally, RPBs have real clout only with regards to subjects over which they have the right of *co-determination*—that is, the right to insist that no change be made without RPB approval. This gives them the right of veto.

Practice may differ from law.[11] For example, German RPBs may be more powerful than their Swedish local unions, even though German law gives its RPBs power over a narrower range of issues (Thelen 1991; Brulin 1995: 389). In many situations RPBs fail to exercise the authority which is legally theirs, at times because of lack of knowledge, training, or skills. This may happen for a variety of reasons: because of a desire not to antagonize management, because management is able to persuade RPB members that its proposals are in the best interest of all parties, or frequently because the parties reach agreement informally without the RPB exercising its formal powers. According to Visser (1995: 95, citing Teulings 1989*b*), only one-third of the Dutch RPBs exercise their full legal rights. By contrast, among large German manufacturing firms, '85 per cent had formal bilateral regulation on matters not covered by legal rights to co-determination' (Muller-Jentsch 1995: 61).

Militant RPBs are able to 'leverage' their perhaps limited legal powers to influence decisions regarding which their legal right is merely to be informed and consulted or less. The main source of clout for German RPBs is their power to veto a range of management activities, especially the use of overtime. Using this power, works councils are able to win concessions with regards to issues regarding which management's legal requirement is merely to consult. At Ford-Cologne, for example, when the company threatened to move its motor line to Britain, the works council banned overtime, and management withdrew its threat.

One crucial source of works council power is the withdrawal of (or threat to withdraw) its active (or even passive) cooperation in day-to-day decision making. This distinction—between the threat to disrupt production (which works councils do not have) and the threat to make routine plant decision making more cumbersome and possibly expensive—is analogous to Alexander Pizzarno's . . . distinction between 'market exchange' and 'political exchange'. (Thelen 1991: 147)

Similarly, Dutch and Spanish RPBs have the legal right to delay employer actions and to appeal these actions in the labour court. Visser (1995, citing Teulings 1989*b*), compares the 'ability of councils to delay the labour process of management, with the union ability to interrupt the labour process of workers'. In such negotiations the RPB is able to trade consent to the implementation of a management policy for greater influence over the terms of the policy itself.

RPBs rarely have the legal right to strike (exceptions: Italy and Spain); German law specifically denies them this.[12] But in Britain in the BBC the union's 'ability to disrupt or halt broadcast transmissions was used quite strategically to obtain their objectives in joint consultative meetings' (Campling 1995: 12). At one time Dutch RPBs engaged in 'unionist' pressure tactics, such as lunchtime demonstrations, sit-ins, work-to-rule and actual strikes, but as RPBs have learned to use other forms of power these primitive tactics have become less common (Visser 1995: 93).

In a limited set of situations (for example, safety issues in Sweden) the employees' views prevail in case of deadlock. Even in Germany, however, management has the final word with regards to most topics; nevertheless, RPBs can often make it expensive for management to make too blatant use of its authority.

In short, while unions' main source of clout may be the strike, RPBs exercise their power in more subtle ways.

RPBs in a System of Conflicting Power Centres

German industrial relations are often said to be characterized by a 'dual system' (or parallel) of unions and works councils, each performing its unique function. Actually it is more complex than this. In practice—and not just in Germany—there are quite a number of sometimes competing, sometimes cooperating power centres.

Apart from the government, these power centres include the union (both national and local), participative bodies at various levels (shop-level work teams, works councils, and employee representatives on boards of directors), and management. Management itself is hardly monolithic: top management has different interests from supervisors; the Human Resources Department has different responsibilities from Production. Thus, as discussed in Chapter 2, works councils occupy a boundary position, wedged in between management, union (both national and local), and employees (independently and as organized into teams).

The existence of competing power centres leads to numerous possibilities for clashes and cooperation, divided individual loyalties, and alternative career tracks. We discuss this below.

Apart from management, three conflicting interests may be involved, those of: (1) the national union, which represents workers in the industry as a whole, (2) RPB members who are concerned with the long-term interests of the plant or company, and (3) shop-floor workers who are concerned primarily with their own (often short-term) interests. For example, an individual employee may argue she should get a pay increase, the RPB says its particular plant cannot afford it, while the national union wants a uniform across-the-board increase for all its members.

The section below examines the relationships between RPBs and four other power centres: (1) national unions, (2) local unions, (3) direct participative bodies, such as QCs and work teams, and (4) individual employees. A fifth relationship, between RPBs and management, may be the most important of all, but will not be discussed further because it has been covered briefly already in Chapter 1 and more extensively by other authors (e.g. Rogers and Streeck 1995).

RPBs and National-Union Relations

There are tensions between national and local-level bodies (both RPBs and local unions). The national union typically:

- has political interests, especially if it is linked to a political party (as in France, Spain, and Italy);
- seeks to establish and maintain uniform pay scales throughout the industry (a major problem in many countries in an era of union weakness);
- advocates a well-trained labour force (such as provided by the German apprenticeship system) and broad social goals (for example, the Swedish equalitarian wage policy);
- may enjoy relationships with nationwide companies which conflict with a given plant's special interests (examples of this below);
- has institutional goals—for example, maintaining membership and dues or improving its position *vis à vis* other unions; and
- is guided by officers who have personal and political interests of their own, especially if they want to be re-elected.

Many of these national-level interests clash with corresponding interests at the local levels. In the USA these clashes typically get played out in terms of tensions between national and local unions. In Europe, by contrast, they are more likely to be evidenced by tensions between national unions and their RPBs. The nature of these tensions are discussed below.

In theory, union functions and those of participative bodies can be strictly segregated, thus avoiding conflict. 'In a majority of member states of the European community a clear distinction is made between rights associated with collective bargaining . . . and rights concerned with information, consultation' (Gill and Krieger 1992: 342). Unions are supposed to handle collective bargaining and RPBs participation. In practice, however, this traditional distinction is often blurred. RPB activities may serve as either a substitute or a supplement to collective bargaining. Dutch RPBs, for example, are in principle prohibited from renegotiating issues already in bargaining agreement, but they can 'apply' the agreement's principles (Visser 1995). German RPBs have the power to 'adopt' contract provisions to meet the needs of individual plants, especially with regards to 'humanization of work' and in reducing hours of work (Thelen 1991: 156; Muller-Jentsch 1995).

Clashes. RPBs' exercise of these powers may lead to RPB–national union friction. 'Subtle and less subtle power struggles between external unions and workplace representatives' occur even in Sweden (Streeck 1995: 667). From the national union's viewpoint, RPBs may engage in 'plant egotism' or 'cooperative syndicalism'. Unions fear that, especially when jobs are at stake, RPBs will cooperate with management to improve the firm's position as against competitors and, in so doing, make agreements which put the welfare of their own constituents above that of the union movement or society generally. 'National unions have an interest in a low unemployment rate but not necessarily in saving particular jobs, whereas the reverse is true for labour representatives at the plant level' (Thelen 1992: 217). In Germany 'Local worker representatives, the shop stewards or work councillors, show a stronger identification with plant survival than national union officials' (Mueller and Purcell 1992: 24).

Clashes occur perhaps most frequently with regards to wages. Depending on the economic situation, RPBs (often with the cooperation of their local unions) may negotiate wages which are either higher or lower than those negotiated nationally. When faced with job loss, RPBs may accept wages and working conditions below those set in regional or national contracts. For example, the RPB at GM's Kaiserlauten plant broke with its regional union to negotiate changes in work hours in order to save the plant, thus leading to strained relations between the RPB, the regional unions and other GM plants (Mueller and Purcell 1992: 20–1). During the mid-1990s RPBs in former East Germany at times negotiated wages below regional union standards, often doing so with the consent of the local union leadership (who typically controlled the RPB anyway). Given their weakness in East Germany, the national unions were in a poor position to object (Turner, forthcoming).

On the other hand, in a tight labour market, German RPBs' 'actual strength often exceeds their legal power' in that they can achieve wage premiums above the industry standard (Schnabel 1991: 20). Often they negotiate a 'second round' of wage increases (Thelen 1991: 176), thus contributing to wage drift. Similarly Austrian works councils, it is complained, undercut solidaristic wage policies through negotiating above-average wages (Duda and Todtling 1986).

National unions sometimes charge RPBs with being too cooperative with management—and at other times with not being cooperative enough. In the 1970s the German Media Workers' national union opposed management-sponsored forms of participation, such as QCs, work teams, and profit-sharing, even though the works council of a major firm, Bertelsmann, accepted them (Jacobi *et al.* 1992: 247). In the 1960s, when union influence over Dutch RPBs was still relatively weak, there was considerable concern that these RPBs were engaged in 'wildcat cooperation' (Visser 1995: 90). By contrast, relations between the rather conservative German chemical workers union and the militant works council at Betrix, a cosmetic firm, 'have historically been conflictual . . . Central union representatives believe the council chair to be too active and confrontational' (Wever 1994: 470).

Strains between national and local levels are illustrated by two cases, both involving the US Auto Workers' union and plants engaged in well-publicized participation programmes. As discussed in Chapter 1, GM's highly experimental Saturn division was designed by a joint committee representing the national union and top management. The plan called for extensive work-team autonomy, bonuses based on divisional profits, and union and company co-managers at all but the highest levels. Though the new local union and the new joint plant management worked closely together, strains rapidly developed between both sets of local leaders, on one side, and their national counterparts, on the other. Local union leadership attacked the national union for calling a strike against GM suppliers which hurt Saturn productivity and union members' chances for profit-sharing bonuses. For its part, the national union opposed Saturn's plan to expand operations at a time when members at other divisions were out of work. National leaders, both union and management, saw Saturn as a loose cannon, out of control. At one point the national union took control of contract negotiations away from the local. The contract it negotiated increased the role of seniority in job assignments, made the grievance procedure more conventional, and reduced the power of teams to select their own members (Shaiken, Lopez, and Mankita 1997). In short it increased the role of rules and decreased workplace discretion.

Somewhat the opposite occurred at Mazda Flat Rock. Here the national Auto Workers' union was anxious to demonstrate to a Japanese company that employee–management participation would work even at a unionized plant. Thus the national union did its best to support a local leadership which supported cooperation with management against a more militant faction which was eventually voted into power (Fucini and Fucini 1990).

Cooperation. Though strains develop between national unions and local RPBs, perhaps more frequently they cooperate to strengthen one another. 'In practice unions and works councils are dependent on each other' (Muller-Jentsch 1995: 61).

RPBs often enable unions to enter the workplace, win elections, and, by effectively representing employees' interests, extend union membership and influence

(Wever 1994; Regalia 1995: 438). In addition, they may also support national-union bargaining objectives—for example, by banning overtime while a new national contract is being negotiated or by organizing demonstrations in support of these objectives (Muller-Jentsch 1995). Indeed union supporters on participative bodies sometimes hold the participation process hostage until the union's demands are met.

An example of hostage-taking occurred in the USA when the Steel Workers' union had developed a smoothly working set of joint participative committees with National Steel at its steel mills. However, relations were far from smooth at the company's mines, which eventually went on strike. To show mill workers' support for the strikers, every time a steel-plant joint committee met, the employee members present raised the issue of the mines and refused to discuss other issues. Eventually the matter was settled when the company CEO resigned.

The national union may assist RPB members in their own negotiations. IG Metall, for example, has developed a series of handbooks for RPB members. Wever (1994) describes a series of German cases in which unions helped RPB members formulate proposals for training, job rotation, job upgrading, and the like. And the councillors involved ascribed their success in part to help from union staff as well as to advice from works councillors from other companies.

Decentralization. A worldwide trend towards decentralized industrial relations is increasing RPBs' power, relative to national unions (Looise 1989; Katz 1993; Walsh 1993; Tchobanian 1995), with the notable exceptions of Norway, Denmark, and Finland. The reasons for this are manifold. Unions have lost members almost everywhere, due in part to a shift away from manufacturing and blue-collar work. Unemployment and growing international trade have made it more difficult for them to preserve uniform industry-wide wage levels and so to take labour costs out of competition. Neo-liberal economic policies have largely disposed of corporatist tripartite bargaining, eliminating one of the peak labour organizations' key roles. Management itself is decentralizing (Streeck 1995).

Also new technology raises numerous issues which are best negotiated at the plant level. These include work structure, incentive pay rates, retraining, work schedules, and, above all, job protection. These 'qualitative' issues are difficult to handle at the national level; at that level the most the parties can achieve are 'frame agreements' which require local implementation.

All these developments are reducing national union opposition to firm- and plant-level decision-making and somewhat increasing RPB influence: 'plant- or firm-level corporatism . . . has replaced tripartite corporatist arrangements at the national level' (Pontusson 1992: 31). Especially in France, as national unions have weakened, participative bodies have helped fill the representation gap, but only somewhat because, as we have discussed, RPBs rely heavily on union support, so the factors that weaken unions may also lead to RPBs being less effective. Moreover, there are still many problems best negotiated at the national level.

RPBs and Local-Union Relations

In most matters the interests of national and local unions are generally the same, but differences do occur. In this section we look specifically at the relationships between local- or branch-level unions and RPBs. Analysis is difficult because in only a few countries (for example, Sweden and the USA) are there institutionally strong, single, enterprise-level local unions. There are competing unions in France, Spain, and Italy, and in countries with single unions, such as Germany, the enterprise-level organization may be institutionally weak.

At one extreme, the local union is non-existent or powerless, or it serves a function other than employee representation (as was the case in former Yugoslavia). When this happens, the RPB may serve as the employees' chief form of representation. In France, when unions are weak on the shop floor or the company refuses to engage in formal bargaining, the Enterprise Council may take over the bargaining role.

At the other extreme, the union and the RPB may be so closely linked that meaningful distinctions are difficult to make. As mentioned earlier, the RPB performs the function of the local union in Austria; there is no separate local union organization (Traxler 1992). By contrast, in Sweden there are no independent RPBs. Much the same result obtains when RPBs serve as the primary forum through which collective bargaining occurs, such as in Spain, where the works council is 'a workplace union organization, pure and simple' (Streeck 1995: 651; see also Escobar 1995).

In between no local union and complete union–RPB identity are situations where local unions and RPBs can be viewed meaningfully as separate bodies. RPBs in Germany, for instance, are legally separate from the union, even though most (but not all) RPB members are elected on a union-nominated slate. In Germany the RPB handles plant-level collective bargaining. Elsewhere whether the local union or the RPB deals with bargaining depends on their respective strengths. There are big differences in every country in the power of shop-floor unions, both absolutely and compared to RPBs. In part this is a function of history. For example, compared with the Netherlands, collective bargaining and shop-floor unions are more important in Belgium and RPBs are weaker, perhaps because Belgium became industrialized earlier (Leisink 1996; Visser 1995; Vilrokx and Van Leemput 1992). Thus the relationship between RPBs and local unions may vary considerably from being quite distant to very close, depending on the relative powers of the two institutions. The range of relationships is discussed below.[13]

Unions ignore RPBs. One approach, once common in Britain (Chell and Cox 1979), was for the union to ignore the participative activity and play no role in it at all. If employees want to participate in RPBs, fine, but this is a matter of no concern to the union, particularly if the RPB keeps its hands off topics subject to collective bargaining.

Unions treat RPBs as rivals. Alternatively the union may treat the RPB as a potential rival and seek to restrict its power and its legitimacy as an employee representative. This kind of relationship was fairly common in Britain, Italy, and the Netherlands forty years ago, when joint consultative committees (in Britain) and works councils (in Italy and the Netherlands) existed alongside increasingly militant stewards (Chell and Cox 1979; Regalia 1995: 429; Visser 1995). Once the stewards and their unions gained substantial strength, joint committees atrophied in Britain (Batstone 1976). By contrast, German works councils quickly co-opted and contained a movement sponsored by militant union members to establish a really independent shop-steward system (Hartmann 1979; Auer forthcoming). 'Today it is no longer control but support of RPB activities that unions expect from' stewards (Muller-Jentsch 1995: 64). Indeed, 'the system of Vertrausensleute has typically evolved into an organizational infrastructure for the works council' (Streeck 1995: 665).

Formal division of responsibilities. Still another alternative is the formal division of responsibilities. In theory, separating distributive from integrative issues makes it possible for the union to handle the first and RPBs the second. Further, separation of functions may reduce the possibility that union leaders will become so closely connected with participative activities that they are co-opted. To take an extreme example of concern with co-option, union leaders were allowed to take only a limited role in Chilean self-management under Allende, purportedly because, 'if the union assumed management functions, then it would cease to lead the workers effectively in the class struggle' (Zimbalist 1976: 50). Similarly in the employee-owned UK bus lines, 'union representatives have . . . sought to avoid co-operative structures . . . which [might] . . . influence operational management decisions', whilst management 'believed it preferable to channel employee demands for greater say primarily through trade unions . . . rather than through direct forms of employee participation' (Pendleton *et al.* 1995: 599–600).

From a very different perspective, a sharp division of functions may prevent the adversarial, divisive zero-sum orientation of bargaining from infecting the more cooperative orientation presumably essential for participation. At one time Kochan, Dyer, and Lipsky (1977: 43) recommended that union and management negotiators should not sit on safety committees 'because essentially different kinds of behaviors are required to make problem-solving work compared to the roles that must be played in contract negotiations'.[14] For the same reasons, McGregor and Knickerbocker (1942) once argued that union stewards should not sit on the Scanlon Plan (joint union–management cooperative) committees.

To maintain separation of functions, US unions frequently negotiate 'shelter agreements'. These provide that the collective-bargaining agreement is not to be superseded except by specific, joint consent. At one time at Xerox, for example, the parties distinguished between 'on-line' topics, which were to be discussed by participation teams, and 'off-line' subjects, which were covered by collective bargaining and therefore outside the team's purview (Kochan *et al.* 1984).

There is some evidence that separation of function has 'proved helpful in the early stages' of participation (Bushe 1988: 145), especially where previous union–management relations were poor. Over time, however, a rigid separation between participative and collective-bargaining issues is difficult to maintain (as it proved at Xerox). All is simple as long as the participative teams confine themselves to purely housekeeping issues. But, once groups begin exploring possible means of cutting costs or making changes in job assignments or pay, they inevitably impinge on matters which relate directly to the heart of US collective bargaining.[15] To control this tendency US unions often establish coordinating bodies (typically joint union and management) whose function is to monitor RPBs' performance to ensure that their activities are consistent with union and management policies (Cutcher-Gershenfeld *et al.* 1991: 14)—in other words, as a unionist put it, 'so they don't give away the store'.

On balance the evidence suggests that participative programmes are more likely to survive if institutions are established which permit issues of possible conflict between collective-bargaining agreements and participative proposals to be squarely faced, with a decision being made to modify either the agreement or the proposal (Eaton 1994).[16] 'Forcibly keeping the two processes [participation and collective bargaining] apart strangles the program' (p. 385). Indeed, most US observers now argue that separation of functions is both undesirable and impossible. Instead, unions should actively participate in determining company strategy.[17]

Rivalries and adjustments. Regardless of the formal relationship, *opportunities* for local union–RPB rivalry are legion especially where, as in some European countries, works councils' members are independently elected and there are several competing unions. To prevent such rivalry, unions in most European countries devote considerable effort to ensure that the leadership of works councils consists of sturdy unionists.[18] As mentioned earlier, most RPB members in Germany are elected on the union slate and most are active unionists (Muller-Jentsch 1995: 135). Indeed, union slates may be elected even if as few as 10 per cent of the workforce are union members (Wever 1994). Similarly in other countries the percentage of union members in works councils is higher than it is in the workforce generally (Regalia 1995: 228; Visser 1995: 104). It is common through much of Europe for local union leaders to serve simultaneously as RPB members—for example, in Spain (Escobar 1995) and Britain (Clegg 1979).

Where there are competing unions, as in France, Belgium, Spain, Italy, and (less so) the Netherlands, it is harder for any one union or for unions generally to control RPBs. Although unions have a legal monopoly of proposing candidates in the first round of French RPB elections (Goetschy and Rozenblatt 1992), recently the percentage of union votes has decreased, especially in small companies (Tchobanian 1995: 140).[19]

However, the fact that a majority of RPB members belong to a union or that they are elected on a union slate does not mean that the union necessarily dominates the RPB or that RPB members put union loyalty first (Visser 1995). When individuals wear two hats, one as union leader and the other as RPB member, they may suffer role conflicts. In Germany, Muller-Jentsch (1995: 64, citing Schmidt and Trinczek 1991) estimates that less than 20 per cent of RPB members see themselves 'primarily as union activists'. For roughly 30 per cent 'the interests of the workforce, and even the firm, come first'. And about half seek to compromise between the conflicting demands, but 'if compromise is impossible, they side with the workforce'.[20]

In practice, adjustments can be made. Indeed the lines between the integrative and distributive functions tend to blur and adversarial and cooperative relations can coexist to a limited degree in most relationships (Walton and McKersie 1965). Eaton (1994: 387) summarizes US research as follows: 'in most cases union–management relations remained adversarial and tense, even as the parties jointly, or management more or less unilaterally, experiments with new participative forms'. Indeed the union may absorb the stress of the adversarial, distributive part of the relationship, leaving the RPB free to pursue integrative channels.

On the other hand, the union may let the RPB handle difficult plant-level problems which might divide the membership, such as distribution of overtime. With regards to these problems, RPBs can take the blame for unpopular decisions, thus shielding unions from workplace militancy (Thelen 1991: 18) and dampen spontaneous workplace actions (Ferner and Hyman 1992: 553). In Germany 'Grievances and local disputes are usually settled by the works council in such a way that the union is relieved of the responsibility of the representation of group interests, allowing the union to concentrate on common interests' such as obtaining wage increases (Muller-Jentsch 1995: 62).

It was partly to avoid union-RPB conflict that UK unions argued for 'single-channel' selection of worker directors, a position supported by the Bullock report (1977), and some UK unions reconsidered their original opposition to having current union officers serving on company boards (BSC Employee Directors 1977).

Even in the USA, where the union appoints 'jointness' (participation) committees, there is, in effect, a dual system of representation, consisting of union stewards and the various 'jointness' committee members. Rivalries between the two may be particularly acute when both offer career ladders for ambitious workers. Some agreements call for union-selected, but company-paid part-time or full-time 'facilitators'. These people may develop interests and approaches which are quite different from those of the old-time, adversarially oriented stewards. Having been trained in consensus-building skills, they often develop political constituencies of their own (Cutcher-Gershenfeld *et al.* 1988; Cutcher-Gershenfeld 1991: 14–15). As a dissident union magazine put it, commenting on the GM relationship:

> Already, many of these facilitators think of themselves as representing the 'joint QWL process' rather than the union . . . The program has expanded chiefly because the company and the union have 'institutionalized' it by rapidly increasing the number of full-time QWL jobs and QWL perks . . . These are especially attractive now that job losses have caused a cutback in the number of union positions. (Parker 1984: 2)

Similar rivalries occur between job involvement specialists in the USA and line-management and industrial-relations departments (Strauss 1989).

RPBs and Direct Participation

The growth of direct participation threatens RPB power if for no other reason than it leads to more flexible work rules and personnel policies. QCs for example, 'provide mechanisms for the resolution of problems . . . previously . . . handled by local collective bargaining or consultation' (Terry 1994: 235). As Turner (forthcoming) puts it, referring to Germany:

> To push decision making about resources allocation down to the shop floor or office level . . . can significantly interfere with the process of co-ordination between the Personnel or HR department and the works council about the terms of resource deployment. For if the shop floor production managers and workers on the shop floor are empowered to negotiate over the shape and movement of internal labour markets, one of the chief issues of negotiation between the works council and HR department is captured at a lower level.

QCs and work teams may be seen as making deals with management which bypass both union and RPBs and violate their policies.[21] At times rank-and-file employees may resist decisions made for them by representative groups.[22] At the highly participative Gaines Dog Food in the USA, 'The norm had developed that employees did not support solutions developed by problem-solving groups in which they had not been directly involved. They reflected a strong preference for "participatory democracy" over a "representative" form of self-government. As a result, committee actions were not truly accepted by the larger work force' (Walton 1980: 226). In some places work teams have become strong enough to be seen as a third source of power (Looise 1989; Wever 1994). Muller-Jentsch (1995: 75) concludes: 'Sooner or later . . . the (German) dual system might give way to a triple system, with sectoral bargaining between trade unions and employer associations, enterprise negotiations between works councils and management, and direct participation by works groups and elected team leaders.'

RPBs feel ambivalence regarding direct participation even when they have originally sponsored the activity themselves. Considerable adjustments may be required. Under what the German metal workers' union calls 'co-determination at the workplace', the RPB's role may change somewhat from that of a negotiator with management to being a consultant to shop-floor work groups, in much the same way as national unions may provide advice to RPBs (Wever, forthcoming).

RPBs and Individual Employees

RPB members run the risk of becoming alienated from the employee constituents they presumably represent. Indeed, as we argued in Chapter 2, there is a danger that employee representatives will develop into a quasi-professional élite apparently clinging to their roles and thus keeping their clienteles in a dependency relationship. There are several reasons for this.

In the first place, as previously mentioned, RPB members are pulled in three directions, towards (1) the immediate interests of their constituents, (2) their national union's policies, and (3) the long-run interests of their employer. For example, German law gives RPBs

> a lever for influencing managerial decision-making to defend the interests of their constituents. On the other hand, being plant-based gives works councils an equally strong incentive to cooperate with managers in the interest of the firm, which of course dovetails with the longer-term interest in the job security of the workers they have been elected to represent . . . [So] works councils tread a fine line between defending the interests of workers and taking into account of the market situation and the economic interests of the firm. The outcome is a balance of conflict and co-operation that varies across plants. (Thelen 1991: 122–3)

In short, RPB members often both represent employees and help run the company. As partners in management, they may be asked to assent to actions that, as employees' representatives, they should oppose. Beyond this, they typically owe some allegiance to their union. In Italy, for example, it was hotly debated whether 'works councillors were to be primarily responsible to the workers who elected them or to the external union or unions' (Regalia 1995: 222).

Many of the issues facing RPB members require technical knowledge which ordinary employees rarely have. Over time these members may become more knowledgeable. But knowledge comes at a price. The more familiar they become with management problems and the more involved they are dealing with them, the less sensitive they may be to their constituents' needs and the more dependent they become on the management which provides their information. Eventually union representatives may see themselves as co-managers, and put the long-run interests of the organization as a whole above the immediate interests of their constituents (Streeck 1984). As Wilpert (1975: 61) explains, the 'professionalization of the representative functions could easily create an estrangement from the constituency. Representatives may now appear part of "them", the upper management' (see also Thorsrud and Emery 1970: 209; Mulder 1971: 36). As some put it, representative participation is 'participation by elites'.

At Saturn 'the relation of the union and the company is so interwoven that many workers begin to perceive the union partners as simply one more face of management' (Shaiken 1995: 264). For example, when a company-appointed co-manager goes on vacation, the union co-manager has sole charge of the department. Understandably when relations are this close, employees may sometimes complain that management is more sympathetic to their grievances than are their own representatives. If joint committees handle substance-abuse problems, as is common in the US auto industry, an aggrieved employee feels he has no recourse if the committee rules against him. Understandably RPB members can easily be charged with selling out to management (Collins 1995).

(Parenthetically it should be noted that the dilemmas just discussed are not unique to RPB members; union leaders are also torn between the often conflicting interests of their national and local unions and the rank-and-file members. Further, they too must balance the short run against the long.)

These problems may be complicated by poor communications. The quality of communications between RPB members and their constituents varies. The relationship is relatively good in the Netherlands, where 40 per cent of the RPBs hold regular meetings with their constituents, while another 40 per cent send out bulletins (Visser 1995: 106). But when such meetings are held in Germany, they are often poorly attended (Adams and Rummell 1977). Reports from other countries (Kolaja 1966: 71; Sachs 1975: Johannesen 1979; Galin 1980: 190) suggest there is often little or no communication at all.

Another problem: RPB members often come from different occupations and reflect different values from the people they represent (Fürstenberg 1978; Batstone 1976: 23–4; Berenbach 1979). Just as do faculty academic senates, RPBs consist of an older established élite. In Germany (Muller-Jentsch 1995: 73), the Netherlands (Visser 1995: 104) and probably elsewhere they tend to be disproportionately better educated, skilled, male, and have long service; by contrast part-time and minority ethnic group may be under-represented[23] (though all this may be changing). An early Norwegian study suggests that those who seek RPB membership may be 'management oriented' and suffer from blocked aspirations for upward mobility (Holter 1965); and in Germany RPB membership may be the first step in a career outside the plant (Adams and Rummel 1977); in the USA it may lead to a management position (Schuster 1984).

The more experience RPB members and management gain in working together, the less they check up on each other and the more likely they assume their interests are mutual. But the assumption of mutuality may block consideration of problems where there is in fact a genuine conflict of interest.

Ironically, representative participation may increase discontent by preventing it from being brought out in the open. Unless discontent is adequately expressed through regular union or participative channels, employees may become alienated from both participation and their union. This may occur particularly in self-managed organizations (Strauss 1982: 230–1). Failure to consider employees' interests as employees, not just as owners, led to strikes in Mondragon (Whyte and Whyte 1992), US 'buyout' firms (e.g. Hammer and Stern 1986), and Yugoslav self-managed companies in the 1970s (Jovanov 1978; Lydall 1989).

Checks and balances. So how can the system be kept responsive to employees' wishes? Perhaps checks and balances are needed. In democracy responsiveness is enhanced by contested elections and competitive political parties. Competition in RPB elections occurs on a regular basis in Belgium, France, Spain, and Italy, where politically or religiously oriented unions vie for employee support—and in Austria, where there are organized factions within a single union. However, since RPB elections in these countries are often fought on the basis of national political issues, they may do little to foster responsiveness to employees' local needs. Even in countries such as Germany, where single-union representation is the rule, incumbent RPB members face frequent electoral opposition.

Contested elections do not necessarily provide adequate representation for minority or individual interests. From the viewpoint of full expression of individual employees' interests a case can be made for separating the participative, integrative function which promotes the long-run interests of the organization as a whole from the ombudsperson function which protects and advocates the often short-run rights of individual employees. Summers (1987: 350) argues that the German works-council system denies employees the kind of aggressive representation of individual rights that a strong adversarial union might provide:

> In lay off cases the American worker participates through his union's negotiation of objective and visible rules, and the union enforces these rules on his behalf. The German worker often has no voice in establishing applicable rules but is subject to the discretion or passivity of works councils over which he has little control. In discharge cases the American worker has a spokesman who vigorously advocates his interest. The German worker has a representative who in most cases opposes his interest. The difference here is rooted largely in the adversary attitude of American unions as contrasted with the non-adversary attitude of German works councils. American union stewards and officers are advocates; German works council members are co-managers.

Though Summers may overstate the extent to which works councils are non-adversarial and non-responsive to their members' interests, the point is relevant. When RPB and union are largely independent of each other, the union may perform the adversarial function. Otherwise a separate institution may be needed to serve employees' individual interests. The Governing Council of the typical Mondragon cooperative is elected by its employee-members, but on an at-large basis. There is a separate Social Council, elected on a plant and departmental basis. The Governing Council represents employees' interests as owners and the Social Council their interests as employees. The Social Council functions somewhat as a combination of a US union and a European works council, bringing grievances to management's attention and negotiating with the Governing Council 'over a broad range of issues' (Whyte and Whyte 1992: 232). When the two bodies are unable to resolve their differences, the final decision is made by the Annual Meeting of all employee members. As Whyte (1967: 25) puts it:

> Since conflicts are an inevitable part of organizational life, it is important that conflict-resolution procedures be built into the design of organizations . . . [Cooperative relationships] do not arise when underlying conflicts of interest are ignored, but rather when the two parties have worked out procedures whereby the problems each face are argued vigorously with each other.

While formal checks and balances may not be required, certainly representative participation increases the need for effective member–leadership communications. As more decisions are made jointly by management and RPBs (or, as in the USA and Sweden, by management and the union), it becomes increasingly important for employee representatives to understand what their constituents want and for the constituents themselves to be familiar with the issues their leadership is facing.

Of course, the danger of RPB co-option may be exaggerated. The high turnout at most Continental European RPB elections, often between 50 and 70 per cent of the eligible voters (Lucio 1992: 570; Vilrokx and Van Leemput 1992: 376; Muller-Jentsch 1995: 74; Regalia 1995: 235; and Visser 1995: 87), suggests both that employees value representative participation and that they believe their ballot makes a difference.

Employer/Union Representation on Boards of Directors

Employee or union representation on firms' boards of directors or supervisory boards is required by law in a number of European countries and in the USA employees are represented on the boards of all major steel companies and many airlines. Further there are employee representatives on the boards of most employee-owned firms, including producer cooperatives, the Israeli kibbutzim, and Mondragon. But who serves as Employee Board Members (EBMs) differs greatly within and between countries. EBMs may be (1) present employees, (2) present full-time local or national union officials, (3) retired officials, or (4) friendly 'outsiders', such as professors or lawyers. Regardless, EBMs face a variety of problems.

Role conflict and uncertainty. Like RPB members, the roles of EBMs are uncertain (Hammer, Currall, and Stern 1991). Are they co-managers, primarily responsible for the firm's welfare, or is their primary job to represent employees' often short-term interests? How should they deal with such issues as retrenchment (Pendleton *et al.* 1995) or union–management negotiations? The practice in Sweden (Brulin 1995) and normally in the USA is for EBMs to absent themselves when labour negotiations are discussed. But this strategy is inconsistent with the alternate view that EBMs' main role is to influence industrial-relations decisions. In any case there are strong, frequently stated expectations that EBMs will represent the organization as a whole, not just their immediate constituents (Thorsrud and Emery 1970; Brannen 1983).

Limited knowledge. As we discuss in our next chapter, a basic dilemma faced by all employee representatives—whether on RPBs or company boards—is that many of the problems faced by participative bodies require technical skills which rank-and-file employees rarely have. In particular, they lack the background to deal with the legal, accounting, marketing, and general-strategy issues which take up much board time. By contrast, union-appointed outsiders may have the technical skills, but typically are unfamiliar with employees' problems and opinions. The answer to limited technical knowledge may be training; unions in a number of countries provide extensive training programmes for their EBMs. The answer to outsiders' lack of familiarity with shop-floor problems is better communications. As EBMs become better informed, their influence increases.

Confidentiality. By custom or rule, board members are expected to keep board deliberations confidential. In theory this could be a major block to communications. Certainly it provides an excuse for those who do not want to communicate. Nevertheless most observers agree that confidentiality is not a serious problem in practice (Strauss 1982).

Rubber-stamp decisions. Despite popular understanding, key decisions in many companies are not made at the board level. Indeed, the board's main function is typically to ratify management's decisions. Since management controls the agenda and the relevant information, it normally controls the results. (If necessary, management representatives can caucus earlier and so transform the official board meeting into a formality.) Top management does most of the talking (Taylor and Snell 1986). As a result, employee directors generally defer to management's expertise (but, *nota bene*, so do other outside directors).

Communications. Failure to communicate back to the rank-and-file employees is commonly cited as a problem. But US experience in the steel industry suggests this problem can be partially overcome. Here a common practice is for EBMs (typically eminent 'outsiders') to meet with the union executive board prior to the directors' meeting and then to report to a union mass meeting once the directors' session is over. And for the benefit of those who do not attend union meetings, EBMs are encouraged to spend time chatting with employees on the shop floor.

Given these problems, what do unions expect to achieve when EBMs constitute only a minority on the board? Among the gains reported are information, the opportunity to ask questions, and a chance to raise concerns. Thus minority board membership is valued for improving upwards and downwards communications, not for participation in decision-making as such.

Conclusion

As methods of employee voice and influence, representative participation and collective bargaining have much in common. Though there are differences in emphasis and symbolism, in practice both contain mixtures of adversarial (distributive) and cooperative (integrative) relations with management.

Representative participation can be viewed as both a substitute and a supplement for collective bargaining. In general, both direct and representative participation are more effective when they have the support of a strong union. But in some instances (especially in France and Italy), where workplace unions are weak, RPBs help fill a representation gap.

The ability of RPBs to exert influence depends to a considerable extent also on their legal and union support. Both unions and law provide 'clout'. True, there have been some instances of successful representative participation in the USA despite its uncertain legal position—and in non-union firms in Britain and elsewhere. However successful, representative participation on a widespread basis seems to require both legal norms and a strong union to ensure that these norms are obeyed.

Union attitudes toward participation vary, depending on a variety of factors. Among these are the union's collective-bargaining relationship with management, the extent to which there are external threats to employment, the extent to which participation is seen as an effective way of saving jobs, and the extent to which participation impinges on already existing collective-bargaining relationships. A key question throughout is whether participation is viewed as weakening or strengthening the union's influence. Often it is seen as a threat.

As we have stressed, RPBs exist in a political world and must coexist with other power centres, especially national and local unions, direct participative bodies, and, above all, management. Unions and RPBs must balance three often-conflicting interests, those of individual workers, the company for which they work, and the industry as a whole. Finally, neither unions nor RPBs perfectly represent their constituents. Both tend to oligarchy, and neither provides much opportunity for individual employees to participate. This requires direct participation.

NOTES

1. *Caveat*: this chapter is written from an Anglo-Saxon perspective, which may emphasize unionism and participation as alternatives rather than as complements or equivalents.
2. Portions of the discussion of participation and democracy are adopted from Strauss 1991; Gallagher and Strauss 1991.
3. Maybe the officers are right. Members want attention to their short-term, immediate problems. Officers may have a better understanding of what is needed for the long-term good of the union membership as a whole (Kelley and Heery 1994). As we discuss later, we run into the same problem again with regards to works councils and ordinary employees. Council members may have a better feel for the long-term survival needs of the organization for which they work.
4. The US distinction between rights and interests should not be confused with the German distinction between topics subject to bargaining and those subject to co-determination, though both distinctions are important.
5. Some US contracts require the employer to pay 'supplemental unemployment benefits' in addition to those provided by the government.
6. The structure of the US grievance handling encourages adversarialism. A US grievance alleges that management broke its promise (the contract). This is a legalistic and often moralistic approach. Understandably it encourages hard feelings. The

many steps through which major grievances go (minor ones may be settled at local levels) are often devoted to sharpening arguments rather than finding solutions.

7. In some countries participation was introduced alongside corporatism and seen as a form of 'micro-corporatism'.
8. Broad banding reduces the number of demarcation disputes, 'yet in British Steel, the erosion of traditional demarcations has challenged the basis of trade union power and control in the steel labour process' (Bacon *et al.* 1996: 38).
9. According to Turner (1991), opposition to cooperation is often led by younger militants and by older employees who oppose giving up their privileges.
10. This is not to argue that without strong union backing RPBs serve no function at all. Particularly in France, Italy, and Germany, RPBs fill the representation gap which occurs when local-level unions are weak or badly divided (Regalia 1995).
11. The IDE group (1981*b*; 1993) makes the important distinction between '*de jure* power' and '*de facto* influence'. However, for the purposes of their analysis, works councils and 'union representative bodies' are lumped together into a single category, 'permanent representative bodies at the establishment level'. Unfortunately this study tells us relatively little about the relative powers of unions and RPBs, to the extent that these two can be distinguished.
12. Of course, works councillors, in their capacity as union leaders, can provide strike leadership (for example, see Turner, forthcoming). According to Streeck (1995: 676), most informal strikes in Germany are more or less openly led by works-council members. And it was works councils, rather than the official union branch, which led the German counterpart to the French demonstrations of 1968.
13. Marchington (1994) suggests a somewhat similar typology.
14. Basing their opinions on US experience, Kochan (and most other US observers) now believe that separation of function is both undesirable and impossible. Instead, unions should take an active part in facilitating participation.
15. 75 per cent of QWL programmes deal with matters subject to collective bargaining (Cohen-Rosenthal 1980; Sockell 1984).
16. Eaton (1994) found that the existence of formal rules regarding the relationship between participative programmes and collective bargaining did not increase programme viability.
17. By contrast, Looise (1989, as cited in Leisink 1996: 82) argues that in the Netherlands 'the relationships between unions and works councils have grown increasingly tense because of the unclear demarcation of responsibilities'. He prefers the Belgian model with its 'a clear division of labour' (Leisink 1996: 82).
18. According to Hancke (1993), unions have been more successful in 'colonizing' works councils in Germany, Belgium, and Sweden than they have been in the Netherlands, France, or Italy.
19. Nevertheless, despite a fall in union membership through much of the world, the percentage of votes cast for union candidates in works council elections appears to remain fairly constant (Terry 1994).
20. There has been a variety of schemes to catalogue the roles of works-council members. For example, as adversary (who puts the members' immediate interests first); as co-manager (responsible for the organization's long-run welfare); and as an expert on shop-floor matters and workers' opinions (which is the most that most paternalistic employers want). Bothe (1987) distinguished among three roles: conflict oriented, passive, and appeasement oriented. According to Bothe, the conflict-oriented provided

more effective representation. Collins (1995) distinguishes among participation supporters, opponents, and fence sitters.

21. Cutcher-Gershenfeld and Verma (1994) argue that coordination between direct and representative participation is easier in the USA and Canada than in Continental Europe because of the closer integration between US–Canadian steward structures and their local and national unions.
22. See the classic Coch and French (1948) experiment in which groups which engaged in complete (direct) participation adjusted more rapidly to workplace changes than did those with representative participation.
23. Muller-Jentsch (1995: 73) reports that foreign workers see German works councils 'as mainly representing the interests of the German workforce or the employer' and further that works councils 'often tacitly approve "soft" discriminatory measures aimed at filtering out foreign workers'.

5. Playing the Devil's Advocate: Limits to Influence Sharing in Theory and Practice

Playing the devil's advocate, we will now explore the varied evidence on problems associated with the democratization of organizational life over the last half century. It will be shown that organizational democracy has spread very slowly, if at all, and has had many setbacks. The literature is full of contrasts. There is near euphoria about the achievements of employee involvement and similar influence-sharing measures in some circumstances and despondency in others. It is not easy to come to a balanced judgement, because the variability of circumstances under which different forms of participation operates is considerable.

This chapter sets out to find and explore the shadow side of organizational developments trading under a variety of names, such as participation, involvement, influence- and power-sharing, industrial democracy, self-management, and empowerment, to name only the best known. Conforming to our overall plan, we will use the term 'participation' to describe the variety of influence-sharing phenomena, although occasionally other terms are used to specify particular variations.

The first part of the chapter deals with the theoretical considerations that set limits to the distribution of influence and power in organizations, in particular resistance to change, dependency needs, inauthentic participation, and some aspects of economic theory. In the second part we give research evidence in support of the shadow side—that is to say, findings and interpretations of evidence bearing out the expectations raised by the theoretical considerations demonstrating many obstacles to genuine and effective participation. Looked at by itself, the research evidence comes to pessimistic conclusions. First, the total amount of participation—that is, influence—given to lower levels of organizations is very limited and in general, people want more than they get. Secondly, even where fairly extensive participation schemes are in operation, they do not always fully deliver the promised benefits.

Of course, this is only one side of the story. There are many theoretical models which anticipate favourable outcomes and elsewhere we cover this material. Furthermore, it must be recognized that success or failure is a function of expectations and, when academics as well as practitioners set very idealistic goals, disappointment is an almost inevitable consequence. For this reason we believe that an exploration of the limit of what participation is likely to achieve, and the circumstances under which it is most likely to fail, will help us to set up more realistic expectations.[1]

Overall, the findings justify caution rather than despondency. After all, political democracy took a long time to establish itself and has suffered many well-documented setbacks right up to the present.

Chapter 6, and to some extent Chapter 7, will have a look at the overall evidence to see whether one can discover positive as well as negative contingencies. After all, where there is shadow, there must also be light.

Theoretical Limits to Power Diffusion

To help understand, and perhaps overcome, the problems described in the second part of this chapter, it is necessary to give some of the principal theoretical reasons which currently limit the democratizing process in organizations.

Resistance to Change

In spite of early attempts by a few pioneers like Robert Owen, most medium- and large-scale modern organizations were built on very centralized hierarchies and had established routinized and outwardly successful patterns of top-down communication and command structures. Generations of owners and managers were brought up to regard benevolent autocracy as the appropriate way to run business organizations. To move away from this established equilibrium requires a very special effort. We know from the extensive literature on change that equilibria are difficult to disestablish and that the process comes up against powerful resistances.

In some individual cases the transition from autocracy to a variety of organizational forms where influence is more widely distributed can be achieved by deliberate intra-organizational processes, as for instance in the formation of the Scott Bader Commonwealth (Hoe 1978) or the democratization of the Glacier Metal Company (Jaques 1951; Wilfred Brown 1960). In the case of Scott Bader, the founder of the business was a devout Christian who, after a prolonged strike of his workforce, came to the conclusion that he no longer wished to be the sole owner. In the Commonwealth he created, every employee became formally a part owner[2] and two potentially participative decision-making councils were set up. The Managing Director of the Glacier Metal Company, Wilfred Brown, was a very unusual person. He combined intellectual and socio-political interests (he was for a time a Minister in the British Labour Government) with a very sympathetic attitude to social science which led him to engage a psychoanalytically oriented consultant, Elliot Jaques from the Tavistock Institute in London, to help introduce a participative–humanistic organization (Jaques 1951).

These two well-documented cases, while not unique, are examples of substantial structural and to a lesser extent behavioural changes consequent on a policy decision by a Chief Executive Officer (CEO). In both cases the CEO stayed on the scene for sufficiently long to consolidate the structural changes and in both cases these changes survived the death of the founder for a number of years.[3] More usually, however, the break-up of a given equilibrium has to wait until powerful external agents force the pace of change—such as wars or political pressures reinforced by laws (like the various industrial democracy schemes in Europe). Alternatively, change is precipitated by the impact of economic pressures (such as competition from Japan or technological changes which require decentralized decision structures and more flexible work patterns).

Charismatic leadership is sometimes credited with the role of change agent, as in the case of Lee Iacocca, who helped to rescue the Chrysler Corporation but then, to win government and union support, had to invite the trade-union leader, Douglas Fraser, to join the Chrysler board. This certainly set a new precedent in the USA, but it is doubtful whether the gesture would have been made if Chrysler had not been on the brink of collapse. Unfavourable economic conditions similarly helped Lynn Williams, recently retired President of the US Steel Workers, to succeed in a personal crusade and put union representatives on the boards of steel companies. In most cases, the democratization achieved by leaders is combined with one of the external levers, like economic competition or changes of technology, and even then the changes do not always last and rarely penetrate deep into the bowels of the organization.

These various examples point to a very powerful, but often neglected explanation of resistance to change based on equilibrium theory and supported by biological and evolutionary research. All living beings thrive on stability, continuity, and predictability and have a natural tendency to oppose any force which attempts to upset what biologists call homeostasis. For the social sciences, this explanation of resistance to change has been well explained by Schön (1971) and is extensively documented (J. A. C. Brown 1963; Staw 1982; Staw and Ross 1985; Holden 1987). One recent analysis by two experienced researchers has come to the conclusion that, in general, claims by consultants and change agents of having achieved lasting and successful reforms are greatly exaggerated, while evolutionary changes in response to changing conditions can be documented everywhere (Brunsson and Olsen 1993).

The need for stability and continuity coupled with human ingenuity for rationalization allows resistance to take on an enormous variety of forms from the banal to the very sophisticated. Here we will give only one example derived from one of the oldest but still quite topical arguments against organizational participation. It is based on the dictum that 'management must manage'. The evidence in support of this dictum is weak and derives from the uncontentious knowledge that all organizations of any size have a hierarchy (Abell 1979). However, even in a multi-tier hierarchy, it is perfectly possible to distribute decision-making and influence so that every level has a measure of discretion and a degree of autonomy over some aspects of the organization's task. Moreover, in Chapter 2 and again below we give evidence that managerial prerogative theory lacks empirical support. In fact, as we shall see, employees' desire for more participation is very limited.

Furthermore the kind of issues employees are interested in (apart from remuneration, which is the subject of bargaining rather than participation) are routine decisions—for instance, over holiday timing or the layout of work, rather than tactical or strategic issues, which are rarely challenged.

Among the reasons why participation is often resisted is the belief that it leads to embarrassing levels of conflict, and most managers prefer harmonious, uncontested relationships. However, the evidence is far from clear and depends on whether one equates conflict with disagreements or even exploration of differences. Almost by definition, participation in a decision-making process, or even participation in a forum where information is shared, will allow people to ask questions and to voice opinions. It is unrealistic to expect all questions to be uncontentious and all opinions to be identical or favourable. The research evidence, in fact, suggests that participation allows disagreements to increase (IDE 1981*b*). But there is also evidence that, when participation works well, disagreements are resolved smoothly (Heller *et al.* 1988: 218–19) and that a fair measure of disagreement in decision-making processes can be a sign of organizational health since it reduces the opportunity for Groupthink (Janis 1982).

Dependency and Skills

Another obstacle to employee participation is employees' sense of dependence. Bowlby describes the origins of attachment in an emotional relationship, in the first place usually to the mother, as the prototype for later relationships. He calls this 'libidinization'. If the early relationships were satisfactory, they produce a sense of being valued, tolerance, and a cooperative attitude. Even so, cooperation has costs; it requires denial, reduction, or postponement of immediate private interests of individuals. For many people and in many situations it is therefore easier to use the libidinization energy only for the in-group, reinforced by a denial of equality to the out-group. Bowlby (1946) also explores the relationship between democracy and psychoanalytic theory. He starts from the proposition that cooperation between individuals is not easily achieved because it always requires a sacrifice of private goals. This conflict can be observed in small children playing with a ball. The tendency is to keep the ball to themselves until they slowly learn to give it up when they become aware of the pleasure of a game of catch. Cooperation, once established, creates in-group feelings and dependency, which in turn produce hostility towards non-group members.

Bowlby was also one of the first to see a further limit to democracy in the inequality of technical knowledge among people in organizations. When tasks and the formulation of goals are complex, groups must be guided by leaders because, as in the modern army, the necessary skills can only be mastered by some. Here Bowlby fails to distinguish between influencing choices about ends which can be made by the public in general, and choosing the means to the end, which may well require considerable expertise (Bowlby 1946).

Mace (writing in the same year as Bowlby) also sees democracy limited by lack of ability and differential needs: 'The optimum distribution of responsibility and power . . . would seem to be that in which each man enjoys responsibility and power in accordance with his capacity and needs' (Mace 1946: 22). This limitation due to lack of competence has been extensively neglected in later decades, but has recently re-emerged. It has already been referred to in previous chapters and will come up again later in this chapter. Dependency can be created by lack of skill.

Dependency needs and dependency behaviour are explained by theories from social psychology and psychoanalysis, which differ in their attribution and causality but attempt to account for well-documented phenomena. Dependency can be analysed at different levels, from the individual via a group, to social class, or even economic–political entities. Miller (1993: 270–1), for instance, sees a relationship between entrenched social welfare institutions, as in Great Britain starting at the end of the Second World War and continuing into the 1970s, and the dependency behaviour and lack of initiative of large groups of citizens. Institutions create dependency through acculturation, reinforced by the growth of large corporations, on the one hand, and relatively powerful trade unions, on the other. The individual abrogates his autonomy and self-reliance in favour of the succour and protection afforded him by various outside support systems.

On the level of the individual, Miller accepts that a degree of dependency is realistic given role differentiation along hierarchical boundaries, but those who control the boundaries tend to assume more power and prestige than the role requires. Inevitably, without some counterbalancing structures—like participation—the dependency culture grows and establishes roots which resist displacement or extirpation.

East Germany provides a good testing ground for this theory. Is it really true that when Easterners became united with the West they were unwilling or unable to take initiatives and preferred to be told what to do, if not what to think? This was certainly the popular perception in what was formerly West Germany. It was tested by Frese, Erbe-Heinbokel, Grefe, Rybowiak, and Weike (1994) and Frese, Kring, Soose, and Zempel (1996), whose findings support the assumption that members of the former German Democratic Republic (GDR), compared with samples of the West German population, were less inclined to take initiatives. Dependency theory would fit this evidence very well. It would forcefully demonstrate what forty-five years of top-down, highly centralized dirigism can achieve in creating dependency thought habits and compliant behaviour. In the West, dependency symptoms have to be seen against a background of a culture which emphasizes independence and individuality and would judge a high degree of dependency as deviant. The case of Japan, as we shall see in a later section of this chapter, is different. There, it is claimed, dependency is a fairly central cultural characteristic and some would argue that it has had positive consequences for Japan.

Dependency theory, then, is one way to explain why people who are given the opportunity to participate, to take initiatives, or to change over to more autonomous working conditions frequently refuse to take on the extra responsibility this entails.

Inauthentic Participation and Voluntary Non-Participation

Apart from dependency theory, several other explanations for voluntary non-participation have been put forward, but few are research based. McCarthy (1989) starts by quoting Leitko, Greil, and Peterson (1985), who take the pessimistic view that 'Non-participation is the modal response of workers to worker participation schemes' (p. 285). However, empirical evidence is difficult to obtain and most researchers in the area of social science are 'strong advocates of participation . . . (and) are reluctant to provide evidence which might diminish enthusiasm for participation' (McCarthy 1989: 125).

Neumann (1989) pursues a number of theoretical arguments and possible explanations for non-participation. Most human-resources management, for instance, is based on assumptions about hierarchy, leadership behaviour, control mechanisms, and motivation, which are not supportive of participative practices. Participation schemes often run parallel to the main decision-making processes, deal with less crucial issues, and therefore fail to show what influence-sharing behaviour could achieve. More subtly, our whole socialization process, which we imbibe from the nursery and throughout the education system, assigns highly differentiated roles to people—teaches some to be active and take initiatives, while others take on more dependent, subordinate roles which are difficult to shake off later in life.

Marchington and Loveridge (1979) try to identify the real and voluntary constraints that limit the involvement of employees in the decision process. They identify two constraints as seen by management. One is the time element and the claim that there are many decisions that have to be taken quickly and cannot wait on the necessarily time-spaced schedule of consultative meetings. The second constraint is the problem of 'the interference by allegedly non-qualified individuals in decisions that are felt to require management's expertise' (p. 172). There are, of course, occasions when non-participation becomes mandatory—for instance, during crises.

The qualification issue has already been mentioned in the work of Bowlby and Mace and will be supported by extensive further evidence below. The time-constraint argument, except for crises, is weak for two reasons. One is the well-documented evidence of the Japanese consensus management and their *ringi seido* system, both being time consuming but highly efficient (Misumi 1984). It is also worth distinguishing influence-sharing on basic aims and objectives, for which time constraint is not an issue, and an implementation of these agreed policies which may sometimes require quick or even hasty decisions.

Disillusionment with participation leading to frustration and a withdrawal from participation can be traced to pseudo or inauthentic participation, which has been widely observed (Argyris 1951, 1970; Verba 1961; Miles 1965; Etzioni 1969;

Pateman 1970; Heller 1971; Hopwood 1976; Hickson *et al.* 1986; McCarthy 1989). There are various inauthentic managerial tactics to participation, but they all avoid genuine influence-sharing. A phrase very widely used by management as well as by some social scientists is 'creating a feeling of participation'. March and Simon (1958: 54), for instance, argue that what they call 'felt participation' is an important variable, and, however it is achieved, its effect is in many respects equivalent to actual participation. French, Israel, and Ås (1960) go even further. They use the term 'psychological participation' to refer to a person's perception of the amount of influence he or she has on jointly made decisions and emphasize the difference between 'psychological' and 'objective' participation, but then go on to say that 'whenever perception appears accurate, the amount of psychological participation is equivalent to the amount of objective participation' (p. 4).

With the support of such eminent social scientists, it is not surprising that managers often choose the easy option of creating a feeling rather than the reality of participation. It is an easy option, because management does not give up its prerogative but nevertheless hopes to achieve the alleged advantages of participation. There are at least three advantages widely canvassed in the popular literature. One is to conform to the image of a modern progressive manager; secondly, it is believed that participation reduces resistance to change; and, thirdly, according to the Human Relations and Human Resources models, participation leads to greater job satisfaction and higher productivity.

However, the easy option has been challenged. Hopwood (1976) criticizes managers who induce a feeling of participation in situations which provide little freedom (p. 72), but he admits that 'there is no doubt that participation can be counterfeited and, prior to its detection, it may lead to higher morale' (p. 82). A tougher line is taken by Hickson, Butler, Gray, Mallory, and Wilson (1986), who criticize the use of a procedure sometime called 'quasi-decision-making' which attempts to give a measure of dignity to a process of involvement that really amounts to 'a charade because the decision has effectively already been made' (p. 52). Etzioni (1969) uses the term 'inauthentic participation' and predicts that this type of deception on employees will not remain undetected, which then inevitably leads to conflict.

During field research among senior levels of management, Heller (1971) finds evidence of manipulative participation which came to light when the results of decision-style analysis were fed back to the group of managers who had supplied the data. It soon became obvious that quite a number of managers had interpreted 'prior consultation' as discussions with subordinates at a time when the decision had already been taken (p. 63). Similar deception was detected when managers described 'joint decision-making'. In the discussion they were asked 'What if the decision comes out against what you want?'; the answer of one manager speaking for many was 'That's why you are there, that's your job, that's why you are there.' In this way manipulation was justified by reference to the managerial role.

Since this research was carried out with both the boss and his most senior immediate subordinate, it was possible to show that March and Simon's and French, Israel, and Ås's argument that deceptive participation comes to the same thing as actual participation is not correct in this sample of senior managers in large American companies. Subordinates expressed frustration and hostility towards various forms of inauthentic behaviour and this was borne out in a much larger eight-country comparative study using a similar feedback method (Heller and Wilpert 1981).

The evidence suggests that inauthentic decision-making is not a new phenomenon and it seems to have been strengthened by the increasingly pervasive management education and development programmes which proselytise the participative philosophy (see also Alvesson 1993).

One of the main dynamic factors behind inauthentic influence-sharing was observed in the classic Miles (1964) study, as well as in Haire, Ghiselli, and Porter's (1966) fourteen-country study on Managerial Thinking and in several other studies reported by Argyris (1970: 62–3). Managers espouse the virtues of participative management for a variety of reasons, but they do not trust their subordinates to have the necessary capacity or judgement to make useful contributions to the decision process. Argyris has shown again and again that these espoused values frequently bear no relationship to reality and the kind of learning required to move from espousal to reality has to penetrate deeply entrenched resistances.

The Need for Competence

The sociological analysis in Chapter 3 begins with a discussion of the division of labour and the consequent and apparently unavoidable differentiation in the distribution of information in relation to manual as well as intellectual work. As complexity increases, differentiation becomes more noticeable and produces what we have called a gradient of inequality among members of organizations.

Although the division of labour is central to the work of many eminent scholars, including Frederick Winslow Taylor, Emil Durkheim, Max Weber, and Chester Barnard, the consequences of the unequal distribution of experience and skill on the participative potential of individuals and hierarchical groups has not always been recognized. On the contrary, egalitarian assumptions pervade most of the theories and research on participation. They are derived from the long and bitter political struggle to achieve a universal franchise for all men and women above a certain age. Equal voting rights for all is the foundation stone for political democracy, and it seemed sensible to extend this principle, without discrimination, to the place of work, the division of labour notwithstanding.

Somehow the transmutation of the egalitarian principle from politics to work has not been as successful as had been hoped. Increasingly in recent years the literature has thrown up doubts and caveats, several of which have been raised in previous chapters. We have already mentioned the reservation of Mace (1946) and Marchington and Loveridge (1979), who thought that democracy can be achieved only when people have adequate ability. Similarly Bowlby (1946) believed that it is difficult to sustain democracy when technical knowledge is unequally distributed, and when tasks are very complex; in these circumstances, only some will fully master them, and this, he thought, was an adequate justification for hierarchy. A careful reading of the literature shows that comments of this kind occur frequently but are usually embedded in evidence or arguments which are focused on a different topic. It is possible that the submerged nature of this evidence is due to an understandable reluctance to specify limits to the democratic potential at the place of work; it could be seen as discrimination against people who, at a given time, lack appropriate experience or skill. It is safer to stay with assumptions based on the analogy derived from political science.

However, gradually, evidence has built up to show that the decision processes and issues at work are different from political processes and issues to which universal franchise applies. One difference is in the language used. Accountants, economists, marketing managers, engineers, and even human-resources specialists have developed vocabularies that do not appear on television and radio or in non-technical newspapers. These specialized vocabularies are often embedded in turgid sentence constructions and form obstacles to communication in consultative or decision-making meetings. Secondly, it seems that many organizational issues are highly complex and require technical knowledge and experience—for instance of civil, commercial, and criminal law, taxation, investment, and city finance, as well as specialized technologies and statistical interpretations. The rate of change in some of these subjects has been considerable, so that even experienced managers frequently have to seek advice from specialists. Management consultants are called in to provide esoteric knowledge or to give second opinions.

One way to make the necessary know-how available for formal participative structures is to give employee representatives the right to engage consultants. This has received legal support in Norway, Sweden, and Germany and could play an increasingly important part in enriching the democratic process. So far it seems to have played a very limited role. One well-documented case suggests that employee representatives are sometimes reluctant to seek outside help. A three-year study in twelve German companies investigated the introduction of Computer Integrated Manufacturing (CIM) and the associated Computer-Aided Production and Management (CAPM) system. These changes are meant to increase flexibility of production to respond to market needs, but they will also impinge on the social system of the factory. What role does participation play in such circumstances? Being in a high-technology industry, employees were technically competent in the pre-CIM methods. The demands imposed by the new system, however, were quite different, and the investigator came to the conclusion that the project has 'become so complex in its technical and social interpretation that it would be senseless even to consider that an individual shop-steward could assimilate all these modernization measures entirely by way of plant information and advanced training . . . Thus the need arises for a division of labour within the works council, implying specialization' (Hildebrandt 1989: 189). However, although the works council was given early and extensive information, it was, in the event, unable to exert any influence, as mentioned in Chapter 4. The Works Constitution Act gives German works councils the legal right to engage scientific experts at the cost of the company. This would obviously have been a great help to the elected representatives and it was therefore astonishing to find that no external scientific experts were consulted in any of the twelve plants studied in this research (p. 189). Hildebrandt is aware that, in comparison with other countries, works councils in West Germany are given a high level of formal influence through the co-determination laws. His own detailed investigation, however, 'leads to the conclusion that their access to the re-organization of planning, steering and control functions is slight' (p. 186).

It is not surprising that the escalation in the requirement for depth and variety of competence has led to difficulties in establishing or maintaining democratic participative structures in spite of training programmes for union leaders—for instance, in Norway (Gustavsen 1986), Sweden, and Germany (Eiger 1986), and India (Virmani 1986). The competence deficit applies as much to representative as to direct participation and somewhat more to senior level structures. A substantial investment in creating appropriate experience and training is required, but the available evidence suggests that, with few exceptions, skill development to support participation has received inadequate attention. For instance, the two major British experiments of having trade-union representatives at board-room level in the steel industry and the post office were preceded by only token efforts to prepare people for their new responsibilities (Brannen *et al.* 1976; Batstone *et al.* 1983; Brannen 1983). See also Chapter 4.

The problem of reconciling influence with competence has been recognized by Wilfred Brown and Elliot Jaques, respectively the Managing Director and Social Science consultant of the Glacier Metal Company who devised a policy of joint consultation for all levels of the organization for the purpose of making policy, but left it to line management to execute that policy. This alleged solution has a number of problems; to begin with it assumes that policy-making requires no competence, or less than implementation; Child (1976) also points out that values enter into policy as well as into the execution of policy, and, if values of the executive system are substantially different from the values of the consultative system, serious distortion will result. Nevertheless, this approach seems to have worked quite well at this company over more than thirty years (Wilfred Brown 1960; Heller 1986: 131–2). A similar distinction is made by Branco Horvat (1983), who talks of two different spheres of activities: one relates to interests and is enshrined in policy; the other relates to professional work and administrative routines. 'Policy decisions are legitimised by political authority, executive and administrative work by professional authority. The former represents value judgements, the latter represents technical implementation. In the interest sphere, the rule "one man one vote" applies; in the professional sphere vote is weighted by professional competence' (Horvat 1983: 281).

Let us also remember evidence presented earlier. Chapters 2 and 3 have presented theory as well as rapidly growing evidence of the need to pay much more attention than previously to the crucial role of competence (skill and experience). In Chapter 2 we argued that competence was a necessary precondition for effective participation, but, at the same time, that existing reservoirs of competence will remain underused unless the decision process gives people access and involvement. Furthermore, through participation employees can become more interpersonally competent, and, finally, the various interactions between competence, influence, and skill utilization create motivational energy. Yetton and Crawford (1992) show that participation among managers is used inauthentically and therefore ineffectively because people lack the necessary skills. Obradović (1975) carefully documented the limitations of the Yugoslav system of self-management, which, like Democratic Dialogue (a concept we discuss later), falsely assumes that everybody is capable of engaging in discourse and decision procedures. The history and development of the kibbutz movement shows that success in the early days coincided with high motivation and above average levels of ability (Helman 1992). The failure to recognize competence as an antecedent to effective participation comes out particularly strongly in Scandinavian work, where the justification for democratic strategies as a way of improving a country's competitive strength is likened to the strength of the Athenian society and their egalitarian, communicative, and participative system, 'which made it possible to bring up to 40,000 people . . . into one and the same discussion . . . ensure support for decisions and a high motivation to carry them through from everybody . . .' (Gustavsen 1992: 120). Were the Athenians supermen, all equally capable of understanding the political–philosophic issues and complex strategic decisions to which they gave assent and participated in defending with their own lives? If so, we are lesser mortals today.

There is some preliminary evidence that motivation, competence, and trust are interrelated. We have seen that managers who have doubts about the competence of their subordinates are reluctant to involve them in decision-making (Miles 1964; Haire *et al.* 1966; Heller and Wilpert 1981; Yetton and Crawford 1992; Koopman *et al.* 1993). If they involve them in spite of doubts about their competence or their adherence to common values and goals, participation is inauthentic. Inauthentic participation is associated with frustration, poor motivation, and low trust.

Few would deny that trust is an essential precondition for successful participatory practices and we have just reviewed some relevant evidence to show that it is frequently absent. In the next section we will describe important economic theories based on the notion of distrust.

It is difficult to know which of these factors comes first; few studies trace processes over time to establish causal relationships, but the DIO research we have mentioned provides some preliminary evidence that the utilization of existing skills is contingent on trust and is an outcome of power-sharing. Motivation in the form of satisfaction with the process as well as with the results of participation is best treated as a consequence of the participation–skill utilization process (see, for instance, Koopman *et al.* 1993: 118, 126–8).

We sum up this section by arguing that the literature on the relationship between competence and participation is quite compelling, but, for whatever reason, and perhaps because of the role democracy plays in the social-science paradigm, the academic community has been slow to realize the critical part competence plays as a necessary input to effective participation. What we need is a new theoretical model which, *inter alia*, postulates that relevant competence (experience, skill, etc.) has to precede effective influence- and power-sharing (Heller 1992*a*).

The Economists' Point of View

Economists have a set of theories which, if valid, might also explain why participation would be resisted. Over the last few decades, economists have become interested in applying their models to an analysis of organizational behaviour. Several aspects of their theory would make economists and managers, as well as shareholders who share their assumptions, resist participative structures. The economists' approach is quite distinct from that of the behavioural social sciences, such as anthropology, sociology, and psychology, which derive their understanding of social reality from painstaking field investigations. Economics tends to be more deductive, starting with assumptions about the nature of men and women and deriving from this logically consistent models which can be, but frequently are not, tested in real life. A very large and intellectually challenging field, called 'managerial economics', has grown up and has put forward advice to policy-makers. Three of its concepts can be related to participation and would predict negative consequences for influence-sharing behaviour. All three are based on similar highly debatable assumptions about motivation and behaviour. Agency Theory assumes that employees, and managers in particular, have different interests from owners, such as shareholders, who are called principals. Agents and principals, like all humans, are rational and want to maximize their own interests, but, since these interests diverge, agents will cheat and deceive, and principals will try to control the agents' opportunistic and responsibility-shirking behaviour. Distrust is therefore a necessary aspect of all relations between principals and agents. Donaldson (1990) has called this a narrow model of human behaviour. There is no reason why the distrust between agents and principals should be confined to senior staff, although they are the more powerful players; a sustained climate of distrust fortified by various control mechanisms will percolate through a whole organization and inhibit or prevent the free and frank interchange between groups on which consultative and influence-sharing democratic structures have to be built.

The 'free-rider' concept in economics (Olsen 1971) argues that people shirk the responsibility of participating in decision-making meetings because they realize that their personal contribution to the final outcome is minimal and they prefer to use their time to pursue more personal goals; instead, they rely on 'free riding' on the hard work of a minority of activists who like to spend their time in participative meetings. It would follow that voluntary attendance is low and Olson gives the example of trade-union meetings where over 90 per cent do not attend but nevertheless behave perfectly rationally in so doing.

More generally, Olson does not believe that groups of individuals obtain any substantial benefit by trying to organize themselves to achieve some common objective. Rational individuals will not take part in such collective action, certainly not if the groups are large, because they realize that their own input has little effect on the final outcome. Although the theory was designed to apply to large-scale democratic institutions, such as trade unions and political parties, it could be applied to multinationals and other fairly large organizations, and therefore, for instance, to German works councils and plenary meetings of the former Yugoslav self-management boards. Since collective action does occur, Olson has to find an explanation. He believes there are two. First, there is coercion—for instance, by some enabling legislation, such as the 1935 Wagner Act in the USA or various industrial democracy legislation in Europe. Secondly, there is the option of providing some plausible incentive for people to attend; trade unions, for instance, provide what he calls 'private goods' such as legal advice services or pension schemes.

Evidence in support of the 'free-rider' phenomenon is patchy and Abrahamsson (1993), in examining this thesis, finds no difficulty in demonstrating its inadequacy as far as Sweden, Norway, and Austria are concerned. Within the sphere of collective action, is the American culture so radically different from the European one as to justify the 'free-rider' thesis? Or is it simply one of many bold but unsubstantiated economic theses?

The theory of transaction-cost economics goes back to the 1930s but lay dormant for nearly forty years because economists were not interested in examining what happens at the level of organizations, preferring to concentrate their analyses at the macro-level of the total economy. When the progenitor of the theory was given the Nobel Prize for Economics, it was no longer possible to downgrade attention to the micro-level of organizational analysis (Coase 1991: 63). The discovery of the importance of costs other than those for land, labour, and capital—namely, the costs of time and effort spent on making contracts among agents and supervising the fulfilment of these contracts—was an early critique of the invulnerability of the market as the basic mechanism of exchange and determination of prices. As Coase (1991) says, 'All that was needed was to recognize that there were costs of carrying out market transactions and to incorporate them into the analysis, something which economists had failed to do' (p. 48). He also drew attention to the fact that since markets were essentially about determining costs and prices, they existed within organizations as well as between them (p. 55).

Unfortunately, and probably unnecessarily, transaction-cost economics is permeated by the same assumptions about human motivation as agency and free-rider theory. Coase sees the achievement of quality in the transaction of goods and services as equivalent to the risk of being defrauded. He also explains the organization's choice of integrating operations within the firm compared with subcontracting as a choice based on the differential risk of fraud, and he gives the example of somebody profiting by substituting material of inferior quality (p. 58).

Furthermore, and from the point of view of participation more importantly, transaction-cost theory has been used to argue that organizations that seek to reduce hierarchy and establish consultative participatory structures will incur greater transaction costs than traditional non-participatory firms. If the market works as it should, this will produce an incentive for companies to avoid participation. Williamson (1980) in pursuing this argument goes so far as to suggest that, if employees want to have influence-sharing forums, they will have to accept a lower wage to compensate for the higher transaction cost. It is an extraordinary argument and could, of course, apply to any set of regular meetings at any organizational level, including the board of directors. We have not yet come across a suggestion that, in companies that hold frequent and prolonged board meetings, directors should accept reduced compensation.

Many arguments pushed to an extreme become nonsensical or unfeasible. Moreover, Williamson neglects or is not convinced by what can be called the 'transaction gain' of participative information-sharing meetings, or by the improvement in efficiency and quality of decisions carried out through influence-sharing procedures. There is an enormous literature on this subject, some of which we review in this book, which has not been evaluated by managerial economics.

Summary

So far in this chapter we have reviewed a range of theories, evidence, and arguments which suggest that there are obstacles to fully and universally functioning schemas of organizational democracy. There is first of all the socio-biological resistance based on a universal need for continuity, predictability, and safety. Change, particularly rapid or artificially induced change—for instance, through fashions disseminated by consultants—disturbs the socio-biological equilibrium.

A need for dependency among adults, while not universally strong, is a function of existing social structures in families, schools, class, and gender arrangements and is perpetuated in most organizations. These structures explain why people frequently fail to take up participative opportunities. Another reason for refusing to take up apparent offers to participate in some aspect of organizational life is a perception of the inauthenticity of the offer. Asking people to take part in discussions on decisions that have already been taken or, for whatever reason, cannot or will not be changed is often cited under this heading.

Participation will be ineffective, and, if not ineffective, inauthentic, if attempts are made to include people in the process of participation without the necessary antecedent preparation through relevant experience and training. Where competence exists, participation will allow it to become effective and thereby increase the quality of decisions, but its absence stultifies participation.

Finally, participation in decision-making will be resisted by people who accept the theoretical postulates of economists on human motivation and the high cost and low benefit of a democratic dialogue.

To the extent that these theories are valid, there are severe limits to what can be achieved in democratizing organizations, but being conscious of them may change our vision from idealism to realism. Knowing the nature of the obstacles may provide us with the means to circumvent them or at least render them less formidable.

Still investigating the shadow side of organizational democracy development, the next section reviews the research evidence which supports and elucidates the problems organizations encounter.

The Research Evidence

Although the previous section set out to present theoretical considerations, inevitably it was already spiced with examples and evidence. This section will deepen the evidence.

In giving examples of the failure of many attempts to democratize organizational life, we do not prejudge the evolution of future developments and in other places in this book we give evidence of successful participative schemas. This section starts with a series of studies which measure the range of participative opportunities called the Influence Power Continuum (IPC). This has already been referred to in Chapter 1 but here serves as a way of measuring the scope and limitation of the distribution of influence within and between levels of organization.

The subject of semi-autonomous work groups was also initiated in Chapter 1, which also used the term 'decision-making work teams'. In this chapter we look at some evidence on the effectiveness of these arrangements. At the level of a whole country, a fairly extreme example of semi-autonomy was the Yugoslav experiment with self-management which came to an end when the country broke up into a number of national units.

The various aspects of the Japanese approach to group work and consensus management are submitted to a critical analysis and followed up with a short section on the broader question of the difference between espoused participative structures and the reality of achievement—for instance, in a well-known consultancy scheme.

We also look at some recent meta-analyses which are a method of aggregating data from a number of individual research studies, on participation in this case, to see whether valid conclusions can be drawn from this larger sample of data.

Finally, we present the evidence from two very large and well-endowed field studies in Scandinavia which were set up to change the operation of

Norwegian and Swedish enterprises further to encourage democratic–participative behaviour.

The reader will appreciate that, given such a wide range of research areas, each with its own extensive literature, omissions are inevitable. Nevertheless, we use these studies to draw some interim conclusions.

The Extent of and Desire for Participation

A number of research projects conducted in many different countries have described the distribution of influence and power in modern medium- and large-scale organizations. To do this, it is necessary to devise a scale of clearly defined distinct alternatives along a continuum of participatory intensity. Starting with the work of Rensis Likert (1961; 1967) and his colleagues at Michigan, the continuum ranged from authoritarian to participative, later divided into four stages. The final and most democratic stage, described simply as System 4, saw group participation and joint responsibility and agreed decisions as the most desirable and effective outcome.[4] This continuum was later extended by Heller and Yukl (1969) to emphasize the possible rearrangement of power through delegation into an Influence and Power Continuum of five alternative variations.

Variations of the Influence Power Continuum have been developed in various European projects, particularly by the IDE (1981*b*) research group, which made an important distinction between being able to give an opinion and having the opinion taken into account.[5] The IDE research extended the continuum to six positions, finishing up with semi-autonomy (allowing individuals to make certain decisions on their own):

1. I am not involved at all.
2. I am informed about the matter beforehand.
3. I can give my opinion.
4. My opinion is taken into account.
5. I take part with equal weight.
6. I decide on my own.

The Influence Power Continua allow us to assess the average or most frequently used method by organizational level, country, or type of decision issue. The findings of these research reports are interesting and important, but we will confine ourselves here to documenting the limitation of influence-sharing methods. Using a sample of nearly 8,000 people in 134 companies in twelve countries, describing the influence they had over sixteen different decisions, the average for workers did not quite reach point 2, 'being informed beforehand', and for strategic decisions, like investments, was closer to 'not involved at all'. Even at the middle-management level, the average barely exceeded 'informed beforehand and can give opinion'. Only in relation to decisions over holidays could middle managers reach the point of having their opinions taken into account. Foremen did not get that degree of influence even on holidays, and workers even less so. In relation to none of the 16 decisions did workers, foremen, or middle managers on average reach the opportunity to 'take part in decisions with equal weight' (IDE 1981*b*: 186).

Given what in the previous section we said about people being frequently disinclined to participate, even when given the opportunity to do so, the IDE research asked each respondent how much involvement he or she would like to have in relation to each of sixteen decisions. The difference between the influence people had, compared with what he or she would like to have, was surprisingly small. Workers were, on average, quite content to be informed beforehand without having their opinion taken into account except in relation to holidays. Even for middle managers their average desire to influence organizational decisions did not quite reach having their 'opinion taken into account'. Only on task assignment were they ambitious enough to aim at 'taking part in decisions with equal weight'.

The limits to actual as well as desired participation, and the degree of realism of the 8,000 respondents, can be seen when the sixteen decisions are grouped into strategic (long-term), tactical (medium-term), and routine (short-term) issues. Workers, foremen, and middle managers were content to have least influence over strategic and only a little more over tactical and a little more still over routine decisions (IDE 1981*b*: 189). This confirms the importance of situational factors in leadership and participation research. Employees neither get nor desire equal degrees of influence over different areas of decision-making. All together, these findings do not amount to revolutionary demands and certainly do not justify senior management fears of losing their prerogative. The replication study in the same establishments ten years later showed that almost nothing had changed (IDE 1993).

Almost identical results have been found in other research—for instance, a four-year longitudinal study in three countries using an analogous Influence Power Continuum (Heller *et al.* 1988: 87, 121).

Large-scale public-opinion surveys on participation are useful if (1) they are supported by other methods less subject to the 'social desirability' influence derived from public stereotypes, and/or (2) if the surveys are designed to cross validate more in-depth work based on smaller samples. A study of over 7,000 EC managers and employee representatives reported investigating participation in planning new technology found a range of 25–80 per cent of 'no involvement in decisions' and 25–50 per cent of 'information only'; there was a little more influence in implementing new technology (Gill and Krieger 1992: 347, 349), but broadly the results support previous studies of *de facto* severe limits to influence-sharing (Gill *et al.* 1993).

Studies of Direct Participation

The European Foundation for the Improvement of Living and Working Conditions has conducted a number of research studies on participation and most recently on direct participation in fifteen member countries.[6] The stimulus came from the MIT study on lean production methods (Womack *et al.* 1990), which suggested that a major competitive advantage of Japanese car manufacturers was their superior way of organizing work and their use of participative working arrangements. The European economic recession in the 1990s provided a further impetus to look at the European experience with direct participation such as the Swedish methods (see also later in this chapter), the French Group d'Expression, and the German Humanisierung des Arbeitslebens experience. The preliminary results of an inquiry among the European social partners—that is, the employers and trade unions—were in some respects quite unexpected. For instance, the concept of Direct Participation was not clearly understood and was often confused with Representative Participation among both employers and unions. The researchers were also surprised to find that employers were not in favour of management domination of the process and stressed the importance of social as well as economic objectives, but they considered that the primary responsibility for Direct Participation was with management.

The union attitudes were more complex and problematic and emphasized the potential negative consequences on union interests and collective representation. They were for the most part not opposed to Direct Representation but thought it should be clearly formulated and subject to some degree of regulation.

In general, the report concludes that among the social partners there is a 'rather high degree of uncertainty and ambivalent feelings for the future of participative programmes . . .' (Regalia 1995: 229). Overall, this large-scale fifteen-country study gives little support for the enthusiasm shown in the popular literature or the pronouncements of some senior managers and politicians. Perhaps the most positive outcome is to show that 'employee direct participation was substantially conceived by both sides as complementing rather than displacing representative participation' (Regalia 1996: 229).

Further evidence comes from in-depth case studies in twenty-five organizations on thirty-eight sites commissioned by the Department of Employment in the UK. The researchers conclude that employee involvement was management initiated and designed to 'improve communication and enhance employee contribution and commitment to organizational goals' (Marchington *et al.* 1992: 55). It had nothing to do with increasing employee influence. In spite of these managerial aims, employee commitment did not increase.

A large national random sample survey, also supported by the Department of Employment in the UK, concluded that 'by far the most common view was that employee influence was low . . . overall 52 per cent were in organizations where they felt employee influence was low, 30 per cent where it was medium, and 18 per cent where it was high . . . the highest level of influence was over work effort and quality, followed at some distance by decisions about work methods' (Gallie and White 1993).

The importance of trust in relation to participation plays a part in the next two research reports. One recent survey of 2,408 American adults claims special methodological sophistication[7] and comes to conclusions that would support other findings. It identifies two major attitudinal gaps. One gap is on trust and loyalty with a substantial minority having little of both. A second gap is on the amount of participation American employees want and the amount they get; employees believe that if they had more influence it would improve the competitive position of their company (Freeman and Rogers 1994).

A random household survey on 1,725 British adults[8] was designed to check on the reliability of a field study in a group of fourteen companies. This sample constituted the UK representation in the twelve-country IDE (1981*a*, *b*) research. The British part of this field study had been conducted in some depth with fifteen UK companies. In the random household survey which followed the fieldwork three main questions were asked: (i) How much and what kind of participation do people experience in their work (in relation to three decision areas)? (ii) How much do they want? And (iii) What other factors are relevant for successful participation, in particular, skill utilization and quality? In addition, the survey asked questions on trust which were not asked during fieldwork (Heller *et al.* 1979).

Results on questions (i) and (ii) show that, in relation to routine decisions, half the sample experienced moderate participation (being informed beforehand or having opinion taken into account), but only 15 per cent said they had moderate participation on more important decisions. Extensive participation (consensus and semi-autonomy) was significantly lower for all types of decisions. When people were asked how much participation they wanted to have, the answer for routine decisions was exactly the same as the amount they had, while their desire for tactical and strategic decisions was moderately higher. As in all other research, the findings of the random survey show substantial differences in actual and desired participation by level; both are high for senior management and decrease for middle and still further for shop-floor level. For instance, desired involvement for strategic decisions is 66 per cent for senior management, 16 per cent for supervisors, and 7 per cent for manual shop-floor personnel. Given consistently high correlations between actual and desired participation, the researchers conclude that 'slightly over a quarter of all respondents want more involvement than they actually have; whilst the substantial majority, nearly three-quarters of all respondents, appeared to be satisfied with their present involvement' (Heller *et al.* 1979: 30–1).

Several policy-relevant findings emerged from question (iii). Of the people who had taken part in production decisions, 79 per cent felt that the quality of the work had improved, and 89 per cent said that their skills were better used. Of those who felt that their skills were under-utilized, 44 per cent had no involvement in decisions, while only 3 per cent of those who had extensive participation indicated under-utilization of their skills (pp. 33, 37). This evidence on the relationship between participation and the utilization of skills, or more significantly between lack of participation and the under-utilization of skill, is further support for the theoretical position outlined in the section on the role of competence above and in Chapters 2 and 3.

The survey results on trust replicated the questions asked in the well-known Almond and Verba *Civic Culture* 1963 study, which included a British sample. The results, sixteen years later, 'reveal a marked movement towards a more distrustful society' (Heller *et al.* 1979: 37). In answer to the question 'Most people can be trusted' the Almond and Verba UK sample had 49 per cent agree, the IDE UK sample 38 per cent. In answer to the question 'You can't be too careful' Almond and Verba had 9 per cent agree; Heller *et al.* 1979 give 42 per cent. The survey results on questions (i), (ii), and (iii) fully support the conclusions from the field study (Heller *et al.* 1979).

This section on a variety of large field studies and surveys covering US and European samples documents the limited real influence of employees in middle and lower levels of organizations.

Semi-Autonomous Work Groups and teams

The term 'semi-autonomous work groups' is now widely used and refers to organizations giving individual employees a very extensive degree of influence over certain aspects of their work. This subject has been discussed in Chapter 1 under the heading 'decision-making teams'. In this chapter we present evidence of the limited impact of participative designs, and begin with a report on a carefully designed and fairly rigorous test of semi-autonomous work arrangements based on a large company producing confectionery goods (Wall *et al.* 1986).

Using a greenfield site and advised by a consultant from the Tavistock Institute, semi-autonomous groups of 8–12 people were made collectively responsible for allocating work, setting production targets, meeting quality and hygiene standards, recording production data, selecting and training new recruits, ordering and collecting raw material, and delivering the finished goods to the stores. An independent research team from the University of Sheffield was called in to evaluate the results over a period of three years. They were able to use two control groups, using very similar technology and products, but not on the greenfield site.

The outcome of this very thorough study, using validated questionnaires in three waves of measurement, as well as insights derived from interviewing, is largely favourable, but is reported here because it clearly indicates certain limitations to semi-autonomy. There was very clear evidence that the autonomous groups were very aware of the special conditions they operated under and their intrinsic as well as extrinsic job satisfaction was significantly higher than in the control groups. They showed increased intrinsic job satisfaction and a greater awareness of influence over the first two phases of measurement and thereafter retained that increased level. Interviews showed that none of the shop-floor employees preferred the conventional system, of which nearly all had direct experience. One is quoted as saying 'After twenty years of working at two other firms, the conditions here are excellent—managers treat you as people' (Wall *et al.* 1986: 297). However, several of the expected results were not achieved. There was no demonstrable effect on motivation, organizational commitment, mental health, or voluntary labour turnover. There were productivity benefits, but they resulted from the lower cost achieved by eliminating the supervisors rather than from other productivity indices. More surprisingly, labour turnover was higher in the autonomous groups and there were significantly more dismissals for disciplinary reasons. It seems that the autonomous work groups were reluctant to enforce their own discipline. In conventional production, employees who stepped out of line would be called to account by their supervisors before management had to step in, but in autonomous groups the problems were typically more advanced when they were discovered by managers and then led to dismissals.

Managers who introduced and ran the new group arrangements reported high levels of stress, particularly in the early stages. Nevertheless the company seemed satisfied with the greenfield results, although it took some time before their output targets were met.

No two pieces of research are the same, but sometimes there are interesting similarities. Two autonomous work teams were set up in a medium-sized American factory, Sound Incorporated (SI), producing high-fidelity equipment. These work teams were part of a much larger Quality of Working Life (QWL) programme supported by unusually progressive management. The President of the company is quoted as saying 'What we are really talking about is converting this organization from a monarchy to a democracy' (Witte 1980: 14). The research, like the Wall, Kemp, Jackson, and Clegg project, is unusual in being longitudinal and combining a number of different research methods, including two waves of before and after questionnaires, a quantitative analysis of the verbal interaction process in a democratically elected worker–management planning council (based on tape recordings), extensive interviewing, and participant observation of autonomous work-group meetings as well as the Planning Council.

The project started with high expectations, since the impetus came from the President of the parent company, who owned a quarter of the company's stock and had completed a doctoral thesis on work humanization. An elected Planning Council was given responsibility for extending employee participation throughout the company. It set up various joint management–worker task forces in addition to the two fully autonomous work teams which functioned without foremen. A Director of Employee Relations had been hired with the democratization project in mind. In spite of these unusually favourable supportive circumstances, at the end of eighteen months most of the experiments had been abandoned. Although the Planning Council was retained and successfully planned a complicated move to a new site, managers and other employees had lowered their expectations and there was a significant increase in alienation among worker representatives. As in the Wall, Kemp, Jackson, and Clegg research, workers in semi-autonomous work groups were unwilling to discipline colleagues who did not pull their weight, and representatives in the Planning Council, who had received little training, soon felt that their lack of knowledge relating to technical problems made their participation in meetings fairly meaningless. As is frequently documented in projects of this kind, middle management was unenthusiastic and resisted any diminution of their influence.

The researcher's final assessment reflected these disappointments and failures. He felt that the future of participation in America will not easily be achieved if even companies which enjoyed so many unusually favourable conditions, like a knowledgeable, dedicated top management with a belief in innovation and influence-sharing, can show few positive results. He blamed the American ethos and in particular the widely held faith in meritocracy which establishes the purpose of corporations, their authority and reward structures, and the distribution of influence. 'It is this commitment to meritocratic norms that establishes the limits of democracy in the economic enterprise' (Witte 1980: 2).

Under favourable circumstances, as in the original coal-mine studies, when skills and experience are equally distributed and appropriate incentives are available, motivation is high and middle management is not disadvantaged by the arrangements, semi-autonomy can be very successful, as in the assembly of the Saab engine (Norstedt and Aguren 1973). To be effective, semi-autonomy must be based on trust and an adequate level of competence. Unfortunately, as so often happens in the field of management, ideas and practices that are contingently successful become fads, universal prescriptions, and consultancy packages (see Chapter 1). This escalation appears to have happened with team working and has been critically evaluated by Sinclair (1992), who claims that a team ideology has started to 'tyrannize the organizational field because it encourages teams to be used for inappropriate tasks and to fulfil unrealistic objectives' (p. 622). She claims that 'this ideology has been supported by researchers who offer the "team" as a tantalizing solution to some of the intractable problems of organizational life' (pp. 611–12).

The literature on team working and similar titles has exploded in recent years, and there are, of course, many broad and some subtle variations on the basic theme of collaborative group work (Dawson 1994; Mabey and Mayon-White 1993; Cohen and Ledford 1994; West 1994). In Chapter 1 we mentioned some of these variations under the title 'decision-making teams'; they are examples of direct participation, while in Chapter 4 the emphasis was on indirect or representative participation. The variations between different types of semi-autonomous, problem-solving and team groups can be grouped under five headings: (1) degree of permanence of the structure; (2) emphasis on competence creation, i.e. training; (3) genuine dispersal of influence; (4) degree of interchangeability of tasks; and (5) level of task assignment (from routine via tactical to strategic). Failure clearly to recognize these five factors and evaluate them in relation to groups that are given different names must lead to confusion.

Classical Case Examples

Several other American experiments with participation are better known than the study by Witte described above. In the mid-1970s the Ford Foundation and the US Department of Commerce financed a series of carefully monitored joint union–management demonstration QWL experiments (Cammann *et al.* 1984). Demonstration programmes of this sort were introduced into more than a dozen settings. The three most fully documented are described below. Though fifteen years have passed since these studies were completed, the problems they illustrate are still critical and few other cases have been studied so intensively and illustrate so clearly the problems and limitations of the participative approach.

Rushton. This experiment involved a small coal mine and a local branch of the militant United Mine Workers. The programme was initiated largely because of the interest of the company president and a member of the union's national staff (Trist *et al.* 1977; Goodman 1979). Although there was a union–management mine-wide steering committee, the nature of the change—job redesign—was determined largely by the consultant, who had been involved in a similar project in Britain.

Initially the programme was confined to a single section rather than the mine as a whole. Prior to the experiment, the section consisted of three teams, each working a different shift. Each team included a foreman and seven miners, each with his own set of duties and special pay rate. The experiment consisted of making each team self-governing, with the foreman's responsibility being restricted to safety and long-range planning. All participants in the programme were volunteers. Each miner was expected to learn the other miners' jobs. All miners' pay was raised to the top pay rate.

At the beginning of the programme each miner received six days of training (including role-playing how potential problems might be handled). Every six weeks the section was shut down so that all the teams could meet together to improve inter-shift communications and to thrash out common problems. Later the programme was extended to a second section of the mine.

The results? Attitudes in the experimental sections were generally favourable. Safety improved fairly dramatically. The impact on productivity was difficult to measure. On balance it increased slightly. Nevertheless, there were problems. Managers felt threatened. Non-participants began expressing jealousy towards the 'super miners' who enjoyed both high pay and considerable autonomy. Some non-participants feared that the union leadership had sold out.

Meanwhile labour relations began to deteriorate in the coal industry generally, and this had an impact on the mine. After eighteen months' experience with the experiment, the local union leadership gave management a choice: extend the programme throughout the mine—or drop it! The company negotiated a plan for extension, but when this was presented to the union membership, it was voted down 79–75. Management decided to continue the programme unilaterally.

Though union officers offered to cooperate informally, the programme gradually disintegrated.

Bolivar. The genesis of the Bolivar experiment was a US Senate hearing on worker alienation at which Irving Bluestone, Vice-President of the United Auto Workers, and Sidney Harman, chief executive of Harman International, were witnesses. Finding themselves in philosophical agreement as to the value of QWL, they decided to introduce such a programme at Harman's Bolivar plan. Located in a small country town, this dirty, run-down plant made auto parts (Duckles *et al.* 1977; Macy 1982).

Initial support for the plan in local-level union and management was low. An elaborate 429–page report on worker attitudes and perceptions, prepared by a university team, remained largely unread. Early meetings of the steering committee took up such issues as parking problems, ventilation, and the provision of Gatorade (a soft drink) in vending machines. Activities accelerated after Harman replaced the plant manager and Bluestone made a special visit to plead for union cooperation. To inspire interest in change, a worker–management team was sent to observe innovative Swedish and Norwegian factories (many members decided that European approaches would not work in Bolivar).

Meanwhile three experimental groups of workers began discussing possible job redesign. From these discussions arose some changes in work procedures, as well as the suggestion that the company institute Earned Idle Time (EIT), which meant essentially that once a worker had produced his day's work quota he could go home and still earn his full day's pay. Once EIT was introduced in the experimental groups, other workers began demanding the same privilege, a request which the union and management granted reluctantly (since workers had unequal opportunities to earn EIT and inequities would be created). Thereafter thirty-three 'core groups' (really Quality Circles (QCs)) were established to discuss departmental problems.

At one point competitive pressures made it likely that the plant would lose its contract for a key product. To meet this threat, company and union staff people met to plan cost-cutting steps, with management sharing much hitherto confidential information. Production standards were raised. The contract was saved, along with some seventy jobs.

In 1978, after the plan had been in operation for five years, there was extensive but unsuccessful discussion as to institutionalizing it, i.e. making it permanent. By this time Harman had left the company and Bluestone was soon to retire. The consultant role was phased out. QWL continued in one department; otherwise the experiment was over.

What did the experiment accomplish? Employment increased; turnover, absenteeism, and accidents dropped, in some instances dramatically. Both production and quality improved, the former in part due to negotiated changes in work standards and the incentive effects of EIT. Attitudinal changes were mixed. Workers felt they had more influence, but overall job satisfaction was unchanged and there were more reports of physical and psychological stress, in part due to self-induced pressure to earn EIT time. Support for the union increased. Another positive factor is that the plan had continued through periods of recession and job loss.

But the programme was far from a complete success. Initiatives and support for it came chiefly from the consultants and from top union and top management, the last two located miles away. There was local enthusiasm mainly for EIT, which was primarily a plan to make it easier to leave the job, rather than to make the job more satisfying. As in other cases, there was opposition from middle and lower-level management and from the work groups not involved in the primary experiment.

TVA. By contrast with the two previous cases, this one involved graduate professional engineers and technical assistants. TVA, a government-owned utility, had a long history of cooperative labour–management relations and a joint participative scheme, which had gradually decreased in significance. The new experiment, confined to one engineering design division and its two unions, was intended to provide a fresh start (Macy and Peterson 1983; Macy *et al.* 1989; Castrogiovanni and Macy 1990).

The steering committee (half union, half management) selected a group of consultants, who in turn interviewed the vast majority of employees, seeking to determine the problems these employees saw. After a week's retreat, in which the consultants' findings were discussed, the committee set up a series of task forces. Each task force was assigned to deal with a critical organizational problem, such as record-keeping or departmental structure.

Among the task-force proposals were changes in (1) workflow, including the elimination of unnecessary engineering drawings and the creation of a new department for environmental matters, and (2) personnel practices—for example, flexitime, a new performance evaluation procedure, and a ten-hour day, four-day week for employees whose work required them to spend nights away from home. Most of the suggestions were implemented. Among those abandoned was a plan to make special 'merit' awards to employees who had engaged in outstanding service. Stumbling blocks here included questions as to who would do the judging and what would be the basis for comparison.

The programme at TVA was a relative success. At least the changes persisted and some were diffused to other TVA divisions. Further, the parties voted to continue to hire new consultants after the original consultants left. Indeed an attempt was made to integrate the new participative system with the older, broader programme (though this effort too eventually petered out). Nevertheless, by 1989 the division's 'redesign effort' had become 'non-existent' (Macy *et al.* 1989: 1161).

Various measures of job satisfaction and perceived influence increased for the one-third of employees who had participated in the various committees. There was some (but less) change in similar measures for non-participants. Given the nature of the job, measures of productivity were difficult to devise; nevertheless there was some evidence of increased productivity.

The problems here were much the same as in the previous two cases. Initially there was unequal interest among employees in participation. Those who participated felt more involved than those who did not. Middle management was under-represented on the various committees and felt bypassed. The Divisional Manager attended only some of the steering committee's meetings. As in other cases, issues relating to compensation (such as the 'merit' award, or the relationship between draughtsmen's and engineers' pay) were difficult to resolve on a cooperative basis. Over time, as the task forces ran out of easy problems to resolve, enthusiasm for the programme began to decline. Perhaps the original expectations were too high.

Self-Management

As we have just seen, disappointment with results depends on expectations and is not always a useful indicator of success or failure. For about three decades social scientists studied the Yugoslav self-management system, which was based on the assumption that even large organizations such as factories, hotels, airlines, etc. could be run by the totality of their employees operating through elected workers' councils, which excluded top managers but were responsible for appointing and, where necessary, dismissing them. Here we will begin by referring to the research of a Yugoslav social scientist who, with colleagues, conducted an empirical study of the top decision-making council in twenty companies from the republics of Bosnia-Herzegovina, Croatia, and Serbia over a three-year period (Obradović 1975); 900 hours of meetings were observed in which over 1,800 individuals took part and fifteen major agenda items were discussed. In order to get away from the more usual assessment of formal participation, they decided to measure the minute-by-minute activity of people who took part in these top-tier works councils. Under the Yugoslav legal system, all decisions were to be made by workers and the role of management confined to implementation. Technically it was against the law for top managers to be members of workers' councils, although they could attend and speak.

The findings show very clearly that these fairly extreme expectations of participation could not be met. In seventeen of the twenty companies, top management were members of the works council and, although they made up only a fraction of the total employment, they dominated discussions on all strategic and tactical issues. Participation in council meetings was handled largely by the chair and professional specialists who were not members of the council. Top management did more than its fair share of talking and had most of its proposals accepted. Although Communist officials (League of Communist members) constituted only 13 per cent of employees, they participated very actively in each of the fifteen major agenda items. Since most managers were members of the League of Communists, their combined influence was critical for the resolution of all issues.

A major aim of the research was to identify the relationship between the formal blueprint for workers' self-management and what happened in practice. The results, showing an enormous gap between expectation and achievement, were adequately explained by differences in experience and knowledge of the people who were present at the works council meetings. At that time, however, there was no theoretical model linking competence with power-sharing and hence no remedial action was taken—for instance, to increase experience and skill development.

The self-management system was different from any other known formal method of distributing power to the lowest level of organization and for this reason received very extensive attention from social scientists and economists (Rus 1970; 1984; Vanek 1971; Arzensek 1983; Horvat 1983). Self-management began after 1950, when Tito broke with Stalin. Various constitutional amendments, particularly in 1963 and 1974, extended self-management externally to include the educational, health, and social-welfare system, and internally to devolve more power to cost centres in enterprises called Basic Organizations of Associated Labour (BOALs). The purpose of the new legal provision for decentralized participation was to overcome the problems described in the Obradović research—that is, the non-participation of the rank and file and the continuing *de facto* dominance of management. Even so, as the twelve-country comparative IDE (1981*b*) research showed clearly, Yugoslav workers had significantly more *de facto* participative influence than workers in the other eleven European countries, which included West Germany and its co-determination structure.

When the Yugoslav state broke apart in 1990, the self-management system based on federal constitutional provisions disappeared, although research by Pusić (1992) among Croatian managers suggests that most felt quite positively towards it. In Slovenia a new industrial-relations structure has emerged, based on co-determination.

However, even the fully operational self-management system before 1990 was open to critical assessment from within as well as from outside the country (see, for instance, George 1993; Rosser and Rosser 1996). Pusić and Rus, writing the IDE (1981*a*) chapter on Yugoslavia, note that even in 1980 a scientific division of labour derived from the theories of Taylor was still widespread and constituted a main obstacle to the successful implementation of the 1976 Law of Associated Labour. A second major obstacle to the further development of self-management was identified as 'the unresolved status of professionals and professional service' (p. 231). They point to the contradiction between the acknowledged greater need for professional skills which would inevitably lead to professionals having more influence and the fear that a technocracy would make it impossible for blue-collar workers to exercise the influence which successive constitutional amendments had conferred on them. The possibility of training lower-level employees to acquire the necessary skills to fill the hierarchical competence gap was not then identified as a possible remedy. However, on the theoretical level the need to recognize professional competence and give managers freedom to exercise it was made by Horvat (1983), a well-known Yugoslav economist, who also recognized that the decision process operates in phases and that different levels of the organization are competent to intervene in some rather than in all phases. These ideas were not incorporated in practice.

An assessment of self-management by Pribicević from Belgrade University (1994) finds that self-management had a number of faults: it made poor use of available resources and did not deliver the anticipated economic returns, but he is optimistic about the future because, in the long run, true democracy cannot be isolated and confined to the political system. With the experience available today, he felt that a better system could be devised by paying attention to four errors: (1) it was a mistake to expect that all employees in an enterprise could be entitled to take part in all decisions including technology, marketing, and innovation; (2) it was not realistic to reduce the role of professional managers to carrying out decisions made by self-management organs; (3) self-government must link rights to responsibility so that, when things go wrong, all those who took part in the decision (including those who delegated decision power to managers) must pay the appropriate price; and (4) it was incorrect to assume that self-management alone would solve the problems of work motivation.

Another recent assessment by one of us presents a very balanced assessment starting from the recognition that the recent industrial history of the country meant that most workers came from a peasant background (Pusić 1996). Perhaps as a consequence, self-management did not reduce the prohibitive economic inefficiency of the system, including spectacular overstaffing and the concomitant reluctance to let people go. The over-idealization of the system by many academics was not shared by the rank-and-file employees, even at the time the self-management system was well accepted. Pusić quotes 1969 research in Belgrade, Sarajevo, and Zagreb which showed that 81 per cent of respondents agreed with the statement that 'Industry needs decisive managers'. However, Pusić observes that, although self-management did not give legitimacy to the regime that sponsored it, nevertheless there is evidence that it created among Yugoslav workers a very positive attitude towards 'their' enterprise, and when the break-up crisis led to extensive company failures, they rallied to give their support and endured substantial hardship in the process.

It seems that one dominant factor in the failure of the system was to confuse democracy with egalitarianism. This emasculated the role of management without giving lower levels of the organization the necessary tools in the form of experience and skill to play a useful part in helping to run the enterprise. Milovan Djilas, the Yugoslav intellectual and one-time adviser to Tito, recognized the problem when he observed that people who hold ideals verging on Utopianism are dangerous; real life never approximates to these Utopian prescriptions (Djilas 1972).

The Kibbutz

Conditions may be more favourable in another part of the world. Israel certainly is often credited with having evolved some of the most democratic working conditions anywhere. The kibbutz movement was founded at the very beginning of the twentieth century, but grew particularly rapidly in the two decades after 1931, when their population increased sixteenfold from 4,000 to 65,000.[9] This was the period when thousands of Jews fled from waves of anti-Semitism in Europe and settled in the kibbutzim to help build up their new homeland. The design of the organizations was clearly built on socialist principles; the means of production were owned by the community, and all work was shared on the basis of equality and rotation to give every member experience of every necessary activity, including the most routine and demeaning. The more desirable and potentially the most powerful jobs were shared on the same basis through rotation. Nobody received payment, but all basic needs were shared on an agreed basis with equality as the principal arbiter. 'From each according to his ability, to each according to his needs' was the guiding motto. The general assembly to which all adults belonged was the source of all power and every member had equal access to it. A factor that does not always receive the attention it deserves is the above-average level of education and wide range of experience of the refugees from European oppression and persecution, and consequently their high motivation to achieve security and a reasonable standard of living.

Predictably, kibbutzim were criticized by economists, who expected them to fail on the basis of traditional assumptions of 'economic man', who was self-centred and always motivated to maximize his own returns with least expenditure and effort and in a setting of unceasing competition with others. The economists' 'free-rider' phenomenon is a consequence of the assumed selfish opportunism which characterizes human endeavour. People will work as little as they can get away with, free riding on the backs of others as long as they are not coerced or motivated by individualistic incentives. However, the kibbutzim movement disproved all these assumptions; over a sixty-year period it grew from strength to strength, was highly efficient, pioneered new agricultural developments, and converted deserts into exotic flower gardens, orchards, and animal farms (Barkai 1977).

In recent years the situation has become less favourable. Many of the external conditions, both in Israel as well as in the wider world which at one time supported socialistic solutions in Israel, have changed. A greater emphasis on individualism, coupled with change in political orientation supported by ubiquitous, if simplistic slogans like 'value for money', have set a new agenda for many of the more highly industrialized countries to which Israel exports its products and from which it receives ideologies. Helman (1992), an economist of the kibbutz movement, has analysed some of the critical socio-economic conditions which threaten the survival of kibbutzim or at least the basic principles from which they received their inspiration.

Using Abell's (1983) research based on other countries, Helman argues that cooperatives are 'formed mainly when solidarity of purpose is considered more important than material incentives' (p. 172). The members of the younger kibbutz generation no longer experience the need for solidarity as strongly as the preceding one, and within Israel they see themselves surrounded by the appearance of prosperity coinciding with the growth of materialistic values. This has led to a 'brain drain' of some of the abler kibbutzim and an influx by way of 'negative selection' of some weaker members of the community, who can increase their earnings or enhance their security by joining a kibbutz.

The kibbutz movement was built on the production of agricultural products and the manufacture of goods, but it offers nothing to people who want to pursue other worthwhile economic occupations as scientists, artists, lawyers, merchants, or tourist guides. Contrary to expectations based on standard economic theory, which predicted a lack of initiative and interest in investment, the kibbutz managers indulged in considerable amounts of over-investment. This led to a substantial under-utilization of the machine potential and produced an 'investment–consumption ratio in the kibbutz . . . three times higher than that in Israel' (Helman 1992: 175). One reason for the investment spree was a different attitude to risk by kibbutz managers, who would not be judged by the same standards as managers in a market economy. There is also a tendency for younger kibbutzim to avoid routine or hard physical labour and, at the same time, to avoid hiring outside workers to carry out these tasks. Mechanization beyond that which their economy could afford was the apparent answer. The fight against inflation in Israel raised the real rate of interest so high that almost all investment failed.

Two other factors add to the crisis facing the egalitarian aspirations of the kibbutz movement, which Sajó (1992) compares to other socialist systems. The first is their capital debt, which 'exceeds the highest per capita foreign debt ever achieved by a socialist country (the debt per capita of Hungary was about $20 compared to $33 of the kibbutzim)' (p. 184). Sajó feels that this large debt has contributed to the collapse of the system. The second comparative disadvantage concerns the quality of management, 'since the kibbutz is neither ready nor perhaps capable of attracting the best managers. Its managers are simply members who happen to manage for a period of time' (p. 186).

A final assessment of the kibbutz as a democratic work system cannot yet be made, but there are strong indications that adjustments to levels less than the original ideal conditions will be required.

Japanese Participation

Going even further east, we come to Japan, about which an enormous amount has been written—often based on the loosely conceived assumption that they have a more democratic work system than the West (Misumi 1984). Japan's history, economic development, and culture are very different from those of Western countries, making comparisons difficult at best or meaningless at worst. Tomlin

(1987) draws attention to several important characteristics of the Japanese character and outlook 'for which western psychology offers no parallels'. One that is particularly important for understanding their approach to groups and influence distribution is summed up in the word *amae* as 'dependency wish'—that is, 'the need felt by the average Japanese for psychological support, not merely in childhood, but at the adult stage, differentiating him in this respect from the westerner, who strives for ever greater independence or individuality . . .' (Tomlin 1987: 399).

It is easy to confuse a long-established cultural tradition of group consensus with democracy or power-sharing. It can be argued that group consensus imposes enormous constraints on what in the West we call individual freedom and which we value as the right to dissent. The Japanese trade-union structure, usually based on companies rather than sectors, or even higher and more independent levels, is difficult to compare with Western systems, and their much discussed Quality Circles (QCs) have characteristics which we do not replicate when that term is applied to quality improvement groups in Western countries. For instance, in Japan QCs usually meet after normal working hours, reflecting the different value Japanese place on their leisure time and family relationships (MOW 1986). Very frequently Japanese QCs have management-imposed targets for the number of suggested annual improvements or other productivity indices, which constitute an important constraint on the freedom of these groups.

The famous *ringi* bottom-up decision-making is highly participative, designed to encourage initiative and make good use of the experience and knowledge of the human potential, but it is confined to management and confers no influence on lower levels (Heller and Misumi 1987).

A report based on forty-eight Japanese manufacturing firms used the Aston Centralization of Authority scale and showed contingency[10] results broadly similar to studies in Western countries. Decentralization was related to task variability, large size of organization, and multiple levels, while centralization was contingent on spatial dispersion of units and high levels of automation (Marsh 1992). Investigating the locus of decision-making on thirty-seven different issues, he concluded that the authority to make a decision 'is always located above the level of rank-and-file operative, i.e. at the level of first-line foremen or (usually) higher' (p. 273). He also argues that claims relating to Japanese participative decision systems have often failed to distinguish between the right to present ideas and suggestions, on the one hand, and the authority to make and implement decisions, on the other. The former are widely encouraged by Japanese management, but the latter tend, on average, to be reserved for fairly senior levels of management. Contrary to the widely held belief that Japanese, particularly in their practice of management-initiated *ringisho* bottom-up decision-making, are unconcerned about the length of time the method requires, Marsh argues that many Japanese firms use executive meetings called *jyomukai* to speed up the process of arriving at decisions. He quotes Misumi (1984: 533), who describes *jyomukai* as 'the vehicle for reaching decisions on all important matters'.

Marsh believes that the West has tended to misunderstand worker involvement schemes such as QCs and the Zero Defect movement. The Japanese worker influence is confined to making suggestions to foremen, who in turn take these ideas to higher levels for consideration, where they are often revised before approval and implementation.

Robert Cole, who has extensive experience of Japanese organizations, would not disagree with Marsh but would add that participatory practices were introduced more for economic than for social reasons resulting from a very tight Japanese labour market in the late 1960s and early 1970s. He claims that, while there are few really well-documented examples of participation, organizations 'often develop myths about what they are doing in participatory work practices' (Cole 1982: 173). He goes on to accuse social scientists, and in particular Lawler, of making exaggerated, unrealistic claims that are designed to 'drum up support for these developments' (p. 173). In reality, he claims, the Japanese way of running organizations never threatens the hierarchical structure of authority.

A recent analysis by Winfield (1994), who was Personnel Manager in a Japanese factory in the UK, gives further support to those who have become sceptical of the democratic credentials of the Japanese enterprise system. He argues from an analysis of the Japanese literature that most Japanese organizational developments were deliberate adaptations of Western methods; for instance the Just in Time (JIT) system derived from the retailing methods used in American supermarkets and some of their group methods were adapted from cell manufacturing developed in the Stalinist Soviet Union in the 1950s. More importantly, these adaptations were mechanistic rather than humanistic and led to a considerable intensification of pressure on employees at lower levels of organization. Winfield claims that we have 'to understand Japanese manufacturing techniques as simultaneously embracing both the intensification and the rejection of Taylorism' (p. 221). Like Tomlin quoted above, he derives insights from a sociolinguistic understanding of terms like *amae* derived from a description of the mother–child relationship and literally meaning a willingness to lean on a person's good will. This concept continues to be important in adulthood and creates a positive attitude towards dependence and a corresponding positive attitude towards mutual obligation and an acceptance of the command and control structure. When this philosophy is translated into the design of Japanese factories in Western countries it leads to a problematic selection process. In the case of Toyota's UK factory with 40,000 applicants for 600 assembly jobs, the selection criteria included 'temperamental stability, compliance, willingness to adhere to group demands, and minimal manifestation of ego dominance. Radicalism is a trait to be avoided. Total allegiance to the team is expected' (p. 231).

Espousal and Reality

Earlier, in discussing 'inauthenticity' we provided several examples of a hiatus between talk and action and between attitudes and behaviour in relation to participation. We have seen that some writers support the notion of giving people a 'feeling of participation' while others condemn it as manipulative. We have also seen that in several major studies managers espoused the idea of participation but justified not carrying it into practice because they lacked trust in people. According to two large-scale surveys reviewed above, one in the USA (Freeman and Rogers 1994) and one in the UK (Heller *et al.* 1979), trust was in short supply. The importance of trust is widely acknowledged but, like competence, rarely included as a major factor in a theoretical model. The decision-making and leadership model of Vroom and Yetton (1973) is an exception. The model is designed as a decision tree to analyse and train managers to become aware of the various circumstances under which it is appropriate for them to use different degrees of participation. One of the contingencies relates to a manager's judgement on whether the subordinate can be trusted to work within the value framework of his superior and accept similar goals.

An interesting example of how failure to recognize the value of contingencies, in particular the need for trust, can affect a behavioural change programme is described by Yetton and Crawford (1992). The widely used Blake and Mouton leadership training programme is based on a very simple universalistic prescription for a 'one best' management style enshrined in an ideal decision style or grid which gives equal weight to the consideration for people and the need of higher productivity (Blake and Mouton 1964). Yetton and Crawford were involved in a longitudinal research study in an Australian company where a Blake and Mouton leadership programme had been introduced by consultants. They were later asked to find out what had gone wrong with the Blake and Mouton leadership and team-building training. The CEO of the Australian company had commissioned the training to increase participation and improve the quality and acceptability of decisions, and the commitment of staff. The programme involved management at all levels. It happens that the Yetton and Crawford academic team had carried out an interview and questionnaire enquiry with 112 senior staff on a different project in that company, so that, when the CEO realized that something had gone wrong with the training, the academic team could carry out a post-change assessment with follow-up interviews and questionnaires.

The findings show that the training programme had produced high levels of espoused participativeness but almost no increase in actual participative behaviour. The disparity between aspirations and expectations, on the one hand, and the actual level of behaviour on the other, produced extensive frustration and, since the CEO had started the programme and was responsible for it, he became the main target of the dissatisfaction. The grid training had prescribed a universalistic participative style of behaviour which was unrealistic for three reasons. In the first place, managers were expected to use the same degree of participation with subordinates, irrespective of their evaluation of the subordinates' values—for instance, whether they agreed with the organization's goals. Secondly, there were big differences between units; some operated in an environment which had few problems to which collaboration and participation could provide solutions but where quick responses were necessary and participation was seen as an unrealistic investment of time. Thirdly, there were substantial differences in staff skills between units of work. In these circumstances, inviting low-skilled staff to participate in finding new solutions in a hostile environment that demands quick responses made little sense. These findings support the Vroom and Yetton (1973) leadership model, which relates styles of leadership behaviour to the demands of the situation *and takes account of the need for trust and competence*. In this Australian company there were clearly many issues which could be handled most effectively without participation.

On a more general level, the tendency towards inauthenticity and the difference between espoused theories and behaviour have been the subject of extensive work by Chris Argyris (for instance, Argyris and Schön 1974; Argyris 1993). He documents a large number of examples of a trend which he believes to be endemic in organizational life—namely to separate beliefs, attitudes, and values, 'the espoused theories', from everyday behaviour, what he calls 'theories in use'. This gap is often unconscious and is difficult to bridge. The problem becomes particularly obvious when organizations try to introduce new ideas like participative leadership. People can be induced to change certain aspects of their behaviour, at least for a time, by persuasion or by coercion—for instance, by executive policy. Argyris calls this single-loop learning. This kind of learning perpetuates inauthenticity because the new ideas will be accepted superficially, while in practice people fail to listen to what subordinates say or to consult them after decisions are taken. Genuine change will occur only if one learns to understand the need for congruence between values and actions. This is called double-loop learning and is very difficult to achieve because people adopt what he calls 'defensive routines' to cover up and deceive themselves as well as anybody who challenges them.

A recent study by Andrew Brown (1995) provides further evidence on the pervasive and sometimes subtle inauthenticities operating through an espoused belief system. The belief system was based on a modern-sounding stakeholder marketing philosophy used in a British National Health hospital which had decided to introduce a large-scale information technology system.[11] The government had introduced marketing and selling terminology into hospitals to give legitimacy to autocratically introduced changes which were unpopular. To sell the new information technology, management and consultants developed what the author calls 'niche marketing'—that is, radically different explanations of the benefits accruing to a variety of stakeholders to get them to participate in the change programme. Each stakeholder group constituted a different market and was given different arguments to appeal to that group's self-interest and cultural norms. The researchers describe how 'niche marketing' involves withholding, slanting, and transmitting selective information in a sophisticated micro-political process to obtain the voluntary participation of the diverse stakeholder groups. Many people would describe such a consultative process as unethical or inauthentic.

Meta-Research

Some of the studies we have reviewed are large scale and longitudinal but they are individual pieces of evidence. We follow this up with a number of meta-analyses of participation research in the USA. Meta-research attempts to draw superior conclusions about a given research area by using statistical techniques to aggregate research data from a substantial number of individual studies. In this way differences and trends between the individual studies can be examined, leading to conclusions about the reliability and validity of the aggregated data. The research included in meta-analyses has to conform to certain quite strict conditions in terms of the published statistical results. Even beyond the statistical requirements, meta-studies usually impose certain constraints on the sample they include based on the nature of the outcome measures. Most meta-research concentrates on productivity and satisfaction measures and excludes other potentially useful outcomes, such as quality improvement, lower labour turnover, and more flexible work practices.

We begin with three studies reported by Wagner and Gooding (1987*a*). They are confined to American cross-sectional research on participatory decision-making (PDM), as well as to studies on autocratic versus democratic leadership and directive versus participatory goal-setting or performance appraisal. The authors excluded research concerned with greater influence-sharing leading to delegation and similar goal-setting procedures 'because they focused on a shift of influence from superior to subordinates rather than on influence sharing between hierarchical unequals' (Wagner and Gooding 1987*a*: 246). This is an interesting and particularly important exclusion which is more widely accepted in American than European research, where we have seen that a scale of influence frequently includes delegation and *semi*-autonomy (DIO 1979; IDE 1981*b*). It can be argued that, unless research looks at the distribution of influence and power cascading from higher to lower levels, one ends up at the bottom of the hierarchy with little if anything of importance to share. Wagner and Gooding also excluded socio-technical interventions, Scanlon plans, board representation, etc. Many of the studies in their preliminary collection could not be included because they failed to report correlations or transformable statistics; however, their final collection was based on seventy studies.

Wagner and Gooding had two principal reasons for carrying out research on participation. In the first place they show through a review of the literature that 'few other organizational topics have been studied in the United States for a longer period of time and . . . few have been accorded a degree of scholarly attention equal to that of participation' (Wagner and Gooding 1987*a*: 241). Secondly, and in spite of this enormous interest and volume of work, the outcome is uncertain and contradictory. In looking for an answer they speculate that societal values and judgements based on personal values could be responsible for some or most of the discrepancies in the literature. They investigate two possibilities through two different studies. First, they looked at variations in the relationship between participation and outcomes and the methods employed for the research over periods of American history when conservative, or alternatively liberal, values predominated. They found that correlation studies between attitudes to participation and attitudes to outcome were published relatively more often during a period when liberal values and social entitlement norms were strong. By contrast, correlations between attitudes to participation and observable outcomes, such as productivity, were published more often during a period when conservative values based on social order predominated. Furthermore, correlation between participation and attitudes were significantly larger than correlations between participation and observable outcomes, such as productivity. Consequently, at different periods between 1950 and 1985 research methods and results fluctuated.

The second hypothesis suggested that the researcher's own attitudes, be they conservative or liberal, would influence the research questions and the methods used in investigating the relationship between participation and outcomes. Liberals believe in an egalitarian distribution of power and privilege leading to efficient organizational outcomes, while conservatives do not anticipate significant or positive outcomes from participation, which is inevitably seen as embedded in the hierarchy. Using questionnaire surveys, the results suggest that investigators with conservative ideology allowed this to influence their research questions but not their methods, while liberalism had no measurable influence on either.

The overall conclusion from these historico-longitudinal investigations shows that societal values have influenced the way participation research is carried out, the kind of questions asked, and the choice of research method. As a consequence 'discrepancies have resulted in published American research on participation and its outcomes' (Wagner and Gooding 1987*a*: 257). Some research designs, using attitude-to-attitude measures, inflate outcome results and show that people who perceive their workplace as participative take a positive view of their work. Using attitude-to-outcome research designs, which produce much lower participation-outcome correlations, suggests that influence-sharing is 'unlikely to solve many of the productivity problems currently encountered in American work organizations' (p. 258). The authors relate these findings to the belief of many American researchers that 'America's industrial future depends on the adoption of participatory practices in the workplace' (p. 241). By implication, they raise the question whether, given the evidence, these beliefs are justifiable.

A similar somewhat pessimistic note is struck by Yukl (1989), who reviews the extensive literature on participation in the context of leadership studies. 'Overall, the research evidence was not sufficiently strong and consistent to reach any firm conclusions. After 35 years of research on participation, we are left with the conclusion that participative leadership sometimes results in higher satisfaction, decision acceptance, effort, and performance, and at other times it does not' (p. 86).

Finally one is left in no doubt about the importance of participation research by another recent broad overview and meta-analysis by Wagner (1994). One stimulus for this reanalysis of existing data is the continuing differences between two groups of academics. Leana, Locke and Schweiger (1990) consistently oppose the conclusion of Cotton, Vollrath, Froggatt, Lengnick-Hall, and Jennings (1988) and Cotton, Vollrath, Lengnick-Hall, and Froggatt (1990) that certain forms of participation and employee ownership have positive effects on performance and satisfaction. Locke and Schweiger (1979) had always maintained that their definition of participation had no noticeable effect on performance.

Wagner (1994) wants to lay these arguments to rest by undertaking a meta-analysis of the studies reviewed by Cotton and colleagues.[12] His reanalysis produces small but significant correlations between participation and performance or satisfaction, thus supporting the conclusions of the Cotton, Vollrath, Froggatt, Lengnick-Hall and Jennings (1988) and Cotton, Vollrath, Lengnick-Hall, and Froggatt (1990). However, since the size of the impact is not substantial, he goes on to review other evidence by adopting a broader definition of influence-sharing to include job enrichment interventions, management by objectives, socio-technical design procedures, and QWL programmes. However, he still excludes delegation, because this means relinquishing all influence to subordinates, and he excludes consultation, which involves idea generation but excludes the final-idea selection.[13]

This new sample of studies included seven meta-analyses and two narratives and one quantitative study of influence-sharing. The results were separately analysed for their effect on performance and satisfaction (Wagner 1994: 324). From this extensive data, Wagner concludes that the evidence 'is consistent in its support for the statement that research on participation has produced reliable evidence of statistically significant changes in performance and satisfaction that are positive in direction but limited in size' (p. 325).

Wagner goes on to ask whether, in view of the considerable costs involved in training and setting up participative organizations, management will be persuaded by the meagre statistical results. He answers this question negatively but admits that these meta-analyses, by their omissions, may give only a partial picture. For instance, he concedes that the Vroom and Yetton (1973) approach to leadership which concentrates on outputs such as the quality or effectiveness of decisions and stipulates situational moderators may come to quite different conclusions.[14]

Slow Diffusion: Evidence from Scandinavia

Slow diffusion, especially of direct participation, has been a problem recognized by scholars and practitioners the world over—for instance, by the US Dunlop Commission (1994). Scandinavian researchers have gone to considerable lengths to experiment with a variety of different approaches to facilitate diffusion and popular acceptance of participative work designs. Norway and Sweden in particular have, with justifiable pride, claimed considerable progress in the field of participation. Their experience goes back many decades and they have invested substantial intellectual and financial resources in a variety of schemes, many of which have pioneered theoretical as well as applied socio-technical developments that have attracted worldwide attention. Some of the early work started at the Oslo Work Research Institute in the 1960s (Emery and Thorsrud 1969). In contrast with the participation emphasis in Germany, which concentrated on legally backed indirect participation of employees on works councils and at boardroom level, the Norwegians preferred to start at the grass roots. They built up impressive experience of direct participation through a variety of in-depth case studies, most of which were fairly successful, but failed to spread to other sites, as had been hoped (Emery and Thorsrud 1976; Qvale 1976; 1989).

The democratizing work spread from Norway to Sweden in the 1969–73 URAF Programme and the 1982–86 Development Programme (Gustavsen 1992). Many Scandinavian researchers took part in the projects and in the discussions which led to changes in theory and practice. The early work was decisively influenced by Kurt Lewin and the field experiments in the Harwood plant, where Coch and French (1948) had conducted a classic experiment on the effect of worker participation on the acceptability of change and on productivity. The results of three experimental treatments of worker participation intensity were compared to a control group. The experiment supported the hypothesis that greater worker involvement was associated with higher productivity and lower resistance to change. Although these results were not replicated in a later Norwegian study (French, Israel, and Ås 1960), they provided inspiration and a point of departure. Gustavsen (1992) describes how the Scandinavians gradually moved away from the experimental theory-inspired field methodology towards a much more hands-on action-oriented approach to overcome what they saw as the limitation of the classical approach.

In both Norway and Sweden the main disappointment was with lack of diffusion to other sites. Sometimes an apparently successful participation project in one division of a company failed to spread to any other division, and, although positive results were published, there was no queue of new firms eager to get engaged with their work. A long debate about reasons for the lack of diffusion took place and led to various changes of tactic. For instance, it was felt that, in traditional action research, scientists took too prominent a part, thus reducing the motivation of managers and other employees to make changes on their own. Consequently, later project designs substantially reduced the role and visibility of the researcher, but this, too, failed to galvanize participants and organizations to take up what the scientists clearly felt to be potentially very successful lessons.

The original action research methodology had already been modified by abandoning the need for control groups and random sampling and giving greater emphasis to the issue of working life in general, rather than focusing on the work unit in which the experiment took place. Researchers became partners in a joint project with management and employees, and less emphasis was placed on a single theory introduced from the outside, like the socio-technical model. Another approach to prevent participative work designs becoming encapsulated was to organize a number of projects on a larger scale into a programme and so gain momentum (Qvale 1996).

In spite of these adaptations, further partnership between researchers and union–management practitioners had stagnated around 1980, particularly in Sweden; new agreements between the labour-market parties excluded research. The situation changed in the mid-1980s, when two major five-year programmes were launched: LOM in Sweden and SBA in Norway.

The methodology and the theoretical assumptions of these new programmes had become more radical and it is not unreasonable to attribute this to previous failures of diffusion and the crisis created by a drop in research interest around 1980. Gustavsen (1992), speaking about the programme, made this very clear: 'There is in principle only one answer . . . and this is to merge the research process with a restructuring of language . . . The chief purpose of language . . . is to link people to each other through the creation of shared meanings' (p. 33). These ideas are partly derived from the German social philosopher Habermas, and it is claimed that they go back to the way Socrates interacted with his students 2,500 years ago. Thirteen separate criteria are listed to describe the Democratic Dialogue (pp. 3–4) as used in the Swedish LOM programme. We will mention only a few, to give a flavour of what is involved:

- It must be possible for all concerned to participate.
- This is not enough. Everybody should also be active . . . Everybody has an obligation not only to put forward his or her own ideas, but also to help others to contribute theirs.
- Each participant must accept that other participants can have better arguments.
- The dialogue must continuously produce agreements which can provide platforms for practical action.

Further radicalization led to the rejection not only of general theories, but also of the recognition of contingency models which accommodate adjustments to situational factors. Their solution was to rely entirely on 'local theory'; this involves 'the construction of a map of any given organization as a local process which can, however, rely on more general concepts' (p. 20). In moving into the large-scale participatory LOM programme, they decided to break with four traditions. First, they considered it reasonable to assume that field experiments were not possible in the social field. Secondly, they came to believe that diffusion as such was not possible; this did not deny that changes could take place, but it had to be 'seen as re-structuring in parallel rather than as diffusion' (p. 28). Thirdly, they thought it wise to avoid drawing demarcation lines or boundaries that separate the research activities from the rest of the entity in which it is embedded, because these boundaries may obstruct the movement towards change. Fourthly, research should not be considered to be the only way to discover what is true or what is good for people; there are other avenues of discovery.

The Norwegian SBA programme was less theoretically radical but possibly more practical. It accepted the value of workplace designs, but insisted that design, the participatory process, and the implementation are closely integrated. SBA was a national development programme designed to make a direct contribution to the socio-economic problems of the country. In particular it was oriented to increase Norway's international competitiveness and thereby the level of employment. Action Research[15] was used as an instrument to achieve these objectives. It set out to change institutions, like universities, so that they in turn could become change agents and take on new roles in relation to the work life in organizations. SBA's aims were very ambitious, although Thoralf Qvale, its Director, never envisaged the five-year programme could do more than demonstrate to political and industrial leaders that their action-based approach was feasible and likely to bear fruit.[16] The idea was to create a national alliance of organizations and institutions that could independently or through cooperation achieve the necessary improvements in participation, quality, and productivity.

Both the Norwegian and Swedish programmes lasted five years and had assured financial resources. From the beginning both planned to have their work independently evaluated, and this resulted in two extensive reports on which we can now draw for our assessment. It is clear that the research has attracted sufficient interest in Norway to allow the Oslo Work Research Institute to launch a further longitudinal study which is intended to last seven years.

Given the objectives of the present chapter, we will note some of the critical assessments of the two evaluation studies. The Norwegian Report (Davies *et al.* 1993) noted that the Programme has been 'more successful at an individual project level than at a branch or regional and national levels. At the national level the outcome was far below the original goals' (p. iii). At the enterprise level, 64 per cent of the organizations want to continue with the work, although only 30 per cent are prepared to pay for it themselves. Over 50 per cent of the firms who participated in the programme have incorporated or will incorporate some expertise into their own organizations.

It is on the level of the overall mission, which was seen to be to assist Norwegian organizations and industries to become internationally competitive, that the report becomes pessimistic. To begin with, in spite of Norway's long history and international reputation for introducing direct participation measures, few wanted to adopt the SBA approach. There was very little diffusion between enterprises or to regional or national levels and there was little publicity and a noticeable lack of genuine support from key firms. Top Norwegian management, unions, and the government paid only lip-service. A more recent overview of the five-part Norwegian action research programme confirms the view that progress in democratization at the level of organizations has been disappointing and it is hoped that a more total systems-change approach planned for the sixth-generation action-research programme which started in 1996 will be more successful (Qvale 1996).

The LOM programme in Sweden was larger and more substantially financed than SBA. LOM worked with individual companies and a range of measures, including network diffusion, based on previous research evidence, and LOM put more emphasis on establishing clusters and networks between organizations and used extensive communication methods and action research to accumulate local knowledge and produce improved organizational practices.

The results as described in the Evaluation Report (Naschold 1993) are mixed. By its own high expectations a success rate of '33 per cent in innovative communicative development and 15 per cent for innovation in the technology, organization and personnel areas seems meagre' (p. 10). The programme is also criticized for its 'exclusive process orientation (which) . . . precludes any effort towards a design orientation. The programme . . . appears to be seriously under-instrumentalised' (p. 14) and showed serious limitations in the adequate control of processes of communication, which were relied on as the main instrument for introducing change. These limitations 'are reflected in the limited effectiveness of operational process control and level of innovation development achieved by the LOM Programme' (p. 14). Although the intention was to concentrate on bringing organizations together as clusters and networks, 75 per cent of projects were run on an individual basis and in the minority of cases where clusters were formed, 'only one or two meetings were held' (p. 130).

However, these apparently disappointing results have to be put into a comparative framework—for instance, by setting them against the successes and failure of the very large-scale German government-supported 'Humanization of Work', or its successor 'Work and Technology' programmes. The German research investment started in 1974 and so far has 'had little success in establishing intra-sectorial networks' and even less success with encouraging cross-sectorial collaboration (p. 130). By comparison with the heavily financed German programmes, the LOM 'achievement [is something] to be proud of, particularly in view of the short duration of the Programme' (pp. 135–6).

Norway and Sweden have a very long tradition of industrial cooperation, peaceful industrial relations, and concern for democratic issues covering a wider area than business or municipal organizations. Against this background an emphasis on Democratic Dialogue as the main tool for creating a climate of innovation and change in the economy may have a better opportunity of establishing itself than in other countries. It is therefore interesting to hear from Gustavsen (1992), the main architect for the LOM programme, that all is not well on 'the industrial democracy front today. The concept is not overwhelmingly popular among managers in general, and the unions tend to deal with it in a very cautious way' (p. 119). He goes on to wonder whether, in the light of this hostility or indifference, it is wise to emphasize such a term as 'industrial democracy' in a research strategy. It seems that Gustavsen and his colleagues now prefer to use a new and arguably more neutral term, like 'democratic dialogue', as the centrepiece of their strategy. It is probably only the initiated who are aware that behind the new term there is also a different method and philosophy of approach.

Overall support for the somewhat pessimistic conclusions of the LOM and SBA programmes comes from an interview-based survey of 228 private- and public-sector firms in Norway by Hammer, Ingebrigtsen, Karlsen, and Svarva (1994) and colleagues from the Norwegian Institute of Technology. The project was designed to examine the dynamic or large-scale organizational change and the role of worker participation in planning, designing, and executing the change projects. The Norwegian industrial relations system gives employees and their union representatives substantial legislative support for participation in major organizational changes and they operate a highly developed collective bargaining system. In spite of these favourable conditions, the findings show that change is dominated by senior management and neither representative nor direct participation plays a significant role and in particular is clearly excluded in the important design and planning phase of change projects.[17] Furthermore, the investigators conclude that, even where participation occurred, it did not contribute to success, which was more directly affected by conditions that operated from outside the organization; nor did participation reduce resistance to change.

Nevertheless, the Norwegian industrial-relations system operates smoothly, conflict levels are low, direct and representative participation are collaborative, and even the moderate amount of participation observed was associated with satisfaction. Among the reasons for this non-adversarial situation, the researchers mention a high investment in education and training of workers' representatives and worker directors in economic analysis, organizational theory, and strategy. This background, it is claimed, enables them to make appropriate judgements of the degree of realism and urgency of the ongoing change projects.

Many people associate the Swedish participation system with the name of Volvo and the innovative assembly system of motor cars at their Kalmar factory and the later much more radically innovative design at the Uddevalla plant. These developments have received considerable attention in the recent literature and it is claimed that the human-resource management practices in the motor car industry have been a seedbed for more general movements which have emerged world-wide (Rehder 1994: 1). In previous chapters we have already referred to Saturn and the NUMMI car plants. The debate about which of these methods of production is more effective, more employee friendly, or more democratic has been provoked by the $5 million MIT study of car manufacturing methods in fourteen countries, published by Womack, Jones, and Roos (1990). They claimed that the Japanese lean production system pioneered by Toyota and used in Japan as well as in transplant companies in the USA, is substantially more productive than other systems, gives greater job security and considerably less absenteeism, and invests much more in training and team working than standard American or European plants. While these claims are not challenged directly, there have been several very critical analyses of the demanding pressures exerted by the kaizen system, which expects employees to take substantial responsibilities for quality and for continuous improvements in productivity and general efficiency. The team system too has been criticized for being narrowly based and routinized so that, 'if anything, the rhythm and pace of the work on the assembly line is more inexorable under the Japanese management system than it ever was before' (Berggren 1993). Swedes are proud of their humanistic approach to work and Swedish unions seem to support these aspirations in which 'Good work is envisioned as safe while it provides scope for increasing responsibility, autonomy, variety and social interaction' (Sandberg *et al.* 1992: p. vii). Swedish managing directors, in a sample of 293 firms, also seem to have positive attitudes towards employee participation. They believe that it leads to a better quality of decision-making and swifter implementation (Levinson 1997). The arguments about the degree of humaneness, participation, and self-fulfilment between the Japanese and Swedish systems will no doubt continue, though it seems that for the moment the former has had a greater impact on Western managerial philosophy. In 1993 social scientists and other well-wishers were deeply disappointed to hear that Volvo had decided to close down the Kalmar as well as the Uddevalla assembly plants which were relatively small compared with other Volvo factories and not very convincing reasons were offered. Both factories were later reopened, though some of the innovativeness seems to have been abandoned (Sandberg 1995).[18]

The problem of diffusion, even of apparently successful participative practices, remains unresolved. Cole (1989) looks at facilitators and obstacles to diffusion in Sweden, Japan, and the USA and concludes that the process of diffusion of participatory work structures 'does not involve a rational process' (Cole 1982: 220). In a recent analysis, Lillrank (1995) makes the point that, while capital can be transferred from one financial centre to another in seconds, organizational innovations may take years or even decades (p. 971). The time for technical innovations is less speedy than the transfer of capital but faster than the transfer of management concepts. A really new and efficient mousetrap will soon be copied, but for organizational success stories Lillrank uses the analogy of the transfer of electricity over long distances resulting in extensive power loss.

Where Do We Go from Here?

There is an enormous scientific and popular literature about participation and participatory practices and there is some theory and evidence to back it up. How reliable are the conclusions that can be drawn from this evidence? Alternatively, and accepting that influence-sharing practices exist and are often thought to be in varying degrees successful, what are the circumstances that favour or inhibit success? These are big questions to which we hope to give some answers in the next two chapters. The present chapter is intended to lead us into these more testing issues, but has the narrower objective of looking at the evidence, which shows that, inevitably, the prospects for democratic practices in organizations are somewhat limited. There is also some theory to explain why these limitations exist. Lafferty (1975), drawing on a variety of established theorists, concludes that people's capacity and desire for participation depend on very difficult and complex circumstances and motivational patterns so that, in the end, each person will make choices on whether to opt in or out of a constantly shifting perception of social reality.

How serious are these limits? As is usual in the social-science field, reality is often assessed against expectations and the gap can be substantial. We have already noticed that Cole (1982) chastised a well-known colleague for making quite unrealistic claims for participatory methods. Quite independently, Argyris and Schön (1991) have dissociated themselves from the claims made for Participatory Action Research (PAR) by a group of well-known American and Scandinavian social scientists, and they question the value of the results they describe.

This problem was anticipated by Strauss (1963), who pointed out that the movement in favour of participation and power equalization was imbued with value judgements with a 'strong emphasis on individual dignity, creative freedom, and self-development, this hypothesis bears all the earmarks of its academic origin' (p. 47). He goes on to question whether most non-academics share these professorial aspirations and whether these theories are functionally suited to all varieties of jobs, including those where self-actualization is neither feasible nor desired. The moral judgements emanating from the academic literature go beyond description. They suggest that people should *want* more freedom and self-actualization; and that not desiring these things is morally reprehensible or a sign of immaturity. But Strauss argues that 'mature behavior does not mean freedom from all restrictions; it means successful adjustment to them' (p. 50), and he goes on to cite Eric Fromm, who contended that most people do not want complete freedom but prefer to know the limits within which they can act and feel comfortable.

This is very different from the conditions put down as essential for the development of Democratic Dialogue in Sweden—namely, that everybody must participate and everybody has an obligation to be active and that, as a consequence, agreement will be reached resulting in practical action.

Three underemphasized but essential assumptions underlie the belief in successful and voluntary power equalization schemes, or in the Democratic Dialogue: motivation, competence, and trust. Competence was treated at some length in an earlier section of this chapter and the underemphasized role of trust is reflected in the many examples of research throughout this book which imply the need for trustful relations between participants but fail to give it the central explanatory role which it deserves. The relation of motivation to participation has received some attention—for instance, in the human-relations theories of the 1960s which saw a natural progression based on Maslow's hierarchy of needs ending with an allegedly universal desire for self-actualization. As we have just seen, the universality of this progress has been questioned.[19]

Overall, the evidence presented in this chapter suggests that theoretical considerations as well as practical experience and research evidence converge to set fairly narrow limits to the development of substantial and lasting participative practices in organizations. This does not mean that more favourable conditions and superior knowledge may not enable us to do better in the future. Mathews (1994), describing organizational democracy practices in Australia, strikes an optimistic note with an Australian metaphor claiming that firms are learning to catch the wave and ride it.

NOTES

1. This line of thinking is given prominence by sociological theorists who argue that all so-called reality, including classifications such as success or failure and descriptions of power, are subjective and constructed by us through perceptual and social processes (Berger and Luckman 1971). At least one school of psychology takes a somewhat similar approach (Moscovici and Doise 1994) using the term 'social representation'. There is some value in drawing attention to the force of expectations and socially constructed realities, but we oppose nihilistic theories of so-called post-modernism which turn their backs on any form of objectivity and any methods which attempt to evaluate subjective realities like judgements on the distribution of power in organizations (Alvesson 1995). However, as will be seen throughout this book, we are also sceptical of scientistic methodologies which make unrealistic or exaggerated claims about the validity of their conclusions. The term 'scientistic' is used, following Hayek (1952), to describe social-science methods which inappropriately copy the physical sciences.
2. Unlike a cooperative where employees own shares, the Commonwealth shares are owned collectively by the workforce.
3. It is perhaps relevant to point out that both CEOs were natural autocrats who used their power to introduce and sustain the changes they wished to accomplish. The Scott Bader Commonwealth structure has survived but little effective participation is now available to employees. The Glacier Metal Company was taken over by a larger company and the participative structure eventually disappeared.
4. A number of other scales have been used—for instance, by Tannenbaum and Schmidt (1958). Nearly all American work ends the range of alternative decisions styles with interpersonal or group participation. In Europe, as we shall see, the range has been extended to include various forms of decentralization, delegation, or autonomy (see Tables 1.1 and 1.2).
5. This distinction reduces the confusion that produced pseudo-participation based on consultation without influence.
6. Under the acronym EPOC (Employee Direct Participation in Organizational Change). See, for instance, Geary (1994); Regalia (1995); and the *European Participation Monitor*.
7. Starting with a telephone survey, Freeman and Roger (1994) then followed up roughly 1,000 participants to probe responses and obtain additional information on workplace relations and policies.
8. Respondents were in full-time employment and covered the full range of industrial sectors. A response rate of over 90 per cent was achieved.
9. In 1996 there were 280 kibbutzim with a population of 126,000.
10. The term contingency will be mentioned several times in this chapter. It describes a relationship between two variables or conditions which are influenced by or depend on another variable or condition. So, for instance, the effectiveness of participation may be said to be contingent on trust.

11. The article uses the terminology of social constructionism (Berger and Luckman 1971), symbolic acts, myths, metaphors, and stories, but can easily be translated into an account of managers using intensive communication and employee involvement to gain acceptance for the new hospital information system.
12. We will not go into a methodological description of Wagner's research, but the final analysis he uses is 23 per cent smaller than the Cotton *et al.* study in order to achieve a more coherent sample, and he claims that the results are likely to underestimate true population effects.
13. These exclusions are problematic; for instance, most field research on participation fails to identify whether it includes making the final decision. Our own experience suggests that it rarely does.
14. By concentrating entirely on American research, Wagner fails to review the very extensive European literature, some of which anticipated Vroom and Yetton.
15. Action research describes a variety of implementation and action-oriented applied research. The methods derive from early work by Kurt Lewin and are meant to be theory-based.
16. Personal communication from Thoralf Qvale, 21 Feb. 1994.
17. Participation plays a moderate role during the execution or implementation phase. This finding is identical with the results of the three-country Decision in Organization study (Koopman *et al.* 1993) and reinforces the need to use a longitudinal approach.
18. Personal communication from Åke Sandberg, June 1996.
19. While we do not use these terms in the 1990s, they are functionally equivalent to semi-autonomy and to the more extensive levels of power-sharing described in the IPC.

6. Participation Works—If Conditions are Appropriate

The theme of this chapter is that, despite its 'dark side', just discussed, participation frequently 'works'. True it works in a variety of ways. But this is understandable given its many forms. Further, it does not always 'work'. For it to work, certain conditions must be met. Some of these requirements are quite substantial. Participation will not succeed if viewed as merely rhetoric or a gimmick. Success typically requires substantial changes in organizational relationships and values. Nevertheless, taken as a whole, the evidence for participation's success is rather impressive.

This chapter consists of three main parts. The first deals with methodological issues, while the second reviews the evidence as to participation's success. The last and longer one sketches the conditions necessary for this success. In so doing it links up with the caveats of the previous chapter.

Methodological Issues

Participation takes many forms. It is introduced for a variety of different reasons: to humanize work, to reduce power differences, to increase competitiveness, to improve union–management relations, and even for nation-building (for a more complete list, see Chapter 1). Consequently criteria for success differ greatly. Some criteria, such as productivity, can easily be expressed in numbers; others, such as humanization, are more difficult to measure. Indeed efforts to measure participation's success are beset by methodological problems (for a listing, see Ichniowski *et al.* 1996). Here are a few.

- It is assumed that (*a*) the introduction of a formal participation scheme leads to changes in actual behaviour (that is, that *de jure* participation leads to *de facto* participation), and (*b*) this behaviour change has a positive impact on some important output variable, such as satisfaction or productivity. If a study shows negative results, it is important to know whether this is because of a failure of (*a*), (*b*), or both.
- Much research is cross-sectional—that is, it compares organizations at one moment of time with and without a given form of participation. But cross-sectional studies may be misleading, because differences in performance may be due to factors other than participation—for example, to differences in management or union behaviour, investment, products, or markets. While one can attempt to 'control' statistically for these factors, one can never be

sure that the right factors are controlled. For this reason longitudinal comparisons over fairly lengthy periods of time are usually preferable. Short-term comparisons may be misleading, since a participation scheme may be successful for a few years and then peter out.

- Cause-and-effect problems need to be untangled. For example, companies with Employee Stock Ownership Plans (ESOPs) tend to be more successful than those without. But do companies adopt these plans because they already enjoy profits? Or do they become more profitable because they adopt ESOPs? Further, companies that introduce participation may be generally more innovative, 'forward looking' and 'progressive'. So can any seemingly positive results of participation be ascribed to participation itself or to company culture generally? Again, longitudinal studies comparing outputs before and after change may help answer this question.
- Even with a longitudinal study, it is never clear whether an observed improvement in performance is due to participation or to other things happening at the same time. Ideally we should take two matched samples of identical organizations which have identical experiences over a considerable period of time, with the single exception that participation is introduced into one set of organizations and not the other. Such perfect experimental conditions are almost never possible.
- In practice, participation is often introduced along with other 'workplace reforms', such as training, performance-based compensation, and increased job security. Indeed, as we discuss later, considerable research suggests that participation alone is more likely to be successful if introduced as part of package (or 'bundle') of such policies. Unfortunately this makes it harder to measure the impact of participation alone. (Possibly such a measure might be meaningless. Participation will work only accompanied by appropriate other policies. Examining the effect of participation while holding other policies constant is a bit like examining the impact of the length of left legs on running ability, meanwhile holding the length of right legs constant.)
- Research typically requires the cooperation of the people being researched. Firms are more likely to allow researchers to study successes than failures. Consequently, the literature is likely to accentuate successes and disregard failures.
- As discussed in Chapter 5, there can easily be disagreement as to the criteria by which participative efforts are to be judged (Marchington 1994); political liberals may give greater weight to factors such as job satisfaction and mental health, while conservatives are more concerned with productivity (Wagner and Gooding 1987*a*). Those who believe the goal of participation should be humanistic will stress different factors from those who are primarily concerned with organizational efficiency. Businessmen may judge participation of its impact on stock prices (as in Huselid 1995), while the German literature is more likely to use political criteria (Wever 1994). Our own definition of participation reveals our liberal, humanistic bias.

Even were the evidence to suggest that participation actually hurts productivity and quality, an argument could be made that participation could be justified on humanistic grounds (see Chapter 2). Indeed, as Williamson (1980) suggests (see Chapter 5), employees might conceivably accept lower wages in return for the benefits of greater self-determination.

Participation Works

With these reservations in mind, let us examine experience with various forms of participation.

Employee Ownership

Employee ownership has been introduced for a variety of reasons, among others for primarily idealistic reasons, to establish a workplace where there are no bosses and everyone is equal, to save jobs in economically distressed plants which might otherwise shut down, or to motivate employees to work harder.

Mondragon is perhaps the best-known example of employee ownership. Established in part to provide employment in a impoverished section of Spain, it combined a high measure of Catholic-oriented idealism with political opposition to Franco. Taking root in an initially politically quite unfavourable environment, it has grown and been economically successful. By 1995 it employed 27,000 members. Branching into a variety of fields, it exported a considerable part of its production. Though profit levels have fluctuated, it has provided relatively stable employment and good wages for its members.

The fact that Mondragon grew is not particularly remarkable; many firms grow. More important is that, despite its growth, it is still employee-owned and employee-managed. Its leadership is elected, key issues are widely debated, and its members make significant decisions. Further, in the face of the increasing competition caused by Spain's joining the EU, Mondragon made major structural changes, but it did so only after considerable discussion and without changing its basic participative process. Possibly more important, at least in the eyes of its founders, Mondragon helped the economic development of the entire Basque region (Whyte 1991; Whyte and Whyte 1992).

Mondragon is not employee ownership's only success story. Despite current problems (discussed in Chapter 5), until recently Israeli kibbutzim were economically successful and contributed substantially to nation-building. Further, they were successful in developing substantially egalitarian communities (at least for men).

Yugoslav self-management provides a good example of the contrasting 'shadows-and-light' aspects of participation. The former was stressed in Chapter 5, but here we can report that self-management was successful on several counts.[1] According to most of IDE's (1981*b*) many measures of participative structure and influence, Yugoslav industries were the most participative of the industries in the eleven countries studied. Further, 'self-management educated the workers and created a feeling of collective property and collective responsibility for the organization they worked in' (Pusić 1996: 148). It did much to transform a traditional, hierarchical society. Gross National Product (GNP) expanded rapidly, but this growth was achieved with less stress than in most developing societies (Malcolm Warner 1975). Self-management acted as a safety value, co-opting many possible dissenters and directing their energies toward safe-plant-level issues. Finally, self-management trained a whole generation of managers (Dunlop 1958).

Of course, Mondragon, the kibbutz, and Yugoslavian self-management all represent exceptional situations. Yet there are numerous examples of successful employee ownership, accompanied by various degrees of actual employee control. Small producers' cooperatives are quite common in Continental Europe. Outside the USA they have a higher overall survival rate than their capitalist counterparts (Jones 1980; Ben-Ner 1988).

Relative to other firms in the British retail industry, the employee-owned John Lewis Partnership performs well in terms of growth, productivity, and investments. With profit-sharing bonuses, employees earn considerably more than the market average. Employee turnover is low (Bradley *et al.* 1990). Although John Lewis's chairman retains the final word, there is an elaborate committee structure which allows some employee input.

There have been numerous cases of 'plant-rescue' employee ownership in Europe, Canada, and the USA (for summaries of the research, see Bonin *et al.* 1993 and Gunderson *et al.* 1995). In most cases these involved economically distressed enterprises which might otherwise might have closed down altogether. As we have seen (Chapter 1), some have succeeded so well that they were sold back into traditional 'capitalist' ownership, with individual employees earning a substantial profit on the deal. In other instances, the firms were so technologically backward or so badly undercapitalized that, despite often-valiant employee efforts, these plants eventually failed. Even these cases can be judged as partial successes because employees held on to their jobs longer than they might have done otherwise (and many of these cases occurred in communities where equivalent jobs were scarce).

A case in point may be Algoma Steel. Formerly a subsidiary of a larger company, this 6,000-employee plant was the primary employer in an isolated Canadian community. When, in the face of huge losses, the plant's owners threatened to shut it down altogether, a largely union-sponsored plan was developed which gave employees 60 per cent of the stock in return for a 16 per cent wage cut. The union received four seats on the thirteen-member board of directors, with public figures holding most of the rest. Government-financed early retirement was arranged for many employees. Levels of management were reduced and the supervisory ratio was cut with the intent of converting supervisors into 'consultants'. Meanwhile an elaborate set of joint union–management committees was introduced and an effort was made to spread semi-autonomous work teams throughout the plant.

The results? The plant returned to profitability (but this can be attributed partly to more favourable economic conditions). Union grievances have practically disappeared. On the other hand, to raise the capital required to bring the plant up to date technologically, the firm was forced to put majority control back into private hands. Still to be determined is whether the firm can survive an economic downturn. For the moment, however, a large number of employees have saved their jobs (Gunderson *et al.* 1995).

United Airlines, the largest US airline, is now majority employee owned. Its twelve-person board includes three union representatives. An extensive network of participative activities has been established at all levels. One measure of results: the price of stock still in non-employee hands has done very well. On the other hand, as of early 1997, negotiations as to new collective bargaining agreement had become quite adversarial, threatening the continuance of cooperation at lower levels.

Finally, studies of employee stock ownership provide considerable evidence that ESOP firms are more productive, more profitable, and grow faster than non-ESOP firms.[2] But this relationship is much stronger when stock ownership is combined with actual direct or representative participation (see Chapter 1 for citations). Further, survey results generally 'indicate favourable perceived effects [of employee stock ownership] on employee attitudes in such areas as job satisfaction, commitment, and motivation. In such cases these positive effects were stronger if ownership was also accompanied by increased participation in decision-making' (Gunderson *et al.* 1995: 424; see also Tannenbaum 1983, Kruse 1984, and Rosen *et al.* 1985).

Representative Participation

The criteria for success here are rather ambiguous. Given the many varieties of representative participation, generalization is difficult. It has been adapted for a range of reasons, especially to facilitate communication, to improve labour–management relations, and to reduce power differences.

The IDE studies (IDE 1981*b*, 1993) found that high formal power for representative bodies (including unions) translates into high involvement and commitment.

The quantitative evidence as to co-determination's impact on profits and productivity in Germany is mixed.[3] Nevertheless works councils are widely given credit for Germany's high productivity and relative industrial peace (see Chapters 1 and 4). According to case studies and anecdotal reports (e.g. Wever 1994), works councils improve communications, reduce misunderstanding, result in high-quality decisions being made, and smooth the way for technological change. Also they reduce turnover (Sadlowski *et al.* 1995).

For example, they have taken a proactive role in restructuring the German steel industry, sponsoring, for instance, at Hoesch's Dortmund plant, voluntary 'participation groups' which helped reorganize work, shape ergonomic conditions, and discuss the sequence of work and the division of labour. This is in sharp contrast to the entirely reactive and largely ineffective role of the divided unions at British Steel (Bacon *et al.* 1996). True, management often charges that co-determination slows decision-making and reduces flexibility. This may well happen in many cases. Nevertheless, the majority opinion of expert observers appears to be that German co-determination has been a success.

Though works councils are less powerful in other countries, on balance their influence on labour–management relations seems positive. Works councils, for example, have played a key role in many countries in facilitating adjustment to new markets and technological change and even in negotiating capacity cuts. Streeck (1995: 677–8) concludes that 'the parallel evolution of representative consultation in European countries over the last two decades may have virtuously responded to economic needs, and may have helped these countries master the challenges of post-Fordism'.

Not everyone agrees, but there is evidence suggesting that unions in the USA increase productivity but decrease profits (Freeman and Medoff 1984).

Direct Participation

Quantitative measures as to the impact of direct participation are becoming increasingly common. These relate to both individual workplaces and whole industries. The main measures of success have been productivity and satisfaction, but there are data as to other variables such as quality, safety, turnover, absenteeism, profits, return on investment, and even stock prices.[4] A major finding of many studies is that direct participation is unlikely to prosper or even to survive unless it is accompanied by other appropriate human-resources policies.

NUMMI and Saturn have been discussed at some length in Chapter 1. Employees in both US companies have enjoyed considerable influence in designing their jobs. NUMMI has set US records in terms of productivity, quality, low absenteeism, and low turnover. Saturn, which enjoys a high level of joint union–management decision-making, has also done well. Both plants have been marked by intensive employee-training, strong unions, and considerable (at least symbolic) efforts to reduce status differences. Employees in both cases are very proud of their product. The General Motors (GM) Eisenach plant in the former East Germany has much the same teamwork structure as NUMMI and has obtained much the same results (Lowell Turner, personal communication).

Xerox, the copy company, has acquired the reputation of being almost a prototype of good union–management relations. Faced with severe competitive pressures in the early 1980s and the apparent need to close down some of its uncompetitive US operations, a series of largely employee-staffed teams proposed enough cost-cutting changes to save their jobs (Kochan *et al.* 1986). Nevertheless, despite top-level cooperation, the extent of workplace participation and cooperation varied considerably among individual departments.

Cutcher-Gershenfeld (1991) studied the impact of these differences, classifying departments as 'traditional', 'transitional', or 'transformed' on the basis of such variables as the number of autonomous work groups in existence, the number of higher-level grievances, frequency of conflicts and speed of their resolution, the extent of informal autonomy and worker-initiated change in work design, and the average number of formal problem-solving efforts. In other words, the study's emphasis was on the quality of problem-solving and conflict resolution, not just the existence of work teams. 'Transformed' departments were those which showed up better than 'traditional departments' on these measures (there being considerable intercorrelation). As hypothesized, transformed departments enjoyed lower costs, higher productivity, fewer defects, less scrap, and better on-time delivery. Once more, the combination of human-resource practices had greater impact than teamwork alone.

Somewhat similar results were obtained at a US paper mill (Ichniowski 1992). Prior to change, jobs here were narrowly defined, with ninety-four separate job classifications and 160 employees on a given shift. After a bitter three-month strike, the union and management decided to start anew. Team organization was introduced. The ninety-six job classifications were combined into four job 'clusters' and each worker's pay was raised to the highest pay in his or her job cluster. Workers were given extensive training so that they could perform their broadened tasks. Employment security (no lay-offs) was guaranteed. The union-grievance procedure was redesigned.

Once again the results were favourable. Though higher pay increased total labour costs, this was more than offset by extra production and sales and lowered non-labour costs. Absenteeism fell by half, accidents by more than that, union grievances declined by 95 per cent, and plant profits tripled. After seven years, favourable results persisted. Significantly these results were obtained even though the company involved had gone through considerable downsizing.

Chapter 1 contrasted the team-oriented 'module' with the more individualistic 'bundle' form of garment manufacture. Berg, Applebaum, Bailey, and Kalleberg (1996) compared two plants making identical garments, one using the module system and the other the bundle. Module work enjoyed a 30 per cent advantage in terms of overall production costs. Other garment industry research also demonstrates the superiority of the plants with the module system (Dunlop and Weil 1996). But the production system alone may not be responsible: module-system employees are more likely to receive training in problem-solving and other skills and to enjoy profit-sharing or some other form of gain-sharing.

US telecommunications companies have experimented widely with QCs, TQM, and self-managing work teams. Batt (1995) extensively studied these programmes in a variety of departments in two different business units in one such company. Ichniowski *et al.* (1996: 317, 323) summarize this research as follows:

Compared to traditional work arrangements, the quality program made little difference in performance while self-managing work teams made a lot. In network services, the primary effect of self-managing work teams was to reduce the number and costs of middle management. In customer services, self-managing services achieved sales that were 20 per cent higher than sales of traditionally organized work groups. Both sets of self-managed teams reported higher levels of quality . . . Ninety per cent of those in self-managed teams preferred their new work arrangements. . . . [T]he increase in annual sales revenue associated with self-managed groups in customer service translated into more than $10,000 per employee; and in network operations, cost savings due to self-managed teams would exceed $200 million per year for the entire division.

Teamwork in the confectionery factory (discussed in Chapter 5) increased intrinsic and extrinsic job satisfaction and employees much preferred the new arrangements to the old.

Industry studies. A major problem with case studies is that successes are more likely to be reported than failures. Researchers are more likely to be permitted access to successes; further, success stories are more likely to be accepted for publication. Thus case studies may be useful chiefly for raising questions and suggesting hypotheses. Research which covers an entire industry is more likely to develop valid generalizations.

The International Motor Vehicle Program examined the impact of various technological and human-resources practices on productivity and quality (MacDuffie 1995; Pil and MacDuffie 1996). Instead of individual case studies, this programme surveyed sixty-two automobile assembly plants in five continents with a follow-up of eight-six plants five years later. Altogether these plants represented between a half and two-thirds of the assembly capacity worldwide. Among the variables investigated were the use of 'high-commitment' work practices, such as 'on-line' (decision-making) work teams, 'off-line' problem-solving groups, job rotation, suggestion programmes, and the extent to which production employees take direct responsibility for quality-related activities. Another set of variables was concerned with employment conditions, such as extent of job security, training, and compensation methods. A final set focused on technology, especially the use of buffers, extent of automation, and work complexity.

Based on statistical cluster analysis the researchers were able to group these plants into three clusters, depending on the practices followed: 'mass production', 'transitional', and 'flexible production'. For example, 70 per cent of the flexible-production workforce worked in team-based systems and 70 per cent were involved in 'EI, QC' problem-solving groups—as contrasted to 22 and 33 per cents respectively in mass production.

Among the findings was the fact that the plants which practised flexible production considerably outperformed mass-production plants in terms of both productivity and quality. Further, 'innovative HR practices affect performance not individually but as interrelated elements in an internally consistent HR "bundle" or system; and that these HR bundles contribute most to assembly plant productivity and quality when they are integrated with manufacturing policies under the "organizational logic" of a flexible production system' (MacDuffie 1995: 217).

Similarly, Ichniowski, Shaw, and Prennushi (1995) compared the efficiency of very similar production processes in a large number of US steel mills. Plants which combined problem-solving teams and broadly defined jobs with extensive training, employment security, and gain-sharing were 7 per cent more productive than plants with more traditional processes. In the highly competitive steel industry 7 per cent makes a great deal of difference. But this result was obtained only in plants which had adopted 'bundles' of associated work practices and policies. The effect of work teams alone, for example, was negligible. A study of thirty 'mini-mills' yielded similar results (Arthur 1994).

Meta-analyses. Chapter 5 summarized the negative results from meta-analyses which seek to draw generalizations from large numbers of individual surveys. As mentioned, the results of these various compilations vary. A meta-analysis of 131 North American field studies of organizational change (Macy and Izumi 1993) draws somewhat more optimistic conclusions than those previously discussed, finding that a majority of the studies participation had positive impacts on measures of productivity, quality, and cost (called 'financial' measures by the authors). Of these changes, multi-skilling (broad banding), multi-skill training, and autonomous and semi-autonomous work teams[5] had the greatest impact. The impact on behavioural measures, such as absenteeism and turnover, was less, as was the impact on job satisfaction. Further, work changes, including work teams, had a greater impact than changes in human-resource policies. Finally, a combination of changes had greater impact than any single change alone.

Actually, for our purpose here, meta-analyses are of little help. The great variety among the findings of individual cases (technically their high standard deviation) suggests merely that participation works in some places and not in others, under some conditions and not under others. But meta-analysis tells us only a little bit about the particular situations under which participation is most likely to succeed.

Beyond this, when participation works, it works in different ways. The numerous studies of direct participation in the USA (including many not encompassed by meta-analysis) show that more often than not direct participation leads to at least short-term improvement in one or more of the following variables: satisfaction, commitment, quality, productivity, turnover, absenteeism, profits, and stocks. In some cases one factor is improved, in others, a different factor.

Implications of these Studies

In the first place, as just mentioned, participation can work, but not always. It works under appropriate conditions and in different ways.

Secondly, participation is not a cure-all. The cases covered above were successes by many standards, but often less successful by others. Let us return to those just discussed. Co-determination has been charged with reducing flexibility and competitiveness. Until rather recently Mondragon paid little attention to direct participation. Though the John Lewis Partnership allows employee input through an elaborate committee structure, the final word rests with the Chairman. Yugoslav self-management failed to adopt to recent changes in that tragic country; but even before then, political and banking interference severely reduced the extent of self-management. NUMMI workers are tied to a sixty-second job cycle. 'Bundle' workers in the garment industry reported higher levels of tension. Teamwork in the confectionery case had little impact on such measures as organizational commitment and cost gains were due chiefly to the elimination of supervisors.

Finally, participation works best when accompanied with other appropriate human resources policies, a point we enlarge upon later.

To return to our first point, what are the requirements (appropriate conditions) for participative success? Put another way, what are the barriers which must be overcome if participation is to fulfil its theoretical promise? We consider these 'contingency-related' questions next.

The Requirements of Participative Success

Regardless of how 'success' is defined, participation's success seems to depend on a variety of factors. These can be divided into five headings. First, participation should be supported by the major organizational stakeholders, employees, work groups, supervisors and middle managers, higher management, and unions. Secondly, it should be associated with appropriate human-resources policies, especially those relating to compensation, status symbols, job security, and training. Thirdly, the organizational context in which participation occurs should be favourable. Fourthly, what might be called the environmental 'infrastructure' should be favourable. Finally, the entire participative scheme must avoid atrophy; it must survive. We discuss these issues in turn.

Stakeholder Support

Individual employees. Participation is more likely to be 'successful' if employees perceive it to have some sort of pay-off for them. Pay-off from the participative *process* can take a variety of forms: a sense of achievement and autonomy, increased knowledge, increased sense of control, increased competence, or just social satisfaction gained from working with other people. *The results of participation* may also provide pay-offs: more interesting jobs, easier work, or increased job security. Not all these forms of pay-off need to be achieved, but enough so that the costs of participation in terms of time, effort, and uncertainty are counterbalanced.

In the case of NUMMI, the rewards from participation included increased job security, the production of a high-quality product, the elimination of waste motions, and perhaps the social satisfaction derived from the time spent each week in participative activities—short as it was. Few workers reported finding their sixty-second job cycle satisfying in itself. Nevertheless, jobs may be 'socially constructed'. The fact that NUMMI's jobs were participatively designed may have made them intrinsically more motivating (or at least less distasteful) than if their design was imposed.

Yet inducing employees to participate is no easy task. True, according to rhetoric, employees represent 'untapped resources' which they would be delighted to contribute to the organization if given a chance. In practice it does not always work out this way. Not all employees want the added responsibilities of enriched jobs; some would rather not change their secure routines (Fenwick and Olson 1986; Leitko *et al.* 1985). As described in Chapter 5, when polled in surveys, most employees report they want more opportunity to participate than they have now, but not much more (IDE 1981*b*).

More central to the success of participation is the extent to which employees are willing to devote time to participation in practice. Considerable research suggests that, even when given the opportunity to participate, relatively few employees take advantage of this opportunity (Leitko *et al.* 1985; Cutcher-Gershenfeld *et al.* 1991; see also Chapter 5). They want the results of participation, but are reluctant to involve themselves personally to achieve these results.

It is rare for more than a quarter of the employees in any location to participate in QCs or similar time-consuming activities (e.g. Griffin 1988—but see Osterman 1994*a*). (Japan is the major exception: here (according to Lincoln 1989), in those plants which had QCs, 94 per cent participated, though often not voluntarily.) Further, according to IDE (1981*b*: 189, 230), only in former Yugoslavia were as many as 20 per cent of the employees willing to be candidates for positions on the representative participative body. Willingness to participate differs not just by countries, but by education, occupation, and personality. For example, professionals and skilled trades employees seem to have greater than average interest in participation. Nevertheless, it is low.

There are a variety of factors which might affect both general desire for participation as well as the willingness to spend time doing so (Dean 1985; McCarthy 1989; Borzeix and Linhart 1989; see also Chapter 2).

- For fundamental personality reasons or because of culture and upbringing, employees may feel uncomfortable in expressing themselves, especially in the presence of supervisors or people of higher caste or status (see Chapter 5 for a discussion of dependency theory). For example, participation may be seen as criticism and therefore inappropriate. Ganguli (1964) reports that Indian employees feel that decision-making is the job of top management, not of employees. (On the other hand, professionals in Western countries view participation as a right.) Consequently some firms—such as NUMMI—have developed selection procedures to increase the likelihood that new employees will fit into a cooperative environment.
- As the previous chapter stressed, employees may lack the skills and knowledge to participate—or think they do. Further, they may lack the incentives to acquire them.

- Participation is time- and energy-consuming and frequently frustrating. Some employees may be willing to participate in return for extra pay or reduced workload, but not in addition to their other assignments. (Others, however, may be anxious for the challenge participation entails.)
- Employees may feel that their current job is already sufficiently challenging or ambiguous. Like professors overloaded with committee work, they may suffer from 'decisional satiation' (Alutto and Belasco 1972) and so prefer to avoid further responsibilities.
- If their interests lie outside the workplace (i.e. it has little salience for them), they may prefer to spend their participative energies elsewhere, say, in a pub or in community activity.
- Employees may willingly participate with regard to only a limited number of topics. For example, they may enthusiastically participate in decisions to raise wages or improve working conditions, but show little interest in improving quality or rectifying supply imbalances. Further, there is the broader question raised by economists (see Chapter 5): why should people participate if everyone shares in the benefits of participation, whether they participate or not?
- Among the presumed advantages of participation is that employees 'buy into' the system—that is, they become more committed to the organization. But employees may consciously or subconsciously believe they are being manipulated. If they are hostile to the organization, they may have no desire to make it work better. Further, hostility to their particular supervisor or to the organization as a whole may quickly develop into hostility to participation generally (Marchington *et al.* 1993). Many employees have developed a habit or culture of passive resistance to everything management proposes; changing this culture so that employees become actively involved in actively governing the workplace may be difficult (Borzeix and Linhart 1989).
- Even when permitted substantial discretion, employees may resist change. The module system in garments requires not just that employees learn new skills, but that they give up painfully acquired old ones which had once provided status and security (Dunlop and Weil 1996; for a classic older study, which made the same point, see Coch and French 1948).
- Employees may participate for a while and then decide they are accomplishing nothing and so drop out, frustrated. Or they may conclude that they are being offered only 'pseudo-participation' and that they have little real influence (see Chapter 5). According to Fucini and Fucini (1990), participation failed in Mazda's US plant because of great inconsistency between management's stated values and its practice. Teams and team leaders were given little real discretion.

There is some evidence that participation is addictive—that is, the more people have, the more they want (Mulder 1971).[6] On the other hand, participation may also be frustrating and actual experience with it may reduce one's desire for more. Obradović (1970) found that those who had actually served on

Yugoslav workers' councils were more alienated than those who had not. Thus, if participation is a failure, employees can easily become inoculated against it and the organization's immune system may rally against future attempts to reintroduce it (Miles 1974). Hill (1991: 547) blames the failure of quality circles in part on the fact that 'the QC route did not meet whatever aspirations these employees may have had for greater participation'.

Work groups. An important requirement for successful participation is that work groups are both prepared to participate and sufficiently cohesive to exert social pressure to induce their members to accept group decisions.[7] Specifically, groups should reward cooperative behaviour and discipline 'shirkers' or 'free riders'. As economists put it, they should engage in 'horizontal monitoring' (peer persuasion) (Cable and Fitzroy 1980). This does not always happen. Indeed studies of participation in unions suggest that work groups differ greatly in their propensity to participate (Gallagher and Strauss 1991). Some aggregations of individuals may evidence so little sense of cohesion or group identity that it would be a misnomer to call their members a 'group'. This is one reason why participation may be difficult to organize among temporary, part-time, contracted, or telecommuting employees or among any aggregation of employees where turnover is high. If only a few employees are interested in participation, their 'decisions' may have little legitimacy. And, as discussed in Chapter 4, some groups may suspect the motives of those who organized the participative process and so refuse to engage in it.

Past experience can build cohesion. Describing how many post-unification East German factories quickly adapted to work teams, Turner (forthcoming) remarks:

> As a response to the inefficiency of a state-run economy [under Communist rule], groups of workers produced by improvisation and collective effort in the face of persistent material shortages and obsolete equipment . . . Habits bred by years of common effort and adaptation in difficult circumstances provided fertile ground in the 1990s for the introduction of modern group teamwork. Such innovation-suitable traditions arise not from [Communist] formal brigade structures, but as a product of tacit opposition (and in spite of former authoritarian practices).

According to Burawoy and Krotov (1992), there were similar developments in other Eastern European countries.

Inter-group rivalries may also make participation difficult. In Chapter 4 we discussed the problems involved in developing work teams if the employees involved belong to different craft unions. At Rushton Coal, as we saw in Chapter 5, the jealousy of non-participants toward 'super-miner' participants contributed to that programme's collapse.

Supervisors and middle managers. Participation needs the support of supervisors and middle management. This requires that they learn new skills and do not feel threatened by loss of job security. Achieving this is difficult. Indeed, participation is resisted and sometimes sabotaged by middle- and lower-level managers and especially by first-line supervisors (Klein 1984; Bradley and Hill 1987; Walton 1980; Muller-Jentsch 1995).[8] Though, for employees, one of the main advantages of direct participation is greater freedom to make decisions on their own (rather than having managers hover over them), this same freedom may threaten managers. Among the problems are the following:

1. *Participation threatens supervisors' authority and status* (loss of separate parking lots, as occurs in some US plants, is symbolic of wider losses). With direct participation, employees are encouraged to make decisions on their own. Discussions in quality circles may reveal managers' mistakes. In representative participation employees' representatives may bypass supervisors and contact higher management directly.[9] German works councillors, for example, are more likely to communicate directly with higher management than with lower management (Fürstenberg 1978). Similarly employee groups may infringe on subjects such as safety, production scheduling, or purchasing which staff departments had previously viewed as exclusively their own. Such jealousies may occur particularly with TQM (Geary 1994).
2. *In some cases, supervisors' very jobs are threatened.* The introduction of direct participation may lead to one or more levels of management being eliminated. In fact in the USA 'de-layering' is often treated as one of the major advantages of team organization. At Saturn there is one supervisory position for every fifty employees, contrasted with a more traditional auto-industry ratio of 10–15 to one. Understandably, supervisory unions in the Netherlands and Australia have sometimes objected vigorously to direct participation's spread.
3. *Managers are forced to learn wholly new techniques of supervision*, such as soliciting employees' ideas or 'encouraging self-goal setting' (Manz and Sims 1987). It is not enough to call a supervisor a 'coach'. There must be behaviour changes. Supervisors need to perform what has been variously called an 'enabling role' (Likert 1967) or 'empowered leadership' (Steward and Manz 1995). Often these techniques are completely at variance with what tradition has taught them is right. In any case, the appropriate role of supervisors in participative systems is quite uncertain (Dunlop 1993; Strauss 1996).

Supervisors rarely know how to be participative. They look upon participation as 'marshmallow management'. They often take a back seat for a while, pass the buck for problems to the group, and then come back in with a heavy hand if the group's solution fails (Klein 1984). Thus they vacillate between being completely tough and completely hands-off, a behaviour almost guaranteed to persuade employees that these supervisors are insincere. All this is consistent with the evidence, expressed in Chapter 5, that managers have little faith in their subordinates' competence.

One thing seems reasonably sure: for participation to be a success, supervisors need to believe in it: that it will work,[10] that it is not top management's momentary fad, that they can behave appropriately,[11] and that they will be rewarded for doing so. Many have good reason not to believe this. Except in Japan, managers rarely receive rewards for making participation a success (Stephen Hill 1991: 550). Quality circles, for example, 'disrupted managers' lives for small returns and created an organizational complexity that confused existing structures and middle management had no reason to make them work' (Stephen Hill 1991: 548–9).

As a US executive put it, introducing shop-floor participation in his company involved changing 'an old-line hierarchical organization into a more participative company from the executive suite to the shop-floor' (Hoerr 1988: 465). In fact, though firm evidence is lacking, there is reason to believe that, if formal participation schemes are to enjoy long-run success, they must be complemented by informal participative managerial styles.

4. *Finally, supervisors feel discriminated against*. They are forced into a system that typically they had no part designing. Though required to share power with subordinates, they do not see their bosses sharing theirs. Thus participation, from their point of view, is an example of 'the top telling the middle to do something for the bottom'.

Although supervisors and middle managers may have an understandably greater desire to participate in key decisions than do rank-and-file employees, often they are left out of the formal representative participation machinery altogether. Yet managers are 'a distinct class of people with something distinctive to say' (Fogerty 1976: 123). And so, to protect their interests, supervisors sometimes join unions, as did principals in the Los Angeles school system. 'Their main complaint was that the [school] district had bargained away their authority in . . . negotiations . . . to which they were not a party' (Baker and Kleingartner 1992: 10).

Higher management. Whilst direct participation is especially threatening to supervisors, representative participation threatens top management. There is weak evidence that participation reduces top management's absolute influence and stronger evidence that it does so relatively (Strauss 1982). Ideally, however, participation should increase management's effectiveness through improving communications, reducing interpersonal conflicts, and legitimating management decisions.

Again, ideally, top management should support participation by use of symbols, through serving as role models of participative behaviour, by rewarding such behaviour on the part of subordinates, and perhaps by sponsoring an organization-development programme. All these activities may help establish a 'participatory culture', though the process is not simple. In practice, however, top management's support for participation is often symbolic and uncertain. Indeed, many managers view participation either as a form of speed-up or as a low-cost gimmick which is good for public relations.

As Marchington *et al.* (1993) point out, managerial enthusiasm for participation comes in 'waves' or fads. A programme may be adopted (often with much fanfare) because it is highly touted by consultants or management journals or practised by competitors. (As institutional theory suggests, organizations are copycats: they follow the leader.) But, as enthusiasm for one programme wanes, a new one is introduced. At Fawley (in England), announcing a new scheme was 'an important "rite of passage" . . . related directly to the career objectives of members of the management group' (Ahlstrand 1990: 23). Once the managerial champion was transferred elsewhere the programme was quietly dropped or allowed to atrophy.

In any case, the symbolic or political nature of many programmes is easily evident to lower managerial levels and helps explain the low priority which these programmes receive. As we discussed in Chapter 5, employees quickly see through inauthentic participation.

The managers of employee-owned firms, especially producers' cooperatives, are in a particularly difficult position. Yugoslav and kibbutz top managers were less satisfied (and had more ulcers) than their counterparts in conventional US firms (Tannenbaum *et al.* 1974). Turnover among managers of US employee-owned plywood factories has been quite high.

But there are some grounds for hope. As supervisors and managers learn to live with a participative system, they may discover that participation actually makes their life easier and their organization more productive. Possibly this change in attitudes may require a new generation of managers. Certainly, without managerial support, participation has little chance of success.

Unions. Unions' support is another key factor in determining whether either direct or representative participation is successful, and for reasons discussed in Chapter 4.

Human-Resources Policies

A wave of recent research supports the hypothesis that participation alone (especially direct participation) is likely to have a more lasting impact when it is combined with 'bundles' of complementary 'high-performance'-oriented human-resources practices. As MacDuffie (1995: 198) put it '"bundles" of interrelated and internally consistent human resources practices, rather than individual practices, are the appropriate unit of analysis for studying the link to performance, because they create the multiple, reinforcing conditions that support employee motivation and skill acquisition'.

Summarizing broadly, the evidence as to the relationship between formal participation and other 'high-performance' practices suggests that adopting only a few such practices has relatively little impact on performance. A major impact is achieved only when a full bundle (or most of it) is introduced (Long 1990; Levine and Kruse 1993; Macy and Izumi 1993; Cooke 1994; Eaton 1994; Osterman 1994*a*; MacDuffie and Kochan 1995; Ichniowski *et al.* 1996; Pil and MacDuffie 1996).[12]

Here we discuss policies in four areas: compensation, status and symbols, job security, and training. These are hardly the only relevant policies. Osterman (1994*b*), for example, found a positive correlation between family-friendly benefits, such as childcare and maternity leave, and employee discretion over work methods. Other relevant policies include selective hiring and promotion from within.

Compensation. For participative success compensation policies should reward participative efforts, be viewed as fair, and not disrupt social cohesion. Successful direct participation plans have increasingly been accompanied by 'pay for knowledge'[13] (Osterman 1994*a*) and/or some sort of financial participation, such as stock-ownership, profit-sharing, or gain-sharing based on group or organizational performance.[14] A key aspect of the US Scanlon Plan is the careful and well-publicized measurement of productivity and frequent (often monthly) distribution of bonuses based on these measures in accordance with an agreed-upon formula. As psychological theory suggests, financial rewards provide a form of feedback to employees that their participative efforts have been successful. Further, they meet the demands of distributive justice.

Nevertheless compensation is a problem in most direct participative schemes. As productivity and responsibilities increase, employees want to be paid more: they see themselves doing supervisors' work without getting supervisors' pay. Further, if participation contributes to increased profits, employees want to share the benefits. Yet management often thinks psychological rewards should be enough and resists all forms of additional monetary compensation.

Conventional incentive schemes have stressed individual piecework. The traditional argument has been that, unless individual and small groups of employees see a *direct* relationship between their individual efforts and the final payoff, they will have little *individual* incentive not to slack. In other words, they will be 'free riders' (see Chapter 5). However, narrow, individual, small-group-based incentives may discourage cooperation between groups. Broader-based incentives, such as profit- and gain-sharing bonuses, may contribute to teamwork, trust in management, and a sense of common destiny. They may also encourage employees to use group pressures to monitor and discipline 'shirkers' (see Strauss 1990). In any case, successful participative efforts appear to be associated with broad-based incentives (Arthur 1994; Fernie and Metcalf 1995; Ichniowski *et al.* 1995).

Limited evidence suggests that wage differentials tend to be low in successful direct participation plans in the USA as well (Levine 1995). Indeed at NUMMI and other plants where numerous unskilled job classifications have been collapsed into one, the vast majority of employees receive the same pay. Arguably this makes sense: since participation presumably reduces power differentials, differentials in pay should also be reduced. High wage differences may increase jealousy, reduce cohesion, and inhibit cooperation. Compensation differentials were low in Israeli kibbutzim (where compensation traditionally was based on need rather than position or performance) (Rosner 1991) and in Mondragon (Whyte and Whyte 1992). As mentioned in Chapter 5, the fact that at Rushton miners in participating teams earned more than non-participants contributed to that experiment's collapse (Trist *et al.* 1977; for a similar case see Trist 1986).

Where compensation is increased, there is always a problem deciding how to distribute this. For example, if pay for lower-paid employees is adjusted upwards in multi-skilled work teams, the formerly higher-paid employees feel discriminated against. Indeed, the elimination of skill differentials reduces employees' sense of progressing upwards; so does skill-based pay once employees reach the top of the scale. Age-based differentials, common in Japan, may preserve a sense of progression while reducing jealousies.

Status and symbols. Successful participation is often accompanied by reduced status differentials, and not just in pay. Symbols are important here. Some of the best-known experiments in direct participation have been accompanied by the elimination of important symbolic status differentials. All 'team members' at NUMMI (in other places they are called 'associates'), managers and employees alike, wear the same uniform and share common dining rooms and parking lots, in sharp contrast to the practice under the old GM management. Similar changes have been made in other US and British factories (especially Japanese transplants). At Saturn the desks of at least some union and management 'co-managers' are placed side-by-side. Too often, however, participation is just symbolic and nothing more—what Kamoche (1995) calls 'totemism' (see Chapter 5 and Alvesson, 1993).

Job security. Limited evidence suggests that direct participation works best when it is combined with the prospects of future job security and long-term employment. Firms with participative schemes are more likely to provide job security than those without such schemes,[15] and successful schemes are more likely to be coupled with job security than are unsuccessful ones (Eaton 1994; Kochan and Osterman 1994; Levine 1995; contra Drago 1988).[16]

Employees often fear that forms of participation, such as QCs and work teams, may threaten their job security. This is not an unreasonable fear, since management's main purpose in introducing participation is typically to increase efficiency and cut labour costs. Further participation is often introduced in the context of layoffs and crisis.

Worry over possible job loss normally inhibits cooperation. At the least, employees should not fear that their jobs will be endangered if they make suggestions and improve their productivity.[17] 'Even layoffs that are market driven or otherwise unrelated to the efforts of problem-solving groups have the effect of undercutting the sense of common purpose that is supposed to motivate employee involvement efforts' (Cutcher-Gershenfeld *et al.* 1991: 15). Though (as we discuss below) fear of layoffs may provide the 'shock effect' necessary to get the parties to agree, continual layoffs are certainly counter-productive. As *The Economist* (14 January 1995: 55) put it, 'TQM does not readily blend with wave after wave of restructuring, downsizing, and engineering'—and this holds for other forms of participation.

Unions commonly ask for increased job security in return for the introduction of cooperative schemes. Greater job security has been one of the main objectives and accomplishments of representative participation in Continental Europe. As we have seen, works-council assent is required in many European countries before layoffs are made. Mondragon made strenuous efforts to avoid layoffs and to provide substitute employment for those for whom there was no work available (Whyte and Whyte 1992; Bonin *et al.* 1993).

Apart from security against redundancy from lack of work, employees need protection against retaliation from supervisors who object to employees 'interfering' into what had previously been supervisory prerogatives (for a summary of the literature, see Eaton and Voos 1992). Levine (1995) argues that individual 'due-process' rights are essential if employees are to feel free to speak up and participate.

Training. As we stressed in Chapter 5, participation requires that employees have the 'competence' to engage in it. This implies a heavy investment in training and skill development generally. Employees, managers, and union leaders—all require training. Some firms, for example, provide extensive schooling for quality circle leaders and members. Work team members need training in breadth and depth—in breadth so that they can perform each others' jobs and in depth so that they resolve unforeseen problems as they occur without running to staff or management for assistance. If employees are to make important technical and other decisions, they must learn technical, analytic, and planning skills, such as statistical analysis. They may also need interpersonal training (such as in group dynamics) and decision-making skills so that they can function better as committee members and chairs.[18]

Well-trained employees, such as those who have gone through the German apprenticeship system, may absorb additional training more quickly. The fact that participative companies need to invest heavily in training makes them more selective in those whom they hire.

Training is required for representative participation as well. Mondragon was a training programme before it started manufacturing. Today it supports (and is assisted by) an elaborate educational network. German and Swedish unions feel it essential that they train employee directors (Eiger 1986; see also Gustavson 1986 and Virmani 1986).

Training and job security are linked, of course. From the employers' viewpoint, long-term employment makes it more likely that they will recoup the substantial training investment required by most participative schemes. And, from the employees' perspective, training demonstrates that the employer values their skills and so is less likely to make them redundant.

Participation's Context

The context in which participation occurs also appears to affect its chances for success. Though there has been relatively little hard research on these topics, among the relevant issues are those discussed below.

Size, technology, and rate of change. All these factors are presumably related to participatory success. Despite much research, however, the precise relationships are still unclear. Many appear weak (e.g. IDE 1981*b*). Here are some generalizations from the literature (for a review of early research, see Strauss 1982).

Size may place limits on direct participation and on various forms of self-management, such as producers' cooperatives. Small groups and small organizations tend to be more cohesive, have a greater sense of organizational commitment, and enjoy easier communications than do large ones. Representative participation, on the other hand, may be more effective in large organizations because workers' representatives are better able to develop the expertise necessary to counterbalance management.

According to conventional wisdom, participation should work best when jobs are relatively unstructured—for example, in craft and professional work. Indeed, many of the most successful producers' cooperatives have involved craftspeople or professionals. As we have seen, however, various forms of direct participation have been introduced with automobile and garment workers, both unskilled occupations. Perhaps the critical factor here is the relatively low competence or 'knowledge gap' (Strauss 1982) between these workers and management. When work is simple, even unskilled workers can suggest how to improve it. When work is complex, only well-trained, experienced employees may have the competence (see Chapter 5) to make changes. In any case, as MacDuffie (1995: 212) suggests, 'technology must be used in a way which complements rather than minimizes the role of human resources'. (How will computerization affect participation? Our next chapter wrestles with this difficult question.)

Equally uncertain is the relationship between participation and technological change. Participation may facilitate minor changes. Though the participative process is slow, once general consensus has been reached that change should be made, implementation of this change may proceed relatively smoothly. Rapid change may be a different matter, at least to the extent it makes employees' previous experience (competence) irrelevant. A German study concluded that works councils were incapable of influencing the process of introducing information technology into the machine-building industry (Hildebrandt 1989). This process was too complex for them to handle. A related study of a US auto company found that participation was more extensive when technological change was slow than when it was fast (Katz *et al.* 1987).

Markets and strategies. Some markets are more favourable to participation than others. Chapter 1 described the apparent utility of the module (team) system of apparel manufacturing over the traditional, Tayloristic approach. But, despite these advantages, only a small minority of enterprises have adopted it. Why? A prime advantage of the new system is that it greatly shortens the lead time between the receipt of an order and its delivery. But for this shortened lead time to be useful, distributors and retailers must make radical and fairly expensive changes in their methods of restocking and inventory control. Each salesperson's point-of-sales scanner must be linked to the firm's central computer. Warehouses must be redesigned because under the new system the ultimate destination of each garment is codemarked on a stocking label by manufacturer. Since few customers have made this change, only a few manufacturers have found a competitive advantage by switching to modules (Dunlop and Weil 1996).[19]

This raises the hotly contested question of whether 'progressive' human resources policies—including participation—are economically best under all circumstances (the universalistic approach) or only when they are consistent ('fit') with overall organizational strategy (the contingency approach). Cutcher-Gershenfeld *et al.* (1991), argue that, other things being equal, participation is more likely to be successful in firms competing on the basis of innovation, quality, and variety than in firms which compete on the basis of price alone (see also Arthur 1994 and MacDuffie and Kochan 1995). But the evidence in support of this hypothesis is rather weak (Cappelli and Singh 1992; Delery and Doty 1996).

Perceived economic payoffs. People and organizations engage in participation because they expect some sort of pay-off. Of the various forms of pay-off, the economic one may be most important.

The relationship between economic success and the parties' willingness to participate is rather complex. At least in Anglo-Saxon countries both unions and management seem more disposed to introduce participative schemes when economic times are bad.[20] At such times, management hopes participation will cut costs and improve its competitive position while unions and employees see it as possibly saving jobs. Cressey, Eldridge, and MacInnes (1985) call this 'lifeboat democracy'. Indeed economic crisis may provide the shock effect necessary to propel change. During periods of economic trouble many managements of unionized US firms have granted participation rights in exchange for wage moderation and work rule changes. As Jacoby (1983: 31) puts it, 'unfavourable economic conditions appear to facilitate a softening of adversarial postures. Both sides are willing to forgo strategies of maximum offence and resistance when confronted by loss of market share.' A related point: Heller and Wilpert (1981) found that when managers perceive uncertainty they increase participation; the same may hold true for employees and union leaders.

But, as suggested earlier, there is considerable evidence that participation works best when there is job security. How do we deal with this apparent contradiction? The answer, it seems, is that both the introduction and the continuance of participation require that the parties perceive and continue to perceive that participation will provide pay-offs (i.e. contributing to more secure jobs, higher wages for employees, and higher profits for management). For this reason, it is fairly unlikely that crisis-induced participation will persist unless there is some relatively quick evidence that success will in fact be achieved. Nevertheless, even if the employer does poorly, participative efforts may continue as long as participation is still seen as promising benefits for both side. But this may require a high degree of trust (see below).

Eaton (1994: 384) reports 'some support for the view that very good or very poor economic circumstances tend to undermine participative efforts, at least in the union sector'. Jacoby (1983) argues that relationship between economic conditions and labour-management cooperation may be curvilinear. Cooperation is hindered if conditions are too good or too bad. Moderate levels of economic uncertainty are best for cooperation and presumably participation. Put another way, when economic prospects are too dismal, employees see little purpose in participating. But when business is booming, the parties may lack the incentive for doing so. In short, 'the middle range of competitive pressure' may be best for participative success, 'where the relations are unfrozen by adversity, but the parties are not paralyzed by calamity' (Cutcher-Gershenfeld and Verma 1994: 560).

Trust. As the previous discussion illustrates (see also Chapter 5), trust is almost essential if participation is to lead to more than controversy, deadlock, or apathy. Yet trust is difficult to establish and easy to destroy. Unions and managements have traditionally had adversarial relationships. Individual employees have interests different from management's and so are often suspicious of management's motives. Thus trust must be earned and learned. Actually there is something of a prisoners' dilemma here. In the short run, each side may gain by behaving uncooperatively. Even if the parties gingerly experiment with Cupertino, each retains its suspicions. Thus participation is built on a flimsy foundation.

Trust may be particularly fragile in the face of economic adversity. Based on a series of case studies, Cutcher-Gershenfeld *et al.* (1991) warn that economic shocks often lead management to make unilateral decisions which disturb the spirit of cooperation. Indeed, they add that one of the advantages of representative participation is that it provides a forum where both parties can formulate strategies for dealing with these shocks. The disruptive impact of layoffs may be reduced if the union or works council has been kept fully informed of management's predicaments and has had the opportunity to influence the final outcome. Nevertheless, once participation is seen as unlikely to pay off, disillusion can set in, especially if initial expectations were high.

As mentioned earlier, kaizen captures the secret short cuts which employees once used to make their lives easier. Before they reveal their secrets, employees must learn to trust management that this information will not be misused. Put another way, effective participation requires employees to make a certain amount of commitment to organizational goals, in return for which these employees expect a certain amount of employer commitment, especially to provide job security. In short, there is a psychological contract.

If management is unable to fulfil its end of the contract, employees may feel betrayed. Marchington *et al.* (1994: 887) describe a company in which 'employees . . . had long experience of EI [employee involvement] as part of the company's participative style', yet recent redundancies 'caused them to question management's commitment to involvement'. Similarly loss of trust in one part of a relationship may threaten the relationship as a whole. In the USA a relatively successful system of workplace participation at Caterpillar fell apart once top-level union–management relations turned to antagonism in a bitter contract dispute.

Indeed we can think of virtuous and vicious cycles. In a virtuous cycle participation leads to initial pay-offs for both parties. It also teaches them to trust each other. In turn this encourages them to experiment with more ambitious forms of participation. Given the parties' cooperative and trusting attitudes, these new forms also succeed, and so on. In a vicious cycle, however, participation is initially a failure. The parties blame each other. Distrust is accentuated and the parties become inoculated against further participation.[21]

At times the parties move between cooperation to adversarialism in a 'yo-yo' fashion (Hammer and Stern 1986). The problems are illustrated by the experience of Rath, a technologically obsolete, near bankrupt meat-packing firm. Here, in return for concessions, employees won majority ownership of their firm and the right to elect a majority of the board of directors. An elaborate structure of workplace teams was established, but effective union–management collaboration never developed at higher levels. When the initial concessions proved insufficient to restore profitability, management proposed further wage cuts. Employees felt betrayed; the board of directors hired a new management which promoted additional participation. But this and wage cuts were not enough. The cycle was repeated. Now the union president became company president. After a short period of goodwill, he too was unable to arrest the downward cycle. There was more bitterness, lay-offs and at one point union members picketed their own employee-owned plant. Finally, the company expired in bitterness (Hammer and Stern 1986).

Environmental Infrastructure

Most organizations are non-participative, so participation exists in a hostile environment. Producers' cooperatives in particular are strange beasts, 'isolated islands in a capitalist sea' (Clarke *et al.* 1972). Evidence suggests that participation of any kind is more likely to survive if it is sustained by what Blasi, Mehrling, and Whyte (1984) call an 'infrastructure'. Elements of this infrastructure are discussed below.

Ideology and value systems. The most successful examples of employee ownership—the kibbutz and Mondragon, in particular—have been supported by an ideology. In the kibbutz it was one of socialism and nationalism (building a Jewish state in a hostile environment). Mondragon was founded by a Catholic priest. Its leaders were motivated by Basque nationalism and hostility to Franco. Beyond this the Basque culture encourages teamwork (Whyte and Whyte 1992).

The success of Japanese fishery cooperatives has been ascribed to their strong sense of community and strong values as to the desirability of consensus and sensitivity to minority interests (Barrett and Okudaira 1995). Similarly Rosner (1991) argues that the communal social structure and egalitarian distribution of income once prevalent in the kibbutz contributed to 'high ideological commitment' and a high level of solidarity, which in turn contributed to organizational success. As we saw in Chapter 5, once kibbutz members became dissatisfied with communal living, the kibbutz form became less effective.

Japanese culture has much to do with the success of Japanese quality circles. On the other hand, Japanese transplants, such as NUMMI in the USA and Nissan in the UK, have successfully induced strong corporate cultures which stress metaphors such as 'teamwork' and 'organizational learning'. At NUMMI, however, management was forced to adapt to the presence of a strong union.

Beyond this there may be differences in national character or culture, although the nature of these is uncertain. The most widely debated evidence derives from Hofstede's very large 1980 study of IBM managers in forty countries. Significant national differences were found, for instance, in what he calls power distance (an index of three questions) relating to a manager's perception of his superior's decision-making style and colleagues' fear of disagreeing with superiors. Mexico, India, and (surprisingly) Yugoslavia are among the countries high in power distance, while Israel, Denmark, Ireland, and Sweden score low. Also surprisingly and against the evidence of other studies, Great Britain and West Germany are lower in power distance than the USA.

Other significant national differences occur between individualism and collectivism (see also Triandis 1972) and something like this factor is often used as an explanation of the difference between Japanese and Western decision-making patterns. A recent large cross-national study (Smith *et al.* 1996) supports Hofstede, but other research (e.g. IDE 1981*b*) fails to replicate the familiar national clusters and suggests that cultural findings could be an artefact of what are called 'response sets to specific linguistic stimuli' (IDE 1981*b*: 274).

Looking at culture from a different perspective, Tolliday and Zeitlin (1991: 274–5; see also Locke *et al.* 1995) observe that Germany, with its elaborate craft-oriented training system, has a less hierarchical management which is more likely to treat employees as individuals and so is more conducive to participation than is France, where management is more Tayloristic and employees are viewed as being more homogeneous. According to Lowell Turner (personal communication), teamwork was more easily accepted in auto plants in former East Germany than in West Germany because teamwork was more consistent with the collectivist values instilled under communism.

To stress the obvious: participation is most likely to be successful if introduced in a culture which is favourable to it.

Industrial relations. Participation directly impacts industrial relations (Chapter 4). National systems of industrial relations are heavily influenced by patterns of interactions and sets of expectations that are hard to change. This is a major reason, for instance, why attempts to introduce US-style labour relations in Japan after the war and in the UK (through the 1971 Industrial Relations Act) largely failed. Institutions are difficult to transplant in alien environments. Industrial relations tend to be less adversarial in Germany and Scandinavian countries than they are in the UK or USA; this may explain the greater prevalence and success of participation in the former countries. Further, one might predict that, were the German co-determination laws introduced into the UK, they would operate very differently and probably less successfully than they do in their native land.

Legal support. You can lead a horse to water, it is said, but you can't make him drink. Yet the evidence (IDE 1981*b*; 1993) suggests that legal arrangements that require organizations to introduce participation do in fact increase employees' influence (both self-reported and as reported by informed observers). The law legitimates participation. Also it gives the employees clout to insist that participation take place. As we saw in Chapter 4, the success of works councils in Continental Europe, even in Germany, depends heavily on the rights given them by law.

However, legal protection is neither a necessary nor a sufficient condition for participatory success. In communist countries there was a great deal of formal participatory apparatus. However, this was manipulated so as to allow little real influence-sharing. On the other hand, even in the absence of legal support, it is possible for an organization to introduce a formal participation scheme, preferably with a written constitution.[22] Mondragon, for example, developed in a quite unfavourable legal climate. And recently participation has done reasonably well in the USA, even though there is no legal compulsion and some forms are legally suspect.

Some economists argue that, if participation increased productivity, firms would find it to their economic advantage to introduce it without compulsion from either unions or the government. But, on the basis of formal economic analysis, Freeman and Lazear (1995: 29) conclude that, at least in theory, Representative Participative Bodies (RPBs) should increase the firm's 'economic rent', but that management will voluntary give RPBs 'less power than is socially desirable'.

And, to repeat a key argument made in Chapter 4, participation seems more likely to be successful when legal support is combined with strong unionism (IDE 1993: 98).

Advice. Organizations implementing participation schemes need technical advice; and the successful diffusion of participation through an economy seems to require the services of trusted organizations capable of providing this (Cornforth 1989*b*). JUS, a decentralized mass-membership quality-circle society in Japan, provides opportunities for employees and managers from different companies to exchange experiences and to spread the quality-circle movement among the uninitiated. National union and management bodies, such as the Swedish Centre for Working Life, serve somewhat the same function, but on a more decentralized basis (Cole 1989). Caja, the cooperative bank, provides a variety of important planning and technical services for Mondragon members. Laws in a variety of European countries permit works councils to make use of consultants. But, as mentioned in Chapter 5, this right is used fairly infrequently. Consultants are widely used in the USA to help introduce participation and some unions are training members of their staff to serve this function.

Financial support. Employee-owned firms require financial as well as technical support. Banks typically are unwilling to loan money to employee-owned industries. Kibbutz organizations support each other (and are suffering financial difficulties for having done so). Mondragon's Caja has generated the capital required for Mondragon's expansion. Without such support, producers' cooperatives may 'self-strangulate'. Levine (1995) argues that the great emphasis placed by US financial markets on short-run returns has inhibited investment in participation.

Survival

Finally, participation has trouble surviving and growing. Some participation efforts are stillborn: management goes through the motions of consultation but ignores all but the most trivial of suggestions. In some instances committees meet several times, a few suggestions are made (but ignored), and then the process atrophies (Marchington 1994). Alternatively participation may flourish for a while and enjoy a 'honeymoon' but then, as the agenda of easily solvable problems grows smaller, interest begins to wane, meetings become less frequent, and eventually they cease altogether (MacInnes 1985; Chevalier 1991). Research suggests that overall the half-life of direct participation is often short. This is especially the case with quality circles (Cammann *et al.* 1984; Schuster 1984; Katz *et al.* 1985; Rankin 1986; Drago 1988; Griffin 1988; Levine and Tyson 1990; Goetschy 1991; Stephen Hill 1991; Marchington 1992*a*). On the other hand there is recent evidence suggesting that direct-participation schemes are lasting longer currently than they did ten years ago (Eaton 1994).

Even at NUMMI there is some evidence of burn-out. 'Workers' active involvement in improvement efforts was no longer the novel experience that it had been . . . in the early days of NUMMI. It had become a taken-for-granted part of the job.' Teams meet less often. 'After eight years, we have set up all the equipment'. said one employee. 'There's not much left to change.' Jobs are rotated less frequently. There are reports of declining cohesion, fewer suggestions, more tension and increased absenteeism (still only one-third of the industry average) (Adler *et al.* 1995). Despite this, NUMMI is still a major success by most standards.

Initially, direct participation raises expectations of opportunities for steadily increased participation, yet, after employees have successfully coped with the problems of redesigning their jobs and found solutions to production problems and work quality difficulties, a period of let-down ('burn-out' or 'plateauing') is almost inevitable. Employees' decision-making skills have increased but the unresolved problems that can be handled through direct participation have decreased (Walton 1980; Miles and Rosenberg 1982). So groups seek to deal with 'forbidden' topics, such as wages, regarding which management wishes to exercise sole discretion, and this leads to conflict. Or they attempt to deal with problems regarding which they lack the competence or information necessary to solve (Chevalier 1995).

In any case, groups often find that redesigning equipment is not enough; whole systems and organizations may need to be redesigned. But system redesign may involve many departments and so be beyond direct participation's scope. Thus broader forms of representative participation may be required. Finally, regardless of possible long-term gains, the just-discussed transitional, short-run costs of participation in terms of training and various forms of disruption may be high. Management may lose its patience and disband the system.

Representative participation schemes may last longer, especially if they are established by law or through union–management agreement. Nevertheless, it is not uncommon for RPBs, especially those with limited power, to meet less frequently over time and to deal with increasingly trivial problems (for an incisive discussion, see Marchington 1994).

Summary

Much research makes several points clear. First, and most important, participation can work (and by a variety of criteria). Further it can have many forms of important pay-off.

Having formal structure facilitates changes in actual behaviour (IDE 1981*b*; 1993) but it does not guarantee it. Formally proscribed (*de jure*) and actual (*de facto*) participation are far from perfectly correlated. Informal participation can occur at the workplace and unions and management may cooperate at higher levels, both without formal participative structures. On the other hand, many formal structures atrophy quickly. For formal participative schemes to have any lasting effect they must receive strong support from top management and, in unionized plants, from top union officials.

Recent research suggests that one form of participation, if introduced alone, may have little effect, especially if it is incongruent with other managerial and union policies. Formal participation must be reinforced by genuine informal participation at the work place, not 'pseudo-participation' (Heller 1971). Specific formal programmes work best when combined with bundles of other policies designed to develop a 'high-commitment' culture, such as pay for knowledge, gain-sharing, extensive training, and job security. We return to this in our next chapter.

A distinction can be drawn between 'self-contained' and 'integrated' forms of participation (Cutcher-Gershenfeld *et al.* 1991) . The self-contained form is grafted on the larger organization without changes in the organization's typically hierarchical structure or linkage with other forms of participation. Quality circles are typically self-contained; by contrast, TQM, at its best, is closely integrated with managerial procedures. Similarly, a solo employee–management safety committee may have little influence. But linked to a works council it can be much more effective. Integrated systems usually include both direct and representative participation.

Without cooperative relations at the higher levels, cooperation at lower levels will not survive long (Kochan *et al.* 1986). Representative participation can survive without direct participation, but its full benefits are unlikely to be obtained. Employee ownership alone has few significant pay-offs. On the other hand, through providing tangible rewards for participative activities it can reinforce those which are intangible.

Finally, participation may lead only to stalemates and frustration unless overall labour–management relations are reasonably good. Leaders on all levels and both sides must develop new attitudes and skills. This is far from easy. Perhaps most difficult of all, since conflicts of interest are unlikely to disappear, all parties must learn to tolerate the tensions which arise when adversarial and cooperative relations coexist.

To conclude, under appropriate conditions, participation can meet one or more of the goals discussed in Chapter 1: humanistic, power equalization, and organizational efficiency. However, participation is not a cure-all for every societal ill. Further, it may have only limited impact under many circumstances. Given this, what should be participation's role in the society of the future? We turn to this in our next and last chapter.

NOTES

1. Technically Yugoslavia practised 'social' rather than 'employee' ownership.
2. According to some US studies (some with methodological problems), ESOP firms have been more profitable than comparable non-ESOP firms (Conte and Tannenbaum 1978), more productive (Mitchell *et al.* 1990), increased employment faster (Rosen and Klein 1981; Trachman 1985), and enjoyed higher sales growth, and return to equity (I. Wagner 1983). According to Jones and Kato (1993), in Japan employee stockholdings were associated with higher productivity. Other studies are less encouraging. Thus Tannenbaum, Cook, and Lochman (1984) found no significant difference between ESOP and conventional companies in profits, productivity, and technological adaptiveness.

3. Empirical studies of works councils on such measures as productivity or satisfaction are beset with methodological problems (Cable 1985). The results to date are mixed (see Cable and Fitzroy 1980; Addison *et al.* 1993; Stephen Smith 1994; Sadlowski *et al.* 1995). Comparing OECD countries, Kleiner and Ay (1996) found only small impacts of joint consultation or mandated works councils on productivity or productivity growth.
4. The cases which follow are overwhelmingly American, reflecting substantial US research. A drawback, from the point of view of this book, is that the dependent variable in almost all these cases is productivity and so is hardly consistent with our humanization-first theme.
5. Also 'other hierarchical changes' such as product realignment and small business units.
6. According to Drago and Wooden (1991: 178), 'Actual participation in high-level managerial decisions is facilitated by the presence of formal participatory structures, which in turn are often attributable to employee demands. On the shop-floor, however, formal programmes exhibit a weak link to actual participation. Instead, employee demands for shop-floor participation are typically met by informal participation. Finally, there is evidence that participation alters employees' tastes for participation. When employees influence high-level decisions, this induces a desire for more participation at that level. Shop-floor participation is quite different, since it appears to reduce desire for participation at the managerial level, consistent with the hypothesis that shop-floor initiatives—such as quality circles—act to deflect employees' desires away from participation in strategic decisions.' Banker, Field, Schroder, and Sinha (1996) found that the positive effect of teamwork was more likely to occur with cohesive work teams.
7. In a study of Xerox customer service technicians organized into self-managing teams Wageman (1996) found that 'team design' had a greater impact on team behaviour and performance than did leader behaviour, with 'team design' being defined as including such factors as clear direction, team composition (including having a well-balanced set of skills), and a supportive organizational context.
8. TQM is designed largely to motivate managers to participate. Consequently managers are less likely to resist it.
9. Even with QCs there may be a dual ladder. QC members may occasionally bypass their supervisors and communicate directly with higher management.
10. In a field experiment involving four plants, managers were given 'artificial' information as to the expected results of a new job enlargement and rotation programme. Some managers were told it would increase production, others merely that it would 'improve relations with employees'. Productivity improved significantly more in the first set of plants than in the second (King 1974).
11. As Stewart and Manz (1995) would put it, leaders need 'high efficacy and outcomes expectations' to be effective as managers of participative work teams.
12. Based on their studies, Huselid and Becker (1995) propose a more complex model. Without singling out participation for special attention, they suggest that the relationship between the adoption of 'progressive' human resources and organizational performance is curvilinear. As organizations adopt an increasing number of such practices, they go through phases. During the first phase, as it adopts a few practices, the results are favourable. The second phase, as more policies are introduced, has little added impact. But in the final phase, as a full bundle of practices is adopted, the results is once again more favourable.

13. By contrast with unions in the UK and USA, which have been generally suspicious of skill-based pay. In Germany 'IG Metall has offensively moved toward a primarily skills-related remuneration system' (Bacon *et al.* 1996: 44).
14. However, Eaton (1994) finds that participative programmes combined with profit-sharing are less likely to survive than those without. According to Cooke (1994), participation programmes in unionized companies without gain-sharing contribute more to productivity than do similar programmes with gain-sharing. The reverse is true in non-union companies. Possibly, as Eaton suggests, employees in unionized firms share in profits through negotiated wages increases and so a formal profit-sharing plan is not needed.
15. Sometimes job security is extended only to permanent 'core' employees, with temporary employees carrying the burden of employment fluctuation. Under these circumstances temporary employees are unlikely to engage in participation.
16. On the other hand, based on Australian data, Drago (1996) finds direct participation most common in two forms of organization: (1) 'transformed workplaces' which are marked by typical 'progressive' human-resources policies, such as high wages, training, and job security, and (2) 'disposable workplaces', where QCs and work teams are combined with low wages and little job security. In the latter, management's motto appears to be, 'Participate or be fired.'
17. Fear and insecurity may lead to groupthink. Neck and Manz (1994) suggest ways of avoiding the danger through a more constructive pattern which encourages divergent views and an open expression of ideas.
18. Training may be a form of indoctrination. Its function at Izusu, according to Graham (1995: 58), was 'to create a co-operative workforce willing to conform to company demands'.
19. Drago (1988: 344) suggests that 'increased product market competition encourages cooperative attitudes . . . [S]evere competition destroys cooperation.' But this may be because the extent of competition affects economic pay-offs, as we discuss below.
20. This may be a reason why participation has been adopted so slowly in Anglo-Saxon countries.
21. As voluminous research concludes, trust is highly dependent on perceived 'substantive' and 'procedural' justice—that is, the participative decision-making procedures are just and the results of participation are just. However, in bad times, when economic pay-offs decline, employees may conclude that the results are unjust and, for all the reasons mentioned in Chapter 4, that the participative machinery is unjust as well (irresponsive, excessively bureaucratic, or just ineffective).
22. In the DIO study such a formal structure was called Status Power and was found to have a positive effect on participation (Heller *et al.* 1988: 209–10).

7. Myth and Reality: Valediction

We call this chapter Valediction rather than Conclusion because it attempts to close a period of very intensive activity in thinking and research, and it is, perhaps, a farewell to certain aspects of myth and reality implied by our topic.

In this chapter we set ourselves two objectives. One is to pull together the main streams of arguments and evidence produced in previous chapters. We will do this indirectly rather than by straight summaries, since Chapter 1 has already presented an extensive overview of the main topics and most chapters provide their own interim conclusions. So, in the next two sections we will review some of the early writing of Fred Emery as a way of drawing attention to the tendency in much of the literature to encapsulate participation narrowly within one or two levels of organization. We then go on to argue that the tentative and in part contradictory evidence from research on these encapsulated phenomena, including the policies often flagged under the banner of Human Resources Management (HRM), leads us to suggest that better results would be obtained from a coordinated approach which makes systematic use of consistent policies. Recent research seems to confirm this (see Chapter 6).

Our second objective is to broaden the topic of participation as an influence-sharing process. We do this first by relating it to certain aspects of the societal environment and in particular to technological decisions—taken without the sanction of democratic processes—that can produce serious risks for which no one is responsible. Secondly, we will attempt to assess likely developments over the first two to three decades of the twenty-first century and in particular the impact of technology on participation.

The Beginning of a Myth

The 1960s and 1970s were periods of irrepressible optimism, well illustrated in the writing of Fred Emery, one of the most important social-science thinkers and pioneers in the area of participation. In a piece published in 1976 he argued that there was hard evidence that all forms of productive and learning systems are much more efficient if they are designed to utilize the multiple capabilities of workers (Emery 1976). As we will see, more than a quarter of a century later, this remains a leading-edge statement. He further argued that, irrespective of the technology, all forms of work which require coordination can be more effectively carried out by incorporating a degree of self-management in the work design. These ideas are now widely accepted by social scientists, but he probably went further than most of us would three decades later by postulating that 'the basic theoretical problems of democratizing work have been confronted and have been solved' (Emery 1981: 391–2). In short, he contributed to the mythology now surrounding participation.

In the 1976 article, he tempers his optimism and enters an area of controversy which has not yet been resolved in theory or practice—namely, boardroom representation. He argued that employee participation should not reach the board, either in private or in nationalized industry. This was a position he and his Norwegian colleague, Thorsrud, had championed a decade earlier when they had briefly looked at the German co-determination system (Emery and Thorsrud 1969) and had not liked what they found, although many other observers took a more positive view of it.

Emery thought that the board which represented shareholder interests should not be disturbed by the invasion of partisan interests on behalf of employees or customers. Participation should not only be confined to lower levels, but is most necessary and most effective at the very bottom of the organizational pyramid. As a consequence of this untested view, most organizational democracy experiments in Norway and Sweden, until relatively recently, favoured concentration on shop-floor participation and work redesign at that level (see Chapters 4 and 5).

Nevertheless, as a result of political pressures, Norway, Sweden, and many other Continental European countries introduced boardroom representation of employees through legislation without noticeable negative effect. In countries where boardroom representation was not supported by a legal framework, as in Britain and the USA, the results were more equivocal, particularly in Britain.

Since arguments for and against employee boardroom representation continue, it is worth looking at the alternatives Emery had in mind. He advanced four, starting with an explicit policy statement in which the board would unequivocally accept that the company and its managers must recognize the 'social character of the resources they use' and get this view across to the shareholders. Secondly, the board must formulate an explicit statement of their management philosophy to be observed by management. Thirdly, boards should work with local-sector organizations to devise suitable societal objectives. Finally, he recommends that the board should be made aware of their joint responsibility for all actions.

The difficulty with implementing prescriptions of this kind, based on the goodwill of individual companies, can be gauged from the experience of a well-known experiment with the introduction of a new management philosophy at Shell UK. This was followed up by the introduction of participative schemes and sociotechnical designs; Emery was one of the principal consultants. The climate for change was favourable, the chief executive took a lead role, and a capable, sympathetic Shell personnel team worked closely with the consultants. It took about a year to work through several drafts of a company policy document and have it accepted at top management level. Implementation of the programme took two years and was interrupted by an external crisis (the threat to the Suez Canal) and a change of the chief executive, as a result of which much of the achievement was dissipated (Hill 1972; Blackler and Brown 1980).

Towards a Systems Approach

There has been a tendency, both in the literature and in practice, for participation to be treated narrowly and segmentally. In most industrial countries the practical work in the field of participation has concentrated at the lowest level of organization. There has been further segmentation by treating topics such as financial participation, job design, collective bargaining, training, and team working in separate administrative and logical compartments. Conceptually, too, involvement, cooperative, and consensus behaviour have been separated from decentralization, delegation, and autonomy on the doubtful ground that group-centred and individual behaviour work with different dynamics. Furthermore, levels of organization have received different treatment and tend to appear in different sections of the literature. Participation at and between senior levels is part of the management literature, while most of the work at lower levels, as well as employee representation on boards, tends to appear under industrial-relations and human-resource headings.

Changes in work design at the operator level are rarely seen to be part of the mainstream participation literature and workers are rarely involved in designing jobs. This function tends to be left to managers, engineers, or specialist consultants. Despite the considerable interest in individual forms of participation, such as job enrichment and job enlargement, during the 1970s, these topics are given little attention in the participation literature. Yet, as we have seen in earlier chapters, when operators are asked about the kind of task they are keen to be involved in, decisions about their own work came top of the list.

Some of the divisions and segregations we have mentioned have been bridged to a certain extent in countries that introduced industrial democracy legislation. In Germany, for instance, the very first law in 1951 prescribed structures which would operate at the top (the Supervisory Board), at the senior function level (the Work Director, chosen or approved by the union, and at the operational level (through Works Councils). However, these strictly structural provisions ignored direct participation through informal channels which allows individuals or groups to participate in *ad hoc* discussions and suggestions on a variety of topics, including quality.

This splitting-off and encapsulating of different aspects of organizational participation have had some undesirable consequences. Most discussions and practices fail to fit into a systems theoretical framework. A system can be described as an assembly of entities (people and structures, for instance) which operate in *reference to* each other and which are to some extent interdependent. From such a point of view, the long-term viability of any part of the system is threatened by a gross lack of congruity between the interdependent entities. Translated into organizational-democracy terms, participation works poorly if it is confined to a single level (see also Chapter 6).

At the lowest level of an organization, the most effective way to give employees a measure of influence is through the design of the job. This is where the skill and experience of employees present a range of job-design options. Other forms of effective grass-roots participation include structures such as suggestion schemes,[1] quality circles, Scanlon plans, etc., which give people an opportunity to contribute to decision-making within their accumulated experience (see Chapter 1). If the jobs people carry out throughout the working day are mechanistic, repetitive, monotonous, unvarying, and therefore without meaningful content, little energy or enthusiasm for participation in other issues may be available, nor will meaningless work contribute to the necessary experience and skill which are a prerequisite for participation in most other topics.[2]

The next level of participation relates to departmental issues and could include subjects such as bonuses and incentives, administrative problems, supply of materials, customer relations, safety, technology, and so on. Handling problems of this kind is not itself an adequate preparation for participation at the highest organizational levels, but it is certainly a useful starting point. Representative participation often operates at this level (see Chapter 1).

At boardroom level, effective employee participation requires careful preparation because the topics covered and the language customarily used would not be familiar to lower-level employees. Lack of preparation and relevant competence account for most of the documented failures (see Chapters 4 and 6). Once the problem is recognized, it can be overcome in a variety of ways, such as extensive training and familiarization, using head-office trade-union officials (as in Germany where they frequently had advanced university preparation), and/or by allowing employee representatives the same right of access to consultants enjoyed by managers.

Given the available evidence, it is puzzling to see that until now researchers and consultants, as well as managers and politicians, have, with few exceptions, failed to see the advantage of a holistic systemic approach to employee participation. The patchy results and short duration of many employee-participation schemes which we reviewed in Chapters 5 and 6 could be due to a lack of firm policy-integrated support from the highest levels of organization, including the board. Research in the 1970s as well as the 1980s has shown that, where legal or other formal participative support structures exist at senior levels, influence sharing at lower levels is greater (IDE 1981*a*, 1993). The follow-up in-depth study (DIO 1979) tested the proposition that non-legal but formally approved participation policy (called Status Power) would also have the effect of increasing real influence at lower levels. This was the case and it further strengthens the argument for a holistic approach (Heller *et al.* 1988).

More recent evidence gives further support for a systemic approach to organizational design including participation. Ichniowski, Kochen, Levine, Olson, and Strauss (1996) (see also Chapter 6) present convincing data from several studies to show that the introduction of single isolated participative practices is ineffective. What is needed is a bundle of measures designed to give employees more influence over relevant aspects of their work, including job design. This has to be part of a policy of organizational decentralization which rearranges tasks and responsibilities in a meaningful manner. However, even given this knowledge, there is at the moment little evidence that countries or organizations which have industrial democracy schemes at senior levels are aware of the value of designing jobs which allow lower-level employees to have a fair measure of control over their daily work.

Lack of systems thinking is very noticeable in the almost total absence of higher-level democratic decision structures and policies in the very large case study literature on team working, semi-autonomous working groups, quality circles, and similar schemes. For practical purposes one can disregard the ritual reference to schemes having the support of the Chief Executive Officer (CEO). Acceptance by a CEO is very different from a well-considered policy-integrated support from the board as well as from the CEO which is likely to have a longer lifespan and more power than simple, often ephemeral support from a CEO alone. In this connection it is worth remembering that the pioneering research on semi-autonomy which occurred in British coal mines in the 1950s came to nothing, although these units were shown to be economically very successful. The findings met with incomprehension and hostility from senior management, which operated within a traditional autocratic structure and probably saw these new developments as a threat to their way of life (Trist *et al.* 1963: pp. xi–xii).

Returning to Emery's four-point suggestion for enlisting the support of the board and shareholders on an *ad hoc* and voluntary basis, it is fairly clear that nothing like this has happened, nor have schemes of employee directors at board level been concerned with introducing job designs that give employees participatory opportunities over their daily tasks.[3] This lack of systemic integration has had negative consequences for industrial relations and has seriously affected trade-union attitudes to a variety of policies and practices loosely described under the banner of HRM.

Human Resources Management and Participation

The term HRM became popular in the 1970s in the USA and the1980s in Europe, and in many organizations has replaced or superseded practices and structural arrangements previously described under the heading of personnel management (Guest 1990; Blyton and Turnbull 1992; Sparrow *et al.* 1994). In the USA terms such as 'high performance' or 'high-commitment workplace' or even 'workplace innovation' are used rather than HRM. The vogue of HRM as a supposedly new concept, or at least a new term, is a sign of the rapid organizational developments in the 1980s as a result of *far-reaching* economic recession, changes in technology, increased competition, worldwide deregulation, increased unemployment in many countries, and the consequent universal drive for higher productivity.

The central practices now subsumed under HRM are not new. They require increased levels of employee involvement at lower organizational levels, group working, a wider range of staff skills, and greater flexibility in work arrangements. As we have seen in previous chapters, all these ideas were the subject of research and were found to be fairly successful in the 1960s and 1970s. However, since their gradual acceptance by management a decade or so later took place in an unfavourable economic climate, the practices were frequently introduced piecemeal and without the necessary careful preparatory work. There can also be little doubt that HRM was often deliberately introduced by management as a way of undermining trade unions (see Chapter 4). Trade unions, for their part, were slow to see that participation, skill-training, and job flexibility were inevitable developments that could be incorporated into their policies as long as they included certain safeguards and could be shown to give their members some advantages. In the 1960s and 1970s when economies in most countries were expanding and unemployment was relatively low, HRM practices could have been supported by trade unions and strengthened their position *vis-à-vis* management as well as their own members.

The Shell UK experiment mentioned earlier provided such an opportunity and many Shell shop stewards rose to the challenge, but the shop steward in charge of the craft unions refused to accept that the company's new approach was serious and continued to use all meetings and all discussions solely for bargaining purposes (Hill 1971: 103–4). In general this scepticism prevailed among British unions and in this context it is interesting to look at a comparative study by Lowell Turner (1991), who showed that other opportunities for trade-union initiatives occurred in the 1980s and were used in Germany and to some extent in Sweden. Against the background of a worldwide decline in union strength, he argues that in Germany and Sweden unions have done better in membership and influence than in other countries, notably the USA, and that one element in their success is the more positive attitudes they have taken to participation at all levels. In both Germany and Sweden unions were supported by a political party, and obtained boardroom representation, used centralized bargaining, but also supported workshop participation, group working, and semi-autonomy. In Germany, particularly in the auto industry and during the 1980s, unions took the initiative in developing new forms of teamwork operating through the legally prescribed works councils. This achieved 'a well developed union-promoted concept of group work that is now being put forward for negotiation at most West Germany auto assembly plants' (Turner 1991: 113). This is in contrast to the USA where 'in all cases, the initial planning and proposals have come from management' (Turner 1991: 111).

Even with representative participation there are important differences. In Sweden and in Norway, as we saw in Chapter 5, HRM initiatives in participation, group work, and semi-autonomy came from academics and were supported by governments. Employees in larger companies had been given boardroom representation. Unions were gradually persuaded to experiment with these measures. Volvo and the Swedish blue-collar union LO signed a co-determination agreement in 1984 and 'the union began to advance proposals for group work that greatly extended workers' and groups' autonomy and responsibility' (Turner 1991: 213).

In Britain unions have neither asked for nor received co-determination rights[4] and have opposed or been lukewarm towards employee participation and joint consultative procedures (except in state industries). As in the USA, the development of these democratizing procedures and group working have generally been initiated by management. However, a recent British trade-union report (TUC 1994) tries to allay union suspicions by putting forward a balanced view on HRM. Nevertheless, the trade-union authors point out that in many companies HRM is seen only as a way of reducing jobs and increasing efficiency and is described as 'a slippery concept that means different things to different people' (TUC 1994: 9).

Although in theory HRM could help to initiate a truly integrated schema of functionally relevant participation schemas, in practice this is rarely achieved.

Towards a Wider Horizon

In line with nearly all the literature on participation we have concentrated on its intra-organizational role, although we have noted in passing the intervening power of political and economic circumstances. We know that these external factors can influence what happens to the decision process inside organizations, but what about the mirror image? What effect do intra-organizational decision processes have on extra-organizational events?

While these considerations are not usually covered in the literature on participation and our self-imposed brief does not allow us to enter deeply into this discussion, we wish to point to a few relevant argument. Some preliminary extra-territorial considerations have already been raised in Chapters 1, 2, and 3. If participation is not simply a potential for higher enterprise efficiency but is an ontological requirement of human maturation, then enterprise behaviour has repercussions for human development in the wider community. This can also be stated negatively by saying that there is a carry-over effect impoverishing the human community from a lack of participative opportunities at work.

Chapter 3 discussed the interdependence between internal and external participants (now often called stakeholders) and the effect of decisions about the division of labour on gradients of inequality and the distribution of competence. Are the effects of these intra-organizational decisions capable of influencing employee behaviour outside the enterprise? These questions are rarely asked and even more rarely investigated except through the blunt instrument of psychological studies of satisfaction. Chapter 3 also looks at the relation between intra-organizational technical change and repercussions on the standard of life of a community through increases in affluence, an extension of lifespan, and its consequence for population density. Increases in affluence and social density naturally affect how people organize themselves individualistically or cooperatively in the wider community.

Elsewhere a few scholars have looked at the connection between what happens at work and leisure and more specifically between participative aspects of work and mental health (Kornhauser 1965; Karasek and Theorell 1990).

A series of studies in Sweden and the USA have concentrated on the relation of work design to mental and physical health and heart disease. Kornhauser interviewed over 1,000 US employees and wives and obtained extensive company records on absences and visits to medical clinics. Using a range of mental health indices he found that 'mental health is intimately associated with the nature of the work in which men are engaged' (Kornhauser 1965: 76). In particular he found a significant association between mental health and the question whether the job 'gives you a chance to use your abilities'. High scores on skill utilization related to high scores in mental health. We have shown elsewhere that participation and skill utilization are closely associated.

The problem of increasing stress apparent in modern organizations is extensively documented and discussed (for instance, Cooper and Smith 1992). Karasek (1979) develops a theory which associates mental strain with the amount of influence and scope people have in carrying out their job. This approach is developed in much greater depth in large-scale samples of US and Swedish working men by relating the influence and scope in employee job design (he calls it 'decision latitude') to physical and mental health symptoms (Karasek and Theorell 1990). They conclude that physical as well as mental problems are related to the lack of control people have over their work rather than simply the demanding or stressful nature of the job. Job designs that underutilize the skills people are interested in using in their work are identified as important preconditions to ill health.

Even wider concerns with organizational and societal issues can be inferred from the socio-political critique by Habermas, who has written extensively about the legitimation crisis of capitalism derived from false concepts of rationality and over-reliance on science and technology. To engage with these issues, he argues, it is necessary to establish extensive means of human communication or dialogue and to aim at a socially acceptable consensus based on the force of superior arguments (Habermas 1971). These global theories are not often translated to the level of organization, but we saw towards the end of Chapter 5 that the Swedish LOM programme of introducing organizational change uses Habermas's democratic dialogue as its major instrument. Operating within a different tradition, but aiming at a similar transformation of consciousness and understanding as a preliminary to achieving change, is the methodology of 'search conferences' which have been developed by Emery and Trist and others who have had considerable influence in the design of workshop-participation schemes (Weisbord 1992).

If the intra-organizational dialogue were to succeed in achieving consensus, would technology develop differently? Would the socio-technical model, to which we referred previously, be more extensively used so that antagonisms between technology and people were reduced? This is clearly an aspiration of the Scandinavian research programme. Intra-organizational participative dialogue would also affect what Dahrendorf (1979) calls 'life chances'—that is, opportunities for individual growth and for the realization of wishes and hopes. These life chances are provided by social opportunities and 'where there is co-determination they can turn mere membership of an organization into participation in running it' (p. 11).

In the absence of co-determination, decisions about life chances and scientific–technical changes may be taken in the privacy of boardrooms and management committees; they may be narrowly conceived and based on short-term enterprise requirements. There is no social or legal legitimation of even the more important life-threatening decisions involving the use of toxins and pollutants which have carcinogenic effects and may affect populations far removed from the enterprise where the decision is made. This is the subject of an extensive analysis by Ulrich Beck (1992), whose writings are very widely read on the Continent of Europe.[5] In the past there was, of course, always some risk associated with wealth creation, but Beck argues that these risks tended to be localized and were usually perceptible to our sense organs. The new risks are quite different. The fallout from the Chernobyl disaster spread over vast areas and could not be seen, smelt, or felt by people thousands of miles away who might suffer serious illness long after the event. Beck was writing before BSE, the so-called 'mad cow disease' which invaded Europe in the 1990s and has an incubation period of many years. These mega risks threaten all forms of life and affect more than one generation. More mundane but perhaps only slightly less dangerous are risks traceable to the chemical industry and ingredients of agricultural products—for instance, due to over-fertilization. The people who take these risks on behalf of society are often scientists who have no formal social responsibilities and bureaucrats who do not understand the premisses or the evidence on which scientific recommendations are made. Who participates, who helps to make these momentous decisions which affect us as citizens, if not as employees?

The questions raised by Beck and Habermas and others who call themselves postmodernists are not easily answered but they clearly relate to the distribution of power in our society as well as in organizations. The normal political process over which we have democratic rights as citizens rarely touch the mega-risk issues. Unlike political topics, the available choices are usually not widely disseminated or debated before decisions are taken and they are not topics on the agenda of formal or informal participative meetings in the organizations responsible for offloading the risks and associated social costs on the rest of society. Should democratically run organizations have an opportunity to discuss and perhaps even influence mega-risk decisions? Who would put these topics on the agenda of participative meetings?

One possible answer is provided by the stakeholder concept that has recently received considerable attention. In its original and simplest formulation it challenges the idea that shareholders, by virtue of ownership, are entitled to make all major decisions and that managers, acting on their behalf, are expected to organize the enterprise to obtain maximum benefits for them. The over-simplicity of this conceptualization was exposed by Cyert and March (1963) and more recently by Russell Ackoff, who, in his 1994 book *The Democratic Corporation*, develops a systems model of the enterprise which must be able to act and not just respond to initiatives from other parts of the system in order to adjust successfully to turbulence and increases in complexity. In a democratic enterprise every part has to exercise authority and responsibility for the good of the whole and can therefore be considered as a stakeholder. Ackoff claims that this is already happening in some corporations which include on their boards representatives of customers, wholesalers, or retailers; he could have added banks and employees.

This notion of the stakeholder corporation is very broad and Ackoff's preference for considering all stakeholders as equal is almost certainly unworkable. Some ranking of preferences must exist and this will depend on circumstances. The role of suppliers, for instance, is more important in enterprises using a 'just-in-time' method than in one which works with an inventory. Finance and banks are important to most businesses, but particularly where gearing is high. Employees are important to all enterprises, but particularly when skill requirements are considerable. In any case, the discussion of the merits and limitations of the shareholder-versus-stakeholder model is likely to grow over the twenty-first century and is already receiving attention from political theorists, politicians and economists (Hutton 1995; Perkin 1996). A stakeholder organization would be a step towards solving some of the problems of irresponsible societal decision-making described by Beck.

A Window into the Future

For the moment, however, we remember that, when we had finished planning and editing the six reference books on Organizational Democracy and Participation to which we referred in the Introduction, we decided to use our collective experience to write this book, and an attempt to anticipate the future of organizational participation was part of our design. Now, the prospect of keeping to this part of our plan seems daunting and excessively ambitious. True, forecasting ten, twenty, or thirty years ahead has fewer hazards than forecasting tomorrow's weather. Few readers of this book will in the year 2020 go back to this chapter and check on the validity of our anticipation. Furthermore, we would not expect to be right all along the line; there are too many socio-economic, technological, and political imponderables, but we believe that the attempt to look ahead is a healthy exercise of the mind.

Hamish McRae, an economics journalist of considerable experience, has written a book on *The World in 2020* (McRae 1994) in which he distinguishes between two major paths taken by futurologists. One is scenario building 'Where different possibilities are outlined and the reader is left to choose between them' (p. xi). This method was used by Shell UK to plan strategy with considerable success. The most usual alternatives, however, are to paint a picture of exaggerated optimism or pessimism. McRae chooses a middle way which starts from the here and now and then examines the various trends which are likely to affect the world over the next quarter of a century. We will follow this approach in an abbreviated version and finish with two scenarios. So far, our book is a reasonable inventory of recent and current organizational experience with participation methods. To arrive at tentative forecasts, we will add our anticipation of major societal trends likely to impinge on organizational life in the more highly developed countries.

The Global and the Local Workforce

Globalization is an incipient phenomenon coexisting with extreme forms of nationalistic protectionism in many parts of the world. Multinational companies have been the spearhead of transnational developments and have clearly affected the distribution of power at national as well as organizational level. Employees in any given location find it more difficult to participate in decisions, even in the operation of their own jobs, without being informed about the extent of international competition and similar considerations relating to their product or service. A factory in the UK producing plastic bags for the market relocated to China and found it economical to import machines and raw material to China and export millions of plastic bags to Europe on a daily basis. Even strong trade unions can exert very limited influence over these developments.

In recognition of the trend towards globalization, the European Union (EU) has developed a 1996 directive which requires all transnational companies with at least 1,000 employees, including at least 150 in two separate member states, to set up European Works Councils (EWC). At least one observer believes that with EWCs the 'European trade unions now hope to regain some of the power which they lost at national level because of the growing globalization of capital' (Schulten 1996: 303).

Collective Representation

Collective representation among employees developed in the nineteenth century as a way of limiting the arbitrary rule of employers and gradually achieved legal and political recognition. In the great majority of countries today, trade unions are accepted as legitimate institutions to carry out collective bargaining as part of the democratic process. Chapter 4 describes some of the ways trade unions operate in exercising influence in organizations and how their policies relate to formal representative as well as more informal methods of participation.

Because the exact manifestation of unionism varies enormously by industrial sector and country, generalizations about their future are hazardous. In the majority of countries, but perhaps especially in the USA, unions have lost ground in the last three decades of the twentieth century and have found it difficult to adapt to economic, technological, and political changes. Some observers believe that decline is inevitable as the ferocious process of competition and globalization accelerates.

At the same time it is argued that some form of collective representation is a fair and practical way of balancing interests among the major stakeholders and that this facilitates rather than obstructs the competitive strength of organizations. Of course, the nature of collective representation may change substantially and is likely in future to depend much more on knowledge-based processes of accommodation between different interest groups than on primitive adversarialism. The withdrawal of labour as a last resort will remain a legally enshrined right in most democratic societies, but the need to use it will diminish. Modern information technology will reduce the scope for basing claims on guesswork by giving accurate and relevant information to all stakeholders. Because in a very competitive fast moving world no stakeholder will gain from disruption, new mechanisms for conflict resolution are likely to emerge and be used.

In Chapter 4 we saw that the structures that evolved in nineteenth-century unionism of local face-to-face meetings often lost their original democratic credentials in the twentieth-century. With the enormous increase in part-time work and the participation of women, new mechanisms for collective representation through the extensive use of technology will emerge. They will be less time-consuming, more effective, and more closely related to rapidly increasing educational standards of employees.

The theoretical background developed in Chapter 3 stressing the perennial ambiguity between cooperation and conflict and dependence and independence will continue to operate in organizations, but in that chapter we also made the distinction between participating through sources of energy—that is, manual work—or through sources of information performance or intellectual work. Traditional unionism evolved from the need to represent the interests of manual workers and the structures that were appropriate for this task have not changed sufficiently to make collective representation meaningful and useful to the majority of employees in the highly developed countries who participate through non-manual work.

Some changes of attitude can now be observed. For instance in Australia, although unions followed the British tradition of charging low fees and consequently lacked the resources to participate effectively in technological changes—unlike

Swedish and German unions (Davis and Lansbury 1989)—they have embraced an innovative forward-looking educational and training policy that recognizes the need for extensive collaboration between management and unions. According to one of their leaders, they are more concerned to increase the size of the organization's output and profits than to claim a larger share of the existing cake (Ogden 1982).

We have also seen that the British Trades Union Congress (TUC) recently produced a policy document based on a review of social-science research on developments of HRM. Although understandably sceptical of some of the modern manifestations of HRM, the document takes a few tentative steps in the direction of proactively forging a new approach to relationships between union and management (TUC 1994: 20–3). European unions are now taking positive steps, in collaboration with management, in developing the new EWCs (Rivest 1996).

In the USA from as early as the 1920s there have been sporadic union–management efforts to reduce adversarialism and to foster what is often called 'union–management cooperation' or 'partnership'. Although these have had various degrees of success, recent years have seen an intensification of these activities, with numerous union and management groups taking training courses in 'mutual gains bargaining'.

By showing that the historic roots of unions have made it difficult for them to engage fully with changing realities, we do not mean to imply that management does not bear a substantial responsibility for the existing maladjustment between stakeholders. In his forceful book *Competitive Advantage through People*, Pfeffer (1994) accuses American managers of having a number of dysfunctional ideas about employees as shirkers and opportunists who must be subdued through strong-arm tactics and constant monitoring. Pfeffer blames economists for filling managers' heads with these beliefs, which lack empirical foundation and, in any case, prevent the emergence of functionally adequate labour–management relations based on trust. He could add that the prevailing idea about management's sole responsibility towards shareholders neatly avoids any accountability for collective representation.

Other Labour-Market Changes

In addition to globalization—that is, a tendency for businesses to trade as if national frontiers did not exist—there are other broad-based trends that cover many parts of the world, like the movement from traditional mass production to specialized flexible processes; from large highly hierarchical to small network-oriented organizations; from self-contained and vertically integrated to highly interdependent outsourcing and subcontracting enterprises. These diverse structural arrangements have clear and often obvious implications for employee participation and have been accompanied by other labour-market changes such as declining job security and a considerable increase in temporary jobs and a larger proportion of women in the labour force. Furthermore, a greater emphasis on competition and the market and on job mobility has inevitably changed, and in many cases reduced, the traditional role of industrial relations. This is a point emerging from Qvale's (1996) review of over thirty years and four generations of workplace democratization research in Scandinavia. In the plan of the latest programme called 'Enterprise Development 2000' he notices a 'clear sign of a certain reorientation among leaders of the labour market organizations' (p. 39). In the future, it seems, democratization if it comes about 'will follow from implementation of new technology and intertwined organizational concepts, or from general organizational development/productivity drives, rather than from specific democratization programs' (p. 39).

We will not be able to analyse the relations of each of these developments to participation beyond what we have already said in previous chapters. Furthermore, many of them—such as flexible specialization, networking, smaller units, and subcontracting arrangements, and even the trend towards more part-time work—have some association with technology. We feel that technology will have a particularly important role in facilitating or obstructing the future of organizational participation.

The European trade-union movement has taken the new legislation seriously and has organized a number of training courses and seminars for the officials who will be expected to take part in EWCs. They have also started a number of research projects. The British TUC, for instance, commissioned a survey of union representatives on EWCs already established and reports that the key areas covered by the meetings were company strategies and markets, company products, financial results, and investment; all these were reported by over 70 per cent of trade-union members of EWCs. Discussions on pay were reported by only 14 per cent.

It seems that the examples set by the companies who have anticipated the September 1996 deadline have induced other organizations that do not have to comply with the EU directive to set up their own works councils—for instance, the large clothing and food retailer, Marks & Spencer.

Technology

The relationship between technology and participation is complex and often subtle, or at least not obvious in the short term. In this section we cover those aspects of technological development which separate people from each other and thereby make interpersonal relations and participation impossible or difficult. This approach extends the term participation beyond its normal use, but seems justified in view of its potential long-term effect of reducing the scope of formal as well as informal participative opportunities.

It is now widely accepted and fairly certain that educational standards will continue to rise and that the rate of technological change will continue, though possibly at a less ferocious pace than in the 1980s and 1990s. Higher technology and higher education go together and reinforce each other. In the recent past and for some time to come, technology favours decentralization of problem-solving activity and makes knowledge more widely available. This means that decisions can be taken at lower levels and, in many cases, have to be taken at lower levels because this is where the experience comes from.

However, the first two decades of the twenty-first century will develop different scenarios. At lower levels tasks will become more and more computerized, based on knowledge derived from the decentralized experience. At the moment, many tasks require that people come together to exchange views and solve problems. This explains the need for committee work, to which one must add the advantage of clarifying differences, achieving agreement based on convergence or consensus, and the further advantage of motivating people who have participated in the formulation of the outcome. This is the basis of QCs and similar group activities where personal experiences are interchanged. Once automation is introduced, most of these activities may be redundant. We will come back to this topic in discussing the work of Zuboff.

Team working, particularly at lower organizational levels, is based on the multi-skilled requirements of modern technology which benefit from multi-skilled cooperation between employees. However, as more tasks are automated or computerized, the need for interpersonal cooperation at the lower levels is reduced or eliminated (West 1994). Quality is a good example. Robots need maintenance and occasional adjustment, and can be programmed to cooperate with each other, but the people who write programs or carry out maintenance on robots may not need to collaborate extensively (Boonstra and Vink 1996).

The completely automated factory is already feasible and by the year 2020 more examples will be developed, but we expect progress to be slow because many modern manufacturing processes are carried out in Third World countries where the cost of labour is low.

The major developments in automation will come in subsystems in the industrialized world, particularly in communication technology and in service industries. In supermarkets, for instance, the checkout points already use machine-reading of bar-coded prices though transactions are handled by a human operator. In some more advanced supermarkets customers can scan prices as they load their trolleys and pay at the checkout with a direct-debit card without the need for sales staff, except possibly to supervise the operation.

Other forms of computerized distant buying and distant banking are already used and will develop rapidly. At the moment, banks still have a very large number of branches staffed with managers, counter staff, and specialists in investment, insurance, etc. Each local bank is a small organization with various participative arrangements. These branch offices occupy prime sites and are expensive. Competitive banks based entirely on telephone communication have already captured a sizeable share of the market and many of the major banking groups have introduced supplementary distant banking services which will later enable them to close most of their high-street branches. In some US banks any face-to-face contact between customers and bank staff is handled by representatives stationed in supermarkets, but increasingly business, including loans, will be arranged through computers. All these changes reduce opportunities for person-to-person participation, but the staff reductions due to the use of new technology have already led displaced employees to form new small-scale organizations or to work as sole traders or consultants. This trend is facilitated by computers and will substantially increase the decentralization of decision power and autonomy.[6]

Another communication technology with potential for automation and for reducing group activities and therefore participation is the expert system. An expert system is a constantly updated computerized flow of information for diagnosis and/or treatment of a technico-human problem area. Medicine provides many good examples for the application of expert systems for both diagnosis and treatment. A medical practitioner faced with an unusual or complex situation with which he or she is not fully familiar will normally want to consult colleagues who may have more specialized knowledge. An expert system operating through computer and/or video communications has the advantage of a wider range of expertise, research data, and case examples than any face-to-face meeting; it can be constantly updated with findings and techniques developed in any country and transmitted with the help of any relevant sense. It is also economical in time and can operate in remote geographic areas where interpersonal meetings are not feasible. For these reasons, expert system communication is likely to grow rapidly in medicine and many other fields where complex decisions require up-to-date knowledge. Of course we do not want to oppose this trend or the other instances of technological innovation which we will describe and we recognize that there will be some positive results for participation. Using video conferencing in expert systems may provide face-to-face computer interaction superior to the telephone, fax, e-mail, or written communication which was previously used.

Bill Gates, Chairman of the biggest software company, believes that voice-activated computers would soon render all other hardware obsolete. This will enable people and computers to talk to each other, though people will have to learn to speak in the measured tones computers can recognize.

Given the subject matter of this book, we simply wish to document a range of developments which will impact on future opportunities for participation and influence-sharing.

Work at a Distance

There are important developments in distant learning and distant working, which tend to reduce the need for interaction between people. Distant learning through institutions like the Open University in the UK and many similar centres of learning round the world has spread rapidly and has an enormous future, particularly in countries with very large, dispersed populations, such as India or China. It reduces or eliminates the traditional interpersonal participation between students and between student and teacher.

Distant working started tentatively in the 1970s but has made somewhat slow progress (Holti and Stern 1986; Judkins *et al.* 1987; Haddon and Lewis 1994). Given the multiple problems associated with inner-city life all round the world—traffic congestion, crime, and pollution—distant working offers many attractions which are likely to become more obvious over the next decade. Of course distant working does not necessarily eliminate face-to-face meeting and conferences. At Rank Xerox it was discovered that a number of managers who had agreed to distant working lived on the periphery of the city within an easy commuting area. So a satellite office was set up and the head-office-connected computers were moved to it. Distant working saves head offices a lot of money. Rank Xerox calculated that, before distant working, the total overheads at head office, including office and garage space, doubled the cost of the executives' salaries.

Distant working will not be confined to one country. With e-mail and information available through the Internet, there is no reason why certain functions —for instance, costing and accounting procedures—of a European-based multinational should not be carried out in South America or Africa. American Airlines already handles much of its accounting in Barbados. Some globally dispersed work in multinationals is already being done through e-mail, but in the future a single trader of reasonable size may find it more economical to subcontract certain activities to professional specialists in low-cost countries in the same way as fashion houses now source their supply of clothes in China or Korea (Jackson and van der Wielden 1996).

Women as a group are likely to reap substantial rewards from distant working. Women with or without children often retain some responsibility for domestic activity which makes it convenient to have flexible arrangements and save the not inconsiderable time needed to travel to offices or factories.

A limiting factor in the adoption of distant working is the conventional attitude to supervisors and control. In distant working it is more difficult to rely entirely on the usual mechanisms, many of which are eyeball to eyeball, as, for instance, when we notice that somebody comes in late, leaves early, or reads a newspaper when this is not part of the job specification. Distant working requires a high degree of trust unless the product—for instance, so many metres of cloth or pages of typing—is readily measurable.

The possibilities for dispersed work arrangements based on the new information technologies, including the use of satellites and mobile telephones, are much broader than the examples given so far. They include certain forms of subcontracting and new types of contractual arrangements which allow services as well as manufacturing processes to be spread over a wider geographic area. Holti and Stern (1986) have argued that the great variety of tele or distant work developments have identifiable social or economic objectives, but increasing the democratization of working life is not among them. However, participative arrangements are not necessarily ruled out. We have to distinguish two aspects of participation more clearly than was necessary in relation to conventional work designs. One is the interpersonal, which includes face-to-face direct participation, as well as communication through representatives. The other is influence as such. Distant working will usually reduce or even eliminate interpersonal participation but has a more complex and difficult-to-predict relationship to the distribution of influence and power. In the original mainframe technology, the size and cost of computers made their location within a given business division a political issue because of the implications of access to information. Senior managers would fight bitter battles to have a mainframe computer under their control. Desktop, laptop, and palmtop miniaturization, the World Wide Web, and the vastly increased memory and speed available to even very small units has clear democratization potential. However, raw information is not always useful. It has to be conceptualized, analysed, and frequently reworked before it reveals its full potential. This means that experience and competence, including new specialized advanced technology skills, are, as before, a prerequisite to the exercise of influence. There is also the question of access. People cannot participate in the solution of problems unless they know the location and timing of the events that are planned to solve the problems. This need for access is often overlooked in research and discussion on participation. People in positions of power can exclude the influence of others by denying access. With the World Wide Web, denying access becomes more unlikely. We have already noted that, when we use a phase model of decision-making, we see that certain groups have very little influence in one or more phases. These results are often due to the manipulation of access. Modern information technology may make it more difficult to deny people the geographic and timing knowledge for access to decision-making or problem-solving, but even if one stands outside the right door at the right time, it may still be locked.

The Quality of Life

One of many unanswered questions is whether dispersed work and lack of face-to-face contact will reduce the motivation to participate and, as a consequence, whether it will affect the work ethic. Even more critical are the escalating changes in what economists call the internal labour market characterized by 'downsizing' as well as growth in part-time and temporary employment. These trends increase insecurity, lower inter-group trust, and reduce opportunities for participation. On this level of analysis there is also the question about the quality of life raised by philosophers and a few unusual economists like Amartya Sen. Traditional economists measure the quality of life by statistics like Gross National Product (GNP)[7] and this would fit well into the theoretical framework of those social scientists and managers who see the primary function of organizational democracy measures like participation as having a positive influence on economic indices such as increased productivity and quality.

As the reader will be aware, our position is different. While we regard improvements in economic indices as a useful bonus, we see participation at work as a way of enhancing the human condition, its dignity, and its developmental potential. Our position is similar to that taken by an interdisciplinary study prepared by the World Institute for Development of Economics Research (WIDER) which asked what is meant by the quality of life and what is required in terms of social policy for improving it. The organizers of this conference, Martha Nussbaum and Amartya Sen (1993), start from the position that GNP per capita is quite inadequate as an indicator of the quality of life, and among the multiple human conditions that have to be assessed, they say, 'We need to know about labour—whether it is rewarding or grindingly monotonous, whether the workers enjoy any measure of dignity and control, whether relations between employers and 'hands' are human or debased.' (p. 1).

From this perspective it would seem that the effect of certain information-technology developments may not enhance the quality of life. The various technology-derived trends we have mentioned so far have the effect of reducing social intercourse and increasing isolation. Some counter-trends, like teleconferencing, are already being experimented with, and an increased use of cable transmission of pictures and videos will give people 'virtual reality'. However, there is no such thing as 'virtual influence', unless we include here what we have previously called pseudo participation.

We have so far mentioned distant learning and distant working with the aid of new technologies. As we have already said, in the near future, and in some parts of the world now, buying goods and selling services such as banking and insurance can be done by telephone, television, or other special apparatus, thus further reducing interpersonal opportunities. Given the well-documented nature of human gregariousness, particularly among the young, the question has to be asked whether in another decade or so social isolation will be resisted or whether people will be able to compensate work-based deprivations by increased face-to-face leisure activities. Leisure compensation already occurs in many routine, repetitive, content-lacking occupations which also allow for little meaningful employee involvement.

Although a leisure explosion has been predicted for decades, it has so far been replaced by a slow incremental progress through a gradual reduction in working hours. However, the pace is likely to be accelerated as a higher life expectancy is added to a later entry into work. More time will be spent on education and training so that at the higher skill levels people may enter occupations in their mid-twenties and many will retire before they are 60 years old.[8] If life expectancy goes up to 80, this would give an average of just over thirty years of work and nearly twenty-five years of post-work activity, which at the moment we usually call retirement. As work and non-work become more nearly balanced, people may decide that gardening or watching television is not enough to sustain the post-work period and they may choose from a range of possibilities that complement or extend whatever they had been doing at work. These post-work activities could give people a large measure of influence or self-determination, since whatever they choose to do is voluntary. But is it too late to learn about participation and influence-sharing at 60?

Many problems remain. For instance, in relation to distant working, it is difficult to see a role for collective representation by bodies like trade unions. As we learnt from Chapter 4, collective representation is historically the most important power-balancing mechanism in organizations, and only legally prescribed organizational, democracy measures, as in some European countries, come anywhere close to exercising this function.

Can History Help us to Look Ahead?

Another way of looking ahead is to ask how long a given trend—for instance, social isolation through new distance-spanning technology—is going to last. Certain historic trends are cyclical. The Industrial Revolution decisively changed the location of work from being based on the home or small local workshops to large factories and, later, equally large offices. This was due to the use of new technologies based on water and later on steam. In England, these changes started in the second half of the eighteenth century. Perhaps 250 years later the new information technologies will enable us to reverse the process and go back to working in the home or in smaller local units. The new cycle will, of course, not take us back to exactly where we were before the Industrial Revolution. For instance, the basic work unit in society, the family, is now and will then be much less stable than in the eighteenth and nineteenth centuries and this will affect the desirability and feasibility of home-based industry.

Will it then take another 250 years to discover a new way of living and working? A lot will depend on whether we can improve our handling of the relationship between people and technology.

One of the important developments introduced through the factory system was a change in the power relationship between people engaged in the manufacturing process. The so-called 'putting-out' system allowed cottage craftspeople who usually owned their own machines to negotiate freely with intermediaries about price and delivery time of home manufactured textiles. They were free, multi-skilled agents subject to competition and had control over the sequence of work.[9] The moment manufacture moved into factories it was subjected to a formal division of labour under a strict boss–subordinate hierarchy based on property rights. A division of labour nearly always results in an increase of power distance.

In the twentieth century three influences gradually reduced the power distance: firstly, an increase of skill requirement for many jobs organized under batch rather than mass production; secondly, the growth of trade unions; and, thirdly, the introduction of universal education and higher levels of expectation. Nevertheless, technology, and in particular the technico-organizational designs developed by

Henry Ford and Frederick Winslow Taylor, have imposed considerable constraints on democratic organizational procedures all over the world, in the former Soviet Union as much as in the USA. The term 'Fordism' is now used to describe a production system which separated workers from one another and divided the production process into a fragmented series of tasks more easily controlled by supervisors and management. Taylorism devised methods of work that extracted the knowledge and skill base from the operator level and relocated them at supervisor or management level, thus supporting a division of labour and hierarchical concentration of power. Many practical manifestations of these two philosophies are still in evidence today.

Cycles of change do not have to be spaced in 200-year intervals. There are a number of well-established theoretical cycles, one called Kondratief, that lasts about fifty years from one economic depression to another. Some commentators give this cycle substantial status (for instance, Emery 1993: 235) and then go on to claim that influence-sharing procedures are relaxed or even abandoned during the topsy-turvy conditions and pressures businesses experience in a depression.

The impact of economic cycles on participation strengthens the case for a legal or structured underpinning of organizational democracy, since, without it, abandoned or emaciated schemes may not recover in the upswing of the economic cycle (see also Ramsay 1977).

Alternative Scenarios

The question we raise here, and our justification for having a brief glance back into history, is to judge whether in the future, as in the past, technology will set the pace and people will be expected to fit in as best they can. An alternative scenario is to anticipate the possibility that a more equal distribution of organizational influence in the twenty-first century will impose conditions and constraints on technological developments to accommodate human preferences. This would take a giant step in the direction indicated by Beck and Habermas, mentioned earlier, who in different ways critique the interaction between social power and technology.

The second scenario is compatible with the socio-technical model described in previous chapters which grew out of an analysis of an organizational change from a small-scale, very humanistic work design based on semi-autonomy, to a conventional division of labour and skill (Emery 1993). In this connection it is important to look at Zuboff's (1988) analysis of 'the smart machine' which explores the dilemmas and options posed by computer-mediated information systems. Zuboff concludes that all the dilemmas presented by computerization point to two alternative uses for information technology: *automating* and *informating*.

The logic of *automating* is to extend the trajectory of the machine in replacing the human body with a technology that enables the same process to be performed with more continuity and control. As one worker put it: the computer 'takes the human factor out of running the machine'. Work itself becomes abstract. And concomitantly workers experience loss of control and loss of action-centred, sentient, and tacit competencies acquired over long years of being on the job. New 'intellective' competencies then become necessary.

The second, or *informating*, aspect of computer-mediated work not only translates work operations into an explicit electronic text (the program), but it even generates new information and a database revealing the past and present state of any given work operation. Such data become transparent: they can be shared; they can be centralized or decentralized; they can be manipulated—that is, changed or linked to other databases. Data banks and electronic texts increasingly expropriate the skills of both industrial and service workers.

Two possibilities follow from those two uses: one is the increasing impoverishment (deskilling) of work activities; the other, more promising, is a more comprehensive understanding (by the worker) of one's work in an elaborated language that introduces the possibilities of questions, choice, and innovation.

The first possibility leads to centralization and control; that is, it exploits the automating function of the smart machine to foster traditional managerial privileges. The second or informating option leads in the opposite direction of decentralization and the formation of an open participative organization that democratizes skills in the interests of maximizing the information function of the new technologies.

Most managers are likely to favour the first possibility and try to maintain the traditional division of labour that emphasizes control and minimizes the need to train workers.

In attempting to come to a conclusion about the role of technology in relation to participation, influence and power-sharing, organizational democracy, empowering, etc. in the future, we have reviewed some of the main trends that are likely to influence the nature of organizational life in the early part of the twenty-first century. We have concentrated on the role of technology rather than other areas of life, such as education and political–economic development and organization structures, because we think that, even if the rate of technological change may not quite sustain its recent momentum, it will still dominate the shape of organizations and their interaction with people.

Here, as well as in Chapter 3, where theoretical aspects of technology are discussed, we have refrained from using currently popular terms such as telematics, cyberspace, the superhighway, and the constantly changing range of acronyms that refer to the finer elements of technological innovations. Using a broad brush we have painted an easily recognizable picture from which we obtain two scenarios. One is based on the assumption of the maximization of technology; the other on the possibility of its joint optimization with the human component. This dichotomy will be familiar and we do not apologize for this. It derives from experience mediated by a considerable literature.

If the technological imperative prevails in the future, as it has to a large extent in the past, then the range of opportunity for participation at the workplace will inevitably diminish.

However, we are inclined to speculate that technological dominance may recede later in the twenty-first century as more people assert their preference for social interaction as against semi-autonomous isolation.

Towards a Conclusion

We return to the point made in the Introduction about the 'myth and reality' title of this book, where we referred to the original Greek contrast between *mythos* and *logos*, the latter suggesting a completely rational account of reality while *mythos* embodies the notion of something popular but fictitious. The reader of the preceding chapters will have had little difficulty in recognizing examples of both in our review of theory and practice of organizational participation. From time to time we have also warned of the dangers from high expectation and idealism which easily transcend into Utopia.

We have attempted to present a fairly balanced account of putative successes and failures and the large grey area in between where so many factors are involved that dichotomous attributions like success or failure are simply not feasible.

In this book, the term participation is given an unusually wide frame of reference. We have included processes of communication, influence, power-sharing, cooperation, and democratization as well as the work structures which encourage or discourage these processes. While concentrating on the workplace and organizational dimensions within which work takes place, we have argued that the wider socio-political–economic environment plays an important part in the development and survival of participation. Finally, we recognize that an absence of democratic participative processes inside organizations may spill over into the socio-political environment and produce societal risks.

To do justice to this wide-ranging approach, we have conceptualized participation in the form of a 'mapping sentence' in Chapter 2 and have concentrated on tracing important antecedents and consequences of the various influence-sharing processes we cover with the term participation. Among the consequences, while we do not ignore efficiency, effectiveness, and satisfaction, we stress that an ethical and practical case has to recognize that participation, in at least some of the important activities that take place at work, is a requirement for human development. Most people spend at least half their waking life at work, inevitably affecting the other half through their work-derived feelings of self-worth, dignity, and competence.

We have attempted to produce a balanced picture by drawing on the major disciplines of sociology, psychology, and industrial relations and by reviewing a range of important individual and meta studies. Balance is not the same as neutrality; we believe there is a case for blending the political goals of freedom, liberty, and democracy with organizational policies which recognize and respect human needs for continuous growth, dignity, and feelings of self-worth (Wilpert 1989).

As we review significant sections of the evidence, through our own experience and the literature, we have paid particular attention to the reasons why participation is often resisted, why it frequently fails to spread, even from successful examples, and why it sometimes fails altogether. One can learn a great deal from understanding the limitations that prevent success. One major reason for failure is the absence of a systemic approach to participation both in theory and in practice which hinders the development of effective organization. If this argument, which was anticipated in the two previous chapters, is accepted, it provides an answer for those who ask why, in spite of sound theoretical support and extensive positive empirical evidence, the overall participation picture is very uneven.

There is, secondly, the well-documented human tendency to resist change, which, in Chapter 5, we explained as due to a basic and biologically understandable need for homeostasis—that is, balance—which increases security and predictability. Based on detailed examples, two very experienced organization researchers argue that, in most cases, organizational reform is stillborn, costly, and undesirable. They even give advice to managers on how to prevent reforms which they see as frequently inspired by the self-interest of consultants (Brunsson and Olsen 1993). However, they have no problem with natural evolutionary developments in response to changing environmental conditions. They also demonstrate that structural reforms are more easily achieved than reforms which require direct changes in human behaviour. From this it might follow that legal–structural measures in support of organizational democracy introduced over a period of time—as in most European countries in the 1960s and 1970s, for instance—have a good chance of being successful. They have lasted well and have not held up the economic progress of the countries that pioneered these schemes.

Thirdly, most of the literature as well as most applications have implicitly assumed that participation can be applied to all or most situations. However, research tells us that this is not the case (Heller and Yukl 1969; Vroom and Yetton 1973; IDE 1981*a*, *b*; IDE 1993). Some early classic and controlled experiments on communication networks demonstrated the contingency nature of tasks. For instance, in the solution of simple tasks a centralized wheel communication structure with one member in the centre made fewer errors and was more effective than a circle network, which made the largest number of mistakes and required more messages to solve the problem. However, although the democratic circular structure was relatively ineffective, the people working in it were more satisfied than in the centralised wheel structure (Leavitt and Mueller 1951; Sabini 1992). Now the situation was quite different when the same design was used on complex tasks; there the centralized structures were less satisfactory and the decentralized circle arrangement was faster (Shaw 1954; Sabini 1992). These controlled laboratory results gave further support to the view that efficiency as well as satisfaction were dependent on the nature of the task.

In spite of the evidence which in this case reinforces common experience that complex or crisis issues have to be handled differently from routine, simple situations, the importance of relating the extent of communication and influence-sharing to certain contingencies has been slow to infiltrate the design of participative schemes.

Fourthly, the importance of skill and experience as necessary antecedents to meaningful, non-manipulative participation has also been slow to enter theory or practice. The evidence of an essential and positive relationship between competence and influence-sharing has been given in most previous chapters. One reason why supporters of participation and influence-sharing did not want to acknowledge the competence–participation relationship was based on an inappropriate identification between organizational and political democracy (Heller 1992*a*). The hard-won battle for a universal political franchise irrespective of property rights, education, or gender convinced many people that the same principle can be applied to business. But there are differences, particularly when it comes to direct informal participation, which has no equivalent in politics.

Even with representative participation there are important differences. In small and medium-sized companies the range of talent and motivation is significantly more restricted than in the larger political scene and the specific expertise expected of office-holders is also different. Failure to see a relationship between competence and participation led to a gross underemphasis on the need for training.

Fifthly, there is the more recent evidence that influence-sharing is not equally distributed over the decision cycle. Few issues are resolved instantaneously and some take months and even years from initiation to implementation. We have reviewed this evidence in Chapter 5. Problem-solving and decision-making are processes that have a beginning, a middle, and an end, and the content of these phases are not identical. This applies to all levels of organization and to most tasks. The most appropriate way to divide a given process into phases may vary, but we have found reliable evidence that the amount of influence people exercise in a given phase of a decision differs significantly by task and by level. Lower levels of the organization will have more influence during implementation than in the initiation of decisions relating to new products, but in relation to people-oriented tasks they have most influence during the early phase. It would seem that participatory behaviour over a decision cycle adjusts itself to the experience and competence of people. This makes a lot of sense, but since these findings are not yet incorporated into policy and design, we must expect some frustration and failures.

Sixthly, in several chapters we have mentioned that participation cannot prosper in the absence of trust. Trust cannot be built up quickly and cannot easily coexist with redundancy. The critical importance of trust in successful organizational development has recently been analysed by Zand (1997), who has enunciated a triadic theory of high-performance leadership in which trust is the key to achieving collaborative committed action leading to knowledge acquisition and the acceptance of a contingent use of power.

Seventhly, there is the evidence that representative as well as direct participation is more easily sustained when it is underpinned by formal or legal support measures.

A number of other problems and limitations to effective participation can be mentioned; they are derived from research and documented experience, although with varying degrees of rigour and certainty:

- In several previous chapters we have already expressed our doubt about the utility of making productivity gains the main objective for introducing participation. Complete laboratory-like controlled field conditions are not feasible and in all realistic situations there will be a number of other factors influencing productivity. This is particularly obvious at the level of an organization where economic-marketing fluctuations, sometimes simply the weather or exchange rates, government policies, the state of the labour market, the impact of new technology, etc. will be much more decisive than the effects of participation. Participation may lead to superior quality or reliability of a product or service, but the economic effect of this will take time to show up in the balance sheet.
- Where participation is introduced primarily to increase satisfaction, it is often forgotten that satisfaction can be achieved as easily by avoiding as by doing work.
- Participation, whether formal or informal, has to be seen to achieve something worthwhile, otherwise confidence will be lost. This means it is not possible to introduce participation coincidental with redundancies.
- Attempts to introduce participation primarily to obtain commitment can backfire in two ways. If participation is seen to be manipulative it will prevent commitment, but where it succeeds it runs the danger of creating groupthink and reducing organizational flexibility.
- There is a temptation to hold participative meetings to solve complex problems, not primarily to obtain clear solutions, but to shift responsibility for outcomes to a wider constituency. The costs of such procedures are likely to exceed benefits.
- Employees may at first welcome participative meetings as a change from the routine of work, but boredom will return if meetings lack clear objectives and fail to provide palpable achievements.
- The memory of a badly introduced scheme lingers on and may prevent a much better scheme from being successfully introduced later.
- More generally it is worth remembering that all manner of participative arrangements, except delegation, incur transaction costs and, while this is quite legitimate, it has to be borne in mind and justified.

Finally, we have to consider the role of unions. As we have seen in several chapters, they are important players even in countries where their membership is low. In many countries unions have started off by being opposed to all methods of influence-sharing except time-honoured collective bargaining. This has meant that, when formal and informal methods of participation gradually became established and demonstrated certain benefits for organizations and/or employees, unions were put on the defensive, and, more importantly, management was seen to take the lead in sponsoring participative processes and was sometimes tempted to use participation as a way of reducing union influence (see Chapter 4). At this point, union scepticism had become a self-fulfilling prophecy and led to further resistance. However, as national and international competitive pressures increased, and, in continental countries, as legislation forced the pace, unions have adopted more conciliatory attitudes and in some countries positively welcome cohabitation between collective bargaining and various forms of controlled participation. Our analysis of the evidence suggests that, in organizations that have trade unions, the utility and longevity of formal and informal participative structures is considerably increased through a process of symbiosis between management and unions.

From an understanding of these limiting conditions, we can construct the ingredients of a positive scenario, but without in any way implying that it is possible to draw up a blueprint for success. Resistance to change is omnipresent in organizations, particularly where shifts in power are perceived to be a result of the change. That is why some formal or legal support measures are necessary to get a participative system started. The term 'system' implies a totality of coordinated measures within a compatible theoretical framework. Confidence and trust derived from a relatively tranquil history of collective representation would provide a suitable backdrop, as would the development of requisite skill and experience to allow meaningful participation among all levels of employees to take place. Experience and research have shown that the design of a participative system must recognize that not all problems or phases of the decision cycle require the same style of influence-sharing or the same group of people to contribute to its solution. Given these conditions, one could confidently expect positive results in terms of a greater utilization of existing competence and an improvement in outcomes—for instance, the quality of decision, product, or service, as well as the quality of organizational life and the developmental potential and maturity of employees.

A case can be made that participation needs to 'grow'. Otherwise it will atrophy. One can conceive of a natural evolutionary pattern from joint consultative procedures, where most of the time is spent on information-sharing, to problem-solving groups, like QCs, where ideas are likely to be taken seriously. Later, through metamorphosis, additional responsibilities and a wider range of skills can be used in work teams. Gradually, as experience with shop-level problems accumulates, pressure develops to deal with organization-level issues. This requires representative participation, training, and regular feedback to constituents as well as a build-up in confidence and trust best achieved by consistent human resource policies, including as much job security as feasible.

Under appropriate conditions, participation can meet one or more of the goals discussed in Chapter 1: humanistic, power equalization, and organizational efficiency. However, participation is not a cure-all for every societal ill. Given this, what should be participation's role in the society of the future?

Our attempt to look into possible developments in the twenty-first century, particularly in relation to technology, leads us to expect an interim period during which people will become increasingly communicative but, at the same time, interpersonally separated, so that the nature of participation will retreat from reality to virtuality. This need not affect the amount of personal or group influence, although it will be exercised in a more mechanistic mode. Given the long evolutionary history of human gregariousness, we would not expect the technological imperative to act as a permanent obstacle to interpersonal and group-based organizational life. Rather, we would expect a long-term integration of the technological potential with social needs in ways that cannot be precisely anticipated. As people live longer, spend more time on education, and retire earlier, so the time spent in non-work activities increases and with it the possibility of partially compensating for the stress and limitations of working in organizations.

The subtitle of our book indicates that we believe 'myth' and 'reality' both play an important part in the broad organizational phenomenon we call participation, and both terms can be variously interpreted. It is appropriate for a term like 'myth' to have many facets. In the 1990s various areas of theorizing have evolved around socio-anthropological analyses of 'myths, rituals, gossips, stories, symbols, negotiated structures and artefacts or visionary goals—all of which provide the basis of and feed back into organizationally specific sets of shared values and meanings' (Wilpert 1995: 60).

While not denying the importance of these attempts to gain new epistemological insights, we have pursued a simpler and perhaps less sophisticated approach in choosing to contrast 'myth' and 'reality'. We do not take a metaphysical approach to reality as something basic, testable, and real, nor do we believe that subjective assessments are unreal; rather we argue that reality is what people believe to be real, so that, in the case of participation, the evidence we review—in fact the only evidence that is normally available—is judgements made by managers, lower-level employees, trade unionists, or researchers who believe that real influence or power is available to them in their organizational tasks.[10] By contrast, myths are judgements by the same group of people that indicate doubts, scepticism, or judgements that very little genuine influence or power is really available to them or that the process is deceptive or inauthentic. In the literature, inevitably, many of these judgements are made through the interpretation of results by researchers and we assume in good faith.

Overall, we have come to the conclusion that democratizing organizational life through participative arrangements depends on more contingencies than much of the current literature leads us to believe. None of the obstacles we have mentioned is insurmountable. It is possible to overcome resistance to change, cosy feelings of dependency, inauthenticity, neoclassical economic pessimism, lack of trust, and inadequate competence training. Technological development and social needs are capable of being integrated. Formal and informal measures of influence-sharing, incorporating appropriate measures of conflict management, must be seen as complementary rather than antagonistic subsystems. All this can be achieved within a systemic framework that recognizes that the decision-making process in organizations must be sanctioned and agile and will remain hierarchical while recognizing the legitimate interests of employees as stake-holders.

Participation has both advantages and costs. To the extent that technology becomes more complex and the environment more turbulent, management may become increasingly dependent on employees' knowledge, commitment, and ability to exercise discretion. Only then will participation's relative advantages become apparent and participation more widespread.

Will this happen? At the moment the myths surrounding participation are stronger than reality. In future they may be more equally balanced. From the Introduction of this book, let us also remember the lesson about Troy, the mystical city featured in Homer's *Iliad* which, in 1872, as the result of a hunch from an amateur archaeologist, transmogrified from myth to reality.

NOTES

1. Suggestion schemes are often badly designed and administered and frequently provide inadequate awards, but the potential is considerable.
2. NUMMI seems to be an exception; they have a sixty-second job cycle but workers designed the work themselves.
3. In some American companies—for instance, employee-owned United Airlines—written policy supports an elaborate structure of direct and indirect participation, but it is too early to assess the results.
4. See Chapter 4. Many unions were and remain highly sceptical of boardroom representation. There was some support for national legislation under the initiative of a Labour government which resulted in the Bullock report of 1977. Its recommendations were not accepted.
5. Beck's book *Risk Society: Towards a New Modernity* (1992), published in Germany in 1986, sold 60,000 copies in the first five years and has now been translated into many languages.
6. This example highlights the difficulty with the term 'participation', which usually refers to interpersonal or group behaviour. However, as we explained in previous chapters, we use the term to describe degrees of influence- and power-sharing and therefore include delegation and autonomy (usually semi-autonomy).
7. GNP is the sum total of goods and services produced in a country (to the extent they can be assessed in money terms) plus the net income from abroad.
8. Senior executives in large multinational companies sometimes retire at 55.
9. Of course, complete freedom was not always achieved and subcontracting reduced autonomy.

10. It can be argued that at least two aspects of the distribution of power in organization have a degree of objectivity—namely, hierarchy assessed in terms of the number of formal levels of authority and job descriptions for each of the positions on an organization diagram. Even there, however, there is some room for judgements, and behaviour does not always follow the tramlines. In cases of disputes, foremen and even middle managers have been known to be bypassed during formal negotiations and informal contacts are known to circumvent the hierarchy quite frequently. The distinction between so-called line and staff jobs is constantly reinterpreted, and responsibilities between job functions are fluid and frequently decided by strength of personality rather than words on a piece of paper.

REFERENCES

Abell, Peter (1979), 'Hierarchy and Democratic Authority', in T. R. Burns, L. E. Karlsson, and V. Rus (eds.), *Work and Power* (Beverly Hills, Calif.: Sage Publications), 141–71.

—— (1983), 'The Viability of Industrial Producer Cooperation', in Crouch and Heller (1983), 73–103.

Abrahamsson, Bengt (1993), *Why Organizations?: Why and How People Organize* (London: Sage Publications).

Ackoff, Russell L. (1994), *The Democratic Corporation: A Radical Prescription for Recreating Corporate America and Rediscovering Success* (New York: Oxford University Press).

Adams, R. J., and Rummel, C. H. (1977), 'Workers' Participation in Management in West Germany: Impact on the Worker, the Enterprise and the Trade Union', *Industrial Relations Journal*, 8/1 (Spring), 4–22.

Addison, John, Kraft, Kornelius, and Wagner, Joachim (1993), 'German Works Councils and Firm Performance', in Bruce Kaufman and Morris Kleiner (eds.), *Employee Representation: Alternatives and Future Directions* (Madison: Industrial Relations Research Association), 305–38.

Adler, Paul (1992), 'The "learning bureaucracy": New United Motor Manufacturing, Inc., Research', *Organizational Behavior*, 15: 111–94.

—— and Cole, Robert (1993), 'Designed for Learning: A Tale of Two Auto Plants', *Sloan Management Review*, 34/3 (Spring), 85–93.

—— Goldoftas, Barbara, and Levine, David (1995), 'Voice in Union and Nonunion High-Performance Workplaces: Two Toyota Transplants Compared', Paper Presented to the Industrial Relations Research Association Annual Meeting, Washington, 7 Jan.

Ahlstrand, B. (1990), *The Quest for Productivity: A Case Study of Fawley after Flanders* (Cambridge: Cambridge University Press).

Albrook, Robert (1967), 'Participative Management: Time for a Second Look', *Fortune*, 75/5: 166–70, 197–200.

Aldrich, Howard (1979), *Organizations and Environments* (Englewood Cliffs, NJ: Prentice Hall).

Allen, V. L. (1954), *Power in Trade Unions* (London: Longmans).

Allport, G. W. (1945), 'The Psychology of Participation', *Psychological Review*, 52: 117–32.

Almond, G. A., and Verba, S. (1965), *The Civic Culture* (Boston, Mass.: Little, Brown & Co.).

Alutto, Joseph, and Belasco, James (1972), 'Determinants of Attitudinal Militancy among Nurses and Teachers', *Industrial and Labor Relations Review*, 27: 216–27.

Alvesson, Mats (1993), 'Corporate Culture, Participation and Pseudo-Participation in a Professional Service Company', in Lafferty and Rosenstein (1993), 280–99.

—— (1995), 'The Meaning and Meaninglessness of Postmodernism: Some Ironic Remarks', *Organization Studies*, 16/6: 1047–75.

Aoki, Mashahiko (1990), 'Toward an Economic Model of the Japanese Firm', *Journal of Economic Literature*, 28: 1–27.

Applebaum, Eileen, and Batt, Rosemary (1994), *The New American Workplace: Transforming Work Systems in the United States* (Ithaca, NY: ILR Press).

Aram, John D., and Kolhaas, Jan (1984), 'Organization, Dissonance and Change', *Administrative Science Quarterly*, 29/3: 473–5.

Argyris, Chris (1951), *The Impact of Budgets on People* (New York: Controllership Foundation).

—— (1970), *Intervention Theory and Method: A Behavioral Science View* (Reading, Mass.: Addison-Wesley).

—— (1993), *Knowledge for Action: A Guide for Overcoming Barriers to Organizational Change* (San Francisco: Jossey-Bass).

—— and Schön, Donald (1974), *Theory in Practice: Increasing Professional Effectiveness* (San Francisco: Jossey-Bass).

—— —— (1991), 'Participatory Action Research and Action Science Compared: A Commentary', in William F. Whyte (ed.), *Participatory Action Research* (London: Sage Publications), 85–96.

Arthur, Jeffrey (1994), 'Effects of Human Resources Systems on Manufacturing Performance and Turnover', *Academy of Management Journal*, 37/3 (June), 67–87.

Arzensek, Vlado (1983), 'Problems of Yugoslav Self Management', in Crouch and Heller (1983), 303–25.

Ashby, William R. (1963), *An Introduction to Cybernetics* (New York: John Wiley & Sons).

Astley, W. Graham, and Van de Ven, Andrew (1983), 'Central Perspectives and Debates in Organization Theory', *Administrative Science Quarterly*, 28/2 (June), 245–73.

Attali, J. (1972), *Analyse économique de la vie politique* (Paris: Presses Universitaires de France).

Auer, Peter (forthcoming), 'German Industrial Relations: Institutional Stability Pays', in Lowell Turner (ed.), *Negotiating the New Germany: Can Social Partnership Survive?* (Ithaca, NY: ILR Press).

—— and Riegler, Claudius (1990), 'The Swedish Version of Group Work—The Future Model of Work Organization in the Engineering Sector?', *Economics and Industrial Democracy*, 11: 291–9.

Bacon, Nicolas, Blyton, Paul, and Morris, Jonathan (1996), 'Among the Ashes: Trade Union Strategies in the UK and German Steel Industries', *British Journal of Industrial Relations*, 34: 25–50.

Baitsch, Ch. (1985), *Kompetenzentwicklung und partizipative Arbeitsgestaltung. Eine hermeutische Analyse bei Industriearbeitern in einer sich verändernden Arbeitssituation* (Bern: Huber).

—— and Frei, F. (1980), *Qualifizierung in der Arbeitstätigkeit* (Bern: Huber).

Baker, Mei Liang, and Kleingartner, Archie (1992), 'Shared Decision-Making in the Schools: Fad or Fundamental Change?', *California Public Employee Relations*, 92: 10.

Bamberg, E. (1986), *Arbeit und Freizeit* (Weinheim: Beltz).

Bandura, Albert (1977), 'Self-Efficacy: Toward a Unifying Theory of Behavior', *Psychological Review*, 84/2: 191–215.

—— (1986), *Social Foundations of Thought and Action: A Social Cognitive Theory* (Englewood Cliffs, NJ: Prentice Hall).

Banker, Rajiv, Field, Joy, Schroder, Roger, and Sinha, Kingshuk (1996), 'Impact of Work Teams on Manufacturing Performance', *Academy of Management Journal*, 39: 867–90.

Barkai, H. (1977), *Growth Patterns of the Kibbutz Economy* (Oxford: North-Holland).

Barley, Stephen, R. (1990), 'The Alignment of Technology and Structure through Roles and Networks', *Administrative Science Quarterly*, 35/1: 61–103.

Barrett, Gene, and Okudaira, Tadashi (1995), 'The Limits of Fishery Cooperatives? Community Development and Rural Depopulation in Hokkaido Japan', *Economic and Industrial Democracy*, 16: 201–32.

Batstone, Eric (1976), 'Industrial Democracy and Worker Representation at the Board Level: A Review of the European Experience', in Eric Batstone and P. L. Davies (eds.), *Industrial Democracy* (London: HMSO).

—— Ferner, Anthony, and Terry, Michael (1983), *Unions on the Board* (Oxford: Blackwell).

Batt, Rosemary (1995), 'Performance and Welfare Effects of Work Reconstruction: Evidence from Telecommunications Services', Ph.D. dissertation (Cambridge, Mass.: Sloan School of Management, MIT).

—— and Batt, Eileen (1995), 'Worker Participation in Diverse Settings: Does the Form Affect the Outcome?', *British Journal of Industrial Relations*, 33: 353–78.

Baudrillard, J. (1990), *La Transparence du mal* (Paris: Galilee).

Beck, Ulrich (1992), *Risk Society: Towards a New Modernity* (London: Sage Publications).

Becker, Bernd (1989), *Oeffentliche Verwaltung* (Percha und Kempfenhausen: R. S. Schulz).

Becker, Ernest (1968), *The Structure of Evil: An Essay on the Unification of the Science of Man* (New York: George Braziller).

—— (1971), *The Birth and Death of Meaning* (New York: Free Press).

Ben-Ner, Avner (1984), 'On the Stability of the Cooperative Type of Organization', *Journal of Comparative Economics*, 8: 247–60.

—— (1988), 'Comparative Empirical Investigations on Worker-Owned and Capitalist Firms', *International Journal of Industrial Organization*, 6: 7–31.

—— and Jones, Derek (1995), 'Employee Participation, Ownership and Productivity: A Theoretical Framework', *Industrial Relations*, 34: 532–54.

Berenbach, Shari (1979), 'Peru's Social Property: Limits to Participation', *Industrial Relations*, 18: 370–5.

Berg, Peter, Applebaum, Eileen, Bailey, Thomas, and Kalleberg, Arne (1996), 'The Performance Effect of Modular Production in the Apparel Industry', *Industrial Relations*, 35/3: 356–73.

Berger, Peter, and Luckman, Thomas (1971), *The Social Construction of Reality: A Treatise in the Sociology of Knowledge* (Harmondsworth: Penguin Books).

Berggren, Christian (1991), *Alternatives to Lean Production: Work Organization in the Swedish Auto Industry* (Ithaca, NY: ILR Press).

—— (1993), *The Volvo Experience: Alternatives to Lean Production* (Basingstoke: Macmillan; previously published by ILR Press, 1992).

Bertalanffy, Ludwig von (1950), 'The Theory of Open Systems in Physics and Biology', *Science*, 3: 23–9.

Black, D. (1958), *The Theory of Committees and Elections* (Cambridge: Cambridge University Press).

Blacker, F. H. M., and Brown, C. A. (1980), *Whatever Happened to Shell's New Philosophy of Management?* (London: Saxon House).

Blake, R., and Mouton, J. (1964), *The Managerial Grid* (Houston, Tex.: Gulf Publishing Company).

Bland, A. E., Brown, P. A., and Tawney, R. H. (1914), *English Economic History: Selected Documents* (London: G. Bell & Sons).

Blasi, Joseph (1984), 'Ownership: Governance, and Restructuring', in I. W. Liberman and John Nells (eds.), *Russia: Creating Private Enterprises and Efficient Markets* (Washington: World Bank).

—— and Kruse, D. L. (1991), *The New Owners: The Mass Emergence of Employee Ownership in Public Companies and What it Means to American Business* (New York: HarperCollins).

—— Mehrling, Perry, and Whyte, William, F. (1984), 'Environmental Influences in the Growth of Worker Ownership and Control', in Wilpert and Sorge (1984), 289–313.

Blau, P., and Schoenherr, R. (1971), *The Structure of Organizations* (New York: Basic Books).

Blyton, Paul, and Turnbull, Peter (1992) (eds.), *Reassessing Human Resource Management* (London: Sage Publications).

Bonin, John, Jones, Derek, and Putterman, Louis (1993), 'Theoretical and Empirical Studies of Producer Cooperatives: Will the Twain Ever Meet?', *Journal of Economic Literature*, 31/3 (Sept.), 1290–320.

Boonstra, Jaap, and Vink, Mauritius (1996), 'Technological and Organizational Innovation: A Dilemma of Fundamental Change and Participation', *European Journal of Work and Organizational Psychology*, 5/3: 351–75.

Borzeix, Anni, and Linhart, Daniele (1989), 'Participation: A French Perspective', in Lammers and Széll (1989*b*), 130–41.

Bothe, B. (1987), 'Bedingungzumsammenhange fur Partizipationstat von Betriebsräten' (Doctoral Dissertation, University of Berlin).

Boudon, Raymond (1983), *Scientific Advancement in Sociology: The Identification of Progress in Learning: Proceedings UNESCO and the European Science Foundation Sponsored Conference on the State of the Sciences, Colmar, France, March* (Cambridge: Cambridge University Press).

Bowlby, John (1946), 'Psychology and Democracy', *Political Quarterly*, 17: 61–76.

Bradley, Keith, and Hill, Stephen (1987), 'Quality Circles and Managerial Interests', *Industrial Relations*, 26: 68–82.

—— and Taylor, Simon (1992), *Business Performance in the Retail Sector: The Experience of the John Lewis Partnership* (Oxford: Clarendon Press).

—— Estrin, Saul, and Taylor, Simon, 'Employee Ownership and Company Performance', *Industrial Relations*, 29/3: 385–402.

Brannen, Peter (1983), 'Worker Directors—An Approach to Analysis: The Case of the British Steel Corporation', in Crouch and Heller (1983), 121–38.

—— Batstone, E., Fatchett, D., and White, P. (1976), *The Worker Directors: A Sociology of Participation* (London: Hutchinson).

Brass, Daniel J. (1984), 'Being in the Right Place: A Structural Analysis of Individual Influence in an Organization', *Administrative Science Quarterly*, 29/4 (Dec.), 518–39.

Brehm, J. W. A. (1966), *Theory of Psychological Reactance* (New York: Academic Press).

Brown, Andrew (1995), 'Managing Understandings: Politics, Symbolism, Niche Marketing and the Quest for Legitimacy in its Implementation', *Organization Studies*, 16/6: 951–69.

Brown, J. A. C. (1963), *Techniques of Persuasion: From Propaganda to Brainwashing* (Harmondsworth: Penguin).

Brown, Wilfred (1960), *Explorations in Management* (London: Heinemann).

Brulin, Goran (1995), 'Sweden: Joint Councils under Strong Unionism', in Rogers and Streeck (1995), 189–216.

Brundtland, G. R. (1989), 'The Scandinavian Challenge: Strategies for Work and Learning', in Lammers and Széll (1989*b*), 103–12.

Brunsson, Nils, and Olsen, Johan (1993), *The Reforming Organization* (New York: Routledge).

BSC [British Steel Corporation] Employee Directors (1977), *Worker Directors Speak* (Westmead, England: Gower Press).

Bullock, Lord Alan (1977), *Report of the Committee of Inquiry on Industrial Democracy* (London: HMSO).

Bunmdesmann-Jansen, J., and Frerichs, J. (1996), *Betriebspolitik und Organisationswandel* (Cologue: Westfalisches).

Burawoy, Michael, and Krotov, Pavel (1992), 'The Soviet Transition from Socialism to Capitalism: Worker Control and Economic Bargaining in the Wood Industry', *American Sociological Review*, 57: 16–38.

Burkhardt, Marlene E., and Brass, Daniel J. (1990), 'Changing Patterns or Patterns of Change: The Effects of a Change in Technology on Social Network Structure and Power', *Administrative Science Quarterly*, 35/1 (Mar.), 104–27.

Bushe, Gervase (1988), 'Developing Cooperative Labor–Management Relations in Unionized Factories: A Multiple Case Study of Quality Circles and Parallel Organizations within Joint Quality of Work Life Projects', *Journal of Applied Behavioral Science*, 24: 129–50.

Cable, John (1985), 'Some Tests of Employee Participation Indices', in Derek Jones and Jan Svejnar (eds.), *Advances in the Economic Analysis of Participatory and Labor-Managed Firms*, ii (Greenwich, Conn.: JAI Press), 79–90.

—— and Fitzroy, Felix (1980), 'Cooperation and Productivity, Some Evidence from West German Experience', *Economic and Social Democracy*, 14: 163–80.

Callus, Ron, Morehead, Alison, Cully, Mark, and Buchanan, John (1991), *Industrial Relations at Work: The Australian Workplace Industrial Relations Survey* (Canberra: Australian Government Publishing Service).

Cammann, Courtlandt, Lawler, Edward E. III, Ledford, Gerald, and Seashore, Stanley (1984), *Management–Labor Cooperation in Quality of Worklife Experiments: Comparative Analysis of Eight Cases* (Report to the US Department of Labor, Ann Arbor: Survey Research Center, University of Michigan).

Campling, John (1995), 'From Rigid to Flexible Employment Practices in UK Commercial Television: The Case of Government Led Reform', *New Zealand Journal of Industrial Relations*, 20: 1–22.

Cappelli, Peter (1985), 'Plant-Level Concession Bargaining', *Industrial and Labor Relations Review*, 39: 90–104.

—— and Singh, Harbir (1992), 'Integrating Human Resources and Strategic Management', in David Lewin, Olivia Mitchell, and Peter Sherer (eds.), *Research Frontiers in Industrial Relations and Human Performance* (Madison: Industrial Relations Research Association), 165–92.

Carrie, L., Ahlbrandt, R., and Murrell, A. (1992), 'The Effects of Employee Involvement on Unionized Workers' Attitudes, Perceptions, and Preferences in Decision Making', *Academy of Management Journal*, 35/4: 861–73.

Carroll, Glenn R. (1990), 'On the Organizational Ecology of Chester I. Barnard', in Oliver E. Williamson (ed.), *Organization Theory: From Chester Barnard to the Present and Beyond* (New York: Oxford University Press), 56–71.

Castrogiovanni, Gary, and Macy, Barry (1990), 'Organizational Information-Processing Capabilities and Degree of Employee Participation: A Longitudinal Field Experiment', *Group and Organizational Studies*, 15: 313–36.

Chell, Elizabeth (1983), 'Political Perspectives and Worker Participation at the Board Level: The British Experience', in Crouch and Heller (1983), 487–504.

—— and Cox, Derek (1979), 'Worker Directors and Collective Bargaining', *Industrial Relations Journal*, 10/3 (Autumn 1979), 25–31.

Chevalier, Françoise (1991), *Cercles de qualité et changement organisationnel* (Paris: Éditions Economica).

—— (1995), 'Change and Managing Contradictions', Paper Presented at the European Group for Organizational Studies, Istanbul.

Child, John (1976), 'Participation, Organization and Social Cohesion', *Human Relations*, 29/5: 429–51.

Clark, A. W. (1976) (ed.), *Experimenting with Organizational Life: The Action Research Approach* (New York: Plenum).

Clarke, R. O., Fatchett, D. J., and Robert, Ben (1972), *Workers' Participation in Management in Britain* (London: Heinemann).

Clegg, H. (1979), *The Changing System of Industrial Relations in Great Britain* (Oxford: Blackwell).

Clegg, Stewart (1981), 'Organization and control', *Administrative Science Quarterly*, 26/4 (Dec.), 545–62.

—— (1990), *Modern Organizations: Organization Studies in the Postmodern World* (London: Sage Publications).

Coase, Ronald (1991), 'The Nature of the Firm: Influence', in Oliver Williamson and Sydney Winter (eds.), *The Nature of the Firm: Origins, Evolution and Development* (New York: Oxford University Press), 48–60.

Cobble, Dorothy (1994), 'Making Postindustrial Unionism Possible', in Sheldon Friedman, Richard Hurd, Rudolf Oswald, and Ronald Seeber (eds.), *Restoring the Promise of American Labor Law* (Ithaca, NY: ILR Press), 285–302.

Coch, Lester, and French, John R. P. (1948), 'Overcoming Resistance to Change', *Human Relations*, 1: 512–32.

Cohen, Michael D., March, James G., and Olsen, Johan P. (1972), 'A Garbage Can Model of Organizational Choice', *Administrative Science Quarterly*, 17/1 (Mar.), 1–25.

Cohen, Susan G., and Ledford, Gerald E. Jr. (1994), 'The Effectiveness of Self Managing Teams: A Quasi-Experiment', *Human Relations*, 47/1: 13–43.

Cohen-Rosenthal, Edward (1980), 'Should Unions Participate in Quality of Worklife Activities?', *Quality of Worklife: The Canadian Scene*, 3/4: 12–17.

Cole, Robert (1982), 'Diffusion of Participatory Work Structures in Japan, Sweden and the United States', in Paul Goodman (ed.), *Change in Organizations* (San Francisco: Jossey-Bass).

—— (1989), *Strategies for Learning. Small Group Activities: America, Japan and Sweden* (Berkeley and Los Angeles: University of California Press).

Collins, Dennis (1995), 'Self-Interest and Group Interests in Employee Involvement Programs: A Case Study', *Journal of Labor Research*, 16: 57–80.

Commission on the Future of Worker Management Relations (1995), *Final Report and Recommendations* (Washington: US Departments of Commerce and Labor).

Conte, Michael, and Svejnar, Jan (1990), 'The Performance Effects of Employee Ownership Plans', in Alan Blinder (ed.), *Paying for Productivity: A Look at the Evidence* (Washington: Brookings Institution), 144–71.

—— and Tannenbaum, Arnold (1978), 'Employee Owned Companies: Is the Difference Measurable?', *Monthly Labor Review*, 101: 22–8.

Cooke, William (1988), *Labor–Management Cooperation and Work Place Innovations* (Report to the Michigan Department of Commerce).

—— (1989), 'Improving Productivity and Quality through Collaboration', *Industrial Relations*, 28: 299–319.

—— (1994), 'Employee Participation Programs, Group-Based Incentives and Company Performance: A Union–Nonunion Comparison', *Industrial and Labor Relations Review*, 47: 594–609.

Cooper, Cary, and Smith, Mike (1992), 'Job Stressors and their Impact on Decision Making and Leadership in Organizations', in Heller (1992*b*), 156–71.

Cornell Participatory Action Research Network (1997), *The World Congresses: Background and Information*, on Internet http:www.parnet.org/calendar/5 June 1997/background.cfm.

Cornforth, Chris (1989*a*), 'Workers' Cooperatives in the UK: Temporary Phenomenon or growing trend?', in Lammers and Széll (1989*b*), 38–49.

—— (1989*b*), 'The Role of Support Organizations in Developing Worker Cooperation: A Model for Economic and Industrial Democracy', in Széll, Blyton, and Cornforth (1989), 107–24.

Cotta, Alain (1976), 'An Analysis of Power Processes in Organizations', in Hofstede and Kassem (1976), 174–92.

Cotton, J. L., Vollrath, D. A., Froggatt, K. L., Lengnick-Hall, M. L., and Jennings, K. R. (1988), 'Employee Participation: Diverse Forms and Different Outcomes', *Academy of Management Review*, 13/1: 8–22.

—— —— Lengnick-Hall, M. L., and Froggatt, K. L. (1990), 'Fact: The Form of Participation Does Matter—A Rebuttal to Leana, Locke, and Schweiger', *Academy of Management Review*, 15/1: 147–53.

Craig, Ben, and Pencavel, John (1992), 'The Behavior of Worker Cooperatives: The Plywood Companies of the Pacific Northwest', *American Economic Review*, 82: 1083–105.

Cranston, Maurice (1994), *The Romantic Movement* (Oxford: Blackwell).

Cressey, P. (1991), 'Trends in Employee Participation and New Technology', in Russell and Rus (1991), 9–27.

—— (1996), 'Direct Participation in Organizational Change: Report on the European Foundation Round Table', *The European Participation Monitor No. 12* (June).

—— Eldridge, J., and MacInnes, J. (1985), *Just Managing: Authority and Democracy in Industry* (Milton Keynes: Open University Press).

Crouch, C., and Heller, F. A. (1983) (eds.), *International Yearbook of Organizational Democracy*, i. *Organizational Democracy and Political Processes* (Chichester: John Wiley & Sons).

—— and Pizzorno, A. (1978), *The Resurgence of Class Conflict in Western Europe since 1968* (New York: Holmes & Meir).

Crozier, M. (1963), *Le Phenomène bureaucratique* (Paris: Éditions du Seuil).

Cutcher-Gershenfeld, Joel (1991), 'The Impact on Economic Performance of a Transformation in Workplace Relations', *Industrial and Labor Relations Review*, 44: 241–60.

—— and Verma, Anil (1994), 'Joint Governance in North American Workplaces: A Glimpse of the Future or the End of an Era', *International Journal of Human Resource Management*, 5: 547–80.

—— McKersie, Robert, and Wever, Kirsten (1988), 'The Changing Role of Union Leaders', *Bulletin 127* (Washington: Bureau of Labor–Management Relations and Cooperative Programs).

—— Kochan, Thomas, and Verma, Anil (1991), 'Recent Developments in US Employee Involvement Initiatives: Erosion or Transformation?', *Advances in Industrial and Labor Relations*, 5: 1–32.

Cyert, R. M., and March, J. G. (1963), *A Behavioural Theory of the Firm* (Englewood Cliffs, NJ: Prentice Hall).

Dachler, Peter H., and Wilpert, Bernhard (1978), 'Conceptual Dimensions and Boundaries of Participation in Organizations: A critical Evaluation', *Administrative Science Quarterly*, 23/1 (Mar.), 1–39.

Dahrendorf, R. (1979), *Life Chances: Approaches to Social and Political Theory* (Chicago: University of Chicago Press).

Davies, Alan, Naschold, Frieder, Pritchard, Wendy, and Reve, Torger, with the assistance of Bjørn Olsen, Thorbjørn Sørum, Ragner Saeveraas, and Bjørn Willadssen (1993), *Evaluation Report* (commissioned by the Board of the SBA Programme, June 1993; Work Research Institute, Norway (Oslo)).

Davis, Edward (1987), *Democracy in Australian Unions* (Sydney: Allen & Unwin).

—— and Lansbury, Russell, D. (1989), 'Worker Participation in Decision on Technological Change in Australia', in Greg J. Bamber and Russell D. Lansbury (eds.), *New Technology: International Perspectives on Human Resources and Industrial Relations* (London: Unwin Hyman), 100–16.

Dawson, Patrick (1994), *Organizational Change: A Processual Approach* (London: Paul Chapman).

De Charms, R. C. (1968), *Personal Causation* (New York: Academic Press).

Dean, J. (1985), 'The Decision to Participate in Quality Circles', *Journal of Applied Behavioral Sciences*, 21: 317–27.

Deci, Edward L. (1975), *Intrinsic Motivation* (New York: Lexington Books).

—— (1981), *The Psychology of Self-Determination* (New York: Lexington Books).

—— and Ryan, Richard M. (1985), *Intrinsic Motivation and Self-Determination in Human Behavior* (New York: Plenum Press).

Delbridge, Rick, Turnbull, Peter, and Wilkinson, Barry (1992), 'Pushing back the Frontiers: Management Control and Work Intensification under JIT/TQM Regimes', *New Technology, Work and Employment*, 7: 97–106.

Delery, John, and Doty, Harold (1996), 'Modes of Theorizing in Human Resources Management: Tests of Universalistic, Contingency, and Configurational Performance Predictions', *Academy of Management Journal*, 39: 802–936.

DIO (1979), Decision in Organization, 'Participative Decision Making: A Comparative Study', *Industrial Relations*, 18: 295–309.

—— (1988), *Decisions in Organizations: A Three Country Study* (London: Sage Publications).

Djilas, M. (1972), *The Unperfect Society: Beyond the New Class* (London: Unwin Books).

Dolvik, Jan, and Stokland, Dag (1992), 'Norway: The "Norwegian" Model in Transition', in Anthony Ferner and Richard Hyman (eds.), *Industrial Relations in the New Europe* (Oxford: Blackwell), 143–67.

Donaldson, Lex (1990), 'The Etherial Hand: Organizational Economics and Management Theory', *Academy of Management Review*, 15/3: 369–81.

Dore, Ronald (1973), *British Factory—Japanese Factory* (London: George Allen & Unwin).

Drago, Robert (1988), 'Quality Circle Survival: An Exploratory Analysis', *Industrial Relations*, 27: 336–51.

—— (1996), 'Workplace Transformation and the Disposable Workplace: Employee Involvement in Australia', *Industrial Relations*, 25: 526–43.

—— and Wooden, Mark (1991), 'The Determinants of Participatory Management', *British Journal of Industrial Relations*, 29/2: 177–204.

Drenth, P. J. D., and Koopman, P. (1984), 'Experience with "werkoverleg" in the Netherlands', *Journal of General Management*, 9/2: 57–73.

Duckles, Margaret, Duckles Robert, and Maccoby, Michael (1977), 'The Process of Change at Bolivar', *Journal of Applied Behavioral Science*, 13: 387–99.

Duda, Helene, and Todtling, Franz (1986), 'Austrian Trade Unions in the Economic Crisis', in Richard Edwards, Paolo Garonna, and Frank Todtling (eds.), *Unions in Crisis and Beyond* (Dover, Mass: Auburn House Publishing Co.), 227–68.

Dunlop, John T. (1958), *Industrial Relations Systems* (New York: Holt, Rinehart, and Winston).

—— (1993), The Future of Labor–Management Relations', in James Auerbach and Jerome Barrett (eds.), *The Future of Labor Management Innovation* (Washington: National Planning Association).

—— (1994), *Commission on the Future of Worker–Management Relations. Fact Finding Report* (Washington: Department of Labor and Commerce).

—— and Weil, David (1996), 'Diffusion and Performance of Modular Production in the US Apparel Industry', *Industrial Relations*, 35: 334–55.

Durkheim, Émile (1933), *On the Division of Labor in Society* (New York: Macmillan).

Eaton, Adrienne (1994), 'Factors Contributing to the Survival of Employee Participation Programs in Unionized Settings', *Industrial and Labor Relations Review*, 47: 371–89.

—— and Voos, Paula (1992), 'Unions and Contemporary Innovations in Work, Organization, Compensation, and Employee Participation', in Lawrence Mishel and Paul Voos (eds.), *Unions and Economic Competitiveness* (Armonk, NY: ME Sharp), 173–215.

—— —— (1994), 'Productivity-Enhancing Innovations in Work Organization, Compensation, and Employees' Participation in the Union versus Non-Union Sectors', in David Lewin and Donna Sockell (eds.), *Advances in Industrial and Labor Relations*, vi (Greenwich, Conn.: JAI Press), 63–110.

Edelstein, J. D., and Warner, Malcolm (1975), *Comparative Union Democracy: Organization and Opposition in British and American Unions* (London: Allen & Unwin).

Ehrenreich, Richard (1983), 'Consumer and Organizational Democracy: American New-Wave Cooperation', in Crouch and Heller (1983), 407–32.

Ehrlich, Eugen (1913), *Grundlegung der Soziologie des Rechts* (Munich: Duncker & Humbolt).

Eiger, Norman (1986), 'Education of Workplace Democracy in Sweden and West Germany', in Stern and McCarthy (1986), 105–24.

Elden, Max (1986), 'Socio-Technical Systems ideas as public policy in Norway: Evolving Participation through Worker-Managed Change', *Journal of Applied Behavioral Science*, 22/3: 239–55.

Emery, F. E. (1959), *Characteristics of Socio-Technical Systems* (Document No. 357; London: Tavistock Institute).

—— (1976), 'Adaptive Systems for our Future Governance', *National Labour Institute Bulletin* (New Delhi), ii. 121–9; repr. in Emery (1981), ii.

—— (1981) (ed.), *Systems Thinking*, ii (Harmondsworth: Penguin).

—— (1993), 'Characteristics of Socio-Technical Systems', in Eric Trist and Hugh Murray (eds.), *The Social Engagement of Social Science*, ii (Philadelphia: Philadelphia Press), 157–86.

—— and Thorsrud, E. (1969), *Form and Content in Industrial Democracy* (London: Tavistock Publications).

—— —— (1976), 'Democracy at Work', *A Report of the Norwegian Industrial Democracy Program* (Leiden: Martinus Nijhoff).

—— and Trist, Eric L. (1965), 'The Causal Texture of Organizational Environments', *Human Relations*, 18/1 (Feb.), 21–32.

Erez, M. (1993), 'Participation in Goal Setting: A Motivational Approach', in Lafferty and Rosenstein (1993), 73–91.

Escobar, Modesto (1995), 'Works Councils or Unions?', in Rogers and Streeck (1995), 153–88.

Estrin, Saul, and Jones, Derek (1992), 'The Viability of Employee-Owner Firms: The Evidence from France', *Industrial and Labor Relations Review*, 45: 332–8.

—— Jones, Derek, and Svenjnar, Jan (1987), 'The Productivity Effects of Worker Participation: Producer Cooperatives in Western Economies', *Journal of Comparative Economics*, 11: 40–61.

Etzioni, Amitai (1969), 'Man and Society: The inauthentic condition', *Human Relations*, 22: 325–32.

European Participation Monitor (1996), 12 (June).

Fayol, Henri (1949), *General and Industrial Administration* (London: Pitman & Sons) (first published 1916).

Fenwick, Rudy, and Olson, Jon (1986), 'Support for Worker Participation: Attitudes among Union and Non-Union Workers', *American Sociological Review*, 51/4 (Aug.), 505–22.

Ferner, Anthony, and Hyman, Richard (1992), 'Italy: Between Political Exchange and Micro-Corporatism', in Anthony Ferner and Richard Hyman (eds.), *Industrial Relations in the New Europe* (Oxford: Blackwell), 524–600.

Fernie, Sue, and Metcalf, David (1995), 'Participation, Contingency Pay, Representation, and Workplace Performance Evidence from Great Britain', *British Journal of Industrial Relations*, 33/3: 379–415.

Finlay, William (1987), 'Industrial Relations and Firm Behavior: Informal Labor Practices in the West Coast Longshore Industry', *Administrative Science Quarterly*, 32/1: 49–67.

Finseth, Eric (1988), 'The Employment Behavior of Profit-Sharing Firms: An Empirical Test of the Weitzman Theory', unpublished senior thesis (Harvard).

Fisher, Roger, and Ury, William (1981), *Getting to Yes: Negotiating Agreements Without Giving In* (Boston: Houghton Mifflin).

FitzRoy, F. R., and Kraft, K. (1987), 'Efficiency and Internal Organization: Works Councils in West Germany', *Economica*, 54: 493–504.

Flanders, Allan, Pomeranz, Ruth, and Woodward, Joan (1968), *Experiments in Industrial Democracy* (London: Faber).

Fogerty, Michael P. (1976), 'The Place of Managers in Industrial Democracy', *British Journal of Industrial Relations*, 14/2: 119–27.

Fombrun, Charles J. (1986), 'Structural Dynamics within and between Organizations', *Administrative Science Quarterly*, 31/3 (Sept.), 403–21.

Freeman, Richard, and Lazear, Edward (1995), 'An Economic Analysis of Works Councils', in Rogers and Streeck (1995), 27–50.

—— and Medoff, James (1984), *What Do Unions Do?* (New York: Basic Books).

—— and Rogers, Joel (1994), *Worker Representation and Participation Survey* (Princeton: Princeton Survey Research Associates).

French, J. R. P. Jr., Israel, J., and Ås, D. (1960), 'An Experiment on Participation in a Norwegian Factory: Interpersonal Dimensions of Decision-Making', *Human Relations*, 13/1: 3–19.

Frese, Michael, Erbe-Heinbokel, Marion, Grefe, Judith, Rybowiak, Volker, and Weike, Almut (1994), 'Mir ist est lieber, wenn ich genau gesagt bekomme, was ich tun muß: Probleme der Akzeptanz von Verantwortung und Handlungsspielraum in Ost und West', *Zeitschrift für Arbeits-u. Organisationspsychologie*, 38 (NE12) I.

—— Kring, Wolfgang, Soose, Andrea, and Zempel, Jeannette (1996), 'Personal Initiative at Work: Differences between East and West Germany', *Academy of Management Journal*, 39/1: 37–63.

Fricke, W. (1975), *Arbeitsorganisation und Qualifikation* (Bonn: Verlag Neue Gesellschaft).

Friedkin, Noah E., and Simpson, Michael J. (1985), 'Effects of Competition upon Members' Identification with their Subunits', *Administrative Science Quarterly*, 30/3: 377–94.

Friedmann, Georges (1956), *Le Travail en miettes* (Paris: Gallimard).

—— (1961), *The Anatomy of Work, Labor, Leisure, and the Implications of Automation* (New York: Free Press).

Fröhlich, D., and Krieger, H. (1990), 'Technological Change and Worker Participation in Europe', *New Technology, Work and Employment*, 5/2: 94–106.

Fucini, Joseph, and Fucini, Suzy (1990), *Working for the Japanese: Inside Mazda's American Auto Plant* (New York: Free Press).

Furby, L. (1978), 'Possessions: Toward a Theory of their Meaning and Function throughout the Life Cycle', in P. B. Baltes (ed.), *Life Span Development and Behavior* (New York: Academic Press), 293–336.

Fürstenberg, Friedrich (1958), 'Der Betriebsrat—Strukturanalys einer Grenzsituation', *Kölner Zeitschrift für Soziologie und Sozialpsychologie*, 14: 418–29.

—— (1978), *Workers' Participation in Management in the Federal Republic of Germany* (Research Series No. 32; Geneva: International Institute of Labour Studies).

—— (1984), 'Personale Selbstgestaltung in sozialen Systemen', in F. Fürstenberg, Ph. Herder-Dorneich, and H. Klages (eds.), *Selbsthilfe als ordnungspolitische Aufgabe* (Baden-Baden), 200–18.

Galin, Amira (1980), 'An Evaluation of Industrial Democracy Schemes in Israel', in Russell Lansbury (ed.), *Democracy in the Workplace* (Melbourne: Longmans Cheshire), 183–94.

Gallagher, Daniel, and Strauss, George (1991), 'Union Membership Attitudes and Participation', in George Strauss, Daniel Gallagher, and Jack Fiorito (eds.), *The State of the Unions* (Madison: Industrial Relations Research Association), 139–74.

Gallie, Duncan, and White, Michael (1993), *Employee Commitment and the Skills Revolution* (London: Policy Studies Institute).

Ganguli, H. (1964), *Structure and Process of Organization* (New York: Asia Publishing).

Gardell, Bertil (1977), 'Autonomy and Participation at Work', *Human Relations*, 30/6: 515–33.

—— (1983), 'Worker Participation and Autonomy: A Multi-Level Approach to Democracy at the Work Place', in Crouch and Heller (1983), 353–87.

Gaus, John M., White, Leonard D., and Dimock, Marshall E. (1947), 'The Frontiers of Public Administration', in Leonard D. White (ed.), *Introduction to the Study of Public Administration* (New York: Macmillan).

Geary, John (1994), 'Task Participation: Employee Participation Enabled or Constrained?', in Keith Sisson (ed.), *Personnel Management* (Oxford: Blackwell).

George, Donald A. R. (1993), *Economic Democracy: The Political Economy of Self Management and Participation* (Basingstoke: Macmillan).

Georgiou, Petro (1973), 'The Goal Paradigm and Notes toward a Counter Paradigm', *Administrative Science Quarterly*, 18/3 (Sept.), 291–310.

Gershenfeld, Walter (1987), 'Employee Participation in Firm Decisions', in Morris Kleiner, Richard Block, Myron Roomkin, and Sydney Salsburg (eds.), *Human Resources and the Performance of the Firm* (Madison: Industrial Relations Research Association), 123–58.

Gilding, Jack (1995), 'Developing Applications in Context', *CIRCIT (Centre for International Research on Communication and Information Technologies) Newsletter*, 7/1.

Gill, Colin, and Krieger, Hubert (1992), 'The Diffusion of Participation in New Information Technology in Europe: Survey Results', *Economic and Industrial Democracy*, 13: 331–58.

—— Beaupin, Thérèse, Fröhlich, Dieter, and Krieger, Hubert (1993), *Workplace Involvement in Technological Innovation in the European Community*, ii. *Issues of Participation* (Dublin, Ireland: The European Foundation for the Improvement of Living and Working Conditions).

Gladstein, Deborah L. (1984), 'Groups in Context: A Model of Task Group Effectiveness', *Administrative Science Quarterly*, 29/4: 499–517.

Glaser, Hermann (1988), *Das Verschwinden der Arbeit—Die Chancen der neuen Taetigkeitsgesellschaft* (Dusseldorf: ECON Verlag).

Goetschy, Janine (1991), An Appraisal of French Research on Direct Worker Participation', in Russell and Rus (1991), 232–47.

—— and Rozenblatt, Patrick (1992), 'France: The Industrial Relations System at a Turning Point', in Anthony Ferner and Richard Hyman (eds.), *Industrial Relations in the New Europe* (Oxford: Blackwell), 404–44.

Goodman, Paul (1979), *Assessing Organizational Change: The Rushton Quality of Worklife Experiment* (New York: Wiley).

Goodrick-Clarke, Nicholas (1994), 'The Scientific Measure of Man', *The Times* (24 Sept.).

Gorz, Andre (1986), *Wege ins Paradies, Thesen zur Krise: Automation and Zukunft der Arbeit* (Berlin: Rotbuch Verlag).

Gould, William B. IV (1993), *Agenda for Reform: The Future of Employment Relationships and the Law* (Cambridge, Mass.: MIT Press).

Goyder, George (1987), *The Just Enterprise* (London: Andre Deutsch Ltd.).

Graham, Laurie (1995), *On the Line at Subaru-Isuzu: The Japanese Model and the American Worker* (Ithaca, NY: ILR Press).

Griffin, Ricky (1988), 'Consequences of Quality Circles in an Industrial Setting: A Longitudinal Assessment', *Academy of Management Journal*, 31: 338–58.

Grunberg, Leon (1991), 'The Plywood Cooperatives: Some Disturbing Findings', in Russell and Rus (1991), 103–22.

Guest, David E. (1990), 'Human Resource Management and the American Dream', *Journal of Management Studies*, 27: 377–97.

Guest, Robert (1983), 'Organizational Democracy and the Quality of Worklife: The Man on the Assembly Line', in Crouch and Heller (1983), 139–53.

Gulick, Luther, and Urwick, Lyndal (1937) (eds.), *Papers on the Science of Administration* (New York: Institute of Public Administration).

Gunderson, Morley, Sack, Jeffrey, McCartney, James, Wakely, David, and Eaton, Jonathon (1995), 'Employee Buyouts in Canada', *British Journal of Industrial Relations*, 33: 417–42.

Gurdon, Michael (1985), 'Equity Participation by Employees: The Growing Debate in West Germany', *Industrial Relations*, 24: 113–29.

Gustavsen, Björn (1973), 'Environmental Requirements and the Democratization of Industrial Relations', in E. Pusić (ed.), *Participation and Selfmanagement* (Zagreb: Institute of Social Research), iv.

—— (1983), 'The Norwegian Work Environment Reform: The Transition from General Principles to Workplace Action', in Crouch and Heller (1983), 545–64.

—— (1986), 'Training for Work Environment Reform in Norway', in Stern and McCarthy (1986), 125–40.

—— (1992), *Dialogue and Development: Theory of Communication, Action Research and the Restructuring of Working Life* (Assen: van Gorcum).

Guzzo, R. A., Jette, R. D., and Katzell, R. A. (1985), 'The Effects of Psychologically Based Intervention Programs on Worker Productivity: A Meta-Analysis', *Personnel Psychology*, 38: 275–91.

Habermas, Jurgen (1971), *Towards A Rational Society* (London: Heinemann).

—— (1976), *Legitimation Crisis* (London: Heinemann).

—— (1990) *Moral Consciousness and Communicative Action*, trans. C. Lenhardt and S. W. Nicolson (Cambridge: Polity).

Hackman, J. R., and Oldman, G. R. (1976), 'Motivation through the Design of Work: Test of a Theory', *Organizational Behavior and Human Performance*, 15: 250–79.

—— —— (1980), *Work Redesign* (Reading, Mass.: Wadsworth).

Haddock, Cynthia Carter, and Guy, Mary A. (1987), 'Professionals in Organizations: Debunking a Myth', *Administrative Science Quarterly*, 32/2: 297–9.

Haddon, Leslie, and Lewis, Alan (1994), 'The Experience of Teleworking: An Annotated Review', *International Journal of Human Resource Management*, 5/1: 193–223.

Haire, M., Ghiselli, E. E., and Porter, L. E. (1966), *Managerial Thinking* (New York: John Wiley & Sons).

Hammer, Tove, and Stern, Robert (1986), 'A Yo-Yo Model of Cooperation: Union Participation in Management at the Rath Packing Company', *Industrial and Labor Relations Review*, 39: 337–49.

—— Currall, Steven, and Stern, Robert (1991), 'Worker Representation on Boards of Directors: A Study of Competing Roles', *Industrial and Labor Relations Review*, 44: 661–80.

—— Ingebrigtsen, B., Karlsen, J. I., and Svarva, A. (1994), 'Organizational Renewal: The Management of Large Scale Organizational Change in Norwegian Firms', Paper Presented at the Conference on Transformation and European Industrial Relations, Helsinki, Finland, August 1994.

Hancke, Bob (1993), 'Trade Union Membership in Europe 1960–90: Rediscovering Local Unions', *British Journal of Industrial Relations*, 31: 593–614.

Hanford, Terry, and Grasso, Patrick (1991), 'Participation in corporate performance in ESOP firms', in Russell and Rus (1991), 221–31.

Hannan, Michael, and Freeman, John (1977), 'The Population Ecology of Organizations', *American Journal of Sociology*, 82: 929–64.

Hartmann, Heinz (1970), 'Codetermination in West Germany', *Industrial Relations*, 9: 137–47.

—— (1979), 'Work Councils and the Iron Law of Oligarchy', *British Journal of Industrial Relations*, 17/1 (Mar.), 70–82.

Hayek, F. v. A. (1952), *The Counter Revolution of Science* (Indianapolis: Liberty Press).

Heider, F. A. (1958), *The Psychology of Interpersonal Relations* (New York: Wiley).

Heller, F. A. (1971), *Managerial Decision-Making: A Study of Leadership and Power Sharing among Senior Managers* (London: Tavistock Publications).

—— (1977), 'Comparing American and British Managerial Attitudes to Skill and Leadership', in T. D. Weinshall (ed.), *Culture and Management* (Harmondsworth: Penguin Books), 341–53.

—— (1986), *The Use and Abuse of Social Science* (London: Sage Publications).

—— (1991), 'Participation and Competence: A Necessary Relationship', in Russell and Rus (1991), 265–81.

—— (1992*a*), 'Decision Making and the Under-Utilization of Competence', in Heller (1992*b*), 71–89.

—— (1992*b*) (ed.), *Decision Making and Leadership* (Cambridge: Cambridge University Press).

—— (1997), 'Leadership and Power in a Stakeholder Setting', *European Work and Organizational Psychologist*, 6/4.

—— and Misumi, J. (1987), 'Decision Making', in B. Bass, P. Drenth, and P. Weissenberg (eds.), *Organizational Psychology: An International Review* (Beverly Hills: Sage Publications).

—— and Wilpert, Bernhard (1981), *Competence and Power in Managerial Decision Making: A Study of Senior Levels of Organization in Eight Countries* (Chichester: John Wiley & Sons).

—— and Yukl, G. (1969), 'Participation and Managerial Decision-Making as a Function of Situational Variables', *Organizational Behavior and Human Performance*, 4: 227–41. Also in Ervin Williams (ed.), *Participative Management: Concepts, Theory and Implementation* (Atlanta, Ga.: Georgia State University, 1976).

—— Wilders, M., Abell, P., and Warner, M. (1979), *What do the British Want from Participation and Industrial Democracy?* (London: Anglo-German Foundation).

—— Drenth, P. J. D., Koopman, P., and Rus, V. (1988), *Decisions in Organizations: A Three Country Comparative Study* (London: Sage Publications).

Helman, Amir (1992), 'The Israeli Kibbutz as a Socialist Model', *Journal of Institutional and Theoretical Economics*, 148/1: 168–83.

Hickson, David, Butler, Richard, Gray, David, Mallory, Geoffrey, and Wilson, David (1986), *Top Decisions: Strategic Decision Making in Organizations* (Oxford: Basil Blackwell).

Hildebrandt, Eckart (1989), 'From Codetermination to Comanagement: The Dilemma Confronting Works Councils in the Introduction of New Technologies in the Machine Building Industry', in Lammers and Széll (1989*b*), 185–96.

Hill, Paul (1972), *Towards a New Philosophy of Management* (London: Gower Press).

Hill, Stephen (1991), 'Why Quality Circles Failed, but Total Quality Management might Succeed', *British Journal of Industrial Relations*, 29: 541–68.

Hilmer, Frederick, and Donaldson, Lex (1996), *Management Redeemed: Debunking the Fads that Undermine our Corporations* (New York: Free Press).

Hobson, John (1894), *The Evolution of Modern Capitalism* (London: Allen & Unwin).

Hoe, Susanna (1978), *The Man who Gave his Company Away: A Biography of Ernest Bader, Founder of the Scott Bader Commonwealth* (London: Heinemann).

Hoerr, Joseph (1988), *And the Wolf Finally Came: The Decline of the American Steel Industry* (Pittsburgh: University of Pittsburgh Press).

Hoffman, L. R., Harburg, E., and Maier, N. R. F. (1962), 'Differences and Disagreement as Factors in Creative Group Problem Solving', *Journal of Abnormal and Social Psychology*, 64: 206–14.

Hofstede, Geert, and Kassem, M. Sami (1976) (eds.), *European Contributions to Organization Theory* (Assen: van Gorcum).

Holden, Constance (1987), 'The Genetics of Personality', *Science*, 237: 598–601.

Holter, Harriet (1965), 'Attitudes toward Employee Participation in Company Decision-Making Processes', *Human Relations*, 18: 297–321.

Holti, Richard, and Stern, Elliot (1986), *Distance Working: Origins—Diffusion—Prospects* (Luxembourg: Commission of the European Communities FAST Programme).

Hopwood, Anthony (1976), *Accounting and Human Behavior* (Englewood Cliffs, NJ: Prentice Hall).

Horvat, Branko (1983), 'The Organization Theory of Workers' Management', in Crouch and Heller (1983), 279–300.

Huczynski, Andrzej (1993), 'Explaining the Succession of Management Fads', *International Journal of Human Resource Management*, 4: 443–63.

Huselid, Mark A. (1995), 'The Impact of Human Resources Management Practices on Turnover, Production, and Corporate Financial Performance', *Academy of Management Journal*, 38: 635–72.

—— and Becker, Boris (1995), 'High Performance Work Systems and Organizational Performance', Paper Presented at the annual meeting of the Academy of Management, Vancouver.

Hutton, Will (1995), *The State We're In* (London: Jonathan Cape).

Ichniowski, Casey (1992), 'Human Resources Practices and Productive Labor–Management Relations', in David Lewin, Olivia Mitchell, and Peter Sherer (eds.), *Research Frontiers in Industrial Relations and Human Resources* (Madison, Wis.: Industrial Relations Research Association), 239–71.

—— Shaw, Katherine, and Prennushi, Giovanna (1995), 'The Impact of Human Resources Management on Productivity' (Working Paper No. 5333; Cambridge, Mass.: National Bureau of Economic Research).

—— Kochan, Thomas, Levine, David, Olson, Craig, and Strauss, George (1996), 'What Works at Work: Overview and Assessment', *Industrial Relations*, 55: 299–333.

IDE (1976), Industrial Democracy in Europe research group, 'Industrial Democracy in Europe: An International Comparative Study', *Social Science Information*, 15/1: 177–203.

—— (1981*a*), *Industrial Democracy in Europe* (Oxford: Oxford University Press).

—— (1981*b*), *European Industrial Relations* (Oxford: Oxford University Press).

—— (1993), *Industrial Democracy in Europe Revisited* (Oxford: Oxford University Press).

Jackall, Robert (1984), 'Paradoxes of Collective Work: A Study of the Cheeseboard, Berkeley, California', in Robert Jackall and Henry M. Levin (eds.), *Worker Cooperatives in America* (Berkeley and Los Angeles: University of California Press), 109–36.

Jackson, Paul, and van der Wielden, Jos (Organizers) (1996), *Report: Workshop: New International Perspectives on Telework* (Brunel University, July 31–August 2; 2 vols.; Netherlands: WORC Tilburg University).

Jacobi, Otto, Keller, Berndt, and Muller-Jentsch, Walther (1992), 'Germany: Codetermining the Future', in Anthony Ferner and Richard Hyman (eds.), *Industrial Relations in the New Europe* (Oxford: Blackwell), 218–69.

Jacoby, Sanford (1983), 'Union–Management cooperation in the United States: Lessons from the 1920s', *Industrial and Labor Relations Review*, 37/1: 18–33.

James, W. (1950), *Principles of Psychology* (New York: Dover; first published 1890).

Jamieson, Suzanne (1992), 'Trade Unions in 1991', *Journal of Industrial Relations*, 34: 162–9.

Janis, Irving (1982), *Groupthink* (Boston: Harcourt-Brace).

Jansen, K. D., Schwitalla, U., and Wicke, A. (1989) (eds.), *Beteiligungsorientierte Systement-wicklung Computer-gesetzter Arbeitssysteme* (Opladen: Westdeutscher Verlag).

Jaques, Elliott (1951), *The Changing Culture of a Factory* (London: Tavistock Publications).

Jelinek, Mariann, Smirchich, Linda, and Hirsch, Paul (1983), 'Introduction: A Code of Many Colors', *Administrative Science Quarterly*, 28/3: 331–8.

Johannesen, Janette (1979), 'VAG: A Need for Education', *Industrial Relations*, 18: 364–9.

Jones, Derek (1980), 'Producers' Cooperatives in Industrialised Western Economies', *British Journal of Industrial Relations*, 18: 141–54.

—— (1984), 'American Producer Cooperatives and Employee Owned Firms: A Historical Perspective', in R. Jackall and H. Levin (eds.), *Worker Cooperatives in America* (Berkeley and Los Angeles: University of California Press), 37–56.

—— and Kato, Takao (1993), 'Employee Stock Ownership Plans and Productivity in Japanese Manufacturing Firms', *British Journal of Industrial Relations*, 31: 331–64.

—— and Pliskin, Jeffrey (1991), 'The Effects of Worker Participation, Employee Ownership, and Profit Sharing on Economic Performance: A Partial Review', in Russell and Rus (1991), 43–63.

Jovanov, Neca (1978), 'Strikes and Self-Management', in Josip Obradović and William Dunn (eds.), *Workers' Self-Management and Organizational Power in Yugoslavia* (Pittsburgh, Pa.: University of Pittsburgh Press), 339–73.

Judkins, Phillip, West, David, and Drew, John (1987), *Networking in Organisations: The Rank Xerox Experiment* (Aldershot: Gower Press).

Kalleberg, Ragnvald (1993), 'Implementing Work-Environment Reforms in Norway: The Interplay between Leadership, Labour and the Law', in Lafferty and Rosenstein (1993), 404–31.

Kamoche, Ken (1995), 'Rhetoric, Ritualism, and Totemism in Human Resources Management', *Human Relations*, 48 (4 Apr.), 367–86.

Kaplan, N. (1960), 'Theoretical Analysis of Balance of Power', *Behavioral Science*, 5/3: 240–52.

Karasek, Robert (1979), 'Job Demands, Job Decision Latitude and Mental Strain: Implications for Job Design', *Administrative Science Quarterly*, 24: 285–308.

—— and Theorell, Töres (1990), *Health Work: Stress, Productivity and the Reconstruction of Working Life* (New York: Basic Books).

Kassem, M. Sami (1976), 'Introduction: European versus American Organization Theories', in Hofstede amd Kassem (1976), 1–17.

Katz, Harry (1986), 'The Debate over the Reorganization of Work and Industrial Relations within the North American Labor Movement', Paper Presented at the Conference on Trade Unions, New Technology, and Industrial Democracy, University of Warwick, 6–8 June.

—— (1993), 'The Decentralization of Collective Bargaining: A Literature Review and Comparative Analysis', *Industrial and Labor Relations Review*, 47: 3–22.

—— Kochan, Thomas, and Weber, Mark (1985), 'Assessing the Effects of Industrial Relations and Quality of Worklife Efforts on Organizational Effectiveness', *Academy of Management Journal*, 28: 509–27.

—— Kochan, Thomas, and Keefe, Jeffrey H. (1987), 'Industrial Relations and Productivity in the US Automobile Industry', *Brookings Papers on Economic Activity*, 3: 685–715.

Keeley, Michael (1980), 'Organizational Analogy: A Comparison of Organismic and Social Contract Models', *Administrative Science Quarterly*, 25/2: 337–62.

—— (1984), 'Impartiality and Participant-Interest Theories of Organizational Effectiveness', *Administrative Science Quarterly*, 29/1 (Mar.), 1–25.

Kelley, John, and Heery, Edmund (1994), *Working for the Union* (Cambridge: Cambridge University Press).

Kelley, Mary Ellen, and Harrison, Bennett (1992), 'Unions, Technology, and Labor–Management Cooperation', in Lawrence Mishel and Paula Voos (eds.), *Unions and Economic Competitiveness* (Armonk, NY: Sharp), 247–84.

Kern, H., and Schumann, M. (1984), *Das Ende der Arbeitsteilung? Rationalisierung in der industriellen Produktion: Bestandsaufnahme, Trendbestimmung* (Munich: Beck).

Kieser, Alfred (1997), 'Rhetoric and Myth in Management Fashion', *Organization*, 4/1: 49–74.

King, Albert (1974), 'Expectation Effects in Organizational Change', *Administrative Science Quarterly*, 19: 221–30.

King, Charles, and van de Vall, Mark (1978), *Models of Industrial Democracy, Codetermination, and Workers' Management* (The Hague: Mouton Publishers).

Kirsch, W., Scholl, W., and Paul, G. (1984), *Mitbestimmung in der Unternehmenspraxis* (Munich: Planungs- und Organisationswissenschaftliche Schriften).

Kißler, Leo (1980), *Partizipation als Lernprozes* (Frankfurt: Campus).

Kjellberg, Anders (1992), 'Sweden: Can the Model Survive', in Anthony Ferner and Richard Hyman (eds.), *Industrial Relations in the New Europe* (Oxford: Blackwell), 88–142.

Klandermans, Bert (1986), 'Psychology and Trade Union Participation: Joining, Acting, Quitting', *Journal of Occupational Psychology*, 59: 189–204.

Klein, Janice (1984), 'Why Supervisors Resist Employee Involvement', *Harvard Business Review*, 62: 87–95.

Kleiner, Morris, and Ay, Change-Ruey (1996), 'Unionization, Employee Representation, and Economic Performance: Comparisons among OECD Nations', *Advances in Industrial and Labor Relations*, 7: 97–121.

Kochan, Thomas (1994), 'Principles for a Post-New Deal Employment Policy', in Clark Kerr and Paul Staudohar (eds.), *Labor Economics and Industrial Relations* (Cambridge, Mass.: Harvard University Press), 646–72.

—— and Osterman, Paul (1994), *The Mutual Gains Enterprise* (Cambridge, Mass.: Harvard Business School Press).

—— Dyer, Lee, and Lipsky, David (1977), *The Effectiveness of Union–Management Safety and Health Committees* (Kalamazoo, Mich.: Upjohn).

—— Katz, H. C., and Mower, N. R. (1984), *Worker Participation and American Unions: Threat or Opportunity?* (Kalamazoo, Mich.: Upjohn).

—— —— and McKersie, Robert (1986), *The Transformation of American Industrial Relations* (New York: Basic Books).

Koenig, Richard (1984), 'Conrail', *Wall Street Journal*, 14 Feb., as cited in Jack Barbash, 'Do We Really Want Labor on the Ropes?', *Harvard Business Review*, 63 (July 1985), 5.

Kohn, M. L., and Schooler, C. (1983), *Work and Personality* (Norwood, NJ: Ablex).

Kolaja, Jiri (1966), *Workers' Councils: The Yugoslav Experience* (New York: Praeger).

Kolarska, Lena (1984), 'The Struggle for Workers' Control: Poland, 1981', in Wilpert and Sorge (1984), 425–42.

Koopman, Paul, Drenth, Pieter, Bus, Frans, Kruyswijk, Agaath, and Wierdsma, Andre (1981), 'Content, Process and Effect of Participative Decision Making on the Shop Floor: Three Cases in the Netherlands', *Human Relations*, 34: 657–76.

—— —— Heller, Frank, and Rus, Veljko (1993), 'Participation in Complex Organizational Decisions: A Comparative Study of the United Kingdom, the Netherlands and Yugoslavia', in Lafferty and Rosenstein (1993), 113–33.

Koopman-Iwema, A. M. (1977), 'Participation and Power Distance Reduction', Paper Presented at the Second International Conference on Participation, Workers' Control, and Self-Management, Paris.

Kornhauser, Arthur (1965), *Mental Health of the Industrial Worker* (New York: John Wiley & Sons).

Kostova, Dobrinka (1993), 'Workers' Participation in Bulgaria: Past and Present Developments', in Lafferty and Rosenstein (1993), 205–13.

Koubek, N. (1985), 'Technischer Wandel, Unternehmensplanung und Mitbestimmung', in P. Warneke (ed.), *Technischer Wandel und Einflussmöglichkeiten der Arbeitnehmer in Europa* (Berlin: Duncker & Humbolt), 75–87.

Krafcik, K. (1989), 'A Comparative Analysis of Assembly Plant Automation', Paper Presented to the International Motor Vehicle Program Policy Forum, Acapulco, Mexico, May.

Kruse, Douglas (1984), *Employee Ownership and Employee Attitudes* (Norwood, Pa.: Norwood Press).

—— and Blasi, Joseph (1995), 'Employee Ownership, Employee Attitudes, and Firm Performance' (Working Paper 5227; Washington: National Bureau of Economic Research).

Lafferty, W. M. (1975), 'Participation and Democratic Theory: Reworking the Premises for a Participatory Society', *Scandinavian Political Studies*, 10: 52–70.

—— (1979), 'Participation, Personal Choice, and Responsibility', Paper Presented at the Conference on Hierarchical/Nonhierarchical Systems and Conditions for Democracy, Dubrovnik, 16–18 Jan.

—— and Rosenstein, E. (1993) (eds.), *International Handbook of Participation in Organisations*, iii. *The Challenge of New Technology and Macro-Political Change* (Oxford: Oxford University Press).

Lammers, C. J. (1967), 'Power and Participation in Decision Making in Formal Organizations', *American Journal of Sociology*, 73/2: 201–17.

—— (1989), Competence and Organizational Democracy: Concluding Reflections', in Széll, Blyton, and Cornforth (1989), 339–57.

—— (1992), 'Organizational and Interorganizational Democracy', in Széll (1992), 585–97.

—— (1993), 'Interorganizational Democracy', in S. Lindenberg and H. Schreuder (eds.), *Interdisciplinary Perspectives on Organization Studies* (New York: Pergamon), 323–37.

—— (1993), 'The Intermediary Organization and the Problem of Interorganizational Democracy', in S. Lindenberg and H. Schreuder (eds.), *Interdisciplinary Perspectives on Organization Studies* (New York: Pergamon).

—— and Széll, Gyorgy (1989*a*), 'Concluding Reflections', in Lammers and Széll (1989*b*), 315–30.

—— —— (1989*b*) (eds.), *International Handbook of Participation in Organizations*, i. *Organizational Democracy: Taking Stock* (Oxford: Oxford University Press).

Lang, R., and Hellpach, W. (1922), *Gruppenfabrikation* (Berlin: Springer).

Lawler, Edward E. III (1986), *High-Involvement Management: Participative Strategies for Improving Organizational Performance* (San Francisco: Jossey-Bass).

—— Mohrman, Susan, and Ledford, Gerald (1992), *Employee Involvement and Total Quality Management* (San Francisco: Jossey-Bass).

Lawrence, P. R., and Lorsch, J. W. (1967), *Organization and Environment: Managing Differentiation and Integration* (Cambridge, Mass.: Harvard University Press).

Leana, C. R., Locke, E. A., and Schweiger, D. M. (1990), 'Fact and Fiction in Analyzing Research on Participative Decision Making: A Critique of Cotton, Vollrath, Froggatt, Lengnick-Hall, and Jennings', *Academy of Management Review*, 15: 137–46.

Leavitt, Harold, and Mueller, Ronald (1951), 'Some Effects of Feedback on Communications', *Human Relations*, 4: 401–10.

—— Pinfield, L., and Webb, E. (1974) (eds.), *Organizations of the Future: Interactions with the External Environment* (New York: Praeger Publications).

Leisink, Peter (1996), 'Dutch and Flemish Industrial Relations: Theory and Practice', *European Journal of Industrial Relations*, 2: 69–92.

Leitko, T. A., Greil, A. L., and Peterson, S. A. (1985), 'Lessons at the Bottom: Worker Nonparticipation in Labor Management Committees as Situational Adjustments', *Work and Occupations*, 12: 285–306.

Leontiev, A. N. (1977), *Probleme der Entwicklung des Psychischen* (2nd edn., Frankfurt: Fischer-Atheneum).

Levine, David (1995), *Reinventing the Workplace* (Washington: Brookings Institution).

—— and Kruse, D. (1992), *Employee Involvement Efforts: Incidence, Correlates, and Effects* (Berkeley, Calif.: Center for Research on Management).

—— and Tyson, Laura (1990), 'Participation, Productivity, and the Firm's Environment', in Alan Blinder (ed.), *Paying for Productivity* (Washington: Brookings Institution), 183–243.

Levinson, Klas (1996), 'Codetermination in Sweden: From Separation to Integration', *Economic and Social Democracy*, 17: 131–42.

—— (1997), 'Swedish Codetermination in Transition—20 Years with the Act of Codetermination', *Paper of the National Institute for Working Life* (Apr. 1997).

Lewin, Kurt (1950), *Field Theory in Social Science* (New York: Harper Brothers).

Likert, Rensis (1961), *New Patterns of Management* (New York: McGraw-Hill).

—— (1967), *The Human Organization: Its Management and Value* (New York: McGraw-Hill).

Lillrank, Paul (1995), 'The Transfer of Management Innovation from Japan', *Organization Studies*, 16/6: 971–89.

Lincoln, James (1989), 'Employee Work Attitudes and Management Practices in the US and Japan', *California Management Review*, 32: 89–106.

—— Kerbo, H. D., and Wittenhagen, E. (1995), 'Japanese Companies in Germany', *Industrial Relations*, 34/3: 417–40.

Locke, Edwin (1968), 'Toward a Theory of Task Motivation and Incentives', *Organizational Behavior and Human Performance*, 3: 157–89.

—— and Schweiger, David M. (1979), 'Participation in Decision-Making: One More Look', in Barry Staw (ed.), *Research in Organizational Behavior* (Greenwich, Conn.: JAI Press), i. 265–340.

—— Feren, D. B., McCaleb, V. M., Shaw, K. N., and Denny, A. T. (1980), 'The Relative Effectiveness of our Methods of Motivating Employee Performance', in K. D. Duncan, M. M. Gruneberg, and D. Wallis (eds.), *Changes in Working Life* (New York: Wiley).

Locke, Richard, Kochan, Thomas, and Piore, Michael (1995), 'Reconceptualizing Comparative Industrial Relations: Lessons from International Research', *International Labour Review*, 134: 139–61.

Long, Richard (1989), 'Patterns of Workplace Innovation in Canada', *Relations Industrielles*, 44: 805–25.

—— (1990), 'The Effects of Various Workplace Innovations on Productivity: A Quasi-Experimental Approach', Paper Given to the 1990 Administrative Sciences Association of Canada Conference, Whistler, British Columbia.

Looise, Jan (1989), 'The Recent Growth of Employees' Representation in the Netherlands: Defying the Times?', in Lammers and Széll (1989*b*), 268–84.

Lowin, Aaron (1968), 'Participative Decision-Making: A Model, Literature Critique, and Prescriptions for Research', *Organizational Behavior and Human Performance*, 3: 68–106.

Lucio, Miguel (1992), 'Spain: Constructing Institutions and Actors in a Context of Change', in Anthony Ferner and Richard Hyman (eds.), *Industrial Relations in the New Europe* (Oxford: Blackwell), 482–523.

Luhmann, Niklas (1964), *Funktionen und Folgen formaler Organisation* (Berlin: Duncker & Humbolt).

—— (1976), 'A General Theory of Organized Social Systems', in Hofstede and Kassem (1976), 96–113.

—— (1984), *Soziale Systeme, Grundriss einer allgemeinen Theorie* (Frankfurt am Main: Suhrkamp).

Lydall, H. (1989), *Yugoslavia in Crisis* (Oxford: Oxford University Press).

Mabey, Christopher, and Mayon-White, Bill (1993) (eds.), *Managing Change* (2nd edn., London: Paul Chapman Publishing Ltd. in association with The Open University).

McCarthy, Sharon (1989), 'The Dilemma of Non-Participation', in Lammers and Széll (1989*b*), 115–29.

McClintock, Cynthia, Podesta, Bruno, and Scurrah, Martin (1984), 'Latin-American Promises and Failures: Peru and Chile', in Wilpert and Sorge (1984), 443–72.

MacDonogh, Giles (1994), 'From Piety to Art and Politics', *The Times*, 24 Sept.

MacDuffie, John Paul (1995), 'Human Resource Bundles and Manufacturing Performance: Organizational Logic and Flexible Production Systems in the World Auto Industry', *Industrial and Labor Relations Review*, 48/2: 199–221.

—— and Kochan, Thomas (1995), 'Do US Firms Invest Less in Human Resources? Determinants of Training in the World Auto Industry', *Industrial Relations*, 34: 145–65.

Mace, C. A. (1946), *Democracy as a Problem in Social Psychology* (Inaugural Lecture Delivered 8 May—Chairman: Rt Hon. Earl Russell FRS; London: Birkbeck College, University of London).

McGregor, Douglas, and Knickerbocker, Irving (1942), 'Union–Management Cooperation: A Psychological Analysis', *Personnel*, 19: 520–39.

MacInnes, John (1985), 'Conjuring Up Consultation: The Role and Extent of Joint Consultation in the Post-War Private Manufacturing Industry', *British Journal of Industrial Relations*, 23: 93–112.

McRae, Hamish (1994), *The World in 2020* (London: HarperCollins).

Macy, Barry (1982), 'The Bolivar Quality of Worklife Program: Success or Failure?', in Robert Zager and Michael P. Rosow (eds.), *The Innovative Organization* (New York: Pergamon Press).

—— and Izumi, H. (1993), 'Organizational Change, Design, and Work Innovation: A Meta-Analysis of 131 North American Field Experiments', in R. Woodman and W. Passmore (eds.), *Research in Organizational Change and Development*, 7: 235–313.

—— and Peterson, M. F. (1983), 'Evaluation Change in a Longitudinal Quality of Work Intervention', in Stanley Seashore, Edward Lawler, Philip Mirvis, and Cortoland Camman (eds.), *Assessing Organizational Change* (New York: Wiley), 453–76.

—— —— and Norton, Larry (1989), 'A Test of Participation Theory in a Work Redesign Field Setting: Degree of Participation and Comparison Site Contrasts', *Human Relations*, 42: 1095–165.

Maffesoli, Michcl (1988), *Le Temps des tribus: Le Déclin de l'individualisme dans les sociétés de masse* (Paris: Méridiens).

Mambrey, P. (1985), *Arbeitnehmerbeteiligung beim Einsatz informationstechnischer Systeme im Betrieb* (Munich: Gesellschaft für Mathematik und Datenverarbeitung).

Manz, Charles (1992), 'Self-Leading Work Teams: Moving beyond the Self-Management Myths', *Human Relations*, 45/11: 1119–41.

—— and Sims, Henry P. Jr. (1987), 'Leading Workers to Lead Themselves: The External Leadership of Self-Managing Work Teams', *Administrative Science Quarterly*, 32 (1 Mar.), 106–29.

March, J. G., and Olsen, J. P. (1989), *Rediscovering Institutions: The Organizational Basis of Politics* (New York: Free Press and Collier Macmillan).

—— and Simon, H. A. (1958), *Organizations* (New York: John Wiley & Sons).

Marchington, Mick (1992*a*), 'The Growth of Employee Involvement in Australia', *Journal of Industrial Relations*, 34/3 (Sept.), 472–81.

—— (1992*b*), 'Surveying the Practice of Joint Consultation in Australia', *Journal of Industrial Relations*, 34: 530–49.

—— (1994), 'The Dynamics of Joint Consultation', in Keith Sisson (ed.), *Personnel Management in Britain* (2nd edn., Oxford: Blackwell), 662–93.

—— and Loveridge, Ray (1979), 'Non-Participation: The Management View', *Journal of Management Studies*, 16: 171–84.

—— Goodman, John, Wilkinson, Adrian, and Ackers, Peter (1992), *New Developments in Employee Involvement* (Manchester School of Management (UMIST); Published by the Department of Employment, London).

—— Wilkinson, Adrian, Ackers, Peter, and Goodman, John (1993), 'The Influence of Managerial Relations on Waves of Employee Involvement', *British Journal of Industrial Relations*, 31: 553–76.

Marginson, P., Edwards, P., Martin, R., Purcell, J., and Sisson, K. (1988), *Beyond the Workplace: Managing Industrial Relations in the Multi-Establishment Enterprise* (Oxford: Blackwell).

Marin, Bernd, and Mayntz, Renate (1991) (eds.), *Policy Networks: Empirical Evidence and Theoretical Considerations* (Frankfurt: Campus/Westview Press).

Marks, Mitchell, Morvis, Philip, Hackett, Edward, and Gradt, James (1986), 'Employee Participation in a Quality Circle Program: Impact on Quality of Worklife, Productivity, and Absenteeism', *Journal of Applied Psychology*, 71: 61–9.

Marsh, Robert M. (1992), 'A Research Note: Centralization of Decision-Making in Japanese Factories', *Organization Studies*, 1312: 261–74.

Marshak, J. (1955), 'Elements for a Theory of Teams', *Management Sciences*, 1: 127–37.

Marx, K. (1889), *Capital: A Critical Analysis of Capitalist Production* (New York: Appleton & Co.).

Maslow, Abraham H. (1968), *Toward a Psychology of Being* (Princeton: van Nostrand).

Mathews, John (1994), *Catching the Wave: Workplace Reform in Australia* (Sydney: Allen & Unwin).

Meadows, Donella H., Meadows, Dennis L., Randers, Joergen, and Behrens, William W. III (1972), *The Limits to Growth* (New York: Universe Books).

Meardi, Guglielmo (1996), 'Trade Union Consciousness, East and West: A Comparison of Fiat Factories in Poland and Italy', *European Journal of Industrial Relations*, 2/3: 275–302.

Meidner, R. (1980), 'Capital Formation through Employer Investment Funds: A Swedish Proposal', in Benjamin Martin and Everett Kassalow (eds.), *Labor Relations in Advanced Industrial Societies: Issues and Problems* (Washington: Carnegie Endowment for International Peace).

Michels, Robert (1958), *Political Parties* (Glencoe, Ill.: Free Press).

Miles, Raymond E. (1964), 'Conflicting Elements in Managerial Ideologies', *Industrial Relations*, 4/3: 77–91.

—— (1964), 'Theories of Managers' Conflicting Attitudes among Managers and their Bosses', *Personnel* (Mar.), 51–6.

—— (1965), 'Human Relations or Human Resources?', *Harvard Business Review*, 43: 148–63.

—— (1974), 'Organization Development', in George Strauss, Raymond Miles, Charles Snow, and Arnold Tannenbaum (eds.), *Organizational Behavior: Research and Issues* (Madison: Industrial Relations Research Association), 165–92.

—— and Rosenberg, Howard R. (1982), 'The Human Resources Approach to Management—Second Generation Issues', *Organizational Dynamics*, 10/3: 26–41.

—— and Snow, Charles (1978), *Organizational Strategy, Structure and Process* (New York: McGraw-Hill).

—— —— (1986), 'Network Organizations: New Concepts for New Forms', *California Management Review*, 26/3: 62–73.

—— —— (1994), *Fit, Failure, and the Hall of Fame* (New York: Free Press).

Miller, Eric (1993), *From Dependency to Autonomy: Studies in Organization and Change* (London: Free Association Books).

Miller, K. I., and Monge, P. R. (1986), 'Participation, Satisfaction, and Productivity: A Meta-Analytical Review', *Academy of Management Journal*, 29/4: 727–53.

Millward, Neil, Stevens, Mark, Smart, David, and Hawes, W. R. (1992), *Workplace Industrial Relations in Transition* (Dartmouth: Aldershot).

Mintzberg, H., Raisingham, D., and Theoret, A. (1976), 'The Structure of "Unstructured" Decision Processes', *Administrative Science Quarterly*, 21: 246–75.

—— and McHugh, Alexandra (1985), 'Strategy Formation in an Adhocracy', *Administrative Science Quarterly*, 30/2: 160–97.

Misumi, Jyuji (1984), 'Decision-Making in Japanese Groups and Organizations', in Wilpert and Sorge (1984), 525–39.

Mitchell, Daniel, Lewin, David, and Lawler, Edward E. III (1990), 'Alternative Pay Systems, Firm Performance, and Productivity', in Alan Blinder (ed.), *Paying for Performance* (Washington: Brookings Institution), 15–87.

Moire, C. (1987), 'Cercles de qualité et groupes d'expression', *CFDT aujourd'hui*, 84: 23–35.

Morgan, Gareth (1986), *Images of Organization* (Beverly Hills, Calif.: Sage Publications).

Morishima, Motohira (1991), 'Information Sharing and Firm Performance in Japan', *Industrial Relations*, 30: 37–61.

Moscovici, Serge, and Doise, Willem (1994), *Conflict and Consensus: A General Theory of Collective Decisions* (London: Sage Publications).

MOW (1987), Meaning of Working, *The Meaning of Working* (London: Academic Press).

Mueller, Frank, and Purcell, John (1992), 'The Europeanization of Manufacturing and the Decentralization of Bargaining: Multinational Management Strategies in the European Automobile Industry', *International Journal of Human Resources Management*, 3: 15–34.

Mulder, Mauk (1971), 'Power Equalization through Participation', *Administrative Science Quarterly*, 16: 31–8.

—— (1974), *Power Distance Reduction Tendencies: Problems of Power and Power Relations* (Delft: Foundation for Business Sciences).

—— (1977), *The Daily Power Game* (Leiden: Martinus Nijhoff).

Muller-Jentsch, Walther (1995), 'Germany: From Collective Voice to Co-Management', in Rogers and Streeck (1995), 53–69.

Mygind, Niels (1992), 'The Choice of Ownership Structure', *Economic and Social Democracy*, 13: 359–400.

Nagel, Stuart S. (1970), 'Overview of Law and Social Change', *American Behavioral Scientist*, 13/4: 485–92.

Naschold, F. (1993), *Evaluation Report Commissioned by the Board of the LOM Programme* (Berlin: Science Center).

Neck, Christopher, and Manz, Charles (1994), 'From Groupwork to Teamwork: Toward the Creation of Constructive Thought Patterns in Self Management with Teams', *Human Relations*, 47: 929–52.

Neumann, Jean (1989), 'Why People Don't Participate in Organizational Change', *Research in Organizational Change and Development*, 3: 181–212.

Newton, Tim (1996), 'Postmodernism and Action', *Organization*, 3/1: 7–29.

Nightingale, D. (1982), *Work Place Democracy* (Toronto: University of Toronto Press).

Norstedt, Jan Peder, and Aguren, Stefan (1973), *The SAAB-Scania Report* (Stockholm: Swedish Employers' Confederation Technical Department).

Nussbaum, Martha (1993), 'Non-Relative Virtues: An Aristotelian Approach', in Nussbaum and Sen (1993), 242–69.

—— and Sen, Amartya (1993) (eds.), *The Quality of Life* (Oxford: Clarendon Press).

Obradović, Josip (1970), 'Participation and Work Attitudes in Yugoslavia', *Industrial Relations*, 9: 161–9.

—— (1975), 'Workers' Participation: Who Participates?', *Industrial Relations*, 14/1: 32–44.

Oesterreich, R. (1981), *Handlungs regulation und kontrolle* (Munich: Urban & Schwarzenberg).

Ogden, S. G. (1982), 'Trade Unions, Industrial Democracy and Collective Bargaining', *Sociology*, 16: 544–63.

Ohman, Berndt (1983), 'The Debate over Wage-Earner Funds in Scandanavia', in Crouch and Heller (1983), 35–52.

Olson, Mancur (1971), *The Logic of Collective Action: Public Goods and the Theory of Groups* (2nd edn., Cambridge, Mass.: Harvard University Press).

Osterman, Paul (1994*a*), 'How Common is Workplace Transformation and Who Adopts It?', *Industrial and Labor Relations Review*, 47: 173–88.

—— (1994*b*), 'Supervision, Discretion, and Work Organization', *American Economic Review*, 84: 380–5.

Parker, Mike (1984), 'Appoint QWL facilitators from the Top, UAW officials urge', *Labor Notes*, 66 (26 July): 2.

—— (1985), *Inside the Circle: A Union Guide to Workers Participation in Management* (Boston: South End Press).

Parkinson, Northcote C. (1965), *Parkinson's Law and Other Studies in Administration* (New York: Ballantine).

Pateman, Carole (1970), *Participation and Democratic Theory* (Cambridge: Cambridge University Press).

Paton, Rob (1991), 'Worker Take-overs of Failing and Bankrupt Enterprises in Europe', in Russell and Rus (1991), 28–42.

Pendleton, Andrew, Robinson, Andrew, and Wilson, Nicholas (1995), 'Does Employee Ownership Weaken Trade Unions? Recent Evidence from the UK Bus Industry', *Economic and Industrial Democracy*, 16: 577–605.

Perkin, Harold (1996), *The Third Revolution: Professional Élites in the Modern World* (London: Routledge).

Peterson, Kent, D. (1984), 'Mechanisms of Administrative Control over Managers in Educational Organizations', *Administrative Science Quarterly*, 29/4: 573–97.

Pfeffer, Jeffrey (1994), *Competitive Advantage through People* (Cambridge, Mass.: Harvard Business School Press).

Pil, Frits, and MacDuffie, John Paul (1996), 'The Adoption of High-Involvement Work Practices', *Industrial Relations*, 35: 423–55.

Piore, M., and Sabel, C. (1984), *The Second Industrial Divide* (New York: Basic Books).

Pontusson, Jonas (1992), 'Organizational and Political–Economic Perspectives on Union Politics', in Miriam Golden and Jonas Pontusson (eds.), *Bargaining for Change: Union Politics in North America and Europe* (Ithaca, NY: Cornell University Press), 1–44.

Poole, M. F. J. (1988), 'Factors Affecting the Development of Employee Financial Participation in Contemporary Britain: Evidence from a National Survey', *British Journal of Industrial Relations*, 26: 21–36.

—— and Jenkins, Glenville (1991), *The Impact of Economic Democracy: Profit-Sharing and Employee Shareholding Schemes* (New York: Routledge).

Pribicević, Branko (1994), 'The End of Second Yugoslavia and the Prospect of Self-Management as an Alternative Model of Society', paper presented at the 7th Conference of the International Association for the Economics of Self-Management, Portoroz, Slovenia, June.

Psczolowski, Tadeusz (1976), 'Praxiological Views of Organization Problems', in Hofstede and Kassem (1976), 148–9.

Pugh, Derek S. (1984) (ed.), *Organization Theory* (Harmondsworth: Penguin).

Pusić, Eugen (1974), *Razvedenost I povezanost: Teoretski problemi sampupravnog modela* [*Differentiation and Integration: Theoretical Problems of the Self-Management Model*] (Zagreb Biblioteke Encyclopaediae Modernae).

—— (1991), 'Property: The Growth and Change of an Institution', in Russell and Rus (1991), 137–48.

—— (1996), 'Participation and Harm Minimization', in Pieter Drenth, Paul Koopman, and Bernhard Wilpert (eds.), *Organizational Decision Making under Different Economic and Political Conditions* (Amsterdam: North Holland), 139–48.

Pusić, Vesna (1992) (in Serbo-Croat), *Vladaoci I upravljaci* [*Rulers and Managers*] (Zagreb: Novi Liber).

Putterman, L. (1984), 'Agricultural Co-Operation and Village Democracy in Tanzania', in Wilpert and Sorge (1984), 473–93.

Qvale, Thoralf (1976), 'A Norwegian Strategy for Democratization of Industry', *Human Relations*, 29/5: 453–69.

—— (1989), 'A New Milestone in the Development of Industrial Democracy in Norway', in Lammers and Széll (1989*b*), 98–102.

—— (1996), 'Local Development and Institutional Change: Experience from a "Fifth Generation" National Programme for the Democratization of Working Life', in Pieter Drenth, Paul Koopman, and Bernhard Wilpert (eds.), *Organizational Decision Making under Different Economic and Political Conditions* (Amsterdam: North Holland).

Ramsay, H. (1977), 'Cycles of Control', *Sociology*, 11/3 (Sept.), 481–506.

—— (1983), 'Evolution or Cycle? Worker Participation in the 1970s and 1980s', in Crouch and Heller (1983), 203–26.

—— (1990), *The Joint Consultation Debate: Soft Soap and Hard Cases* (Research paper No 17; Glasgow: Centre for Research in Industrial Democracy and Participation).

Rankin, Tom (1986), 'Integrating QWL and Collective Bargaining', *Work-Life Review*, 5: 14–18.

Ranson, Stewart, Hinings, Bob, and Greenwood, Royston (1980), 'The Structuring of Organizational Structure', *Administrative Science Quarterly*, 25/1 (June), 1–17.

Reed, Michael (1988), 'The Problem of Human Agency in Organizational Analysis', *Organization Studies*, 9/1: 69–90.

Regalia, Ida (1995), 'Italy: The Costs and Benefits of Informality', in Rogers and Streeck (1995), 217–42.

—— (1996), 'How the Social Partners View Direct Participation: A Comparative Study of 15 European Countries', *European Journal of Industrial Relations*, 2/2: 211–34.

Rehder, Robert R. (1994), 'Saturn, Uddevalla and the Japanese Lean Systems: Paradoxical Prototypes for the Twenty-First Century', *The International Journal of Human Resource Management*, 5/1 (Feb.), 1–32.

Rimmer, Malcolm (1992), 'Wage Determination and Systematic Overtime in Australian Workplaces' (unpublished paper; Melbourne: National Key Centre in Industrial Relations, Monash University).

Ritchie, J. B., and Miles, Raymond (1970), 'An Analysis of Quantity and Quality of Participation as Moderating Variables in the Participative Decision Making Process', *Personnel Psychology*, 23: 347–59.

Rivest, Chantal (1996), 'Voluntary European Works Councils', *European Journal of Industrial Relations*, 2: 235–53.

Roberts, Ben (1956), *Trade Union Government and Administration in Great Britain* (London: Bell).

Roberts, Karlene (1990), 'Some Characteristics of One Type of High Reliability Organization', *Organization Science*, 1: 160–76.

Roethlisberger, Fritz, and Dickson, W. J. (1939), *Management and the Worker* (Cambridge, Mass.: Harvard).

Rogers, Joel, and Streeck, Wolfgang (1995) (eds.), *Works Councils* (Chicago: University of Chicago Press).

Rojek, C., and Wilson, D. C. (1987), 'Worker's Self-Management in the World System: The Yugoslav Case', *Organization Studies*, 8/4: 297–308.

Rosen, Carey, and Klein, Katherine (1981), 'Job-Creating Performance of Employee Owned Companies', *Monthly Labor Review*, 106: 15–19.

—— —— and Young, K. (1985), *Employee Ownership in America* (Lexington, Mass.: Lexington Books).

Rosenberg, Richard, and Rosenstein, Eliezer (1980), 'Participation and Productivity: An Empirical Study', *Industrial and Labor Relations Review*, 33: 355–67.

Rosner, Menachim (1991), 'Ownership: Participation, and Work Restructuring in the Kibbutz: A Comparative Perspective', in Russell and Rus (1991), 170–96.

Rosser, Barkley J., and Rosser, Marina V. (1996), *Comparative Economics in a Transforming World Economy* (Chicago: Irwin).

Rothschild-Whitt, Joyce (1979), 'The Collectivist Organization: An Alternative to Bureaucratic Models', *American Sociological Review*, 44: 509–27.

—— (1983), 'Worker Ownership in Relation to Control: A Typology of Work Reform', in Crouch and Heller (1983), 380–406.

—— and Whitt, J. Allen (1986), *The Cooperative Workplace: Potentials and Dilemmas of Organizational Democracy and Participation* (New York: Cambridge University Press).

Rubenstein, Saul, Bennett, Michael, and Kochan, Thomas (1993), 'The Saturn Partnership: Co-Management and the Reinvention of the Local Union', in Bruce Kaufman and Morris Kleiner (eds.), *Employee Representation: Alternative and Future Directions* (Madison: Industrial Relations Research Association), 339–70.

Rubinstein, S. L. (1977), *Grundlagen der Allgemeinen Psychologie* (Berlin: Volk & Wissen).

Rus, Veljko (1970), 'Influence Structure in Yugoslav Enterprise', *Industrial Relations*, 9: 148–60.

—— (1984), 'Yugoslav Self-Management: Thirty Years Later', in Wilpert and Sorge (1984), 371–90.

Russell, Raymond (1985), *Sharing Ownership in the Workplace* (Albany: SUNY Press).

—— (1989), 'Taking Stock in ESOPs', in Lammers and Széll (1989*b*), 50–60.

—— (1991), 'Sharing Ownership in the Services', in Russell and Rus (1991), 197–217.

—— and Rus, V. (1991), *International Handbook of Participation in Organisations*, ii. *Ownership and Participation* (Oxford: Oxford University Press).

Sabini, John (1992), *Social Psychology* (New York: W.W. Norton & Co.).

Sachs, Stephen, M. (1975), 'Implications of Recent Developments in Yugoslav Self-Management', Paper Presented at the Second International Conference on Self-Management, Ithaca, NY, June.

—— (1987), 'Salvaging Knowledge: Learning from Worker Ownership Failures', *Workplace Democracy* (Spring), 21–2, 26.

Sadlowski, Dieter, Backes-Gellner, Uschi, and Frick, Bernd (1995), 'Works Councils: Barriers or Boosts for Competitiveness of German Firms', *British Journal of Industrial Relations*, 33: 493–513.

Sahiken, Harley, Lopzm, Seven, and Mankita, Isaac (1997), 'Two Routes of Team Production: Saturn and Chrysler Compared', *Industrial Relations*, 36: 18–45.

Sajó, Andras (1992), 'The Failure of the East European System as an Indicator for the Israeli kibbutz?', *Journal of Institutional and Theoretical Economics*, 148/1: 184–9.

Sale, Kirkpatrick (1996), *Rebels against the Future* (London: Quartet Books).

Sandberg, Åke (1995) (ed.), *Enriching Production: Perspectives on Volvo's Uddevalla Plant as an Alternative to Lean Production* (Aldershot, UK: Avebury).

—— Broms, Gunnar, Grip, Arne, Sundström, Lars, Steen, Jesper, and Ullmark, Peter (1992), *Technological Change and Co-Determination in Sweden* (Philadelphia: Temple University Press).

Schmidt, Rudi, and Trinczek, Rainer (1991), 'Duales System: Tarifliche und betriebliche Interessenvertretung', in Walther Muller-Jentsch (ed.), *Konfliktpartnerschaft: Akteure und Institutionen der industriellen Beziehungen* (Munich: Hampp), 167–99.

Schall, Maryan (1983), 'A Communication-Rules Approach to Organizational Culture', *Administrative Science Quarterly*, 28/4: 557–81.

Schnabel, Claus (1991), 'Trade Unions and Productivity: The German Evidence', *British Journal of Industrial Relations*, 29: 15–24.

Schön, D. A. (1971), *Beyond the Stable State* (The 1970 Reith Lectures; London: Maurice Temple-Smith).

Schulten, Thorsten (1996), 'European Works Councils: Prospects for a New System of European Industrial Relations', *European Journal of Industrial Relations*, 2: 303–24.

Schuster, M. (1983), 'Forty Years of Scanlon Plan Research', in Crouch and Heller (1983), 53–72.

—— (1984), *Union–Management Cooperation: Structure, Process, and Impact* (Kalamazoo, Mich.: Upjohn Foundation).

Scott, Jerome, and Lynton, R. P. (1952), *Three Studies in Management* (London: Routledge & Paul).

Seligman, M. E. P. (1975), *Learned Helplessness* (San Francisco: W. H. Freeman & Co.).

Shaiken, Harley (1995), 'Experienced Workers and High Performance Work Organization: A Case Study of Two Automobile Plants', *Proceedings of the Annual Meeting of the Industrial Relations Research Association* (Madison: Industrial Relations Research Association), 257–66.

—— Lopez, Steven, and Mankita, Isaac (1997), 'Two Routes to Team Production: Saturn and Chryster Compared', *Industrial Relations*, 36: 17–45.

Shapley, L. S., and Shubik, M. (1954), 'A Method for Evaluating the Distribution of Power in a Committee System', *American Political Science Review*, 48 (Sept.): 787–92.

Shaw, M. E. (1954), 'Some Effects of Problem Complexity upon Problem Solution Efficiency in Different Communication Nets', *Journal of Experimental Psychology*, 48: 211–17.

Signorelli, Adriana (1986), 'Cooperatives and Public Action', in Stern and McCarthy (1986), 355–74.

Simon, Herbert A. (1945), *Administrative Behavior* (New York: Macmillan).

—— (1946), 'The Proverbs of Administration', *Public Administration Review*, 1.

Sinclair, Amanda (1992), 'The Tyranny of a Team Ideology', *Organization Studies*, 13/4: 611–26.

Smith, Adam (1937), *An Inquiry into the Nature and the Causes of the Wealth of Nations* (New York: Modern Library).

Smith, P. B., Dugan, S., and Trompenaars, F. (1996), 'National Cultures and the Values of Organizational Employees', *Journal of Cross Cultural Psychology*, 27: 231–64.

Smith, Stephen (1994), *Employee Participation Rights, Training, and Efficiency: Hypotheses and Preliminary Evidence from Germany* (Washington: Economic Policy Institute).

Snow, C. C., and Miles, R. (1994), *Fit, Failure and the Hall of Fame* (New York: Free Press).

Sockell, Donna (1984), 'The Legality of Employee–Participation Programs in Unionized Firms', *Industrial and Labor Relations Review*, 37: 541–56.

Sorge, A., Hartmann, G., Warner, M., and Nicholas, I. J. (1983), *Microelectronics and Manpower in Manufacturing Applications of Computer Numerical Control in Great Britain and West Germany* (Farnborough: Gower Press).

Sparrow, Paul, Schuler, Randall, and Jackson, Susan (1994), 'Convergence or Divergence: Human Resource Practices and Policies for Competitive Advantage World Wide', *The International Journal of Human Resource Management*, 5/2: 267–99.

Spitzer, Quinn, and Evans, Ron (1997), *Heads You Win: How the Best Companies Think* (New York: Simon & Schuster).

Srivastva, S., Salipente Jr., P. F., Commings, T. F., Notz, W. M., Bigelow, J. D., and Water, J. A., in collaboration with Chisholm, R. F., Glen, R. H., Manring, S., and Molly, E. S. (1975), *Job Satisfaction and Productivity—An Evaluation of Policy Related Research and Job Satisfaction: Policy Development and Implementation* (Cleveland, Oh.: Case Western University Press).

Staw, B. M. (1982), 'Counterforces to Change', in Paul S. Goodman & Associates (eds.), *Change in Organizations* (San Francisco: Jossey-Bass).

—— and Ross, J. (1985), 'Stability in the Midst of Change: A Dispositional Approach to Job Attitudes', *Journal of Applied Psychology*, 70: 469–80.

Stern, R. N., and McCarthy, S. (1986), *International Yearbook of Organizational Democracy*, iii. *The Organizational Practice of Democracy* (Chichester: John Wiley & Sons).

Stewart, Greg, and Manz, Charles (1995), 'Leadership in Self-Managing Teams: A Typology and Integrative Model', *Human Relations*, 48: 747–70.

Strauss, George (1963), 'Some Notes on Power Equalization', in H. J. Leavitt (ed.), *The Social Science of Organizations* (Englewood Cliffs, NJ: Prentice Hall).

—— (1977), 'Managerial Practices', in J. R. Hackman and J. Lloyd Suttle (eds.), *Improving Life at Work: Behavioral Science Approaches to Organizational Change* (Santa Monica, Calif.: Goodyear), 297–363.

—— (1982), 'Workers' Participation in Management: An International Perspective', *Research in Organizational Behavior*, 4: 173–265.

—— (1989), 'Workers' Participation and US Collective Bargaining', in Lammers and Széll (1989*b*), 227–47.

—— (1990), 'Participatory and Gain-Sharing Systems: History and Hope', in Myron Roomkin (ed.), *Profit Sharing and Gain Sharing* (Metuchen, NJ: IMRL Press/Rutgers University), 1–45.

—— (1991), 'Union Democracy', in George Strauss, Daniel Gallagher, and Jack Fiorito (eds.), *The State of the Unions* (Madison: Industrial Relations Research Association), 201–36.

Strauss, George (1992), 'Workers' Participation in Management', in J. Hartley and G. Stephenson (eds.), *Employment Relations: The Psychology of Influences and Control at Work* (Oxford: Blackwell), 291–313.

—— (1996), 'Some Selected Problems Connected with Formal Workers' Participation', in Pieter Drenth, Paul Koopman, and Bernard Wilpert (eds.), *Organizational Decision-Making under Different Economic and Political Conditions* (Amsterdam: North-Holland), 117–26.

—— and Warner, Malcolm (1977), 'Research on Union Government: Symposium Introduction', *Industrial Relations*, 16: 115–26.

Streeck, Wolfgang (1984), 'Codetermination: The Fourth Decade', in Wilpert and Sorge (1984), 391–422.

—— (1995), 'Works Councils in Western Europe: From Consultation to Participation', in Rogers and Streeck (1995), 313–48.

Summers, Clyde (1987), 'An American Perspective of the German Model of Worker Participation', *Comparative Labor Law Journal*, 8: 333–55.

Széll, G. (1992) (ed.), *Concise Encyclopedia of Participation and Cooperative Management* (Berlin: de Gruyter).

—— Blyton, P., and Cornforth, C. (1989) (eds.), *The State, Trade Unions and Self-Management: Issues of Competence and Control* (Berlin: W. de Gruyter).

Tannenbaum, A. (1983), 'Employee-Owned Companies', *Research in Organizational Behavior*, 5: 235–68.

—— Kavcic, N., Rosner, M., Vianello, M., and Weiser G. (1974), *Hierarchy in Organizations* (San Francisco: Jossey-Bass).

—— Cook, Harold, and Lochmann, Jack (1984), 'The Relationship of Employee Ownership to the Technological Adaptiveness and Performance of Companies' (unpublished paper, Ann Arbor, Mich.: Institute for Social Research).

Tannenbaum, Robert, and Schmidt, Warren (1958), 'How to Choose a Leadership Pattern', *Harvard Business Review* (Mar.–Apr.), 95–101.

Taylor, David, and Snell, Mary (1986), 'The Post Office Experiment: An Analysis of Industrial Democracy', in Stern and McCarthy (1986), 75–102.

Taylor, Frederick W. (1967), *The Principles of Scientific Management* (New York: Norton Library; first published 1911).

Tchobanian, Robert (1995), 'France: From Conflict to Social Dialogue', in Rogers and Streeck (1995), 115–52.

Terry, Michael (1994), 'Workplace Unionism: Redefining Structures and Objectives', in R. Hyman and A Ferner (eds.), *New Frontiers in European Industrial Relations* (Oxford: Blackwell), 223–49.

Teulings, A. W. M. (1987), 'A Political Bargaining Theory of Codetermination: An Empirical Test for the Dutch System of Organizational Democracy', *Organization Studies*, 8/1: 1–24.

—— (1989*a*), 'Eine Verhaltenstheorie der Mitbestimmung', in H. Martens and G. Peter (eds.), *Mitbestimmung und Demokratisierung. Stand und Perspektiven der Forschung* (Wiesbaden: Gabler), 91–121.

—— (1989*b*), 'A Political Bargaining Theory of Co-Determination', in Széll, Blyton, and Cornforth (1989), 273–343.

Teune, Henry, and Mlinar, Zdravko (1978), *The Development of Logic in Social Systems* (Beverly Hills, Calif.: Sage Publications).

Thelen, Kathleen (1991), *Union of Parts: Labor Politics in Postwar Germany* (Ithaca, NY: Cornell University Press).

—— (1992), 'The Politics of Flexibility in the German Metal Working Industries', in Miriam Golden and Jonas Pontusson (eds.), *Bargaining for Change: Union Politics in North America and Europe* (Ithaca, NY: Cornell University Press), 215–46.

Thompson, James D. (1967), *Organizations in Action* (New York: McGraw Hill).

Thorsrud, Einar (1984), 'The Scandinavian Model: Strategies of Organizational Democratization in Norway', in Wilpert and Sorge (1984), 337–44.

—— and Emery, Fred (1970), 'Industrial Democracy in Norway', *Industrial Relations*, 9/2 (Feb.), 187–96.

Tolbert, Pamela, and Stern, Robert (1991), 'Inequality in the Company of Equals: Participation and Control in a Large Law Firm', in Russell and Rus (1991), 248–64.

Tolliday, Steven, and Zeitlin, Jonathan (1991), 'National Models and International Variations in Labor Management and Employer Organization', in Steven Tolliday and Jonathan Zeitlin (eds.), *The Power to Manage: Employers and Industrial Relations in Comparative Perspective* (London: Routledge), 273–343.

Tomlin, E. W. F. (1987), 'Japanese Concept of the Mind', in Richard Gregory (ed.), *The Oxford Companion to the Mind* (Oxford: Oxford University Press).

Toynbee, Arnold (1994), *Lectures on the Industrial Revolution of the Eighteenth Century in England* (London: Longmans Green & Co.).

Trachman, M. (1985), *Employee Ownership and Corporate Growth in High Technology Companies* (Washington: National Center for Employee Ownership).

Traxler, Frans (1992), 'Austria: Still the Company of Corporatism', in Anthony Ferner and Richard Hyman (eds.), *Industrial Relations in the New Europe* (Oxford: Blackwell), 270–97.

Triandis, Harry (1972), *The Analysis of Subjective Culture* (New York: John Wiley & Sons).

Trinczek, R. (1989), 'Betriebliche Mitbestimmung als soziale Interaktion', *Zeitschrfit für Soziologie*, 18/6: 444–56.

Trist, Eric (1986), 'Quality of Working Life and Community Development: Some Reflections on the Jamestown Experience', *Journal of Applied Behavioral Science*, 22: 223–37.

—— and Bamforth, K. W. (1951), 'Some Social and Psychological Consequences of the Long-Wall Method of Coal-Getting', *Human Relations*, 4/1: 3–38.

—— Higgin, G. W., Murray, H., and Pollock, A. B. (1963), *Organizational Choice* (London: Tavistock Publications).

—— Susman, Gerald, and Brown, Grant (1977), 'An Experiment in Autonomous Working in an American Underground Coal Mine', *Human Relations*, 30: 201–36.

TUC (1994): Trades Union Congress, *Human Response Management: A Trade Union Response* (London: TUC Congress House).

Tuckerman, Alan (1994), 'The Yellow Brick Road: TQM and the Restructuring of Organizational Culture', *Organization Studies*, 15: 727–51.

Turner, Lowell (1991), *Democracy at Work: Changing World Markets and the Future of Labor Unions* (Ithaca, NY: Cornell University Press).

—— (forthcoming) (ed.), *Negotiating the New Germany: Can Social Partnership Survive?* (Ithaca, NY: ILR Press).

—— and Auer, Peter (1994), 'A Diversity of New Organization: Human-Centered, Lean and In-Between', *Industrielle Beziehungen*, 1/1: 39–61.

Tushman, Michael L., and Anderson, Philip (1986), 'Technological Discontinuities and Organizational Environments', *Administrative Science Quarterly*, 31/3: 439–65.

—— and Nelson, Richard, R. (1990), 'Introduction: Technology, Organization, and Innovation', *Administrative Science Quarterly*, 35/1 (Mar.), 1–8.

Ulich, E. (1978), 'Über mögliche Zusammenhänge zwischen Arbeitstätigkeit und Persönlichkeit', *Psychosozial*, 1: 44–63.

US General Accounting Office (1987), *Employee Stock Ownership Plans: Interim Report on a Survey and Related Economic Trends* (Washington: US General Accounting Office).

Uvalic, Milica (1991), *The PEPPER Report: Promotion of Employee Participation in Profits and Enterprise Results* (Florence: The Commission of the European Communities).

van Atta, Don (1989), 'A Critical Examination of Brigades in the USSR', *Economic and Industrial Democracy*, 10: 329–40.

van de Vall, Mark (1970), *Labor Organizations* (Cambridge: Cambridge University Press).

van Eijnatten, F. M. (1993), 'The Socio-Technical System Design (STSD): A Full Bibliography of 2685 English-Language Literature References', *Report EUT/BDK/59—Eindhoven 1993*.

—— (1994), 'The Socio-Technical System Design (STSD): A Full Bibliography of 3082 English-Language Literature References', *Report EUT/BDK/59—Eindhoven 1993*.

van Waarden, Franz (1986), 'Corporate, Corporatist, and Cooperative Initiatives for Experiments with Industrial Democracy in the Netherlands' in Stern and McCarthy (1986), 335–54.

Vanek, Jaroslav (1971), *The General Theory of Labor-Managed Market Economics* (Ithaca, NY: Cornell University Press).

Verba, S. (1961), *Small Groups and Political Behavior* (Princeton, NJ: Princeton University Press).

Verma, Anil, and McKersie, Robert (1987), 'Employee Involvement: The Implications of Non-Involvement by Unions', *Industrial and Labor Relations Review*, 40: 556–68.

Vilrokx, Jacques, and Van Leemput, Jim (1992), 'Belgium: A New Stability in Industrial Relations?', in Anthony Ferner and Richard Hyman (eds.), *Industrial Relations in the New Europe* (Oxford: Blackwell), 357–92.

Virmani, B. R. (1986), 'Training Workers for Participation in India', in Stern and McCarthy (1986), 141–50.

Visser, Jelle (1992), 'Netherlands: End of an Era and the End of a System', in Anthony Ferner and Richard Hyman (eds.), *Industrial Relations in the New Europe* (Oxford: Blackwell), 323–56.

—— (1995), 'From Paternalism to Representation', in Rogers and Streeck (1995), 79–114.

Von Neumann, John, and Morgenstern, Oskar (1949), *Theory of Games and Economic Behavior* (Princeton: Princeton University Press).

Voos, Paula (1987), 'Managerial Perceptions of the Economic Impact of Labor Relations Programs', *Industrial and Labor Relations Review*, 40: 195–208.

Vroom, V. H., and Jago, A. F. (1988), *The New Leadership: Managing Participation in Organizations* (Englewood Cliffs, NJ: Prentice Hall).

—— and Yetton, Philip (1973), *Leadership and Decision Making* (Pittsburgh: University of Pittsburgh Press).

Wageman, Ruth (1996), *The Effects of Team Design and Leader Behavior in Self-Managing Teams: A Field Study* (New York: Columbia University Press).

Wagner, I. (1983), 'Report to the New York Stock Exchange on the Performance of Publicly Traded Companies with Employee Ownership Plans', cited in Rosen, Klein, and Young (1985).

Wagner, John A. III (1994), 'Participation's Effects on Performance and Satisfaction: A Reconsideration of Research Evidence', *Academy of Management Review*, 19/2: 312–30.

—— and Gooding, Richard (1987*a*), 'Effects of Societal Trends on Participation Research', *Administrative Science Quarterly*, 32/2: 241–62.

—— —— (1987*b*), 'Longitudinal Trends in American Research on the Outcomes of Participation: Effects of Societal Issues, Methods Behavior: A Meta-Analysis of Situational Variables Expected to Moderate Participation–Outcome Relationships', *Academy of Management Journal*, 30/3: 524–41.

Wall, T. D., and Lischeron, J. A. (1977), *Worker Participation: A Critique of the Literature and Some Fresh Evidence* (London: McGraw Hill).

—— Kemp, N., Jackson, P., and Clegg, C. (1986), 'Outcomes of Autonomous Work Groups: A Long-Term Field Experiment', *Academy of Management Journal*, 29/2: 280–304.

Walsh, Janet (1993), 'Internalization vs Decentralization: An Analysis of Recent Developments in Pattern Bargaining', *British Journal of Industrial Relations*, 31: 409–32.

Walton, R. E. (1977), 'Work Involvement at Topeka after Six Years', *Journal of Applied Behavioural Science*, 13/3: 422–33.

—— (1980), 'Establishing and Maintaining High Commitment Work Conditions', in J. R. Kimberly and Robert H. Miles (eds.), *The Organizational Life Cycle* (San Francisco: Jossey-Bass).

—— and McKersie, Robert (1965), *A Behavioral Theory of Labor Relations* (New York: McGraw-Hill).

—— Cutcher-Gershenfeld, Joel, and McKersie, Robert (1994), *Strategic Negotiations* (Cambridge, Mass.: Harvard Business School Press).

Warner, Malcolm (1975), 'Whither Yugoslav Self-Management', *Industrial Relations Journal*, 6: 65–72.

Warner, Rex (1983), *Encyclopaedia of World Mythology* (London: BBC Publishing Company).

Watson, Tony J. (1994), 'Management "Flavours of the Month": Their Role in Managers' Lives', *International Journal of Human Resource Management*, 5/4: 893–909.

Webb, Sydney, and Webb, Beatrice (1920), *A Constitution for the Socialist Commonwealth of Great Britain* (London: Longmans).

Weber, Max (1921), *Grundriss der Sozialoekonomik,* iii. *Abteilung Wirtschaft und Gesellschaft* (Tuebingen: J. C. B. Mohr–Paul Siebeck).

—— (1968), *Economy and Society* (New York: Bedminster Press).

Weiler, Paul (1990), *Governing the Workplace* (Cambridge, Mass.: Harvard University Press).

Weisbord, Marvin (1992), *Discovering Common Ground* (San Francisco: Berrett-Koehler).

West, Michael (1994), *Effective Teamwork* (Leicester: British Psychological Society).

Wever, Kirsten (1994), 'Learning from Works Councils: Five Unspectacular Cases from Germany', *Industrial Relations*, 39: 467–81.

—— (forthcoming), 'Deformalizing Labor–Management Relations in the New Germany', in Lowell Turner (ed.), *Negotiating the New Germany: Can Social Partnership Survive?* (Ithaca, NY: ILR Press).

White, Robert W. (1959), 'Motivation Reconsidered: The Concept of Competence', *Psychological Review*, 66/5: 297–333.

Whyte, William F. (1955) (ed.), *Money and Motivation* (New York: Harper).

—— (1967), 'Models for Building and Changing Organizations', *Human Organization*, 26: 22–31.

Whyte, William F. (1991), 'Learning from Mondragon', in Russell and Rus (1991), 83–102.

—— and Whyte, K. K. (1992), *Making Mondragon: The Growth and Dynamics of the Worker Cooperative Complex* (2nd edn., Ithaca, NY: ILR Press).

—— Hammer, Tove, Meek, Christopher, Nelson, Reed, and Stern, Robert (1983), *Worker Participation and Ownership* (Ithaca, NY: ILR Press).

Williamson, Oliver E. (1980), 'The Organization of Work: A Comparative Institutional Assessment', *Journal of Economic Behavior and Organization*, 1: 5–38.

Wilpert, Bernhard (1975), 'Research on Industrial Democracy: The German Case', *Industrial Relations Journal*, 6: 53–64.

—— (1977), *Fuhrung in deutschen Unternehmen* (Berlin: W. de Gruyter).

—— (1989), 'Participation Behavior and Personal Growth', in E. Krau (ed.), *Self-Realization, Success, and Growth* (New York: Praeger), 77–90.

—— (1990), 'How European is Work and Organizational Psychology?', in P. J. D. Drenth, J. A. Sergent, and R. J. Takens (eds.), *European Perspectives in Psychology* (Chichester: John Wiley & Sons), iii. 3–20.

—— (1991), 'Property, Ownership, and Participation: On the Growing Contradictions between Legal and Psychological Concepts', in Russell and Rus (1991), 149–64.

—— (1992), 'Organization–Environment Relations—Towards Overcoming a Notorious Blindspot in Organizational Psychology', in J. Misumi, B. Wilpert, and H. Motoaki (eds.), *Proceedings of the 22nd International Congress of Applied Psychology*, i. (Hove/Hillsdale: Lawrence Erlbaum), 66–88.

—— (1993), 'Das Konzept der Partizipation in der Arbeits- und Organisationspsychologie', in W. Bungard and T. Herrmann (eds.), *Arbeits- und Organisationspsychologie im Spannungsfeld zwischen Grundlagenorientierung und Anwendung* (Bern: Huber), 357–68.

—— (1994), 'Participation Research in Organizational Psychology', in G. d'Ydewalle, P. Eelen, and P. Bertelson (eds.), *International Perspectives on Psychological Science*, ii (Hove: Lawrence Erlbaum), 293–310.

—— (1995), 'Organizational Behavior', *Annual Review of Psychology*, 46: 59–90.

—— and Rayley, J. (1983), *Anspruch und Wirklichkeit der Mitbestimmung* (Frankfurt: Campus).

—— and Sorge, A. (1984) (eds.), *International Yearbook of Organizational Democracy*, ii. *International Perspectives on Organizational Democracy* (Chichester: John Wiley & Sons).

Winfield, Ian (1994), 'Japanese Manufacturing Techniques', *The European Work and Organizational Psychologist*, 4: 209–17.

Winther, Gorm (1995), *Employee Ownership: A Comparative Analysis of Growth Performance* (Aalborg: Aalborg University Press).

Witte, John F. (1980), *Democracy, Authority and Alienation in Work: Workers' Participation in an American Corporation* (Chicago: University of Chicago Press).

Womack, James, Jones, Daniel, and Roos, Daniel (1990), *The Machine that Changed the World* (New York: Rawson-MacMillan).

Work Practices Diffusion Team (1994), 'Japan Team-Based Work Systems in North America', *California Management Review*, 37: 42–64.

Wortman, Camille B., and Brehm, Jack W. (1975), 'Response to Uncontrollable Outcomes: An Integration of Reactance Theory and Learned Helplessness Model', in Leonard Berkowitz (ed.), *Advances in Experimental Social Psychology*, viii (New York: Academic Press).

Yankelovich, Daniel (1979), 'Work, Values and the New Breed', in C. Kerr and J. Rosow (eds.), *Work in America: The Decade Ahead* (New York: Van Nostrand), 3–26.

Yanowitch, Murray (1991), 'Worker Participation in the Soviet Union: New Possibilities', in Russell and Rus (1991), 301–22.

Yetton, P., and Crawford, M. (1992), 'Reassessment of Participative Decision-Making: A Case of Too Much Participation', in Heller (1992), 90–112.

Yoshino, M. Y. (1968), *Japan's Managerial System: Tradition and Innovation* (Cambridge, Mass.: MIT Press).

Yukl, Gary (1989), *Leadership in Organizations* (2nd edn., Englewood Cliffs, NJ: Prentice Hall).

Zand, Dale E. (1997), *The Leadership Triad: Knowledge, Trust and Power* (New York: Oxford University Press).

Zimbalist, Andrew (1976), 'The Dynamics of Participation', in G. David Garlson and Michael Smith (eds.), *Organizational Democracy* (London: Sage Publications).

Zuboff, Shosona (1988), *The Age of the Smart Machines: The Future of Work and Power* (London: Oxford University Press and Heinemann).

Zwerdling, Daniel (1979), 'Employee Ownership: How Well is it Working?', *Working Papers for a New Society*, 7: 15–27.

INDEX